STUDIES IN ISRAELI ETHNICITY

STUDIES IN ISRAELI ETHNICITY

After the Ingathering

Edited by
Alex Weingrod

*Ben Gurion University
of the Negev*

GORDON AND BREACH SCIENCE PUBLISHERS
NEW YORK   LONDON   PARIS   MONTREUX   TOKYO

Gordon and Breach Science Publishers

P.O. Box 786
Cooper Station
New York, NY 10276
United States of America

P.O. Box 197
London WC2E 9PX
England

58, rue Lhomond
75005 Paris
France

P.O. Box 161
1820 Montreux 2
Switzerland

14–9 Okubo, 3–chome
Shinjuku-ku,
Tokyo, 160
Japan

Library of Congress Cataloging in Publication Data
Main entry under title:

Studies in Israeli ethnicity.

Includes bibliographies.
1. Israel–Ethnic relations–Addresses, essays, lectures.
2. Ethnicity–Israel–Addresses, essays, lectures. I. Weingrod, Alex.
DS 113.2.S78   1985   305.8'0095694   84–27939

For Aron

CONTENTS

INTRODUCTION

Alex Weingrod

This book offers a retrospective view, as well as fresh anthropological and sociological perspectives, of one of the most fascinating developments in contemporary Israel: the emergence of ethnicity to social prominence. This was by no means an anticipated development. Quite to the contrary, the expectations of the 1940's and 1950's were that Jews then immigrating to Israel from many European and Middle Eastern countries would rapidly shed their different cultures and re-emerge as "Israelis." This expectation was expressed by the ideology of "Ingathering of the Exiles," or, in Hebrew, *mizug ha'galuyoth*. According to the government-sponsored programs and slogans of the 1950's, the immigrants flocking to Israel from such diverse places as Morocco, Yemen, Poland, Hungary, Rumania, Bulgaria, Iraq, Iran would soon become assimilated within the new society and adopt a common culture.

Studies in Israeli Ethnicity looks back on and explores this experience from the perspective of the 1980's. As the chapters in this book make clear, not all the immigrants were "transformed" in the decades following the Ingathering; in fact, Israeli society became increasingly "pluralistic" as ethnicity became more legitimate and Jewish ethnic groups not only maintained their viability but also began to express a new vitality (Eisenstadt, 1967; Lissak, 1973; Deshen and Shokeid, 1974; Smooha, 1978; Weingrod, 1979). Parallel changes also took place among Israeli Arabs: Formally defined as "minorities" within the Jewish State, they too have undergone processes of ethnic mobilization and redefinition (Smooha, 1978; Zureik, 1979; Lustick, 1980). Focusing upon ethnicity does not deny that other important trends—such as the importance of social class identification and the development of new ideologies—are also present. Indeed, some of these processes are also considered, but this book's emphasis is set firmly upon how persons conceptualize and organize their lives in respect to their countries, places, or groups of origin: In a word, the focus is upon ethnicity.

This has been a central motif in many previous studies of Israeli society, and over the years an impressive literature has been built up. To be more specific, since the early 1950's two different perspectives on ethnicity have become established, and they continue to focus and define many of the issues in present-day research. The first perspective conceptualizes ethnicity broadly in terms of what may be called "culture," while the second places emphasis upon "social change." Although these two formulations are not mutually exclusive, most studies have followed one model or the other. In addition, different theories have also been advanced in the attempt to understand the reasons for ethnicity: some scholars have tended to explain ethnicity primarily in terms of "inequalities," while others have preferred to see ethnicity as a "mobilized" feature that emerges during certain periods or under particular circumstances. Explaining how the chapters in this book update, enlarge, and revise these two perspectives and how they contribute to broader theories of ethnicity is the main theme of this introduction.

The cultural perspective was first introduced in Raphael Patai's *Israel between East and West* (1953). As the title of his book intimates (the titles of all the early studies indicate their theoretical orientation), Patai was primarily concerned with the "cultural crisis" resulting from the impact of culturally Western Israel upon the Eastern immigrants then flocking into the country. Indeed, he was not so much concerned with "ethnicity" (the term does not appear in the index) as with the processes of "culture contact" and "acculturation" that appeared to be distorting the Easterners' cultural patterns. His was a plea for moderation, for "cultural synthesis instead of cultural absorption; an ingathering of cultural contributions from each ethnic element in the country, instead of the assimilation of all to the Western culture of Ashkenazi Jewry" (p. 334).

Looking back from the vantage point of the 1980's, the present-day vitality of ethnicity would appear to invalidate Patai's concern regarding overwhelming Western assimilation. Or does it? As will be made clear, cultural assimilation and heightened ethnicity are quite compatible trends; in fact, their linkage may be inevitable! What is important for present purposes is the theory that guided Patai's research. The concept of culture was the core of his approach. More specifically, his analysis was conceived within the frame of reference of anthropology (especially American anthropology) during the 1930's. According to this view, a culture was composed of bundles of traits, patterns, and, ultimately, configurations; moreover, during the process of acculturation, traits or patterns belonging to the dominant group were thrust upon and ultimately adopted by subordinate groups (Kroeber, 1952).

While this view of culture has changed radically during the past three decades, Patai's cultural emphasis has important echoes in several of the essays included in this book. The best example is Harvey Goldberg's analysis of how "culture" influenced the ways in which immigrants responded to their new life in Israel (Chapter 9). Goldberg poses questions such as, How does the immigrants' native culture screen their perceptions? and In what ways does it shape their understanding of Israeli politics? In keeping with contemporary anthropological thinking, his emphasis is upon symbols, meanings, and codes; in passing, he also criticizes Patai's early formulation. The point to be stressed, however, is not that their definitions are different, but rather that both place the "culture concept" at the center of their analyses.

This perspective is also found in Herb Lewis's study of Yemenite town-dwellers (Chapter 11) and Laurence Loeb's analysis of Habbani identity (Chapter 10). Lewis's argument is strongly cultural: In explaining how and why Yemenites who reside in an ethnically mixed small town maintain their separate identity, he argues that it is their "strong sense of values and attitudes [culture] which guides the actions and choices of many members of the group" (p. 315). In somewhat the same vein, Loeb shows that, while the Habbani have undergone enormous changes in Israel, they resist other Israelis' ethnic stereotypes and insist upon their own native categories.

Finally, culture is also at the center of Shiloah and Cohen's ambitious analysis of the changing character of "Jewish Oriental Ethnic Music" (Chapter 16). Of course, the term is employed much differently. Their concern is with a specific "cultural product"—music—rather than directly with culture as a "total design" or a symbolic system. In a sense, their analysis harkens back to Patai's request for an "ingathering of cultural contributions." The authors are able to show how certain Jewish Oriental motifs are maintained by becoming refashioned for different audiences. What this attests to, if it needs to be stated again, is the vibrancy and unpredictability of ethnic themes in contemporary Israeli life.

Culture, that kaleidoscopic term, can also be given a rather different meaning. The term can be used to depict the behavior of particular sets of people as they interact in a variety of situations and contexts. These are the terms of analysis of *a specific culture*—an Indian caste, suburban housewives, or an urban village. In Israel, what might be called "ethnic studies" have frequently focused upon particular immigrant groups residing in urban neighborhoods, development towns, and, most often, in *moshavim,* or immigrant cooperative villages (see, for example, Weingrod, 1965; Deshen, 1970; Shai, 1970; Willner, 1970; Shokeid, 1971; Goldberg, 1972; Marx, 1976). Taking off from these community-based studies, Moshe Shokeid and Shlomo Deshen have recently developed a research genre that illuminates ways in which members of one cultural tradition— North African Jews—reshaped their lives in various Israeli contexts. This viewpoint is best expressed in their book *The Predicament of Homecoming* (1974). Starting from the theoretical slant of British social anthropology, the authors widened their perspective as they show how, in Israel, groups of Moroccan and Tunisian Jews refashion their native understandings, interests, and symbols as they accommodate to their new Israeli circumstances.

This genre is represented in this book by two studies; both focus upon Moroccan Jews, and each casts new light upon their accommodation. The best example is Shokeid's essay (Chapter 14), in which he takes up the vexing problem of violence among Moroccans. By examining a series of "violence cases," Shokeid is able to show the social circumstances in which Moroccans act aggressively and those in which violence is muted. To put it differently: Operating within a specific cultural system (Moroccan Jews), Shokeid suggests social circumstances that either excite or dampen violence. While his topic is much different, Yoram Bilu's analysis of changing patterns of folk psychiatry (Chapter 15) is roughly parallel. Bilu also focuses upon Moroccans—in his analysis he shows how, in Israel, folk healers adopt different strategies in treating their clients' psychic complaints.

There is, in addition, a second major research tradition, and it too needs to be presented in detail. This second perspective can best be introduced by referring to another of the early books on Israeli ethnic themes: Carl Frankenstein's edited volume, *Between Past and Future* (1953).

Frankenstein's collection deals mainly with a number of educational and psychological topics. However, the best-remembered section of this book is a debate between two Israeli social scientists regarding the interpretation of the processes of change taking place among the immigrants who were then flocking to Israel. One of the debaters, Frankenstein, took a view similar to Patai's; he argued that it was important to understand the Oriental immigrants' cultural patterns and that one should therefore adopt a relativist view. The second participant, Ben David, took a much different approach. His essay bears the arresting title "Ethnic Differences or Social Change?" At the outset he makes his own position clear:

> In this country ... there are no ethnic groups possessing definite cultures, but only one society characterized by a rather uniform cultural orientation ... and on the margins an ever increasing number of individuals and groups which have not yet been absorbed in it. The important point is that even groups hailing from the same country do not see, in their common origin or in the cultural tradition therein involved, an important or vital social value ... The frame of reference we suggest instead is that of "social change" (Frankenstein, 1953:33).

This is certainly a radically different theory. For Ben David "culture" was relevant only in the sense that many of the immigrants reject their native traditions, while all (except those "on the margins") strive to adopt the society's "uniform cultural orientation." This represents the second major perspective in Israeli ethnic studies: The focus is upon social change, and the key issues are the processes through which immigrants become "absorbed" within the society.

S. N. Eisenstadt has been the main proponent of this second perspective. His views were first spelled out in *The Absorption of Immigrants* (1954), and the issues raised there have since been refined and elaborated in a series of publications. In keeping with macrosociological theory (Parsons, Shils, and Merton are cited in particular) Eisenstadt's research team identified types of immigrant responses to the new Israeli conditions —the immigrants' adaptation ranged, for example, from "isolated, apathetic" families to "self-transforming cohesive" groups. The focus of these studies was not upon specific immigrant groups (Yemenites or Rumanian Jews) but rather upon social processes taking place throughout the entire immigrant population. As the title indicates, the central issue was "absorption": Were the immigrants becoming dispersed within the institutions and primary groups of the society (and consequently "absorbed") or did they establish separate institutions and maintain different traditions? The goal, in other words, was to understand new forms of social differentiation and stratification then emerging in Israeli society.

This theme has since become the basis for an impressive literature. During the past three decades, "absorption" (Eisenstadt's term) has been far from complete and research has therefore concentrated upon the persisting differences between the "European" and "Asian-African" segments of the population. More precisely, studies identified and sought to explain systematic differences in income, occupation, and education between these two broad social categories; indeed, the issues of social inequality (what in Israel is called the "social gap") have become not merely research topics but also the subject of intense political debate. Among these comprehensive studies one can cite Weingrod's *Israel: Group Relations in a New Society* (1965), Matras's *Social Change in Israel* (1965), Lissak's *Social Mobility in Israeli Society* (1969), Peres's *Ethnic Relations in Israel* (1977, in Hebrew) and, more recently, Smooha's *Israel: Pluralism and Conflict* (1978) and Swirski's *The Exploited* (1981, in Hebrew). While they differ sharply in outlook (Smooha and Swirski are particularly critical of Eisenstadt's early formulations), what these studies have in common is an attempt to demonstrate how ethnicity is relevant to society-wide patterns of social differentiation and integration.

Substantial portions of this book are devoted to re-examinations of these issues. In a synthesizing essay, Peres (Chapter 3) summarizes a wide range of recent data on ethnic stratification and then examines three of the current theories ("absorption through modernization," "conflict between ethno-classes," and "structural pluralism") that attempt to explain the complicated and often contradictory "facts." His comprehensive, balanced analysis succeeds in bringing data and theory up to date. Taking a more pointed view, Matras's essay on intergenerational social mobility (Chapter 1) underscores one of the main trends occurring in the society. Based upon a large-scale study (six thousand households) of young Israeli-reared families, Matras concludes that the contrasts between those of "Europe-America" and "Asia-Africa" origins are becoming increasingly less significant. Moreover, he predicts an "erosion of ethnic solidarity" as mobility continues to proceed apace. This conclusion is shared by Weil's study of children's perceptions of their families (Chapter 5). Weil tested youngsters from European, Iraqi, and Moroccan families; her findings indicate that, while there are systematic similarities within each group, Iraqi and Moroccan youngsters adopt European's descriptions of "ideal family behavior." Although his theme is different, similar trends are also described in Gonen's study of evolving ethnic residence patterns (Chapter 2). Gonen shows how previous patterns of ethnic segregation have broken down, and he intimates that the newer "intermediate" urban zones are likely to serve as arenas for interethnic contact.

Ben-Rafael's study of upwardly mobile Moroccan and Yemenite males (Chapter 4) adds important dimensions to the stratification picture. His data indicate that upwardly mobile people do not identify with their ethnic group–they become "Israelis" instead of "Yemenites"–and Ben Rafael goes on to discuss the implications of this shift for ethnic political mobilization. Finally, set within a much different context–an Arab town with a multiethnic population–al-Haj shows how status and power relations among Muslims, Christians, and Druze changed dramatically as members of these groups interacted differently with the Israeli state and economy (Chapter 6).

Attention has thus far concentrated upon the "culture" and "social change" perspectives and the contrasts between them. There is also, as was noted previously, a second dialectic that runs through these pages. Broadly speaking, two different theories of ethnicity are expressed. One major line of inquiry seeks to explain ethnicity ("why ethnicity?") in terms of equality or, better still, inequality. Although the second main line of analysis does not necessarily disregard inequality, it places more emphasis upon what can be called "mobilization." Both of these theories are represented in this book, and it is worthwhile to explore them in greater depth.

According to the "inequality theory," ethnicity becomes a salient social factor when groups sharing common historico-cultural features (ethnic groups) are clustered together in discrete, usually lower socio-economic niches. Since they are concentrated together (in the same occupations or residential areas) they also join together in various groups and organizations. Moreover, inasmuch as these tend to be low-status occupations and poorer residential zones, the pervading sense of discrimination also generates bonds among them. Members of these groups maintain common cultural traditions–for example, they speak the same "native language," share religious beliefs and symbols, and observe distinctive family or community celebrations. Taking this argument one step further, once inequalities and cultural differences are narrowed or eliminated, ethnicity will also lose its power. Putting it differently, as equality grows so too does assimilation.

This theory has a lengthy history in Israeli ethnic studies. Indeed, although they differ in most respects, both Patai and Ben David share this view: Patai believed that ethnicity was bound to recede in importance if "assimilation of all to the Western culture of Ashkenazi Jewry" continued, just as Ben David argued that ethnic bonds would vanish as a consequence of the deeper processes of social change. More recent studies of the "social gap" also rest upon this approach; these studies assume that, when the "gaps" in income or education between European and Middle Eastern origin groups are eliminated, ethnic associations or expressions will also cease (Lissak, 1973; Ben Porath, 1973; Smooha, 1978). This same point of view is also strongly expressed in this book. Matras's essay (Chapter 1) is an excellent case in point: As noted above, he argues that, when "opportunity structures" become equalized for all groups, there will inevitably be an "erosion of ethnic solidarity." This theory is shared, at least implicitly, in the chapters by Gonen, Ben-Rafael, and, to a certain extent, Peres. However, this latter study is of special interest, since, in effect, it parts company from the inequality theory.

Peres poses the interesting question of why, in Israel, ethnic expressions become more insistent just at the time when the "social gaps" appeared to be closing. In asking this question he points to a quite different interpretation of ethnicity. According to this second theory, ethnicity is not a social feature that is immanent in social systems or social relationships. Whether or not individuals or groups are identified as "ethnic" does not depend upon their failure to assimilate; quite to the contrary, they resist assimilation (or emphasize native cultural features) because they wish to become identified as a separate group for certain specified purposes. This view of ethnicity has been put forward in a number of studies published during the past decade. These studies have highlighted the "situational" (Barth, 1969), "interest group" (Cohen, 1974), "emerging" (Yancey et al, 1976), "symbolic" (Gans, 1979), and "mobilization" (McKay, 1982) bases for ethnic group organization. While the meaning of these terms differ, they share a common base. According to this interpretation, ethnicity can best be seen as a resource that can have political, economic, and symbolic uses. From this perspective, people tend to join together as "ethnics" when it suits their interests; consequently, ethnicity is only one basis of membership or identity among many. Moreover, according to this theory, there is not necessarily a "straight line" process of assimilation (Gans, 1979); instead, ethnic forms of expression may persist, together with others, for long periods of time.

This theory is also well represented in these studies. Arnold Lewis's essay is a fine example (Chapter 7). He begins his analysis by noting a thoroughgoing process of social change but then raises the critical question, If social change runs so deep, why do Israelis insist upon differentiating between various ethnic groups and categories? Lewis's answer runs mainly along political and symbolic lines. He argues that the category

"Oriental Jews" has important symbolic meaning for the dominant European population and that ethnicity must therefore be understood in the contexts of myths, ideologies, and power. This point is explicitly taken up in three other studies. By means of a detailed historical analysis, Hanna Herzog (Chapter 8) is able to show contexts in which ethnic political parties become organized in Israel. Her analysis indicates that, while ethnic political parties have been stigmatized, they nonetheless emerge periodically as part of a "negotiated" process. It is instructive to couple Herzog's historical study with Judith Goldstein's documentation of the early moments in the formation of one particular "ethnic consciousness" (Chapter 12). Goldstein studied a number of structured encounters involving Persian Jews and traces the fascinating process by which myths and symbols are used in fashioning a new Israeli "Persian identity." Finally, Oppenheimer's careful analysis (Chapter 13) indicates the complex political interplay by means of which a separate "Druze identity" has been deliberately fashioned. At certain moments and for some purposes the Israeli Druze may be "Arabs," while at other moments and for different purposes they are separated out and become "Druze."

The dialogue between these two contrasting theories of ethnicity is one of the main dialectics of this book. The point is not that one view is better or more accurate than the other, but rather that, when taken together, they clarify some of the mysteries of modern ethnic group organization. The result is a richer understanding of Israeli ethnicity in the 1980's.

Many of the articles in this collection grew out of a three-day conference held at the Ben Gurion University of the Negev during June 17–19, 1980. The two articles on Israeli Arabs—Oppenheimer's study of the Druze and al-Haj's analysis of group relations in an Arab town—were added later in order to provide a wider understanding of ethnic phenomena.

The following is a list of those who made presentations at the conference: Eliezer Ben-Rafael, Yoram Bilu, Erik Cohen, Sam Cooper, Shlomo Deshen, A. L. Epstein, Harvey E. Goldberg, Judith L. Goldstein, Amiram Gonen, Jeff Halper, Hanna Herzog, Yael Katzir, Arnold Lewis, Herbert S. Lewis, Emmanuel Marx, Judah Matras, Phyllis Palgi, Yochanan Peres, Maurice Roumani, Moshe Shokeid, Sammy Smooha, Pnina Talmon, Shalva Weil, Walter Zenner. The conference was cosponsored by the Chilewich Chair in Studies in Social Integration and the Humphery Center for Studies in Social Ecology. I am pleased to thank all the participants and sponsors for their enthusiasm and help.

Finally, Karen Schachter Weingrod was mainly responsible for turning these manuscripts into a book; her careful creative editing was of invaluable assistance. My thanks too to Faye Popelsky for her skillful typing. I am delighted to be able to dedicate this book to Aron Chilewich. Ethnicity and social integration have been among his concerns and passions, and he has contributed immeasurably to a better understanding of these issues.

REFERENCES

Barth, Frederik. 1969. *Ethnic Groups and Boundaries.* Boston: Little, Brown & Company.
Ben Porath, Yoram. 1973. "On East-West Differences in Occupational Structure in Israel" in M. Curtis (Ed.), *Israel: Social Structure and Change.* New Brunswick: Transaction Books.
Cohen, Abner. 1974. *Urban Ethnicity.* London, Tavistock Publications Ltd.
Deshen, S. 1970. *Immigrant Voters in Israel.* Manchester: Manchester University Press.
——, and Shokeid, M. 1974. *The Predicament of Homecoming.* Ithaca: Cornell University Press.
Eisenstadt, S. N. 1954. *The Absorption of Immigrants.* London: Routledge and Kegan Paul.
——, 1967. *Israeli Society* New York: Basic Books.
Frankenstein, C. 1953. *Between Past and Future.* Jerusalem: Szold Foundation.
Gans, H. 1979. "Symbolic Ethnicity", *Ethnic and Racial Studies,* Vol. 2, No. 1, 1-20.
Goldberg, H. 1972. *From Cave Dwellers to Citrus Growers.* Cambridge: Cambridge University Press.
Krausz, E. 1980. *Studies of Israeli Society.* New Brunswick: Transaction Books.
Kroeber, A. L. 1952. *Anthropology.* Berkeley: University of California Press.
Lissak, M. 1969. *Social Mobility in Israeli Society.* Jerusalem: Israel Universities Press.
——. 1973. "Pluralism in Israeli Society" in M. Curtis (Ed.), *Israel: Social Structure and Change.* New Brunswick: Transaction Books.
Lustick, I. 1980. *Arabs in the Jewish State.* Austin: University of Texas Press.
Marx, E. 1976. *The Social Context of Violent Behavior.* London: Routledge and Kegan Paul.
McKay, J. 1982. "An Exploratory Synthesis of Primordial and Mobilizationist Approaches to Ethnic Phenomena", *Ethnic and Racial Studies,* Vol. 5, 395-420.
Matras, J. 1965. *Social Change in Israel.* Chicago: Aldine Publishers.
Patai, R. 1953. *Israel between East and West.* Philadelphia: Jewish Publication Society.
Peres, Y. 1976. *Ethnic Relations in Israel* (in Hebrew). Tel Aviv: Sifriat Hapoalim.

Shai, D. 1970. *Neighborhood Relations in an Immigrant Quarter.* Jerusalem: Szold Foundation.

Shokeid, M. 1971. *The Dual Heritage.* Manchester: Manchester University Press.

Smooha, S. 1978. *Israel: Pluralism and Conflict.* Berkeley: University of California Press.

Swirski, S. 1981. *The Exploited* (in Hebrew, *Lo Nichshalim ela Menuchsalim*). Haifa: Notebooks on Research and Critique.

Weingrod, A. 1965. *Israel: Group Relations in a New Society.* London: Pall Mall Press.

——. 1979. "Recent Trends in Israeli Ethnicity" *Ethnic and Racial Studies* Vol. II, 55–65.

Willner, D. 1970. *Nation Building and Community in Israel.* Princeton: Princeton University Press.

Yancey, W., Ericksen, E. P., and Juliani, P. N. 1976. "Emergent Ethnicity: A Review and Reformulation" *American Sociological Review,* Vol. 41, 391–403.

Zureik, E. 1979. *The Palestinians in Israel.* London: Routledge and Kegan Paul.

1

Intergenerational Social Mobility and Ethnic Organization in the Jewish Population of Israel

Judah Matras

In this chapter I consider the bearing of variations in ethnic intergenerational social mobility upon socio-economic inequality, intraethnic generation gaps, mate-selection and marriage, and the formation and composition of major occupational strata. Many analysts and observers have found that ethnic differences in the Jewish population of Israel continue to be major axes of social solidarity, differentiation, and segregation. I conclude, however, that although massive intergenerational social mobility has not yet resulted in substantial reduction of ethnic socio-economic inequality, it has led or contributed to the decline in the salience of ethnicity as an axis of social organization and differentiation, to the erosion of ethnic solidarity and continuity, and to a transformation of the Israeli entitlement regime, which has also operated to diminish intergenerational ethnic continuity and the social and political salience of ethnicity.

Intergenerational social mobility will be viewed primarily in terms of intergenerational shifts in educational and occupation attainment. I draw upon data obtained in Israel's first national mobility study, which was carried out in April-June 1974, as part of the Israel Central Bureau of

1

Statistics' ongoing Labour Force Survey.[1] The population studied in that survey included all persons aged 14 and over in 1974, for whom information was available concerning employment status and occupation five years earlier. Their current labour force characteristics and the usual socioeconomic details obtained in the Labour Force Survey were also included. In addition, for heads of households and their wives information was obtained regarding the educational attainment and occupations of their fathers. The sample comprised some 6,000 households.

Most of the analysis and discussion of this subject has centered on heads of households aged 25 or over in 1974 or wives of heads of households. The population aged 25 and over in 1974 had experienced massive intergenerational educational and occupational mobility. This extensive mobility took place in the Jewish and non-Jewish populations, and within the Jewish populations, in the Asia-African and European-American-origin groups alike (designated hereafter as AA and EA, respectively).

The bearing of patterns of intergenerational social mobility on ethnic socio-economic inequality in Israel has been explained in various ways. The general conclusion has been that intergenerational social mobility in Israel has not yet operated to diminish ethnic socio-economic inequality and, indeed, may even have worked to preserve or increase it. The reasons for this failure of massive social mobility to reduce inequality include:

a. The "takeoff" in starting situations differed among the various major ethnic groups: among Jews the EA (European-American origins) group had initially high average levels of educational attainment compared with very low average levels in the AA (Asian-Africa origins) population or among non-Jews. Similarly, the EA population had some previous white collar occupational experience aside from entrepreneurship, while the AA populations had little professional, technical or managerial experience and little white collar experience aside from small entrepreneurship. The non-Jewish population had been heavily concentrated in agricultural employment (Matras and Weintraub, 1977).

b. The different ethnic groups experienced different social-origin specific patterns of mobility. Those of European or American background were much more likely to obtain secondary and post-secondary education than were those of Asian or African background; and among the non-Jews any education beyond the primary school level was quite infrequent (Matras and Noam, 1976). Regardless of occupational origin, AA populations were more likely to enter blue collar occupations, and less likely to enter managerial or academic occupations than were those of EA origin.

Some AA origin men, a large proportion of non-Jewish men, but virtually no EA men, entered unskilled occupations (Matras and Weintraub, 1977). These differences are related to different patterns of geographic distribution. The EA population was heavily concentrated in the metropolitan centers, while those of AA origin were dispersed in the urban periphery. Non-Jews were largely found in separate villages and towns (Semyonov, 1978).

c. The meaning, convertibility or "payoff" of educational and occupational mobility are evidently not identical for all groups. In particular, the occupational status and income "returns" to an "additional year of schooling" are less for non-Jews than for Jews and more for EA origin than for AA origin Jews—though the nature of the average "additional year of schooling" may well vary among these groupings as well (Matras, 1977; Boyd, Featherman, and Matras, 1980).

In the sections that follow, I would like to explore the effects of ethnic social mobility patterns on intra-ethnic generation gaps, mate selection and marriage, and the formation and composition of occupational strata, and then return briefly for another look at ethnic socio-economic inequality.

Social Mobility and "Generation Gaps" Within Ethnic Groups

Perhaps nothing is more obvious than that immigrant groups experience sharp generation gaps. The first generation born or socialized in the new country or community cannot duplicate the socialization, life course, language and cultural features, socio-geographic constraints or options that the adult immigrating group experienced. These generation gaps require more extensive and intensive examination in Israel, both because of the relative size of the immigrant and immigrant-offspring community as well as because of the heterogeneity of both geocultural origins and community settings in Israel. Moreover, patterns of massive intergenerational educational and occupational mobility have operated to increase and sharpen the generation gap in Israel in ways that, in turn, feed back and have direct bearing on the very stability and continuity of the ethnic groups themselves.

Table 1 shows the distribution of 25-34 year-old respondents in the 1974 national mobility survey by intergenerational educational mobility, i.e., by educational attainment relative to their fathers' educational attainment (R Ed and Fa Ed, respectively). The data are arranged to show the large generation gaps in education, and there are many respondent-father

TABLE 1

Israel National Mobility Survey, 1974. Respondents Aged 25-34, by Sex and by Major Ethnic Sub-groups: Percent Distributions Intergenerational Educational Attainment Differences[a]

	Jewish Males				Jewish Females	Non-Jewish Males	Non-Jewish Females
	Asia Born	Africa Born	EA Born	Israel Born			
Estimated number in Population, 1974	30,800	20,000	40,000	34,000	131,600	16,400	17,600
Percent: Total	100.0	100.0	100.0	100.0	100.0	100.0	100.0
R Ed > Fa Ed, Total	56.9	63.2	58.0	56.0	60.1	76.5	33.8
R Elem; Fa No Sch	19.2	21.9	7.2	2.0	14.5	53.5	24.4
R Post Pr; Fa No Sch	10.0	15.2	1.4	2.4	2.8	9.8	3.1
R Post Pr; Fa Elem	20.5	18.8	23.4	24.0	21.9	5.4	6.3
R Post Sec	6.3	7.3	26.0	27.6	20.9	7.8	–
R Ed ≅ Fa Ed, Total	32.5	29.0	34.5	37.8	34.2	23.8	57.8
R No Sch; Fa No Sch	1.3	5.3	1.5	0.4	1.4	5.6	33.6
R Elem; Fa Elem	19.8	11.8	15.5	7.4	14.0	18.2	22.9
R Post Pr; Fa Post Pr	10.8	10.4	12.9	19.3	13.9	–	1.3
R Post Sec; Fa Post Sec	0.6	1.5	4.6	10.7	4.9	–	–
R Ed < Fa Ed	8.4	7.8	7.5	6.4	5.6	–	8.4
Total	100.0	100.0	100.0	100.0	100.0	100.0	100.0

[a]Source: J. Matras and G. Noam (1976), "Intergenerational Educational Mobility in Israel—An Overview," Tables 6, 9, 12, 20, 22, 24 and 26.

differences that are obscured in these data. Reading across the third line of the Table, we can see that a majority of Israeli Jews 25-34 years old—between 56% and 63% of the males, and 60% of the females—had substantially more educational attainment than their fathers. In the top panel we see that for Jewish males born in Asia or Africa, and for non-Jewish males, over half of these were men who had had elementatry or post-primary education while their fathers had had no schooling at all. Of the 25-34 year-old Jewish males born in Israel in this educational generation gap category, half had post-secondary education while their fathers had not gone beyond secondary school of yeshiva; and almost all the rest had post-primary education while their fathers had not studied beyond the elementary level. A similar pattern holds for the Jewish males born in Europe or America and with large educational generation gaps, except that the latter group also includes a fraction whose fathers had had no schooling at all. The data reflect educational attainment differences between respondents and their fathers, but do not show those between respondents and their mothers, which inevitably would be even more dramatic.

Table 2 shows some of the occupational "general gaps" for Israeli males. The table shows all males 25+ in 1974, but I will restrict discussion to those socialized in Israel and whose fathers' occupations were reported in Israel (shown in the first five columns). Almost 19% of Israelis born of Israeli parentage and just under 20% of Israelis born of AA parentage, were in white collar positions, though their fathers were blue collar workers; and 11% of the latter were in manual positions, though their fathers had been in non-manual employment. Large percentages of the men were in non-manual occupations in 1974, though their occupational origins, i.e., their fathers' occupations, were manual occupations. In particular, 9% of the Israeli-Israelis subgroup; 9% of those born in Europe or America but immigrating at age 14 or under; and 11% of the Israeli subgroups were in "high white collar" occupations—professional, academic, or managerial occupations. Smaller, but not insignificant, proportions of the Israeli-socialized males of AA origin were also in the non-manual occupations, though of manual origin: just under 6% of the Israeli-born AA group and 3% of the AA=14. Smaller numbers, but nevertheless substantial proportions of the total, in high white collar occupations are men whose fathers were proprietors or merchants.

Similarly, more than one-third of those respondents who were skilled or semi-skilled manual employees in 1974 reported fathers in non-manual occupations, either as proprietors or as white collar employees. Of the

TABLE 2

Jewish Males, 25+, by Major Ethnic and Age-at-Immigration Sub-groups: Percent Distributions by Own Major Occupation Groups and by Occupational Origins (Father's Occupation Groups); 1974a

Own Occupation Group and Occupational Origins	Israel Isr.	Father's Occupation in Israel Reported					Father's Occupation Abroad Reported	
		Israel AA Origins	AA, Imm Age 14 yrs	Israel EA Origins	EA, Imm Age 14 yrs	AA, Imm Age 15+ yrs.	EA, Imm Age 15+ yrs.
Total: All Respondents	100.0	100.0	100.0	100.0	100.0	100.0	100.0
High White Collar, Total	21.2	13.2	8.7	28.7	20.7	4.6	17.3
Proprietor (W.C.) Origins	4.6	6.3	2.2	4.1	5.6	2.2	7.2
Other Non-Manual Origins	7.3	1.0	3.5	13.8	5.7	1.6	6.5
Manual Origins	9.3	5.9	3.0	10.8	9.4	0.8	3.6
Other White Collar, Total	25.4	22.5	15.2	33.8	32.1	16.0	25.4
Proprietor (W.C.) Origins	9.5	4.3	3.6	5.5	9.2	6.6	11.5
Other Non-Manual Origins	6.4	4.5	2.2	12.4	10.0	3.9	7.0
Manual Origins	9.5	13.7	9.4	15.9	12.9	5.5	6.0
Skilled, Semi-Skilled Employees, Total	26.6	33.2	44.4	18.3	28.9	33.2	25.8
Proprietor (W.C.) Origins	4.4	2.9	10.3	2.7	7.9	14.5	9.7
Other Non-Manual Origins	4.4	8.1	3.3	5.3	3.5	4.0	3.7
Manual Origins	17.8	22.2	30.8	10.3	17.5	14.7	12.4
All Other Occupational Groupsb	26.8	31.1	31.7	19.2	18.3	46.2	31.5

aSource: J. Matras and D. Weintraub (1977), "Ethnic and Other Primordial Differentials in Intergenerational Mobility in Israel." Paper presented in International Sociological Association Committee in Stratification and Mobility Seminar, Jerusalem, May, 1976. Table 7a-h.

bIncludes Proprietors (W.C. and B.C.), Service and Unskilled Workers, and Farm Owners and Workers.

Israeli-born men, in skilled or semi-skilled occupations, whether of EA or of AA parentage, close to one-fourth are sons of white collar employee fathers; and of the immigrant (before age 14) men in the blue collar occupations, about one-fourth are sons of white-collar proprietors. Just under one-third (30.8%) of the respondents born in AA (and immigrating before age 15) and considerably smaller percentages in the other groups reported that they are skilled or semi-skilled employees and that their fathers were manual workers as well. Thus, intergenerational occupational continuity—even continuity in broad categories of occupations—is quite the exception for all major ethnic groupings.

A type of mobility-related generation gap that has not been looked at in this study but bears examination is the entrance of women into the labour force, and the deepening involvement and commitment of women in the labour force, i.e., the shift from casual employment to career paths, among women. Large numbers of women—especially of AA birth or origin, but also of EA birth and origin—whose mothers were never employed outside the home have sought and obtained employment thus extending their social involvement and participation far beyond that of the previous generation.

The Asian and African, and Europe and American subgroups are characterized by extreme "general gaps" as a result of intergenerational educational and occupational mobility; but they are different kinds of gaps. They inevitably erode ethnic continuity and solidarity both because of internal dissimilarities and heterogeneity, which they imply, and also because of their impact on the potential for intergenerational transfer of resources. Knowledge, experience, contacts, human skills, or other "human capital" type resources as well as material wealth are resources typically transferred intergenerationally within families and are major axes of family and group solidarity and, often, of intra-group power, influence, and control. Educational and occupational mobility of the younger generation however, may render it effectively independent of the relatively meager resources controlled by or accessible through the older generation. On the other hand, the mobility of the younger generation may itself be a consequence or function of resources made available by the older generation.

It is precisely at this point that the nature of the generation gaps differs between the AA and EA groups: the mobility of the former tends to be independent of older generation resources and introduces discontinuity; while that of the latter uses resources of the older generation. This is probably best illustrated by the case of preparation for, continuation through, and completion of post-primary schooling. While attendance and completion of primary school has, since the early 1950's, been compulsory and free, financed by the State, and thus entailing relatively minor costs to pupils' parents and families, post-primary education—especially in academic secondary schools leading to university matriculation—have involved both substantial outlays, foregoing time and earnings, and parental support.

Through the 1950's and 1960's relatively few (though increasing numbers and percentages) of the youth of Asian or African parentage continued in post-primary education, and these mostly in non-academic (vocational, agricultural, etc.) tracks (Matras, 1965). The great educational strides—and intergenerational gaps—among the AA group were mostly at the primary and non-academic post-primary levels, involving relatively minor parental or familial support or foregone income; while the great educational increments—and intergenerational gaps—among the EA group were mostly at the academic secondary and post-secondary levels, involving major parental or familial support and extended deferment of income. It is probably correct to note that, even at the primary school level, the support, assistance, encouragement, leverage, and sponsorship that the Asian or African origin child in the 1950's or 1960's was able to command from his parents or nearby community of orientation was considerably less, on the average, than that to which the European or American-origin child had access. This was so both because of the disadvantage of the AA children and families in the per capita resources available (income, parents' educational attainment, housing density, numbers of siblings, etc.) and because of lesser familiarity and lesser ability of the AA families to deal with teachers and school situations that were largely organized by Europeans and tended to be characterized by European-origin norms, values, rhetoric, and operating procedures.

Mate Selection and Marriage

In an earlier study (Matras and Selbee, 1980) it was found that Jewish males in Israel who were occupationally upward mobile intergenerationally were better able to compete for marriage partners of higher occupational origins than they themselves; and they were more often upwardly mobile in their marriages than those of similar occupational origins not occupationally mobile. Conversely, males who were occupationally downward mobile intergenerationally were less well able to compete for marriage partners of the same occupational origins as they themselves; and they were often more downward mobile in their marriages than were other males of similar occupational origins. I will consider the bearing of intergenerational occupational mobility on patterns of mate selection within the major ethnic-origin divisions in the Jewish population. The discussion is restricted to persons married in Israel.

Table 3 shows comparative educational, occupational origin and ethnic origin characteristics of the wives of occupationally upward-mobile, downward-mobile and immobile men who, in turn, are grouped by current (1974) occupation category, ethnic origin and age at immigration to Israel.[2]

The first vertical panel of Table 3 (columns (1)-(3) shows the relationship between respondents' intergenerational occupational mobility and the educational selection of wives. Among men born or with fathers born in Asia or Africa, and among those born in Israel or Israeli-born parentage, there is a tendency for more men to marry women with lower than their own education than with higher. Among men of European or American origin, a pattern of this type clearly appears only for white collar workers immigrating at age 15 or over. Overall, there does not appear to be an important mobility effect. Within each sub-group there is not a great deal of difference between the distributions of the upwardly-mobile, stable, and downwardly-mobile men. There is no clear mobility-related pattern common to all or even some of the sub-groups. Instead, the only patterns that do show up indicate that in all sub-groups, a majority—often quite a large majority—of each mobility category marry women with the same education.

In examining the second vertical panel (columns (4)-(6) of Table 3, which shows the distribution of occupationally mobile men by the occupational origin characteristics of their wives, we find in every sub-group, men who are upwardly-mobile are much more likely to marry women of higher social origins than themselves than are men who are downwardly mobile. Conversely, men who are downwardly-mobile are much more likely to marry women of lower origins than are the upwardly-mobile men. In addition, with only a few exceptions, the likelihood of stable men (not intergenerationally mobile) marrying women of higher or lower social origins tends to fall between that of the upwardly and downwardly-mobile men.

Turning to the question of mobility and ethnic-origin selection of

TABLE 3

Jewish Males, Married in Israel, 25+, by Area of Birth or Origin, Manual or Non-Manual Current Occupation, and by Intergenerational Occupational Mobility: Percent Distribution by Wives' Educational Occupational-Origin and Ethnic-Origin Similarity or Dissimilarity. Israel National Mobility Survey, 1974.

Areas of Birth or Origin and Socialization, Current Major Occupation Category, and Intergenerational Occupational Mobility	Characteristics of Wives									N =100% (10)
	Education Level (1)			Occupational Origins (2)			Ethnic Origins (3)			
	Higher (1)	Same (2)	Lower (3)	Higher (4)	Same (5)	Lower (6)	Same Country (7)	Same Continent Different Country (8)	Different Continent (9)	
Born in Asia-Africa: Age IM ≥15:										
Non-Manual Occupational Mobility:										
up	4.5	50.8	44.7	32.1	45.1	22.8	71.5	16.4	12.1	54
same	11.2	55.3	33.5	18.7	52.3	29.0	69.6	15.2	15.2	42
down	14.7	50.2	35.1	10.7	24.2	65.2	76.4	18.5	5.1	39
total	9.5	52.1	38.5	21.7	41.6	36.7	72.3	16.6	11.1	134
Manual Occupational Mobility:										
up	7.4	79.0	13.7	31.2	60.4	8.4	68.0	15.3	16.7	22
same	6.4	54.8	38.8	34.2	55.3	10.5	74.5	18.3	7.3	75
down	11.0	67.1	22.0	11.9	45.8	42.3	69.2	22.3	8.5	91
total	8.8	63.7	27.6	23.2	51.4	25.4	71.2	19.9	9.0	188

Born in Israel, Father born in
Asia-Africa; or born in Asia-
Africa: Age IM ≤ 14:

Non-Manual Occupational Mobility:

up	16.5	53.3	30.1	30.5	50.4	19.1	42.0	22.3	35.7	99
same	16.9	67.0	16.1	25.2	44.4	30.5	49.4	28.9	21.7	42
down	14.7	64.8	20.5	16.8	10.8	72.3	40.6	33.7	25.7	25
total	16.4	58.4	25.2	27.1	42.8	30.1	43.6	25.7	30.7	167

Manual Occupational Mobility

up	15.1	64.3	20.6	48.0	42.9	9.1	47.0	35.0	17.9	36
same	18.4	66.9	14.7	28.3	65.2	6.5	52.3	38.8	8.9	152
down	18.9	56.4	24.7	5.5	35.7	58.8	60.9	25.2	13.9	87
total	18.1	63.2	18.7	23.6	52.8	23.6	54.3	34.0	11.7	275

Born in Europe-America:
AGE IM ≥ 15

Non-Manual Occupational Mobility

up	12.1	56.0	31.9	36.8	41.0	22.2	51.0	37.7	11.3	140
same	12.3	59.5	28.1	29.8	45.7	24.5	58.1	32.7	9.3	77
down	6.8	67.3	25.9	12.3	19.5	68.2	52.7	43.2	13.1	56
total	11.1	59.3	29.7	29.9	38.0	32.1	53.4	35.5	11.1	273

Manual Occupational Mobility

up	9.9	68.9	21.2	48.1	47.9	4.0	55.0	32.6	12.5	25
same	21.6	56.8	21.6	43.6	44.3	12.1	61.8	22.5	15.7	63
down	22.3	58.5	19.2	20.0	32.5	47.5	47.4	36.5	16.2	90
total	20.0	59.3	20.3	32.1	38.7	29.3	53.5	31.0	15.5	178

TABLE 3 (Continued)

Areas of Birth Or Origin and Socialization, Current Major Occupationa Category, and Intergenerational Occupational Mobility	Characteristics of Wives									
	Education Level (1)			Occupational Origins (2)			Ethnic Origins (3)			
Born in Israel, Father born in Europe-America: Age IM ≤14:	Higher (1)	Same (3)	Lower (3)	Higher (4)	Same (5)	Lower (6)	Same Country (7)	Same Continent Different Country (8)	Different Continent (9)	N =100% (10)
Non-Manual Occupational Mobility										
up	15.8	63.5	20.7	39.4	41.9	18.7	31.6	54.3	14.2	233
same	12.0	72.3	15.7	18.6	24.8	56.5	19.2	46.7	34.1	65
down	25.8	52.5	21.8	3.9	11.8	84.4	23.2	40.7	36.1	38
total	16.2	63.9	19.8	31.5	35.3	33.3	28.2	51.3	20.5	336
Manual Occupational Mobility										
up	18.3	65.0	16.7	49.7	35.0	15.4	33.8	45.4	20.7	38
same	22.7	64.5	12.8	27.4	64.6	8.1	22.3	51.1	26.6	108
down	271.	60.1	12.8	20.8	17.9	61.4	19.6	50.1	30.3	54
total	23.1	63.4	13.5	29.8	46.4	23.8	23.7	49.8	26.5	199
Born in Israel, Father born in Israel										
Occupational Mobility										
up	11.6	56.5	31.9	27.6	49.0	23.4	20.7	—	79.3	39
same	18.2	53.5	28.3	42.5	28.9	28.6	27.3	—	72.7	39
down	9.2	59.5	31.3	11.4	17.0	71.6	17.5	—	82.5	26
total	13.5	56.2	30.4	28.8	33.4	37.8	22.4	—	77.7	104

wives, the first point to be made is that there does not appear to be a very strong or consistent mobility effect on the ethnic character of mate selection. While minor variations do occur, these do not constitute regular patterns within or across sub-groups. However, a number of patterns are of interest.

Men who immigrated at older ages, 15 or over, whether of Asian or African birth, or of European or American birth, were in general most likely to marry women born in or with parents from their own countries of birth. They were least likely to marry women born or originating in different countries and in different continents, i.e. in different geo-cultural areas. These men show high percentages in column (7)-e and low percentages in column (9). Men of EA birth were considerably more likely to marry women from different countries, but in the same continents or geo-cultural areas (Column (8)), while men of AA birth were much more likely to marry women born, or with parents born, in the same countries. Among all sub-groups of males born abroad and immigrating at ages 15 or over, there is virtually no intergenerational occupational mobility effect on patterns of ethnic selection or intermarriage.

Among men born in Israel of AA origin, or born in AA and immigrating at younger (14 or under) ages, there are differences between those in white collar and in blue collar occupations. The former are characterized by somewhat higher percentages marrying women born or originating in different AA countries from their own (column (8)), than were apparent for those immigrating from AA countries at older ages (15+). The upwardly-mobile were slightly more likely to marry "Out" of the ethnic origin group (column (9)) than were the non-mobile or downwardly-mobile.

Among the Israeli-socialized men of EA birth or parentage, there was much more outmarriage (columns (8) and (9) than for either EA-born men who immigrated at older (15+) ages and Israeli-socialized men of AA birth or parentage. However, among these EA-origin men—immigrating at younger ages, or else born in Israel—the upwardly-mobile were most likely to marry wives born in, or with fathers born in, the same countries; and they were least likely to marry wives born or with parents born in AA countries.

Analysis (data not shown here) of the distribution of educationally mobile or immobile women across three variables representing the similarity of dissimilarity of characteristics of their husbands was carried out. The three variables: education levels, occupational origins and ethnic origins are indicative of the degree of marital homogeneity (or heterogene-ity) in mate selection among educationally mobile or immobile women.[3]

A fairly definite mobility effect on mate selection by comparative edu-cation levels appears. Women who are downwardly-mobile are much more likely to marry a man with a higher level of education than are women who are upwardly-mobile. Conversely, upwardly-mobile women are much more likely to marry men of a lower educational level than are the down-wardly-mobile women. This suggests that mobile women tend to select mates from among the men whose educational levels are similar to their own educational origins, and not necessarily men whose education level is more consistent with their present status.

With respect to the effect of intergenerational educational mobility on occupational-origin selection of husbands, two conclusions emerge. First, among all EA women, among the AA women with high education, and among AA women of low education socialized in Israel, mobility pro-duces a distinct pattern of mate selection: upward-mobility combines with the selection of a mate of higher occupational origins and downward-mobility with the selection of mate of lower origins. This combination re-sults in a type of consistency between mobility experience and occupa-tional origin selection. For the AA women of low education who immi-grated after the age of 14, mobility seems to have little effect on mate selection by occupational origins.

Turning finally to educational mobility and the ethnic character of mate selection, we find that, as was the case among the males, across most of the sub-groups of AA and EA women there does not appear to be any systematic way in which mobility shapes the ethnic pattern of mate selec-tion. There is variation, to be sure, in the extent of within-country-of-origin marriage. For both AA and EA origin women married in Israel, those with least education were more likely to marry men of the same countries of birth or origin, while those with higher educational attain-ment were more likely to marry outside their origin groups. Those born in Israel or immigrating at younger ages (=14) were less likely to marry men of the same countries or origin than those born abroad and immi-grating at older ages (15+). But the intergenerational educational mobility factor does not further differentiate the relative frequencies.

Probably the main finding of this analysis, however, is the extent of marriage both outside the respondents' country-of-origin groups and out-side the continent-of-origin grouping (i.e. couples with AA and EA part-ners). Almost 30% of women of AA origin born or socialized in Israel and with some post-primary education (9+ school years) were married to EA-origin husbands; and about 22% of women of EA origin born or socialized in Israel and with some post-secondary education (12+ school years) were married to AA-origin husbands.

Ethnic Social Mobility and Occupational Strata Formation

In this chapter I can only touch briefly on the bearing of ethnic social mobility on strata formation in Israel. The topic of "social strata" in Israel is both complex and elusive. By social strata I refer to some more or less well-defined groupings—usually hierarchically ordered—with institutionalized reward or resource entitlements, control of or access to resource entitlements, or rights to consumption, to associations, to participation of certain kinds. "Strata formation" refers both to institutionalization of such entitlements and rights and/or to changes in the size, composition, internal relationships, etc. of groups with institutionalized reward or cultural entitlements.

For Israel, the first problem is identification of such strata. We certainly can identify strata in Israel—at the very least by identifying the Israeli counterparts of the kinds of strata that have been identified and described in the social scientific literature: elites, classes, the poor, the illiterate, new immigrants, type-of-settlement groupings, occupational groups, educational attainment categories, etc. But these all have a certain fluidity or historical shallowness, in the sense that it is difficult to trace them and their incumbents back over any substantial period of time either in Israel of Palestine or in pre-immigration Jewish communities.

Even "occupational strata" are not well-established, or well-defined in Israel; and the immigration and rapid economic development as well as the massive intergenerational occupational mobility have rendered occupational strata all the more fluid. Nonetheless, it is possible to begin by tentatively identifying four reasonably well-defined occupational strata in Israel:

1. Professionals, scientists, and academic employees
2. Managers and administrators
3. Skilled and semi-skilled manual workers
4. Unskilled manual workers

TABLE 4
Selected Characteristics of "High White Collar" and Manual Jewish Male Occupational Strata. Israel, April-June 1974 (Percent Distribution)

| | Total | "High White Collar" | | | | Manual | |
| | | Professional and Academic | | Management and Administration | | Skilled & Semi-Skilled Employees | Unskilled Workers |
		Self-Employed	Employee	Self-Employed	Employee	11	13
Residence	100.0	100.0	100.0	100.0	100.0	100.0	100.0
T.A., J-m, Haifa	33.4	63.1	47.2	36.7	44.4	28.1	24.6
Other Veteran cities	34.3	30.5	42.4	44.8	29.1	35.9	29.7
New Towns	26.8	6.5	9.9	15.5	21.8	33.0	41.2
Villages	1.6	—	0.3	1.2	1.6	0.9	2.8
Moshavim	3.9	—	0.3	1.8	3.1	2.0	1.6

P1 Birth/Origins:	100.0	100.0	100.0	100.0	100.0	100.0	100.0
AA	66.8	48.7	21.6	17.6	13.5	15.4	40.7
EA	28.4	38.1	50.1	60.1	54.2	55.0	41.8
Is-Fa/Is	1.3	3.3	2.4	8.2	6.7	6.0	3.7
Is-Fa/AA	2.0	4.2	3.2	4.3	1.5	1.8	3.6
Is-Fa/EA	1.4	5.7	22.8	9.8	24.1	21.8	10.2
Father's Education	100.0	100.0	100.0	100.0	100.0	100.0	100.0
None	41.9	23.0	8.6	—	0.6	3.8	18.7
Elementary	39.0	.53.1	36.5	47.3	32.9	34.1	47.2
H.S.	5.8	10.4	24.8	11.9	28.1	39.6	14.5
Yeshiva	12.0	11.3	15.0	34.2	14.5	10.9	13.3
Teach's Seminary	0.7	0.3	1.4	—	2.5	—	0.8
University	0.7	1.9	13.8	6.6	21.5	11.6	5.5
Own Education	100.9	100.0	100.0	100.0	100.0	100.0	100.0
0-7 years	52.4	25.9	3.6	7.0	0.4	4.3	21.4
8 years	27.4	28.1	6.9	13.2	1.0	2.2	19.7
9-11 years	11.3	29.3	19.1	30.4	1.0	10.3	22.2
12 years	7.4	10.9	25.0	27.5	5.4	6.9	16.0
13-15 years	1.6	5.1	20.7	5.9	17.6	20.8	10.0
16+ years	—	0.8	24.8	15.9	74.5	55.5	10.7

Intergenerational occupational mobility into and out of these strata has been studied in earlier works (Matras and Weintraub, 1976, 1977). In Table 4 we show selected compositional characteristics of these strata. All the four occupational strata shown in Table 4 are essentially urban strata. The high white collar strata are concentrated in the three largest cities: Tel Aviv, Jerusalem, and Haifa, and substantially under-represented in the "New Towns." On the other hand, the manual strata, and especially the Unskilled Workers group are highly over-represented in the new towns and somewhat under-represented in the three largest cities.

The high white collar strata were, in 1974 at least, largely composed of people of "European-American" birth or origin-strata, though by no means exclusively so. By contrast the manual strata, while comprising Asian and African-birth or -origin majorities, include also substantial numbers and percentages of European birth or parentage. Israeli-born males of European or American parentage, in particular, were over-represented in the self-employed and employee Professional and Academic groups and in the Managerial and Administrative employee group; while Israeli-born of Asian or African parentage were greatly under-represented in the Professional and Academic groups. Asian or African-born immigrants were greatly under-represented in all the high white collar strata; but they still comprised between 13% and 22% of the total in those groups.

Of the occupational strata shown, only the "skilled and semi-skilled manual employees" group is vaguely "representative" of all the major ethnic categories, with EA percentage "domination" of the high white collar strata and AA percentage "domination" of the unskilled workers stratum. But none of the strata is properly viewed as "excluding" any given ethnic category, nor is any particular ethnic category highly concentrated in a single given stratum (see also Table 2). The composition of the various strata by fathers' educational attainment and by respondents' educational attainment are largely as expected.

Concluding Remarks

I mentioned earlier the familiar conclusion that the extensive intergenerational educational and occupational mobility in all the ethnic categories has not diminished ethnic socio-economic inequality. Moreover, data showing regressions of occupational status on education by country of origin, and percentages of employed males with specified levels of educational attainment in selected occupational groups and economic branches by ethnic groups, suggest ethnic inequality of socio-economic opportunity in the sense of unequal occupational returns or "payoff" for educational attainment, in addition to the ethnic differences in origin-specific and destination-specific rates of mobility. (Israel Central Bureau of Statistics, 1977; Matras, 1977; Boyd *et al.,* 1980; Semyonov, 1978). This point calls for more detailed investigation and analysis. However, these very data show a convergence, across Jewish ethnic groupings in Israel, of the process of occupational and income attainment. This convergence of socio-economic opportunity regimes may be formulated alternatively as an "erosion of occupational disprivilege", or an "erosion of exclusion" of Jews from occupational positions or economic sectors. Credentialled Jews, whatever their ethnic identification or background, are admitted to all occupational status groups or economic branches, though not necessarily with equal frequency, equal promotion or career trajectories or velocities, equal job power or authority for a given work experience or educational credential.

Similarly, there has been some convergence across ethnic groups of schooling and "credentialling" opportunities under way, indexed primarily by sharply increasing rates of continuation in schooling among the Asian- and African-origin groups (Israel Central Bureau of Statistics, 1980: Table XXII). This may or may not be attributable to developments in the school system. Political, economic, and especially demographic trends have been factors in this convergence process, and the school system has adopted a variety of measures and innovations intending explicitly to promote such convergence of educational and training opportunity.

Perhaps the most dramatic and best-documented example of convergence of social opportunity regimes across the Jewish ethnic groups in Israel has been the convergence of marriage and family formation patterns. The Asian- and African-origin population sub-groups, previously characterized by precocious marriage and very high fertility, have experienced upward shifts in age at marriage and widespread institutionalization of small family values and of families limitation. Among recent marriage cohorts whether in European- or American origin or in Asian- or African-origin sub-groups, family size is small and childbearing is terminated early, a trend that bears on per capita income, on cognitive achievements at all levels of school, on women's labour force and social participation, and on other social and economic trends (Bachi, 1977; Friedlander and Goldscheider, 1978, 1979).

I am not sure that I can put an immediate finger on the evidence, but I suspect that several of the important axes and modes of ethnic social organization—especially in the larger towns and metropolitan centers—are undergoing erosion and decline. Migration, intra-city mobility, and expansion of new housing developments have combined to erode the genuine ethnic or place-of-origin ghettos or residential enclaves in the cities—with the possible exception of the ultra-religious community ghettos. If there were in the past ethnic or origin-specific occupations or economic sectors (e.g. German banking, Kurdish porters or earth-moving, Persian rug-dealers, etc), these are disappearing. In this chapter I have tried to indicate that, at least in the major occupational strata, it is impossible to make a case for either ethnic exclusiveness or exclusion. Indeed, it would be difficult to make a case even for any recent past institutionalized exclusion of Jews from social positions or from participation in organized social activity in Israel strictly on grounds of ethnic background, or of country or place of birth or origin. Rather, attributes or characteristics or credentials of some sort—or their absence—have frequently been the bases of social, economic, or political exclusion, and these have very often coincided or been associated with ethnicity or origin.

Numerous ethnic and origin-based voluntary organizations—mutual aid, commemorative, *landsmannschaft*-type organizations—exist and thrive, often with connections to political parties, trade unions, or public institutions. Participation in these, however, generally does not extend beyond immigrants from the places of origin or with similar ethnic origins. Involvement of the younger generations is quite exceptional and there are few prospects for long-term survival of the organizations beyond the lifetimes of present membership. Urban synagogues in old neighborhoods remain organized along ethnic and community-of-origin axes, but they tend to be much less elaborately differentiated in the newer neighborhoods and housing developments; and without large-scale support, e.g. from the Ministry of Religious Affairs or from the religious or right wing parties, the urban ethnic synagogues—again, excepting those of the ultra-orthodox ghettos—seem to have a doubtful future. In the very largest cities, the ethnic or origin-based burial societies have a certain viability related to property ownership and maintenance. But these, too, are by and large in the process of replacement by ethnically less-highly-differentiated organizations and services.

In this chapter I have tried to show some of the intra-ethnic group generation gaps associated with intergenerational educational and occupational mobility. The data connecting mobility with patterns of mate selection suggest that marriage in Israel is supportive of trends in the direction of crystallization of social class groupings, while ethnic or country-of-origin homogamy is declining. More generally, the change among Jews in Israel from a pattern of marriages contracted within small, endogamous ethnically and geographically circumscribed pools of eligibles—either with previous kinship relationships or, minimally, with extended families of orientation mutually acquainted prior to the marriages and mutually visible and accountable after the marriages—to marriages contracted within large ethnically heterogenous, relatively diffuse and mutually unknown pools of eligibles, has been one of the decisive social transformations of contemporary Israel. Taking place, as it has, conjointly with the massive intergenerational educational mobility, the large scale entrance of women into the labour force and a communications revolution which has rendered the various ethnic and social class groupings in Israel and abroad mutually visible, the changing mate selection and marriage regime has made alternative role and activity models, as well as alternative axes of solidarity, patterns of interaction, and social participation options visible and attainable.

Finally, and perhaps most important, shifts in the entitlement regime—institutionalized bases of claims on rewards, on control of resources, or on access to or allocation of rewards or resources—have both resulted in additional intra-ethnic group generation gaps and worked to diminish ethnic solidarity and continuity. These shifts, including the upgrading of educational credentials, skill, work experience, property ownership, and productivity-related entitlements and the downgrading of piety, seniority, past-deprivation, kin, origin, and past-residence-related entitlements, have altered the axes and meanings of social mobility and strata formation in Israel generally and raise questions about the salience and nature of "ethnicity" in Israeli society.

Notes

[1] For a full description of the survey, see Israel Central Bureau of Statistics, 1977, and other references cited herein.

[2] Intergenerational mobility or immobility is reckoned in terms of the differences between respondents' fathers and their own occupational prestige scores, as derived by Kraus (1976). Respondents with scores differing from their fathers by 10 points or more are classified "upward" or "downward" mobile (in accordance with the sign of the difference), while those with less than 10 points are classified "same."

To compare a respondent's occupational origin with that of his wife, the respondent's wife and wife's fathers' respective occupational prestige scores, (as derived by Kraus, 1976) are compared and the difference computed. The wife's occupational origins are denoted "higher," the "same," or "lower" according as the difference is 10 or more points (higher or lower, depending on the sign) or less than 10 points (same). Respondents whose wives or wives' fathers were born in the respondent's own country of birth, or, if born in Israel, in father's country of birth, are classified "same country." Those born or originating in a different country, but in the same area (Europe-America-Oceania, or Asia-Africa) are classified "same continent, different country." Those whose wives are born or originate in different countries and different continents are classified simply "different continents." For those born in Israel with Israeli-born fathers, all who marry wives born either abroad or in Israel, but with foreign-born fathers are classified "different continent."

For purposes of educational attainment comparisons, both respondents and wives are grouped according to whether they did not attend school at all, attended primary school, attended post-primary school or attended post-secondary schools or institutions. Wives are classified as having higher, the same or lower educational attainment compared to the respondents if they are in higher, the same or lower educational attainment groups respectively.

[3]"Upward, "downward" or "no educational mobility" are determined for each female respondent by comparing her own educational attainment groups (none, primary, post-primary or post-secondary) with her fathers' reported educational attainment group.

References

Bachi, R. 1977. *The Population of Israel.* Jerusalem: C.I.C.R.E.D.

Boyd, M, Featherman, L. D., and Matras, J. 1980. "Status Attainment of Immigrant and Immigrant-Origin Groups in the United States, Canada, and Israel," *Comparative Studies in Sociology,* Vol. 3.

Friedlander, D and Goldscheider, C. 1978. "Immigration, Social Change and Cohort Fertility in Israel," *Population Studies* 32, 2 July.

—— and ——. 1979. *The Population of Israel.* New York: Columbia University Press.

Israel Central Bureau of Statistics. 1977. *Labour Mobility Survey, 1974.* Special Publications Series no. 544, Jerusalem.

—— . 1980. *Statistical Abstract of Israel, No. 31, 1980.* Jerusalem. Tables XXII/12, XXII/14.

Kraus, V. 1976. "Social Grading of Occupations in Israel." Unpublished Ph.D. dissertation, the Hebrew University, Jerusalem.

——, Hodge, R. W., and Schild, E. 1978. "Social Grading of Occupations in Israel," *Social Forces,* March.

Matras, J. 1965. *Social Change In Israel.* Chicago: Aldine.

—— 1973. "On Changing Matchmaking, Marriage, and Family Formation in Israel: Some Findings and Some Hypotheses," *American Journal of Sociology,* 79.2 (Sept.).

——. 1977. "Ethnic and Social Origin 'Dominance' in Occupational Attainment in Israel," Brookdale Institute Discussion Paper No. 28-77, Jerusalem, June.

——, and Noam, G. 1976. "Intergenerational Educational Mobility in Israel–An Overview," Brookdale Institute Discussion Paper No. 11-76, Jerusalem.

——, and Weintraub, D. 1976. "Intergenerational Mobility in Israel," Economics Quarterly (in Hebrew, *Riv'on LeKalkala*) No. 90, August.

——, and ——. 1977. "Ethnic and Other Primordial Differentials in Intergenerational Mobility in Israel," Brookdale Institute Discussion Paper No. 25-77, Jerusalem.

——, and Selbee, K. 1980. "On Marriage, Social Stratification, and Mobility in Israel" in U.O. Schmelz, P. Glikson, and S. Della Pergola (Eds.), *Papers in Jewish Demography 1977.* Jerusalem: World Union of Jewish Studies.

Noam, G. 1978. "Patterns of Occupational Authority and Control of Resources" Brookdale Institute Discussion Paper No. D-33-78, Jerusalem.

Semyonov, M. 1978. "Community, Ethnicity, and Achievement: Toward Understanding Contextual Effects." Unpublished Ph.D. Dissertation, Dept. of Sociology, State University of New York at Stony Brook, August.

2

The Changing Ethnic Geography of Israeli Cities

Amiram Gonen

The division of the Jewish population of Israel into two large ethnic categories—Asia-Africa and Europe-America—finds expression in various socio-economic indices. Throughout the past six decades, the Europe-America (henceforward EA) category has been categorized by a higher socio-economic status then the Asia-African one (henceforward AA) (Hartman and Ayalon, 1975; Lissak, 1969; Smooha and Peres, 1975; Weingrod, 1965). These differences can be seen, for example, in contrasting levels of income, education and occupation. Various studies have also found clear intra-urban spatial expressions of the positive correlation between ethnicity and socio-economic status. Urban areas that mainly include persons of a higher socio-economic status also have, in general, a high proportion of EA residents; conversely, areas characterized by lower socio-economic status tend to have higher proportions of inhabitants in the AA category (Borukhov et al., 1979; Gradus, 1977; Hershkovitz, 1979; Klaff, 1973; Shachar et al., 1978).

This chapter reexamines the intra-urban geographical pattern formed by these two social categories. The focus is primarily upon the recent changes which have reshaped the urban ethnic residential map. Only older cities established prior to 1948 are discussed; unlike most of the new towns developed in the 1950's, the older cities are ethnically heterogenous to a degree that warrants a study of their ethnic geography. Analyzing ethnic residential patterns in the new towns is of little significance, since they tend to be ethnically homogeneous, with an overwhelming majority of persons in the Asia-Africa category.

The Residential Pattern Before the 1970's

As mentioned above, there is a broad positive correlation between residence and ethnic membership in older Israeli cities. This ecological pattern is similar in many respects to that of many European and Third World cities. More specifically, many of the zones characterized by high socioeconomic status, and thus predominantly EA in composition, are found in *inner* urban zones. This tendency of higher income groups to concentrate in the inner urban neighborhoods is probably indicative of their preference for accessibility and urbanity over space amenities and a suburban life style (Gonen, 1976). On the other hand, many of the *outer* urban areas tend to be populated by lower socio-economic status groups, with a majority of persons from the AA category. The cause of this AA concentration in the outer areas derives from the locational policies and practices of state public housing agencies, which led them to build new housing estates on the then open periphery of cities (Gonen, 1975). The availability of publicly-controlled land, the need for rapid construction in view of the large influx of immigrants, as well as political and bureaucratic considerations, were among the factors pushing public housing estates towards these peripheral zones. This combination of residential preference among the higher socio-economic strata plus the locational policy of the housing agencies produced a typically concentric residence pattern. The maps in Figure 1 exemplify this format in four medium-sized Israeli cities: Herzliya, Netanya, Petah Tikva and Rishon Letzion.

Figure 2 shows the relationship between ethnic composition, socioeconomic status (as measured by income or housing price) and intraurban location in these cities. As a rule, the proportion of AA residents decreases with rising income or housing price but increases with distance from the urban core. Exceptions to this rule are the higher status "garden neighborhoods" that have a majority of persons from the EA category. These affluent "garden neighborhoods" are either the result of recent suburban development (to be discussed later in this essay) or they were originally "workers neighborhoods" that were lately upgraded.

The pattern in the major cities of Jerusalem, Tel Aviv-Jaffa, and Haifa, is somewhat different. In these cities the inner areas are divided in a sectoral fashion between higher and lower-status neighborhoods, and hence between the two ethnic categories. For example, next to the commercial core of Jerusalem poor and affluent neighborhoods exist side by side and exhibit a high degree of ethnic and socio-economic segregation. This is also true of Tel Aviv-Jaffa, where north of the commerical core one finds a high proportion of persons of higher socio-economic status, most of whom belong to the EA category. The opposite is true south of the commercial core. In Haifa, the ecological differentiation is aligned topographically: socio-economic status increases along the ascending slope of Mount Carmel, as does the proportion in the Europe-America category.

Why lower-status neighborhoods are situated in the inner zones of large-sized Israeli cities can be explained in historical terms. In Jersualem, for example, it was due to the "ethnic migrations" that characterized the city towards the end of the nineteenth and first quarter of the twentieth centuries. When originally developed these neighborhoods were on the urban periphery; as Jerusalem grew in size they became a part of the urban core area. In Tel Aviv-Jaffa, the division between the northern and southern inner areas (near to the commercial core) is related to the northward migration of Jewish families during the 1920's and 1930's. At that time Jewish Tel Aviv was quickly moving away from hostile Arab Jaffa to its south. The older Jewish neighborhoods, those close to or within Jaffa, gradually underwent a decline as many of the upwardly mobile households migrated to the then developing northern neighborhoods.

Finally, in Haifa the division between the "downtown" and "uptown" sections is also associated with the city's recent history. Prior to 1948, the older areas of Haifa at the foot of Mount Carmel were largely inhabited by Arabs, while the newer areas, higher on the slope, were developed by Jews. During the 1948 war the Arab population fled the city and newly arrived Jewish immigrants were settled in the evacuated neighborhoods. These new immigrants lacked resources, and the downtown inner areas of Haifa consequently became a lower socio-economic zone. Over time, differential intra-urban migration tended to increase ethnic segregation: the more upwardly mobile EA families moved to more prestigious areas, leaving behind a high proportion of AA residents. In addition, low-status Arab neighborhoods also re-formed in certain parts of downtown Haifa.

It should be emphasized that although these three older cities include low status inner areas with a majority of AA residents, many other AA's settled in public housing estates built in the *outer* fringe. Thus, the overall geographic pattern, in which a relatively high proportion of AA's reside in the outer city areas, does not differ substantially between large and medium-sized cities.

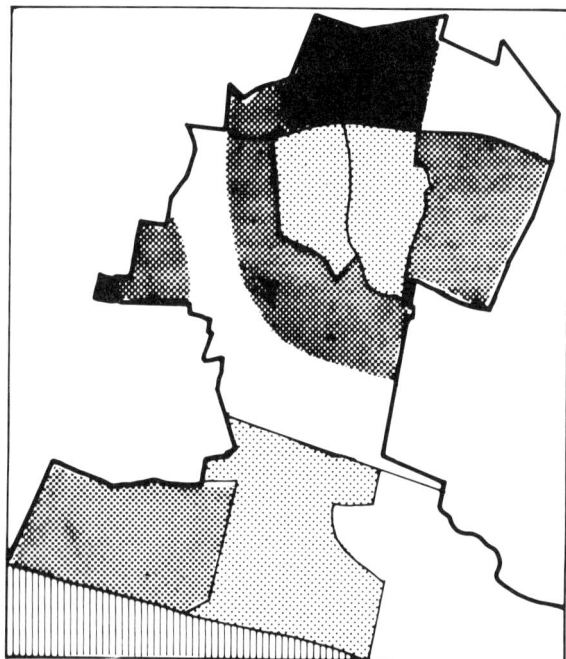

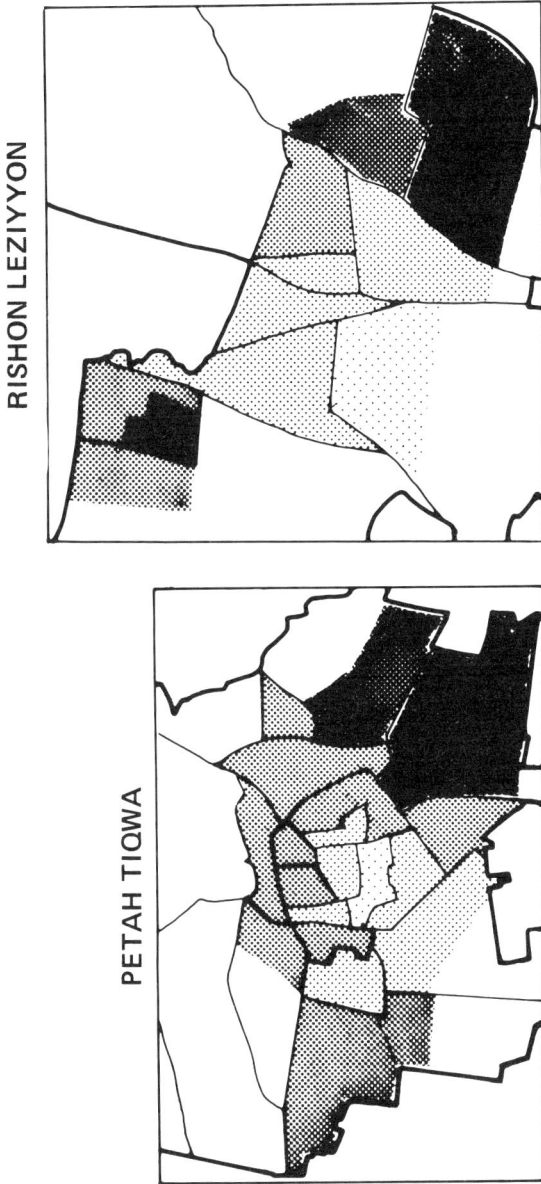

Figure 1. Ethnicity in medium-sized cities in Israel 1972

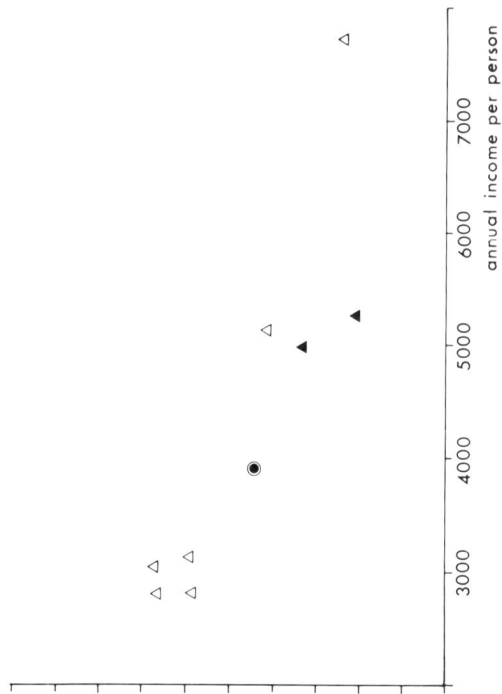

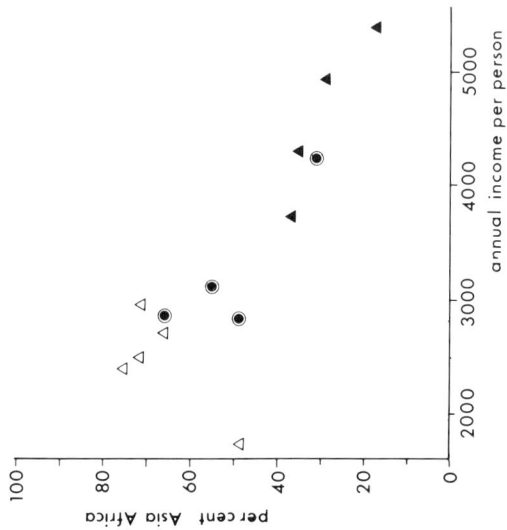

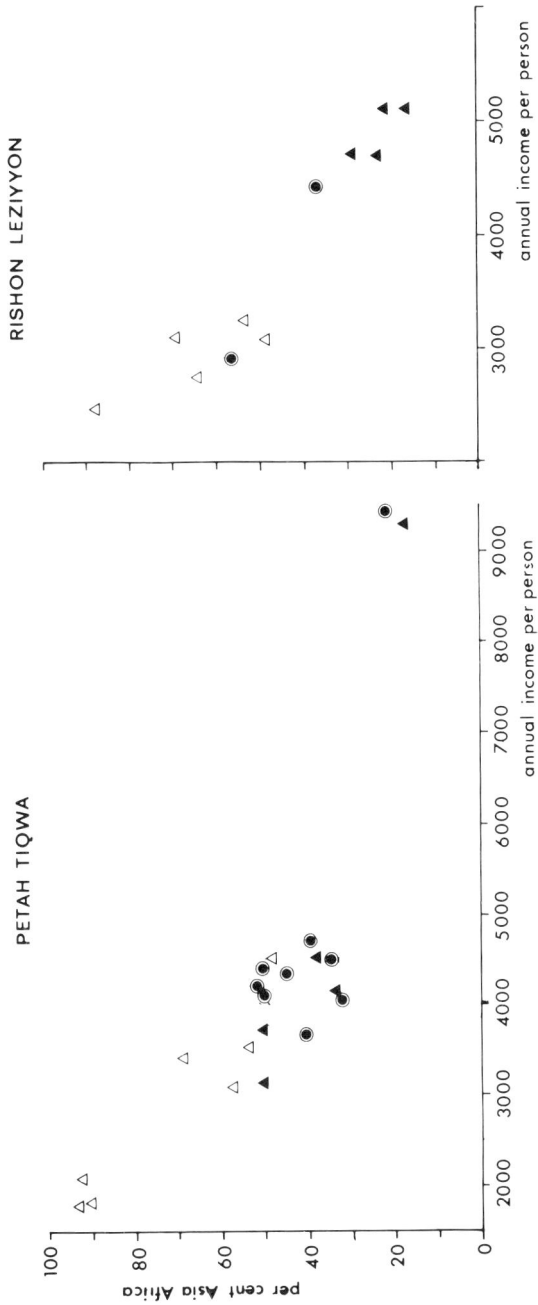

Figure 2. Ethnicity and income in medium-sized cities in Israel, 1972

This characteristic spatial pattern emerged during the first five or six decades of Israeli urban development. It is important to understand how this pattern has continued to evolve. The remaining sections of this chapter analyze some recent directions in ethnic residential continuity and change. Briefly described, the major trends have been: decreasing ethnic segregation in inner urban areas; increasing ethnic segregation in outer urban areas; suburbanization of the EA category; and the emergence of important new areas of ethnic integration.

Decreasing Segregation in Inner Urban Areas

Comparing the 1961 with the 1972 census one discovers a *decrease* in the level of ethnic segregation in the higher status inner areas of the older cities: the EA category has declined from a majority of over 80 percent in the 1961 census to a much smaller majority in 1972.

This decline is the result of concurrent processes of in- and out-migration. In some inner areas it is due to the in-migration of persons in the AA category, while in others it is primarily the incipient out-migration of the EA's.

The migration of AA category persons into these higher status residential areas is mainly the result of increasing upward social mobility. In these areas housing is of better quality, as are neighborhood services, particularly schools. Indeed, one important component of intra-urban migration during the 1960's was the flow of persons from the outlying public housing estates into these inner urban areas, particularly in the medium-sized cities (Gonen and Hasson, 1974).

On the other hand, a principal reason for the out-migration of some EA families is the obsolescence and decay of some inner urban neighborhoods. Older inner areas, particularly those close to the commercial core, lost their residential desirability. This is especially true of younger households, who leave the inner city for newer urban or suburban neighborhoods. Their exit is followed by the entry of AA households, who find housing in the inner areas appropriate to their newly achieved socioeconomic status.

This process of obsolescence and out-migration is restricted mainly to the older neighborhoods in the three large cities. In the medium-sized cities, the encroachment of commerce is still negligible. On the contrary: in these cities the relatively low density of commercial development has made possible a substantial increase in building activities near the urban core. Centrally-located streets built for low density single-family housing (as in the case of the former *moshavot* or rural towns), witnessed the construction of "high-rise" residential buildings. This newly expanding supply of housing attracted upwardly mobile AA households, many of whom migrated from outlying housing estates.

The increasing residential density of the inner areas and the resulting change in their ethnic composition also induced an out-migration of EA households. Many of them moved to new pockets of affluence within the expanding urban core. For example, the northern inner areas of Petah Tikva, which include the commercial streets of the oldest part of town, underwent an increase in the proportion of AA families, while the southern inner areas have become new centers of higher-status families, largely in the EA category. In the northern inner areas the percentage of AA's rose from 28.0 in 1961 to 43.5 in 1972, although in the southern inner zones the percentage of the Europe-America born remained high throughout this period (81.1 in 1972). Comparable changes took place in some of the newly built residential areas in northern Tel Aviv, adjacent to the older inner areas.

Increasing Segregation in Outer Urban Areas

While ethnic segregation was breaking down in inner urban zones, it was strengthened in the outer ones. There are indications that segregation of AA's has intensified in many of the outlying lower income public housing estates. This concentration of population is due to a number of factors. In many of these areas the original EA residents either migrated elsewhere or died of old age; those EA's who remained were either too poor or too old to move, or they were new immigrants who had recently settled there. The proportion of second generation, Israeli born EA's in these housing estates is especially low.

Moreover, upwardly mobile AA households that sought to improve their housing and social conditions also migrated out of these areas. The "weaker" AA families have been left behind, and they form the population majority in these neighborhoods. It is probably inevitable that these clusters are characterized by deviant behavior and social disorganization. Indeed, negative ethnic stereotypes tend to be generated or reinforced in these relatively poor areas.

Suburbanization of the Europe America Category

While a gradual decrease in the level of ethnic residential segregation has taken place in the inner urban neighborhoods, new essentially segregated clusters have emerged in the suburbs. Since the late 1960's, and particularly during the 1970's, there has been a growing preference for a suburban residential setting among the younger upwardly mobile EA households. While during earlier decades most of the higher-status European–American's preferred residing in accessible neighborhoods with an urban ambience, many have recently shown an interest in a suburban life style (Gonen, 1980). This had an added effect on the previously described tendency to withdraw from the older, established EA neighborhoods. Garden-suburbs, so common in the North America urban setting, have thereby emerged as another kind of EA ethnic concentration.

One important consequence of suburbanization is an emerging ethnic mosaic in the suburbs, where side by side one now finds new garden neighborhoods with a majority of EA's and older public housing estates with a majority of AA residents (Gonen, 1976). These two kinds of residential areas differ not only in their ethnic composition, but also vary greatly in their income level and quality of housing.

The question that arises is whether this newly emerging suburban mosaic implies increasing or decreasing ethnic segregation. On the one hand, what stands out are ethnically differentiated clusters, each correlated with contrasting socio-economic status and differing housing quality. These separate clusters undoubtedly emphasize ethnic segregation. On the other hand, however, the proximity of the two kinds of neighborhoods offers opportunities for sharing certain local services, especially schools. These opportunities were non-existent in earlier decades when immigrant housing estates stood alone on the urban fringe. Moreover, the development of higher-status households in the suburbs also strengthened the residential attractiveness of nearby public housing estates, especially in those cases in which these estates were originally built at low densities. In some of these estates housing has been upgraded, thus contributing to the relaxation of tensions between the adjoining neighborhoods.

New Areas of Ethnic Integration

The most striking changes in ethnic residential integration has taken place in what can be described as "intermediate areas": these are new zones built up gradually in undeveloped open spaces situated between the older parts of cities and the outlying public housing estates. These intermediate areas were the scene of much of the residential construction that took place in Israeli cities during the past fifteen or so years. The development and construction of these new areas was financed from both public and private sources—in Israel, public housing has included a wide spectrum of the population and is by no means limited to the poor.

The interesting question is who moved into these zones. Generally speaking, they have been populated by what can be described as young, middle income families. In ethnic terms they include large numbers of *both* EA and AA households (as well as families based upon "mixed marriages"). Many upwardly mobile AA families were attracted to these new areas; for these families they represented a better housing quality as well as improved urban services when compared with the older, mainly AA housing estates. Moreover, a significant number of EA origin families also moved to these intermediate areas; these new residents were attracted by the comparatively lower housing costs as well as the difficulty of finding adequate housing in the older, predominantly EA inner city areas.

In these residential areas, ethnic mixing takes place from the very first stages of development. The households are primarily composed of second or third generation Israeli-born persons, and consequently they typically share important features of culture and life style. Moreover, there are no marked socio-economic differences between the households, and this too reduces segregation. Finally, the comparatively young age of the residents is also conducive to a "smooth" residential mix along ethnic lines. For all of these reasons these zones appear to be arenas in which new cultural formats as well as new inter-ethnic social relations are becoming shaped.

Conclusions

The foregoing description of the changing ethnic geography of Israeli cities indicates a variety of different, and in certain instances, contradictory, trends. Focusing upon the two major ethnic categories—AA and EA—processes of both segregation and integration are apparent. Within the EA category, there has been a general decline in the level of segregation. This trend can be explained primarily as the result of migration of upwardly mobile AA families into the higher status inner city areas. At the same time, however, small clusters of EA's concentrated in the new suburban "garden neighborhoods"; there too the segregation level is relatively low since many of the mobile AA's have joined the Israeli move to the suburbs.

Focusing next upon the AA's, the trend towards residential integration is strongly evident in the migration to the "intermediate areas", as well as in the migration of upwardly mobile AA's to prestigious inner city areas and the suburbs. However, those AA's residing in outlying housing estates or in older inner city neighborhoods have been increasingly segregated within pockets of poverty. Indeed, the AA category is to an increasing extent differentiated between two broad groups–those mobile AA's who have shared in Israel's economic development, and those large numbers who may have entered into a long lasting state of poverty.

What does seem clear is that, in comparison with the 1950's, the urban ethnic residential map has become increasingly complex. From the social policy perspective the continued segregation of poor AA households is a major topic of national concern. New strategies will have to be devised in order to significantly alter and upgrade the urban poverty zones. In addition, however, attention should be given to the new areas of residential ethnic mixing, particularly the new intermediate areas. A more detailed understanding of these zones will help to clarify the directions in which Israeli society is moving in regard to ethnicity, socio-economic status, and their residential and spatial expressions.

References

Borukhov, E., Ginsberg, Y., and Werczberger, E. 1979. "The Social Ecology of Tel Aviv: A Study in Factor Analysis", *Urban Affairs Quarterly,* Vol. 15, No. 2, 183–205.

Gonen, A. 1975. "Locational and Ecological Aspects of Urban Public Sector Housing: The Israeli Case," in G. Gappert and H. M. Rose (Eds.), *The Social Economy of Cities.* Beverly Hills: Sage Publications (Urban Affairs Annual Reviews, Vol. 9), 275–295.

——. 1976. "The Suburban Mosaic in Israel", in D. Amiran and Y. Ben-Arieh (Eds.), *Geography in Israel.* Jerusalem: Israeli National Committee of the International Geographical Union, 163–186.

——. 1980. "A Basic Pattern in the Social Geography of Israeli Cities", in U. O. Schmelz, P. Glickson, and S. Della Pergola (Eds.), *Papers in Jewish Demography 1977.* Jerusalem: Institute of Contemporary Jewry, The Hebrew University of Jerusalem, 351–366.

——, and Hasson, Sh. 1974. "Ethnic Differences in Change of Residence: Immigrant Housing Estates on the Fringe of Medium-Sized Cities in Israel", *Megamot,* Vol. 20, No. 3, 310–315 (in Hebrew).

Gradus, Y. 1977. *The Spatial Urban Ecology of Metropolitan Haifa, Israel: A Factorial Approach.* Unpublished Ph.D. Dissertation, University of Pittsburgh.

Hershkovitz, S. 1979. *The Spatial Structure of the Population in Tel Aviv Metropolitan Area 1961-1972.* Unpublished Ph.D. Dissertation, The Hebrew University of Jerusalem.

Hartman, M, and Ayalon, H. 1975. "Ethnicity and Class in Israel", *Megamot,* Vol. 21, No. 2, 124-139 (in Hebrew).

Klaff, V. Z. 1973. "Ethnic Segregation in Urban Israel", *Demography,* Vol. 10, No. 2, 161-184.

Lissak, M. 1969. *Social Mobility in Israel Society.* Jerusalem: Israel Universities Press.

Shachar, A., Hershkovitz, S., and Stier, M. 1978. "Social Areas in Tel Aviv Metropolitan Region in the 1960's", *Research in the Geography of Israel,* Vol. 10, 1-30.

Smooha, S. and Peres, Y. 1975. "The Dynamics of Ethnic Inequalities: The Case of Israel", *Social Dynamics,* Vol. 1, No. 1.

Weingrod, A. 1965. *Israel: Group Relations in a New Society.* London: Praeger Publishers.

.

3

Horizontal Integration and Vertical Differentiation among Jewish Ethnicities in Israel

Yochanan Peres

The challenge of understanding ethnic relations stems, to a large extent, from a duality between their horizontal and vertical dimensions. By "horizontal distance" between two groups, I mean the aggregate of all cultural differences (values, norms, preferences), which are transferred by socialization and eventually crystalize into a "style of life." The "vertical distance" between two groups is the distance between the groups' positions in the society's stratification system.

Students of ethnic relations as well as political leaders and commentors differ in their emphasis on either dimension. Some define the issue exclusively in terms of social stratification. Diversity of culture, outlook or mentality are simply perceived as manifestations of economic or political inequality and ethnicity is supposed to be social class (or caste) in disguise. An opposing view, represented mainly by anthropologists, considers ethnic groups as authentic cultures that cannot be graded and should not be assimilated.

The task in the following pages is to present a balanced approach that might do justice to cultural diversity as well as to ethnic stratification.

To illustrate a hypothesis that combines the two dimensions, let us imagine two points between which there is an appreciable horizontal, and a small vertical distance:

39

In a situation like this it is difficult to discern the difference in height. If, however, we shorten the horizontal distance without changing the vertical one, the latter will become salient and appreciable:

This example enables us to plunge directly into one of the most crucial problems in Israel in the 1970s. Precisely because of the considerable success of cultural and social absorption, inequality in distribution of economic, political and educational resources is more striking. Not that these gaps have increased: on the contrary, it is possible to prove that they diminished in the 1970s after remaining more or less stable, with only small fluctuations between 1955-1970. The psychological and social significance of inequality has, however, increased considerably, due to the fact that the various ethnic groups in Israel have come closer together in culture, language, behavior and family patterns. Generally speaking, a greater similarity between people intensifies the demand for greater equality between them. For example, siblings who are dissimilar in sex, age, appearance and interests will not be hurt by a slight imbalance in distribution of family resources between them. An identical twin, however, will react with a furious outburst of jealousy if his twin brother is even slightly preferred.

Horizontal Integration

The broadest single evidence of cultural integration is attitudinal. Most Israelis seem to view ethnic differences as a phenomenon that can and should eventually disappear. In a survey conducted in the mid-1960s, respondents were asked whether they considered it desirable for ethnic differences to disappear. About seventy percent of the sample opted for a complete extinction of ethnic differences, while twenty-eight percent justified the persistence of different traditions. Only a negligible two percent preferred that "ethnic differences should remain as they are now." More than eighty percent of the respondents predicted that the cultural gap between ethnicities will decline substantially. Detailed interviews with a subsample verified this impression: feelings of interdependence and a desire for the formation of an Israeli national identity that should replace separate ethnic identities were repeatedly expressed (Peres, 1971:1036-1038; Peres, 1976:99-100).

Several studies performed during the 1970s have convincingly shown that these attitudes have behavioral correlates. The most outstanding behavioral indicator of integration is interethnic marriage. The rate of mixed couples (couples with one partner of European origin (E-A) and the other of Asian or African origin (A-A) among all Jewish marrying couples rose from nine percent (1952) to nineteen percent (1976) (Peres and Schrift 1978:439-440). A parallel rise occurred in the ratio of intermarriage among Orientals originating from different (Asian or African) countries, from twenty-two percent (1952) to forty percent (1975) (Swirski and Katzir 1977:45-57). During the 1970s the patterns of family life drew closer. In 1960 the divorce rate (per 1000) for couples of Asian or African origin (A-A) was 1.2, and for couples of European or American origin (E-A), 1.8. The ratios in 1975 were, respectively, 1.5 and 1.7 (Statistical Abstract: 1962 Table 15: 1977 Table 13). In the early 1960s, E-A tended to marry later than A-A. The groom's age at first marriage was 29 for E-A and 26 for A-A. The bride's age at first marriage was 24 for E-A and 21 for A-A. By 1975 these differences vanished: the mean age of brides and grooms of both ethnicities was 21 and 23 respectively (Statistical Abstract 1977: Table 111/14). It should be noted that these developments are symmetric, i.e., not merely a result of A-A acculturation but of corresponding changes on the part of both ethnicities.

A somewhat different picture emerges when the possession of durable household equipment is examined. Jews of A-A origin modernized their households rapidly. Twenty years ago, there was a difference between ethnic groups as to the numbers of gas ranges, electric refrigerators and washing machines owned (over three times more E-A owned gas ranges than did A-A). Since 1970, modern household equipment has become almost commonplace. Thus, ethnic differentiation has vanished; A-A has adopted a modern style of life (Statistical Abstract, 21:181, 185-6).

Similar trends can be found in cultural consumption (Katz and Gurevitch 1973:104; 230). The ratio of movie-goers among A-A somewhat exceeds that among E-A; the ratio of theater-goers among A-A is lower than among E-A but the gap diminishes substantially if second generation high school graduates are compared. A similar statement can be made about reading habits. Educated A-A read as many books as educated E-A do. The only item of cultural consumption that sharply differentiates ethnicities is music. Among A-A (even second generation possessing high school education) the ratio of concert-goers is low: seven percent compared to twenty-one percent among E-A high school graduates. Smooha (1978:232), after carefully examining the level of structural differentiation between Jews and Arabs, religious and non-religious Jews and, finally, A-A and E-A, concluded that ". . . the Orientals have proved to be an assimilating group." While this statement is evidently true when the relationship between A-A and E-A is compared with such pluralistic situations as the Jewish-Arab or the religious-secular, we have shown that in several crucial areas of behavior (e.g., marriage and birth rates) the term "integration" is a more accurate account of the process, since it was not just the Orientals who have "assimilated;" rather, both ethnicities have drawn closer to each other.

Social and Psychological Roots of Cultural Integration

What are the factors that accelerated the process of cultural integration? To what extent does this process derive from unique Israeli circumstances? The special quality of Israeli ethnic relations will become salient if we define it in general terms. According to Schermerhorn (1970:107-109; 142-147), most ethnic situations originate from conquest, immigration or annexation. One ethnic group usually emerges from such an encounter with superior resources, and aspires to preserve this superiority. Jewish ethnicities in Israel came into contact as a result of immigration. But this immigration was caused by relatively collectivistic motives; not just individual survival or pursuit of private goals, but also a vision of national revival.

Eisenstadt (1954:111-124) hypothesized that the motivation to immigrate will have important implications for adaptive behavior after immigration. Indeed, an overall tendency emerged to change the former Jewish-Yemenite or Jewish-Rumanian identities and to adopt a new common identity of Israeli-Jew.[1] "Nation building" was in this case not just an objective of the leadership or an analytical concept used by social scientists, but rather an explicit and virgorous impulse in the life of individuals.

Attachment to countries and cultures of origin has been further weakened by another phenomenon: most newcomers to Israel have "burned their bridges," i.e., have no hope of returning to their former homes under reasonable terms, because their old countries have turned against them. This sequence of immigration followed by bitter animosity between country and origin and country of destination has been repeated in the case of Russia (shortly after the Bolshevik revolution), the rest of Europe (between 1939-1945), and the Middle East and North Africa (after 1948). Nostalgic feelings for the various "old countries" are far less an obstacle to national integration than in other instances of immigrant societies. Like Lot's wife fleeing from Sodom, most immigrants to Israel cannot look back.

While the conditions of immigration probably started the process of cultural integration, the scope and speed of the process should be attributed mainly to the continuous and all-embracing Arab-Israeli conflict. It is well established that the existence of an external enemy is an effective unifying force. For Israelis the feeling (whether justified or not) that the enemy's aim is the total annihilation of Israel and that no compromise could alter the commitment to this goal, has provided an additional impetus toward national cohesiveness.

If this reasoning is valid, feelings of national unity should arise whenever hostilities break out. In fact, the Institute for Applied Social Research in Jerusalem has inquired repeatedly (in the framework of periodic public opinion surveys) whether respondents considered the relations between Jewish ethnicities to be "very good," "good," "fair" or "bad." Immediately after the Six Day War, eighty four percent regarded ethnic relations as "very good" or "good." In subsequent surveys this percentage declined gradually to 44 percent and stayed on this level until October 1973 when it jumped again to a peak of 84 percent. Similar findings were obtained by the Institute regarding other internal strife (e.g., religious versus secular groups). All these conflicts lost much of their relevance whenever external struggle became more threatening (Peres, 1976:97-98).

The two major ethnicities are affected by the external conflict in the same direction, but probably not to the same extent. To support this last statement, let us underscore the notion that since all Jewish communities have adopted major components of culture from their host societies, integration between Jews of Mid-Eastern and European origins means also integration of Arab and European cultures. During wars, a tendency to devalue the enemy's culture is a rather normal phenomenon. Thus, immigrants from the Middle East felt that in order to become fully accepted as Israelis they should rid themselves of all traces of Arab tradition. The presence of a sizable minority of Israel Arabs (over 15 percent of the total population) who cherish their separate identity as well as their attachment to the Arab world is another inducement for Jews of Afro-Asian origin to mark themselves off. Israeli Arabs are not fully accepted in Israeli society, in spite of their having obtained citizenship. Their social advancement is blocked by suspicion and resentment.[2] Under these circumstances it becomes apparent that the "horizontal" distance between Jews of European and Afro-Asian background is diminished, not only by the attraction of the latter to the former, but also by their impulse to dissociate themselves from anything Arab. The discontinuity in the identity of Afro-Asian Jews in Israel manifests itself in many ways. These include: the claim of newcomers from North Africa that they emigrated from "Southern France," the tendency of second generation Oriental Jews to "forget" their Arabic (or never to learn it), and the underrepresentation of Oriental Jewish scholars among the rather numerous and sophisticated experts on Arab affairs.

A further complication of the Arab-Israeli conflict is a widely accepted wish to accelerate modernization. Israel's relative deficiencies in land and population make adaptation of modern techniques and sophisticated tools imperative. Large capital imports and, lately, enormous military aid, also made such a process feasible. Thus, modernization is not necessarily perceived as an acculturation of A-A to European norms, but rather as an adaptation of all Israelis to economic and geopolitical necessities.

Vertical Differentiation

Few topics have obtained more attention on the part of Israeli social scientists than ethnic inequality. Economists, educators, political scientists, demographers and sociologists have contributed facts and figures as well as their theoretical perspectives. Let us devote several paragraphs to an updated account of the magnitude and trend of ethnic stratification in Israel. During the period between 1955-1970 the relative gap in earnings (measured simply by dividing the mean earnings of A-A by the mean earnings of E-A) was stable (Smooha and Peres, 1975:67; 68). This was not the case for the period 1970-1978 (the latest data obtainable was from 1978). The relative gaps for these years[3] are:

1970	1971	1972	1973	1974	1975	1975	1977	1978
.73	.74	.74	.74	.77	.82	.81	.81	.80

Are these gaps small or large? It is impossible to provide an absolute answer to this question, but the data could be evaluated in the light of some comparative information. Black-White relations in the United States are often referred to as an outstanding example of racial inequality in the midst of an advanced liberal society. The ratio of Black median income to White median income was reported by Farley (1977:198) to be .62 and by Jencks *et al.* (1972:237) to be .65. Similar levels of ethnic inequality were reported for Israel in the late fifties (Levy 1969, Table 17).

A closer and perhaps more relevant analogy is provided by the income gap between Arabs and Jews, which is consistently lower than the gap between Jewish ethnicities (e.g., the Arab-Jewish income ratios, 1973, 84 percent; 1975, 92 percent; 1977, 84 percent). Furthermore, the average incomes of non-European Jews and of Arabs are roughly equal (ratio for 1977, .96; source, Central Bureau of Statistics Special Publication 598 Tab. A/s). It should be emphasized that the overall status of Israeli Arabs is far below that of A-A Jews. This fact is manifested in substantial gaps in education, political representation, occupational prestige, etc. Nevertheless, it seems to be a striking and significant fact that Arab and Oriental Jewish wage earners are equally deprived.

Another angle from which the ethnic income gap can be viewed is the upward tendency of real income. During the decade 1955-1965, the average income of Jews in Israel nearly doubled (Central Bureau of Statistics 510, Table 14). The same tendency persisted during 1968-1977, albeit the pace was slower; the increase in real mean earnings was 82 percent (Central Bureau of Statistics 598, Table A/3). Under such circumstances the issue of ethnic inequality should be rephrased. It is not a conflict over the division of a fixed amount of resources but over the allocation of additional ones. Which ethnicity took more advantage of the growing economic opportunities? Between 1965 and 1977 E-A improved their real income by 41 percent while A-A earned 60 percent more in 1977 than in 1968, and Arabs improved their incomes by 69 percent during the same period (Source: *ibid*). It is thus incorrect to state that in Israel the dominant ethnicity has become more affluent while the deprived groups have become impoverished. Among employed men (for whom data was provided), Orientals as well as Arabs have experienced a relative improvement in their material situations.

Several investigations of ethnic inequality use "gross" income gaps only as points of departure. Their actual target is the "net" or residual gap, which remains after all possible "confounding variables," such as schooling, seniority on the job, area of residence, etc. have been controlled. This residual inequality is sometimes considered an estimate of economic discrimination, since all other components of inequality can be "explained away" as being relevant variations in the quality of human resources (Hanoch, 1961; Levy, 1969; Weiss *et al.,* 1979). It should be emphasized that in contemporary societies the very existence of ethnic inequality is the major issue, while the fact that a group that is economically deprived is also likely to be less educated and located in less desirable areas only sharpens the sense of injustice toward that group. In P. F. Lazarsfeld's terms, the basic relationship between ethnic background and income should be "elaborated" or "interpreted" by taking into account "test variables," such as schooling or age.

If, for instance, we hypothesize that ethnic background → schooling → income, then ethnic background remains the cause of income differentials, even though "schooling" is an intervening variable. The same constellation might be presented as a prediction. If and when A-As acquire the relevant attributes of E-As (e.g., quantity and quality of education), the gaps in income will be reduced to 30-40 percent of their "gross" values. The practical meaning of this prediction depends on the likelihood that educational gaps can be effectively reduced.

This approach was adopted by Hartman and Eilon (1974), who attempted to calculate the chances of an individual to attain a prestigious occupation on the basis of his schooling and ethnic background. Their study, based on 1961 census data and on survey data for 1970, revealed that ethnic disparities in schooling remained stable during the decade 1960-1970, while inequality in occupational prestige increased (p. 129).

In the light of this finding one wonders whether "years of schooling" are an exhaustive measure of education as a base for occupational mobility. Pupils of A-A background seem to receive schooling of lower quality and, at the same time, take less advantage of identical educational input. Minkovitch, Davis and Bashi (1977) conducted careful tests of scholastic achievements and reported appreciable gaps between the mean achievements of E-A and A-A pupils. At about the same time, Chen, Adler and Levy (1978) concluded a comprehensive evaluation research of school integration. While an improvement in interethnic relations (more friendships across ethnic lines, as well as less prejudicial attitudes) was indicated, no significant decrease in the gap of scholastic attainments could be shown.

The overall contribution of the Israeli education system to the social goal of ethnic equality can be best evaluated by comparing ethnic gaps among immigrants (from A-A and E-A) to the same gaps among Israeli-born individuals whose parents migrated from different continents. H. Peres (1969) was the first to point out that income gaps (gross as well as adjusted for schooling) among "native Israelis" were actually larger than gaps among immigrants.

The finding has been replicated by Hartman and Eilon (1974) and by Weiss *et al.* (1979), but the most articulate account was given recently by S. Amir (1980), who calculated personal investment in schooling for Israeli-born and foreign-born male Jewish wage earners. While the ratio on investment in education between individuals born in A-A and E-A was .43, the parallel ratio for native Israelis was only .37. It has thus been shown that ethnic differentiation persists in the school system on two levels, investment and achievements.

At this point another question should be raised: do students of A-A backgrounds obtain the same evaluation if they demonstrate the same achievements as E-A do? This issue was investigated by Stahl *et al.* (1976), who designed a simple but quite convincing experiment. Grammar school teachers were instructed to grade two identical essays. One group of teachers graded the essay when "signed" by a student bearing a European name, while the second group of teachers graded the same essay, apparently written by a student with a typical Oriental name. The grades given to the "Oriental student" were significantly lower than those obtained by the "European student" for identical work. It should also be noted that the "pro-European" bias was almost as frequent among teachers whose own background was A-A, as among Ashkenazi teachers.

In the light of these findings, reported independently by several scholars and based on various methods of research and analysis, yet another question is unavoidable: Is the Israeli educational system an effective tool for the implementation of ethnic equality? The graveness of this question is accentuated when one recalls the enormous material, political and intellectual investments in Israeli education. We should consider the fact that not all returns from the investment in schooling are in to date, as the graduates of Israeli schools who are working already obtained most of their education during the first 20 years of the State's existence. The contributions of the last ten years are not measurable yet. Even when these circumstances are taken into account, the effectiveness of education as a vehicle geared toward promoting ethnic equality remains questionable. Is it feasible for ambitious Orientals to circumvent the school system and achieve advancement in roles that do not require formal education? Or will they confront other forms of unintended, institutional discrimination in these pursuits as well?

A critical contribution to this problem was made by Yuchtman-Yaar and Semyonov (1979), who studied ethnic inequality in professional soccer. The same pattern of progressive reduction in the representation of non-Europeans among the high achievers, which has been reported over and again in the school system, was found among soccer players as well. "Ashkenazim (E-A) are 1.3 times more likely to become professionals than Orientals" (A-A) (p. 583), and among the professionals, the ratio of Orientals at the lowest level (second league) is 76 percent, and at the highest (national team) only 27 percent. Here is a clear cut instance of ethnic inequality that is not mediated by schooling or education. Yaar and Semyonov interpret their findings as indicating that achievements of Orientals are perceived as being of lower quality than parallel achievements of Europeans. Such states of expectation are likely to become self-fulfilling. The underestimated person lowers his level of aspiration and eventually adjusts to the levels of performance expected of him (Rosenthal and Jacobson, 1968).

A balanced account of the dynamics of ethnic stratification should take into consideration as many facets as possible of ethnic differentiation. While it is not feasible to exhaust all manifestations of ethnic inequality within the limits of this study, the issue of political representation should not be neglected. Political representation bears some unique properties: (a) Only a relatively small number of individuals (political leaders of various ranks) are directly involved, therefore it is almost always possible to select some adequate candidates. (b) Allocation of political power approximates a zero-sum-game: the economy may expand, new educational opportunities may be opened, but the overall amount of power than can be mobilized in a particular society is more or less fixed. (c) In a centralized system of government a reallocation of power is likely to affect the allocation of other resources to a greater extent than vice versa. During the last three years, Oriental leaders were nominated to three positions of national significance: the State's President, one of the most influential members of the cabinet, and the vice-secretary of the trade unions (Histadrut). A systematic survey of the ethnic composition of the executive committees of major parties and institutions reveals that the above-mentioned nominations were by no means isolated or accidental as the ratio of Oriental members in all the leadership positions increased during 1973-1979. (See Table 1.)

TABLE 1

Members of A-A Background in the Executive of Major Groups:
1973-1974[a]

	N (All Members)		Percent A-A	
Institution	1973	1979	1973	1979
Labor Party Executive	27	65	11%	20%
Mapam Party Executive	9	25	0	15
Herut Party Executive	31	49	13	26
National Religious Party Executive	16	14	25	29
Trade Unions Party Executive	20	33	25	27
Israel Defense Forces Generals	21	16	0	13
Government Ministers	18	17	11	21
Local Authorities	98	100	34	44

[a]I am grateful to my colleague Sammy Smooha for permission to publish these data and to Rita Bresler for her help in collecting them.

These increases in political representation go far beyond co-optation and their consequences are not limited to the pacification of Oriental masses or to finding outlets for political ambitions of ethnic leaders. The gradual but consistent change in the ethnic composition of so many major institutions indicates a tendency to share political power. Admittedly, this is not an egalitarian sharing—the dominant ethnicity still gets the largest part—but it does not rule alone anymore; substantial portions of authority are transferred to politicians of A-A background.

Three Sociological Perspectives on the Israeli Ethnic Scene

Studies of Israeli ethnic relations gradually accumulate, each scholar contributing convictions and predictions alongside his own data and findings.

Three main sociological perspectives on the Israeli ethnic scene will be briefly summarized and critically discussed in this section. In the conclusion an attempt will be made to reach a new synthesis between these perspectives, and to suggest an integrated interpretation that will more closely correspond to the facts.

Absorption through modernization

This view is justifiably identified with Eisenstadt's theoretical perspective (1950, 1954, 1967), but several other sociologists have contributed to its development (Ben-David, 1953; Lissak, 1969; Bar-Yosef, 1968, 1970). The main feature of this approach, which has drawn attention as well as criticism, is the notion of an asymmetrical process. The veteran European community resocializes the newcomers from Asia and North Africa. The latter gradually are transformed and become "modern Israelis".

Conflict between ethno-classes

This mode of analysis perceives Israeli society as an arena of class conflict. The social system, its needs and values, are interpreted as a convenient cover for the interests of the dominant European ethno-class. Advocates of this viewpoint vary in degree of extremity. Bernstein (1979:65) claims that "in Israel, as in many societies, there are basic contradictions between the interests of various social groups. . . . These conflicts should not be seen as transitory but as a manifestation of divergent conceptions and interests . . . which lead to relationships of control and dependence. . . ."

Swirksi and Kazir (1977) go so far as to reject Israeli society "as the major frame of reference." Instead they focus on the "capitalistic world system."

Oriental Jews in Israel are just an instance of a "peripheral group," which is exploited by the "core." Therefore, the theory predicts a persistence or even increase in economic inequality, a cessation of cultural integration and a reflection of ethnic conflicts in the political realm.

Structural pluralism

The attempt to apply the theory of structural pluralism to the Israeli scene has so far been a one-man job. About twelve years ago, Sammy Smooha initiated a study of ethnic leadership which gradually developed into his comprehensive *Israel: Pluralism and Conflict*. Actually, this book can be viewed as a synthesis between the functionalistic and the conflict approaches, even though it was published before the Swirski and Bernstein studies had appeared. Smooha's comparative analysis of three major divisions in Israeli society (Oriental-Ashkenazi; religious-secular, Arab-Jewish) shows that institutional separation is least developed in the Oriental-Ashkenazi case. In other words, while the notion of pluralism provides a comparative framework, it is by no means an effective model for understanding Oriental-Ashkenazi relationships. The ruling elite did not establish separate institutions for Orientals;[4] furthermore, even where separate organization was legally possible and probably in line with their immediate interests (as in politics), Orientals refrained from it. All attempts to organize ethnic parties failed to gain more than marginal and transitory support. Aware of these facts, Smooha returns to a position that is rather close to the absorption-through-modernization model from which he wanted to mark himself off. In fact, he changed the name of that model to "dynamic paternalism-cooptation" (p. 3), but the predictions derived from his theory are not substantially different from those of his predecessor.

Obviously, total adherence to any one of the three conceptions leads to a disregard of important findings. First, the absorption modernization model cannot account for the fact that the predicted dispersion of Oriental immigrants among places, roles and social positions failed to occur.

Second, the radical conflict approach may be a prophetic revelation, but to date most of its predictions have not materialized. Acculturation is a continuous and even prolific trend; some crucial dimensions of inequality (income, political representation) have recently been diminishing. Nor have attempts to organize ethnic-based political parties been successful.

Furthermore, the attempt by Swirski and Katzir (1977:8-14) to apply dependency theory to the Israeli ethnic scene fails to differentiate between Oriental-Ashkenazi and Jewish-Arab relationships. In the broad perspective of "World Systems," both Arabs and Orientals are semiperipheral communities doomed to the same kind of exploitation. However, in reality, the divergence in institutional structure, patterns of acculturation and political identification between Arabs and non-European Jews is so well established and so heavily documented that it hardly requires further discussion.

Third, while coming closer than the others to being a realistic model, Smooha's approach also faces some difficulties. The consistent increase of intermarriage rates, as well as the appreciable decline in income and political representation gaps, can hardly be predicted from his theory.

Conclusion: The Interplay of Conflict and Integration

Integration, inequality, conflict and pluralism have all been suggested by various scholars as key concepts in analyzing the Israel ethnic scene. None of these, when applied as the sole or dominant analytical tool, seems to yield satisfactory results. Is a combination of the four feasible? Or will this lead to confusion?

At the outset of this study the distinction between cultural integration (a decrease in "horizontal" distance) and inequality (the presistence of "vertical" distance) was introduced. The next step was to identify the factors that motivated immigrants from Asia-Africa to adjust to a new "Israeli" culture, as well as the factors that determined their overrepresentation in the low strata of Israeli society.

The first set of factors has been discussed at length: collectivistic motivation to immigrate, the break with the "old countries," the wish to disassociate themselves from anything Arab and the old commitment to modernization, constitute the major part of these factors. It should be emphasized that they amount to a mutual tendency toward cultural integration. Admittedly the motivation is not exactly the same: Orientals wish to be integrated more than Ashkenazim want to absorb them, but national cohesion and modernization are general concerns.

The outcome is not symmetrical either: modern Israeli styles of life are closer to the Jewish-European culture than to the Middle Eastern tradition. Reality seems to defy clear-cut definitions: what happened among Israeli ethnicities is not "assimilation" (Oriental norms, symbols and attitudes have left their marks on Israeli culture), but neither was it "integration." Orientals have yielded more toward Western behavior than vice versa.

While Orientals have been admitted to Israeli society and are now recognized as an integral part of it, they are by no means distributed proportionally among all strata. In fact, they have been absorbed mainly into the lower strata. The same factors that attracted Orientals to Israeli society also contributed to their relative tolerance toward inequality. The association of Israel with Jewish revival and with a modern standard of living, together with the lack of an acceptable alternative, made their acceptance into Israeli society a major goal. Furthermore, as is predicted from exchange theory, the more interested party gets less out of a relationship (Blau, 1964:68).

In a conflict situation, the party with less internal strife has a clear advantage. On the Israeli ethnic scene the European-American ethnicity is relatively unified. On the average, Ashkenazim have been in the country for a longer period of time and thus have had more time to integrate. The Ashkenazi ethnicity is dominated by the East European subgroup. Immigrants from Russia and Poland were not only the numerical majority among the Ashkenazim, they were also the first to immigrate and founded almost all political, economic and cultural institutions.

The trade unions and industry, the kibbutz movement and the first Jewish cities, the pre-military organizations and the national theater were all started by leaders of Russian or Polish background (higher education and Philharmonic Orchestra are noteworthy exceptions). No other European group ever challenged the supremacy of East Europeans, and thus leaders from Eastern Europe emerged as national leaders.

The internal structure of the Oriental ethnic group is fundamentally different. Dominance among Orientals is divided between Jews of Iraqi background who have a well known advantage in schooling, affluence and political organization, and the North Africans who are the majority. In addition, the most veteran group, the Yemenites, only constitute a small segment of the Oriental population and are strongly attached to various veteran parties (in particular, the religious parties and the labor movement). Under these circumstances, it is very difficult, if not impossible, for the Oriental masses to unite behind a generally accepted leadership. The path toward the crystallization of such a leadership is blocked by additional obstacles: the absence of a common cultural denominator among them has made deprivation the main, if not the only, unifying element. Gradual political and occupational mobility (or "large-scale cooptation" in Smooha's term) has diluted the leadership potential. Qualified and mobile individuals tend to identify with the system into which they have risen, rather than with the deprived and frustrated segments from which they have emerged.

The terms "inequality" and "conflict" have become almost inevitable predictors of social change. However, in some specified circumstances the combination of social economic gaps and internal conflicts might have a stabilizing effect. A social system is in a most vulnerable situation when the elite is divided and the rank and file is united; and in a rather stable state when conflict prevails in the lower and unity in the upper strata.

This postulate is derived from the general notion of the stabilizing effect of crosscutting conflicts. If Dahrendorf (1959) is right in assuming that universal conflict exists between the holders of wealth and power and the "have-nots" in every society, then a split in the ruling elite helps the deprived groups to alter the status quo while a conflict between two (or more) low status groups contributes to the preservation of overall stability.

While this chapter has deliberately taken an eclectic position, applying various apparently contradictory theoretical perspectives, its conclusions are quite clear and definite. Nation building is the concept that best describes what has actually happened among Jewish ethnicities in Israel. Whether one takes immigration (i.e. the motivation to immigrate, the relationship with the country of origin, etc.) as a point of departure or focuses on modernization itself, the data point overwhelmingly to a continued process of integration. In other words, the Oriental ethnic groups have mainly adapted themselves to the norms and values of mainstream Israeli society. Indeed, despite the current fashion of tracing and reviving "original cultures," Israeli Jewish ethnicities are more concerned about reaping a fair share in the present and future then with revealing the roots of the past.

At the same time, however, the adoption of different conceptual frameworks brings into focus various phases of the process and curbs the widespread inclination to view integration (or nation building) in an unqualified optimistic light. The experience of the last several decades indicates that growing cultural proximity will not produce equality (although it sharpens the demand for it) just as extensive cooptation will not do away with poverty and deprivation.

Notes

[1] The dominance of Israeli identity over particularistic loyalties to various countries of origin, has been demonstrated by Herman (1970), as well as by Farago (1977). Of particular interest is the wave of name changing that gained momentum after the mass immigration of the 1950s. A majority of name changers abandoned names that symbolized attachment to a country of origin (by language, style or explicitly mentioning a country or place) and adopted Hebrew names symbolizing attachment to the new country and/or to national goals and values (Bockstein, 1980).

[2] Detailed accounts of anti-Arab prejudice in the Jewish-Israeli population can be found in Peres and Levy, 1969.

[3] Source: Central Bureau of Statistics Special Report 598: Tabl. A/3.

[4] The Chief Rabbinate, which is separated along ethnic lines, was established under Ottoman rule and is therefore no exception.

References

Amir, S. 1980. "Income Gaps, Educational Inequality and Social Opportunity." Lecture at the School of Education, Hebrew University, Jerusalem, February.

Bar-Yosef, R. 1968. "Desocialization and Resocialization: The Adjustment of Immigrants." *International Migration Review* 2:3.

———. 1970. "The Moroccans: Background to the Problem," in S. N. Eisenstadt, Ch. Adler, and R. Bar-Yosef (Eds.), *Absorption and Development in Israel.* Jerusalem: Israel University Press.

Ben-David, J. 1953. "Ethnic Differences or Social Change?" in C. Frankenstein (Ed.), *Between Past and Future.* Jerusalem: Henrietta Szold Foundation.

Bernstein, D. 1979. "The Black Panthers: Protest and Conflict in Israeli Society." *Megamot* 25:1.

Blau, P. M. 1964. *Exchange and Power in Social Life.* New York: John Wiley.

Blockstein, R. 1980. *Name Changing in Israel.* Unpublished M.A. thesis, Tel Aviv University.

Chen, M., Adler, Ch., and Levy, A. 1978. *Process and Outcome in Education: The Contribution of Junior High Schools.* Tel Aviv: Tel Aviv University, The Hebrew University.

Dahrendorf, R. 1959. *Class and Class Conflict in Industrial Society.* Stanford: Stanford University Press.

Eisenstadt, S. N. 1950. "The Oriental Jews in Israel." *Jewish Social Studies* 10:1.

———. 1954. *The Absorption of Immigrants.* London: Routledge and Kegan Paul.

———. 1967. *Israel Society* New York, Basic Books.

Farago, U. 1977. Continuity and Change in the Jewish Identity of Israeli Jews. Unpublished Report, Jerusalem.

Farley, R. 1977. Trends in Racial Inequalities: Have the Gains of the 1960s Disappeared in the 1970s? *American Sociological Review* 42:2.

Hanoch, G. 1961. "Income Differentials in Israel." Jerusalem: Falk Center Research in Economics.

Hartman, M., and Eilon, H. 1974. "Ethnicity and Class in Israel." *Megamot* 21:2.

Herman, S. N. 1970. *Israeli and Jews: The Continuity of an Identity.* New York: Random House.

Jencks, C. 1972. *Inequality.* New York: Basic Books.

Katz, E., and Gurevitch, M. 1973. *The Culture of Leisure in Israel. Patterns of Spending Time and Consuming Culture.* Tel Aviv: Am. Oved.

Levy, H. 1969. *Income Differential Among Wage Earners in Israel 1963-1968.* Jerusalem: Bank of Israel.

Lissak, M. 1969. *Social Mobility in Israeli Society.* Jerusalem: Israel Universities Press.

Minkovitch, A., Davis, D., and Bashi, J. 1977. *An Evaluation Study of Israeli Elementary Schools.* Jerusalem: Van Leer Foundation.

Peres, Y. 1971. "Ethnic Relations in Israel." *American Journal of Sociology* 76:6.

——. 1976. *Ethnic Relations in Israel.* Tel Aviv: Sifriat Poalim.

——, and Levy, Z. 1969. "Jews and Arabs: Ethnic Group Stereotypes in Israel." *Race* 15:2.

——, and Schrift, R. 1978. "Intermarriage and Interethnic Relations." *Ethnic and Racial Studies* 1:4.

Rosenthal, R., and Jacobson, L. 1968. *Pygmalion in the Classroom.* New York: Holt, Rinehart & Winston.

Schermerhorn, R. A. 1970. *Comparative Ethnic Relations.* New York: Random House.

Smooha, S. 1978. *Israel, Pluralism and Conflict.* London: Routledge and Kegan Paul.

——, and Peres, Y. 1975. "The Dynamics of Ethnic Inequality: The Israeli Case." *Social Dynamics* 1:1.

Stahl, A., Agmon, T., and Marchaim, M. 1976. "Teachers' Attitudes Towards Underprivileged Pupils." *Bechinuch,* 11 May.

Swirski, S., and Katzir, S. 1977. "Ashkenazim and Orientals in Israel: An Emerging Dependency Relationship." Paper presented to the A.S.A. Convention.

Weiss, Y., Mark, N., and Fishelson, G. 1979. "Income Gaps Among Men by Ethnic Origin: 1969-1976," In A. Arian (Ed.), *Israel–A Developing Society.* Tel Aviv: Zmora, Bitan, Dotan.

Yuchtman-Yaar, E., and Semyonov, M. 1979. "Ethnic Inequality in Israeli Schools and Sports: An Expectation-States Approach." *American Journal of Socioloty* 85:3.

4

Social Mobility and Ethnic Awareness: The Israeli Case

Eliezer Ben-Rafael

Two of the major characteristics of Middle Eastern and North African Israeli ethnic groups (the so-called Oriental *edot*) are their tendency to remain concentrated in homogenous communities (Weingrod, 1965) and their overwhelming presence in the lower strata of society (Smooha, 1978). In contrast, the various European-origin groups—the Ashkenazim— have gradually evolved into a unified sociocultural category, which is predominantly middle and upper class. In the mind of the Ashkenazim, the two previously mentioned characteristics have merged to form a stereotype of the "Oriental edot" as an undifferentiated entity composed of culturally and socially similar elements.

Despite the strong correlation between ethnic affiliation and class, some persons of Oriental origin do achieve upward social mobility. Recent studies show that about one fourth of the Oriental population was found in middle or higher class occupations and this number is increasing over time (Smooha and Peres, 1974). However, the impact of this social mobility on the ethnic groups has not received detailed study and it is this issue that forms the focus of this chapter.

The determinants of ethnicity are based on a two-fold process of self-identification, which includes both objective and subjective phenomena. An ethnic group is comprised of people who exhibit sociocultural particularism associated with religion, race, origin, language or other primordial attributes, but who also share the more amorphous sentiment of a distinct awareness of kind. Sociocultural particularism refers to the objective featues appearing in a given setting that especially pertain to the group's participation in various spheres of social activity. The subjective phenomenon of the ethnics' awareness of kind concerns the conceptualization of primordial attributes defining the group's collective boundaries and their significance relative to other labels of identity. The intrinsic meaning of this primordial identity affirms the existence of the group so that it is clearly understood to be indicative of a "unique" cultural collective personality.

On the basis of this definition of self-identification, the group may perceive various aspects of its social endeavor in terms of social distances between itself and others. For ethnics, these perceptions represent the practical meanings of ethnicity. Furthermore, beyond these segmented images and in the context of the group's self-definition and expectations, awareness of kind may also include an overall understanding of ethnic reality, which underlines general feelings of deprivation or self-fulfillment.

The objective phenomena of sociocultural particulars are influenced by the effects of upward social mobility, especially in a country like Israel, where ethnic groups can be characterized by community concentration and low (or high) social status. Members of the ethnic group who become upwardly mobile attain a status that is far above the majority of the group and thus become socially and culturally closer to given categories of others. The ethnic group as a whole becomes more heterogenous as it comes to incorporate other elements of culture and class stratification.

Social mobility also influences ethnic awareness of kind. The following questions arise in relation to this issue: (a) Do upwardly mobile ethnics endorse the same definition of primordial identity that is accepted by their group? (b) To what extent do upwardly mobile persons see themselves as representative of what they understand to be the group's "unique" personality? (c) What practical significance do the upwardly mobile give to their own ethnic distinctiveness in comparison with what they associate with their group as a whole? (d) To what extent do the upwardly mobile interpret their individual destiny in society as bound to their group, and how do they define their relation with others?

These questions indicate that social mobility may create a differentiation of ethnic awareness of kind within the group. According to Glazer and Moynihan (1974, XXIV), "Individual choice, not law or rigid custom, determines the degree to which any person participates, if at all, in the life of an ethnic group". Thus, it is only when upwardly mobile ethnics still share a clear awareness of kind and consider themselves an integral part of their group, that the group really includes members of different status as well as diverse cultural variants. If there is no such binding awareness of kind among the upwardly mobile, a different situation occurs, in which the mobile ethnics associate themselves with others and tend to assimilate into outside groups (Gordon, 1975). In this instance, the relationship of ethnicity and lower class is perpetuated, as the ethnic group remains composed of essentially non-mobile elements. This type of ethnic group may be called an ethnoclass.

Several different consequences may occur as the result of an ethnic group's evolution into a heterogenous entity or an ethnoclass. For example, in the case of a heterogenous group, organizational resources may be acquired by middle and upper class ethnics for the benefit of the group as a whole. In the ethnoclass setting, when the successful have left the community, this type of access to resources is not likely to be possible. Similarly, mobile elements in a heterogenous group constitute a natural reservoir of leadership, whereas in an ethnoclass, group leaders—whether or not they are of lower class background—cannot expect even the passive support of upwardly mobile individuals who have left the group. A third aspect of the divergent developments of ethnic groups is that as the correlation between ethnicity and class becomes less blatant in the heterogenous group, the nature of the ethnic's relations with other cultural groups represents an issue of ethnic reality and is part of the fabric of the group rather than a strong indication of class difference. In contrast, the most salient aspect of the ethnoclass condition continues to reside in problems directly pertinent to social stratification.

Several comparative studies have provided insight into the circumstances influencing the development of an ethnic group into a heterogenous or ethnoclass model. These works indicate that two main elements play important roles by shaping the mobile individual's attitudes toward the ethnic group as a whole. The first factor pertains to the group itself and the second to the attitudes of "outsiders."

The existence of any ethnic group is dependent upon and requires that its members identify with it in some measure (Williams, 1966:45). However, the degree and strength of this required identification is linked to the group's basic aspiration as to whether to maintain itself as a distinct entity or to totally integrate into society (Greeley, 1971). If the goal is to assimilate, the group cannot allow itself to discourage the tendency of members, particularly those who are upwardly mobile, to move outward and take advantage of objective opportunities to "escape" from their ethnicity. The attitude of "outsiders" to ethnics who "make it" and are ready to move out of their immediate sphere is important as to how the ethnic group continues to evolve. Many researchers have stressed (Van den Berghe, 1970; Myrdal, 1944) that successful ethnics inevitably endanger the status of others who are not part of the ethnic group. Because there is a threat to the status of the already well-established implicit in the movement of upwardly mobile ethnics as they try to assimilate into the community at large, the "outsider" groups tend to raise social obstacles to the acceptance of ethnics into the new strata. The ease with which upwardly mobile ethnics move out of their group into a larger sphere correlates with their maintaining positive attitudes to their group of origin (Patterson, 1975). The overtness of rejection of upwardly mobile ethnics and consequently its influence on the mobile ethnics awareness of kind, is dependent upon formal or informal discrimination on the part of the dominant culture group (i.e. the cultures represented by the political center). This, as reported by Hoetinck (1972), is primarily a function of the extent to which the dominant culture aspires to socially fuse the ethnic group with society at large.

When considering the Oriental *edot* in Israel in light of this analysis, it should be emphasized that social fusion was fully endorsed by both the ethnic groups and the dominant culture. Each Jewish group that emigrated to Israel was moved by a deep wish to "melt" into a setting that shared its national and religious concepts (Deshen, 1973, 1975). At the same time, the ideals of "Ingathering and fusion of the exiles" are at the root of the Zionist version of Judaism, the official ideology of the State (Peres, 1977:79). Thus, on the one hand, mobile individuals assimilating among "outsiders" are by no means considered "deserters" by their group of origin, and on the other, for the dominant culture, these mobile elements constitute the symbol of fulfillment of a critical ideological value.

Although the previously described relationship between the ethnic group and the dominant culture works in theory, there has been no overall fusion of all groups of origin in modern Israel. However, one would expect that, in accordance with the foregoing discussion, the mobile elements from the Oriental *edot* who gradually dissociate themselves from their ethnic group, show a reduced awareness of kind and a strong tendency to assimilate with Ashkenazim. If this contention is true, it indicates that the Oriental *edot* evolve as ethnoclasses. This analysis presents the results of empirical research designed to test this hypothesis.

The Empirical Study

The empirical study was based on interviews conducted during 1978 and 1979 among two sample groups: 139 Yemenites and 152 Moroccans, selected to represent the urban, upwardly mobile ethnic. Approximately twenty-five percent of the total sample were in business; thirty percent held technical jobs; twenty percent were clerks, and the remaining twenty-five percent were professionals. The age range of the respondents was 28 to 45 years. Those who were not born in Israel had immigrated during childhood. All had completed at least ten years of schooling; eighty-five percent had completed secondary education and sixty-five percent had studied further. Two thirds of this population had achieved at least some promotion in rank during their military service.

The sample of mobile individuals was drawn from the Moroccan and Yemenite communities because they reflect the major shades within Israel's Oriental population. Some twenty percent of the Yemenites came to Israel before the creation of the State and the remainder by 1952. They emigrated from a stronghold of Muslim conservatism where they formed a closed caste. Their immigration to Israel therefore represented the transplantation of a traditional community (Tobi, 1966; Tsadok, 1967). The cultural characteristics of the group were such that they became the most highly esteemed of all non-European groups. For this same reason, they also remained one of the most cohesive groups. While Yemenites account for only six percent of Israel's Jewish population, they may be considered representative of a larger proportion as the characteristics of their Diaspora background are quite similar to those of other groups such as the Kurds or Libyans. In contrast, the Moroccans—most of whom came to Israel in the late 1950s—were characterized by cultural and community disorganization after five decades of French colonialism (Confino, 1953; Weingrod, 1960). They soon became the most ill-esteemed group in Israel though also the largest; accounting for fourteen and one half percent of the entire Jewish population, they are about thirty percent of all Israel's Oriental Jews.

The general hypotheses of the research were derived from both the different aspects of ethnic awareness of kind as defined previously with regard to the issue of social mobility, and the particular Israeli situation.

Thus, the first three hypotheses, which deal with respondents' attitudes toward their group, take into consideration that most mobile ethnics in Israel are the first generation mobile offspring of their group. Accordingly, it was predicted that:

1. Mobile ethnics identify with the concepts of *primordial identity* as they see them generally endorsed by their group. On the other hand, the effect of mobility is that they themselves interpret these concepts in more flexible terms, leaving greater leeway for "escape" from ethnic boundaries.
2. Mobile ethnics emphasize affinity with many aspects of what they see as the ethnic cultural personality, but in many other respects they perceive themselves closer to the dominant culture.
3. They consciously minimize the practical meanings of ethnic distinctiveness for themselves in comparison with what they perceive as the norm for their group.

If confirmed, these hypotheses signify that mobile ethnics do not see themselves as effective parts of their groups; as such these hypotheses also represent a "minimalist" answer to the question of the extent to which mobile ethnics interpret their individual destiny as bound to that of their groups in general.

Given the uniqueness of the Israeli situation, the issue of the upwardly mobile ethnics' relation to outsiders must be clarified. It is necessary to distinguish between two different categories of outsiders: the Ashkenazim, who are prominent in the middle and upper social strata, and the non-Yemenites or non-Moroccan Oriental groups, which are mostly confined to a lower social status.

Two hypotheses can be formulated in relation to these distinct groups of outsiders. The first involves the *Edot Hamizrach* category, which refers to the whole group of Orientals although it is comprised of many different ethnic groups. Because mobile ethnics achieve a status far above most of their fellow ethnics, consequently undergoing a process of "de-ethnicization", it would be expected that:

4. Mobile ethnics dissociate themselves from the *Edot Hamizrach* category at least as much as from their communities of origin as regards self-perceived identity, cultural personality, and practical social endeavors.

On the other hand, since the Ashkenazim are identified with the dominant culture:

5. It is with the Ashkenazim that mobile ethnics feel the greatest affinity in relation to the elements in hypothesis 4.

Ethnic Identity and Boundaries

The first hypothesis posits that mobile ethnics share the general concept of primordial identity held by their group but interpret it less rigidly. As expected, almost all respondents attributed the same importance to their ethnic identity as they assumed that others of the same origin did. More precisely, a majority—ranging from sixty to eighty percent, according to the item—said that they and others of their group put primary emphasis on the Jewish and Israeli identities, giving third place to the ethnic label and only fourth to the concept of "Orientals-as-a-whole". However, additional questions inquiring more closely into emotional identification with the ethnic identity (represented in the questionnaire by the term "pride") brought out substantial differences. As Table 1 shows (item d), both groups, and particularly the Moroccans, tend to assume that their group is more proud of their ethnic identity than they themselves are.

In the same vein, respondents tend to regard children of "mixed" marriages more as "Jews, Israelis without label" than they assume people of their group to regard them (Table 2). This tendency is common for both Yemenites and Moroccans. At the same time there is a general tendency to underrate the perpetuation of the ethnic identity among such offspring, although this is somewhat less pronounced among the Moroccans. In other words, the respondents effectively define ethnic boundaries less rigidly than they perceive that their group does.

Cultural Features

Hypothesis 2 assumed that while mobile ethnics would express an affinity with some aspects of the ethnic cultural personality, they would in some cases consider themselves closer to the dominant culture. In this respect the inquiry focused on attitudes regarding four major parameters of social life: religious and *edah* customs, family and education, criteria of social status, and political concepts. Although by no means exhaustive, the data

TABLE 1
The Various Identities as Sources of Pride

	Yemenite (%)		Moroccan (%)	
	Respondents' opinions	Respondents' perceptions of the opinions of others	Respondents' opinions	Respondents' perceptions of the opinions of others
(a) *Jew*				
1. Small source of pride	12	11	14	57
2. Important source of pride	11	10	60	36
3. Very important source of pride	77	79	26	7
Total	100	100	100	100
(b) *Israelis*				
1. Small source of pride	13	14	18	21
2. Important source of pride	23	32	63	47
3. Very important source of pride	64	54	19	32
Total	100	100	100	100

(c) *"Orientals"*

1. Small source of pride	71	69	98	70
2. Important source of pride	20	20	2	24
3. Very important source of pride	9	11	—	6
Total	100	100	100	100

(d) *"Yemenites" or "Moroccans"*

1. Small source of pride	32	22	73	59
2. Important source of pride	33	33	25	31
3. Very important source of pride	35	45	2	10
Total	100	100	100	100

TABLE 2
The Ethnic Identity of Children of Mixed Marriages

	Yemenites (%)		Moroccans (%)	
	Respondents' opinions	Respondents' perceptions of the opinion of others	Respondents' opinions	Respondents' perceptions of the opinion of others
(a) *Mother from the edah,*[a] *father Ashkenazi*				
Children's identity:				
1. *Edah*	14	22	14	13
2. Father's ethnic identity	14	11	12	17
3. Oriental	4	31	1	6
4. Jew, Israeli, without label	68	36	73	64
Total	100	100	100	100
(b) *Father from the edah, mother Ashkenazi*				
Children's identity:				
1. *Edah*	27	37	31	29
2. Mother's ethnic identity	4	10	2	10
3. Oriental	4	3	2	1
4. Jew, Israeli, without label	65	50	65	60
Total	100	100	100	100

(c) *Mother from the edah, father from another Oriental group*

Children's identity:

1. *Edah*	13	45	10	17
2. Father's edah	12	36	–	3
3. Oriental	22	15	28	22
4. Jew, Israeli, without label	53	4	62	58
Total	100	100	100	100

(d) *Father from the edah, mother from another Oriental group*

Children's identity:

1. *Edah*	32	43	14	34
2. Mother's edah	3	5	1	2
3. Oriental	13	20	23	9
4. Jew, Israeli, without label	52	32	62	55
Total	100	100	100	100

aRespondent's ethnic groups.

clearly show the respondents exhibit an amalgam of traditional and modern attitudes. However, the latter are emphasized more in the respondents' self-images than in those they report for their communities.

With respect to religion, many Yemenite respondents consider themselves more observant than their group in general: no Yemenite defined himself as "secular," but no less than twenty percent referred to their group as such. The Moroccans, in contrast, view themselves as much less religious than their group: twenty-three percent considered themselves "secular," while only one percent placed the Moroccan *edah* as a whole in this category. Despite this, both groups of respondents consider themselves less dedicated to ethnic traditional customs such as pilgrimages to tombs of the saints. While eighty-four percent of the Yemenites and sixty-eight percent of the Moroccans think these customs are observed by their groups only thirteen percent, and fifty-eight percent, respectively, participate in these activities. Similarly, few accord the rabbi a role of community leadership: seventy-seven and one hundred percent, respectively, do not see him on nonreligious matters. Finally, while all Yemenites and half the Moroccans feel that religious education is perceived as important by their communities of origin, only two-thirds of the former and about one-third of the latter share the same attitude.

With regard to family and education, the same trend is prevalent. Although many respondents reported that they maintain strong ties with relatives (forty-five percent of the Yemenites and twenty-one percent of the Moroccans), many more feel that their own family ties are less strong than those of their fellow ethnics in general (sixty percent of the Yemenites and half the Moroccans reported "strong ties with relatives" as a major values of their groups). Even if questions related to authority in parent-child relationships did not show any significant differentiation, attitudes toward the value of formal education—whether academic or vocation—and particularly for girls, contrast with those that respondents reported for their groups (Table 3).

One of the interesting differences between Yemenite and Moroccan respondents concerns the importance of a "cohesive family" as a goal. The Yemenite respondents emphasize this even more than they feel that their group does (eighty-three percent consider it important although only sixty-four percent think it is true for people of their group). The Moroccans, however, see themselves as being less family-oriented than their group (only fourteen percent consider it of major importance for themselves, but seventy percent think it is important to their group).

TABLE 3
Attitudes Toward the Education of Boys and Girls

	Yemenites (%)		Moroccans (%)	
	Respondents' opinions	Respondents' perceptions of the opinion of others	Respondents' opinions	Respondents' perceptions of the opinion of others
(a) *Academic education for boys*				
1. Very important	77	58	36	14
2. Important	15	22	26	38
3. Some importance	8	20	38	48
Total	100	100	100	100
(b) *Academic education for girls*				
1. Very important	75	4	26	14
2. Important	17	7	29	28
3. Some Importance	8	89	45	58
Total	100	100	100	100
(c) *Vocational education of boys*				
1. Very important	43	39	74	30
2. Important	32	28	21	35
3. Some Importance	25	33	5	35
Total	100	100	100	100
(d) *Vocational education for girls*				
1. Very important	36	no data	28	17
2. Important	31	no data	55	51
3. Some Importance	33	no data	17	32
Total	100		100	100

Attitudes toward social status were studied from two angles: factors determining individual success in social life, and worthwhile goals. With respect to the former, respondents' personal attitudes appear to differ little from those they perceive as generally held by their groups in regard to the importance of attributes such as talent, "brains", education, or money. Greater differences emerge, especially among the Yemenites, regarding "uncontrollable" factors more alien to the modern ethos: "luck", for example, is considered "important" in the Yemenite community according to the perceptions of eighty-five percent of the Yemenite sample, but is rated as such by only sixty-three percent of the subjects. The respective figures for the Moroccans are eighty-four and seventy-two percent.

The respondents differentiate themselves from their *edot* with regard to worthwhile goals mainly on two issues: the importance of modern education for children and of a well-established economic position. On the first issue they consider themselves more positive: only forty-four percent of the Yemenite respondents think their group sees modern education as a very worthwhile goal, but seventy-two percent consider it important for themselves. The respective figures for Moroccans are forty and fifty percent. However, the respondents consider themselves less preoccupied with financial success than is the norm in their respective *edot*: sixty percent of the Yemenite sample and ninety-seven percent of the Moroccan respondents think it is a major aim in their groups, but only forty-eight and fifty-five percent, respectively, describe themselves as feeling this way. Thus once again, the respondents see themselves as being closer to the modern ethos, which, at least in its middle-class version, holds education achievements to be no less prestigious than economic standing.

Finally, in regard to political concepts, respondents see themselves sharing attitudes similar to their group on some things, but not on others. The similarities cover a whole range of issues: they share their ethnic group's belief that the government should "serve the citizens" and be deeply involved in all social matters of importance, though, like their fellow ethnics, their awareness of and interest in political issues remains weak. On the other hand, respondents are more emphatic about the representative function of the polity: ninety-six percent of the Yemenites and sixty-percent of the Moroccans consider this attribute essential, but only fifty-four and thirty-five percent, respectively, think their group endorses this stand.

The cultural data reviewed show an emerging pattern, which supports the second hypothesis that although respondents consciously emphasize similarities with the ethnic collective personality, they also deliberately insist on certain differences. This is further confirmed by the respondents themselves: not only do they estimate in general terms that ethnic legacies and outlooks are less characteristic of people of a higher educational level, but they also consider themselves different from their group at least in some aspects, and closer to the dominant Israeli culture.

Attitudes Toward the Ethnic Community

The increasing distance between mobile ethnics and their *edot* anticipated by the third hypothesis was studied under four main headings: attitude toward abandoning the community; feeling of special ethnic obligations; preference for social proximity; and the image of everyday relations between the respondents and their respective groups.

Both Yemenites and, to a greater degree, Moroccans indicate that members of their group leave ethnic neighborhoods once they can afford to do so: only twenty-seven percent of the Yemenites and five percent of the Moroccans consider that such people stay in the community neighborhood; twenty and nine percent, respectively, say that those who leave move to places relatively close to it; while fifty-three and eighty-six percent emphasize their moving completely away. Further evidence of this (see Table 4) is provided by respondents' preferences concerning all types of social proximity, regarding neighborhood, friendship, or friends for their children. In each case, "one's own *edah*", was far less popular a category than "all groups without distinction". Thus, centrifugal attitudes characterize both Yemenites and Moroccan respondents.

These attitudes are reinforced by the description of the nature of respondents' actual links with their *edot*. Only thirty-five percent of the Yemenites and twenty-eight percent of the Moroccans reported that their best friends belong to their own group, and in this regard, respondents generally considered themselves atypical. Similarly, sixty percent of the Yemenites and fifty-two percent of the Moroccans reported that their children's best friends are either Ashkenazi or "from all groups without distinction". Only thirty-four and eight percent, respectively, reported that their children's friends belong to their own *edah*. These findings confirm the image of respondents' loosening links with their groups. In the same vein, Table 5 shows that strong ties with people of

TABLE 4
Preferences for Social Interaction

	Yemenites (%)		Moroccans (%)	
	Respondents' opinions	Respondents' perceptions of the opinion of others	Respondents' opinions	Respondents' perceptions of the opinion of others
(a) *As neighbors*				
1. Ashkenazim	15	7	25	47
2. The *edah*[a]	22	52	9	12
3. Orientals in general	—	1	8	5
4. All groups without distinction	63	40	58	36
Total	100	100	100	100
(b) *As friends*				
1. Ashkenazim	9	7	9	17
2. The *edah*	15	46	23	34
3. Orientals in general	—	1	11	9
4. All groups without distinction	76	46	57	40
Total	100	100	100	100
(c) *As friends for one's children*				
1. Ashkenazim	15	13	9	23
2. The *edah*	3	24	3	4
3. Orientals in general	1	4	4	8
4. All groups without distinction	81	59	84	65
Total	100	100	100	100

[a]Respondent's ethnic groups.

one's group are reported mainly in connection with relatives (although for the Yemenites, they also exist, to a lesser extent, with friends).

Furthermore, only a minority of the Yemenites and Moroccans feel a special obligation toward their groups. Similarly, respondents are not involved in community activities and organizations: sixty-three percent of the Yemenites and eighty-one percent of the Moroccans do not belong to an ethnic synagogue; eighty-two and ninety percent, respectively, have no ties with local charity groups; and eighty-five percent of both samples never or almost never participate in meetings held by national ethnic organizations. (See Table 5.)

Despite the trends shown in the previous data, the respondents do have a genuine concern as to the general social, economic and political status of their groups in society at large. A large majority of the subjects resent what they call "unfairness from the establishment" and they look forward to substantial change in the overall ethnic situation in the sense of more equality between their *edot* and the Ashkenazim. Yet, it is quite evident that they themselves will not take the initiative in this conflict: seventy-five percent of the Yemenite respondents and eighty-six percent of the Moroccans do not endorse ethnic political organizations. The activity of ethnic parties is opposed by eighty-five percent of the Yemenites and ninety-one percent of the Moroccans, with seventy-three and seventy-one percent expressing strong opposition. Moreover, although more positive feelings were expressed concerning community groups that help strengthen their *edot's* status in society, very few are actually ready to join.

This aloofness is not merely the product of cultural distance. The major cause is mobility itself since it is with respect to status distances that the widest gaps appeared between the respondent's perceptions of themselves and of their communities. No Yemenite or Moroccan respondent considers himself a member of the lower class; only a small minority (eight and nine percent, respectively) define themselves as "lower-middle class"; more than half (fifty-six and sixty-two percent) put themselves in the middle class and about one-third (thirty-six and twenty-nine percent) even higher. This is in contrast with the perceptions of the social position of their groups; among Yemenites, thirty percent felt that a "large" or "very large" portion of their ethnic group belong to the lowest stratum in society and forty-four percent responded in the same terms with respect to the lower middle stratum. For the Moroccans, the respective figures were even more extreme, eighty-nine and seventy-three percent.

TABLE 5
Respondents' Ties with People of the Edah in the Various Areas
of Social Life

	Yemenites (%)	Moroccans (%)
(a) *Relations with relatives from the edah*[a]		
1. Strong and continuous	63	29
2. Quite continuous	10	37
3. Weak	27	34
Total	100	100
(b) Friendships with people of the edah		
1. Strong and continuous	45	13
2. Quite continuous	19	44
3. Weak	36	43
Total	100	100
(c) *Contacts with people of the edah in one's social life*		
1. Very important	13	17
2. Relatively important	25	30
3. Weak importance	62	53
Total	100	100
(d) *Contacts with people of the edah in one's occupational life*		
1. Very important	17	12
2. Relatively important	9	20
3. Weak importance	74	68
Total	100	100

[a]Respondents' ethnic groups.

Attitudes Toward Edot Hamizrach

Yemenite and Moroccan respondents share similar images about themselves, which show them closer to one another than to their groups of
origin. However, despite this convergence, and in accordance with our
fourth hypothesis, they are not attracted by the label of the *Edot Hamizrach*. We have already seen some examples of this: Table 1 showed
that the majority (seventy-one percent of the Yemenites and ninety-eight

percent of the Moroccans) do not consider being an Oriental an important source of pride; Table 2 showed that neither group finds much use for this label in defining the ethnic identity of offspring of mixed marriages of any kind—including the cases of parents of two different Oriental *edot*. These data leave no doubt about the respondents' remoteness from the notion of *Edot Hamizrach*.

From the status viewpoint, "Edot Hamizrach" is understood by the respondents mainly in reference to people of lower class; as mobile ethnics, they define themselves in different terms. They also refrain from using the term in the cultural context, as they perceive their own group as distinct from the others. Regarding social contacts, the term has wider currency, particular among Moroccans, thirty-eight percent of whom report that their best friends are recruited among people of the Oriental category in general (as against five percent of the Yemenite respondents). However, when asked with whom they would prefer to have social contact (Table 4), *Edot Hamizrach* emerged as the least favored choice. Clearly, respondents who loosen ties with their *edot* do not identify with a new ethnic label.

Attitudes Toward Ashkenazim

Our fifth hypothesis predicts that mobile Oriental ethnics have a strong tendency to assimilate with the Ashkenazim. Table 1 illustrated how respondents see comprehensive identity labels—Jews, Israelis, without label—that include Ashkenazim as a greater source of pride for themselves than for their groups. Table 2 showed that respondents also have a stronger tendency to define offspring of all kinds of mixed marriage by these labels.

These findings are consistent with the respondents' images of their social milieu as well as their aspirations in this respect. As already discussed, respondents see their own social status as being closer to that of the Ashkenazim; culturally too, they consciously express orientations closer to them than to their own group. Moroccan respondents, in contrast to Yemenites, assume that their group sees Ashkenazim in a far more favorable light than they themselves (see Table 4). However, as also shown by Table 4, Moroccans share the Yemenites' tendency to aspire to social contacts with "all groups without distinction" rather than with any other specific category, including their own group. This pattern is, to a large extent, reflected in their day-to-day contacts. It is no wonder then that as also seen earlier, a low degree of readiness to support ethnic politics and conflict characterizes respondents of both samples, for despite numerous cultural features, which still recall their origins and faithfulness to the ethnic label, respondents consider themselves an integral part of the Israeli middle class. In this overall context, Deshen's (1973:40) description of a special group of mobile ethnics appears as a private case of the general rule:

> The *Yeshivot* (religious academies), mostly founded by European scholars, foster the European variants of Jewish scholarship and religiosity. . . , [In fact] there is comparatively little demand among Oriental youth for advanced Talmudic education. However, a fair number of these attend the more recently established *yeshivot*. . . . These students have become absorbed in the Yiddish language and even switch their particular prayer-ritual to the European style. Hence they emerge, in fact, from their studies more or less acculturated to European tradition.

Conclusions

The two samples studied in these pages originate from groups that differ widely from each other with respect to their Diaspora background, population size and experience in Israel. It is no wonder that as representatives of first-generation mobile elements several differences were found between the two groups of respondents. The major differences relate to the greater ethnic identification of the Yemenites when compared with that of the Moroccans, their deeper religiosity and family orientation, and their greater self-perceived closeness to the ethnic community. These differences may be seen as a reflection of the influence of the stronger traditionalism and cohesion of the Yemenite group as a whole as compared with the Moroccans.

However, the similarities between the samples appear even greater than expected. In regard to almost every issue investigated, Yemenite and Moroccan subjects share many attitudes and see themselves as different from their respective groups of origin. This was especially the case with respect to the flexibility of their concept of group boundaries, their value-orientations regarding the cultures of their respective *edot*, and the more limited meaning they endow to ethnicity regarding almost any aspect of their social activities. Moreover, this twofold comparison between the samples'

attitudes on the one hand, and their views of their respective groups on
the other, highlights common trends of assimilation with the predominantly Ashkenazi middle class.

The reduced awareness of kind among mobile ethnics as well as their
strong tendency to define themselves as a part of new strata, lead to their
assimilation outside their groups of origin. At the same time, this study
as well as many others have shown that the *edot* are maintained as lower
class communities. Hence, our findings all lead to the conclusion that despite the existence of social mobility, these *edot* evolve as ethnoclasses.

A number of general conclusions may be suggested. The findings help
to explain the paradox of the political weakness of the *edot* when contrasted with their demographic weight in the population. Ethnic political
figures are quite numerous in Israel; many of them are typical ethnoclass
leaders who have attained success in places of work or in the neighborhood; others are politicians who have been co-opted by established parties
as symbols of ethnic political integration; a third category consists of
middle-class persons who try their hand at politics as self-appointed ethnic
leaders. In all cases, however, these persons do not succeed in obtaining
the political, organizational and financial support of large numbers of
mobile ethnics. This is well expressed by Sofer, himself an "ethnic activist" (Sofer 1978:9): "many among the intellectual stratum of the . . .
Orientals ignore the people of their *edot* and get away from ethnic activity. They have become successful and prosperous and have left the public
stage . . . There are among them economists and businessmen who could
contribute a lot in all domains, but they do that only for themselves".

The process of ethnoclass formation also explains why, despite the existence of mobility, ethnic problems in Israel are still perceived as issues
of social inequality rather than of cultural pluralism. The typical claim of
the ethnic activist is that (Sofer 1978:29), "thanks to the investment of
serious resources to . . . liquidate the slums, and of good and competent
teachers in development towns . . . the big turn will come toward the creation of One People with a rich and versatile culture conveying the legacies
of all *edot*". Similarly, the establishment's policy toward ethnic issues is
primarily concerned with socio-economic concerns. This policy emphasizes
the Fusion of Exiles, widening the scope of social services for the "underprivileged" and on the other hand, encouraging ethnically integrated frameworks offering opportunity for social mobility. By the same token, however, our research also helps explain the relatively limited success of these
programs. "Underprivileged" pupils, for instance, who succeed in meeting

the requirements of integrated schools are also able to successfully complete their military service, and then, to reach university level. For them, however, ethnicity loses much of its significance; hence, they do not represent any fundamental altering of the ethnic structure. Other data (Ben-Rafael, 1980) indicate that the less successful among the *edot's* offsprings—even those that graduate from the schools and the army and are more accultured than their parents—re-enter the ethnoclass and, thereby, perpetuate the overlapping of ethnic affiliation with lower-class position.

This process also contributes to the relative stability of interethnic relations, as well as to the precarious nature of this stability. The assimilation of the upwardly mobile brings support to the ideal of Fusion and the general consensus of the temporariness of ethnic cleavages (Peres, 1977:79). However, by the same token, it cannot be assumed that this state of affairs will continue indefinitely. Should sharp disparities occur between the cohorts of potential upwardly mobile ethnics on the one hand, and available opportunities on the other (whether as a result of changing economic circumstances, demographic reasons, because of improved school facilities for children of "underprivileged" background, or other reasons), one cannot exclude the possibility that ethnic tensions might be aggrevated by reactions of the threatened predominantly Ashkenazi middle class. Such a rejectionist response could induce mobile ethnics to grow more aware of their ethnicity and to consequently adopt a new attitude toward their groups of origin. In this context of deteriorated inter-ethnic relations, the re-linking of mobile persons to the *edot* and the latter's becoming heterogenous entities could produce a crystallization of their political potential.

References

Ben-David, J. 1969. "Note of Discussion," in *Mizug Galuyot,* Jerusalem, Magnes Press, 89-91.

Ben-Rafael, E. 1980. Realité Ethnique et Conflit Social: Le Cas Israélin," *Cahiers Internationaux de Sociologie,* 68:127-48.

Confino, M. 1953. "North African Jewry," *Mibifnim,* 16/2:566-80 (in Hebrew).

Deshen, S. 1973. "Israeli Judaism, Introduction to the Major Patterns", *International Journal of Middle Eastern Studies,* 9:141-169.

——. 1975. "Political Ethnicity and Cultural Ethnicity during the 1960's" in ASA Monographs—*Urban Ethnicity,* London, N.Y.: Tavistock, 281-309.

——, and Shokeid, M. 1974. *The Predicament of Homecoming*. Ithaca and London: Cornell University Press.

Glazer, N., and Moynihan, D. P. 1974. *Beyond the Melting Pot*. Cambridge, Mass.: Harvard University Press.

Gordon, M. 1975. "Toward a General Theory of Racial and Ethnic Group Relations" in Glazer and Moynihan (Eds.), *Ethnicity*. Cambridge, Mass.: Harvard University Press, 84-110.

Greeley, A. M. 1971. *Why Can't They Be Like Us?America's White Ethnic Groups*. New York: E. P. Dutton and Co., Inc.

Hoetinck, H. 1972. "National Identity, Culture and Race in the Caribbean," in Campbell (Ed.), *Racial Tensions and National Identity*. Nashville: Vanderbilt University Press, 17-44.

Myrdal, G. 1944. *An American Dilemma*. New York: Harper.

Patterson, O. 1975. "Context and Choices in Ethnic Allegiances" in Glazer, N. and Moynihan, D. P. (Eds.), *Ethnicity*.

Peres, Y. 1977. *Ethnic Relations in Israel*. Tel Aviv: Sifriat Hapoalim (in Hebrew).

Shibutani, T., and Kwan, K. M. 1965. *Ethnic Stratification, A Comparative Approach*. London: MacMillan.

Sofer, Y. 1978. "There is No Leading Leadership," in *Bama'araha*, 216; 2-4; 29 (in Hebrew).

Smooha, S. 1978. *Israel: Pluralism and Conflict*. London: Routledge and Kegan Paul.

——, and Peres, Y. 1974. "Ethnic Gap in Israel," *Megamot*, vol. 20/1 (in Hebrew).

Tobi, J. 1966. "The History of Yemenite-Sephardic Relations in Jerusalem from Tarmab to Tarsat," in Ratshavi (Ed.), *Chapters in the History of the Jewish Settlement in Jerusalem*. Jerusalem: Ben Zvi Institute, (in Hebrew).

Tsadok, M. 1967. *Yemenite Jews, Their History and Way of Life*. Tel Aviv: Am Oved (in Hebrew).

Van den Berghe, P. L. 1970. *Race and Ethnicity*. New York: Basic Books.

Weingrod, A. 1960. "Moroccan Judaism in Transition," in *Megamot*, 3:193-208 (in Hebrew).

——. 1965. *Israel: Group Relations in a New Society*. London: Pall Mall Press.

——. 1979. "Recent Trends in Israeli Ethnicity," *Ethnic and Racial Studies*, Vol. 2.

Williams, R. 1966. "Ethnocentrism," in B. E. Segal (Ed.), *Racial and Ethnic Tensions*. New York: Thomas Y. Crowell Co.

5

Ethnicity and the Family: A Q-Study of Israeli Children[1]

Shalva Weil

Conceptual Framework

This study is part of a larger research project in which perceptions of family among 168 Israeli children between the ages of 11 and 12 were examined in the actual and in the ideal.[2] In this chapter, diversity within perception is the focus, the overall aim being a detailed investigation into the implications of family patterns for ethnic continuity (cf.Kobrin and Goldscheider,1978), as well as the implications of ethnicity for diverse family pattern maintenance. This study was undertaken after a preliminary inquiry had established a connection between ethnic origin and children's perceptions of their families by means of one-way analysis of variance.

The purpose of this part of the research was to conduct a more intensive study of three interconnected items: the way children from different ethnic backgrounds view their own family patterns; the way children of different ethnic extraction represent their ideal family; and the degree of congruence between perceptions of the actual and the ideal family. The first subject is designed to describe children's perceptions of existing family arrangements. The second topic aims at delineating children's aspirations with respect to their families; it also points to possible future trends among Israeli families. The third area of interest attempts to assess relative satisfaction with actual family patterns and the direction of desired change.

In attempting to deal with the effect of ethnic origin on diverse family perceptions, the research concentrates upon certain problem areas in the study of ethnicity. Attention is paid to the following four topics: the simplification of ethnic categories to binary oppositions; the lack of common attention to the enduring qualities of ethnicity; the non-predictive character of many ethnicity studies; and the super-imposition of the notion 'ethnicity' without specification as to its meaning in context.

The Simplification of Ethnic Categories to Binary Opposition

While it would be a caricature to suggest that ethnicity studies over-simplify the ethnic reality in order to highlight ethnic difference, a tendency does exist among social scientists to reduce groups to easily-workable binary oppositions, such as Black-White or Eastern-Western, in which ethnic gradations are concealed. This tendency is particularly apparent in Israel where the Jewish population is commonly divided into two sections —Ashkenazi and Sephardi, or Euro-American and Afro-Asian[3] —as if both sections were opposed, separate yet self-contained.[4] While acknowledging that at one level of conceptualization, the Ashkenazi-Sephardi dichotomy exists, at the ground level, ethnic dynamics are far more complex. Depending upon the social context and the frame of reference, the familiar question "Which *eda* (Jewish ethnic group) are you?" most often produces the answer "Ashkenazi" for a European Jew, but "Iraqi", "Moroccan" or "Yemenite" for a Sephardi Jew, who may also define himself as a member of the *edot hamizrach* (Eastern Jewish ethnic groups).[5] The description "Iraqi", "Moroccan" or "Yemenite" refers either to a person's parents (or even grandparent's) country of origin or to his own country of origin, and conveys a significance to the respondent beyond the all-embracing category "Sephardi".[6] In contrast, among European Jews "a broad Ashkenazic culture category has emerged, and less trace remains of the particular European origin groups" (Weingrod 1979:58).

In order to focus upon ethnic difference which goes beyond the binary opposition Ashkenazi-Sephardi, the research reported here concentrated on three groups of Israeli children, two of whom belonged to the wider category edot hamizrach. The idea was to compare the family styles of children of Moroccan and Iraqi origin both with each other and with children from *vatik* (veteran) Israeli Ashkenazi backgrounds.

Of the three types of families studied, the Israeli Ashkenazi family is most familiar to sociologists by virtue of its similarity to their own, largely middle-class, family of origin. Yet, in contrast to the kibbutz family, which has been studied at length, (e.g. Spiro, 1958; Bar-Yosef, 1958; Talmon-Garber, 1972; Tiger and Shepher, 1975), the Ashkenazi family in an urban setting has been relatively overlooked. In Bar-Yosef's pioneering empirical study, role patterns are compared in two groups, the first composed of largely middle-class Jews of Western origin, and the second (Bar-Yosef, 1969) composed mainly of lower-class Jews of Eastern descent, but the distinctiveness of the 'modern' urban Ashkenazi family does not emerge clearly. Palgi (1970) gives an account of the veteran Ashkenazi family in urban and semi-rural areas and Talmon-Gerber (1969) describes the "isolated refugee family in urban centres'. While differences in quality may exist between these family types—the refugee family stressing education as a means to social mobility more that the veteran family—intermarriage between Ashkenazi families and basic similarities between families of Eastern and Western European origin have tended to blur the differences that a more detailed investigation might have shown. In retrospect, therefore, despite the belief in an emerging Ashkenazic cultural category (Weingrod 1979, quoted above), it might have been opportune in this research to specify a more homogenous Ashkenazic group originating from a particular country or part of Europe.

The Persistence of Intergenerational Ethnicity

It has often been posited that ethnicity is a passing phenomenon characteristic of an immigrant society, which will disappear in due course as class or national ties take precedence over local and ethnic loyalties. Indeed, the famous 'melting pot' theory is based upon the premise that ethnic difference will be replaced by a wider, more pervasive national allegiance.

In practice, however, ethnicity has not only persisted, but it also appears to have re-emerged as a viable force in an era of "Neo-Ethnicity" (Kilson, 1975). In Israel, a country where new immigrants brought with them a diversity of ethnic cultures, the interesting feature of ethnicity is the extent to which differences in life-style have persisted intergenerationally (cf. Katz and Zloczower, 1961).

In an attempt to estimate the influence of ethnicity on continuing, diverse patterns, pre-adolescent children were selected as the focus of our research. The children are Israeli by nationality and by birth, but are distinguishable on the basis of the ethnic origins of their parents or grandparents. The aim was to find out whether differences in family patterns are transmitted from one generation to the next so that the children or grandchildren of immigrants perceive their life situations differently.

The Potential for Prediction

In addition to discovering the influence of the past on the perpetuation of ethnic patterns in the present, the research also aimed at making a predictive statement about the persistence of ethnicity in the future. Discovering the unknown is perhaps the most exciting part of research, the potential for prediction so often giving way to caution on the side of the social scientist who contents himself with a study of the familiar and the tangible rather than the prospective and the intangible. This general maxim is particularly true of ethnicity studies, which describe, retrace, reason and rationalize, but which rarely predict. The explanation for this is very simple: in making statements about the future one can easily err and be proven to have erred post hoc.

In order to minimize this possibility, an "emic" (Pike, 1954) interpretation was sought in this research, whereby pre-adolescents describe the types of families they would like to perpetuate. The discrepancy between their actual accounts and their ideal families would indicate the degree of dissatisfaction with existing family arrangements and hence the direction of desired change in the future. In this research, the predictive statement about the future of family patterns in Israel is made by the informants themselves who hail from different ethnic backgrounds and whose ethnicity may influence the types of families they themselves wish to perpetuate.

The Superimposition of an Absolute Notion of Ethnicity

Ethnicity is too often regarded as an absolute category which exists or does not exist, primordially (Geertz, 1973) or non-primordially (Hechter, 1975), according to the specifications of the social scientist. In practice, as I have shown with naming practices among Bene Israel Indian Jews (Weil, 1977a), ethnicity is a phenomenon that is selected according to the definition of the situation in varying contexts. It is the task of the social scientist, therefore, to discover what constitutes ethnicity and what differentiates one group from another in particular spheres, such as the school, the army or work.

In this research, the focus is upon a basic area of social life, the family, and the task undertaken is to discover how children from different ethnic backgrounds perceive their families. The approach is "emic" in that children's own understanding of their family arrangements is sought, the assumption here being that children are too often treated within a normative framework as "unsocialized" or "semi-socialized" adults (MacKay, 1972) in order to assess the degree of their adult orientation (e.g. Singer, 1971) or their perceptions of adult role assignments (e.g. Aldous, 1972). The "emic" approach espoused is manifested primarily in the choice of methodology which is both a source of strength and of weakness in the research.

Methodology

Q-methodology was selected as one that would be sensitive to perceptual style and would operate within a non-formative framework. By virtue of its ipsative nature, Q-methodology elicits person-centered accounts with emphasis on variation within one individual or between groups of individuals.

Q-technique has been championed by Stephenson (1953) and his followers (see Brown and Brenner, 1972), and has been applied in a number of fields such as psychotherapy (e.g. Rogers and Dymond, 1954; Beck, 1972; Butler, 1972; Fiedler, 1972), education (Sontag, 1968; Golding and Wilbur, 1971; Redburn, 1975) and communications (Stephenson, 1967; Brenner, 1972; Schlinger, 1972). In contrast to the more widely-used R-methodology, Q-methodology, which attempts to establish the correlations between people and not variables, remains relatively unknown. The difference between R and Q methodologies is that where R-methodology looks for variables that form factors, Q-methodology seeks to identify clusters of people who sort Q-sorts similarly (cf. Block, 1955).

The Q-sort designed for this research consisted of 50 statements or descriptors of family life derived from pre-adolescent children from varied socio-economic and ethnic backgrounds. The procedure for eliciting the descriptors followed that of the "new ethnography", whereby the trait terms used by members of a society to organize and categorize their lives are elicited. Informants were asked to engage in an open-ended conversation about their own family life. These "interviews" were held with sixth-grade children in different towns in Israel, in their homes, at school and on the street corner. In all cases, interviews were carried out by native speakers; they were taped with the knowledge of the children; and they followed a question-answer format designed so that the relevancy and meaningfulness of the subject matter was left to be determined by the informants (cf. Metzger and Williams, 1966).

When sentences began to repeat themselves irrespective of the social background of the informant, a representative statement on Israeli family life was considered to have been elicited. A pool of several hundred typical sentences was analysed and, after a series of pilot tests, 50 descriptors were finally selected on the basis of frequent repetition and clarity as the components of the Family Q-Sort (see Appendix).

The Family Q-Sort was administered to a total of 168 children in three schools in different urban areas which included: Ramat Gan, near Tel-Aviv, where the population was largely lower middle-class with a high concentration of children of Iraqi origin; Ramat Chen, near Tel-Aviv, where the population was largely upper average Ashkenazi; and Bet Shemesh, a "development town" near Jerusalem, where the population was largely of working-class, Moroccan background. The children were provided with a grid depicting a quasi-normal distribution into which they had to force descriptors along a rank-order continuum ranging from "most like my family" to "least like my family", with degrees of similarity and dissimilarity falling between the extremens.[7] Children were instructed to sort the descriptors, once to describe their families in the actual and a second time to describe them in the ideal.

The Q-Sort Grid.

	Most like my family					least like my family	
Frequency	1	3	6	30	6	3	1
Score	1	2	3	4	5	6	7

In the tradition of Q-methodology, subjects were selected who were "known" to have a specific relevant characteristic (cf. Stephenson, 1953; Kerlinger, 1973-1964).[8] Instead of working with a large random sample, small groups of children were randomly chosen from the wider sample of 168 children, according to their "known" ethnic origin: four children whose parents, though born in Israel, were of Ashkenazi origin; four children whose parents were born in Iraq; and four children of Moroccan parentage. When the sample of twelve was examined, it was discovered that half the children were male and half were female; and that there was no correlation between ethnic origin and class, as judged by the occupational and educational attainments of both parents.

The Family Q-sorts of the twelve children were compared both in the actual and in the ideal by means of factor analysis; each Q factor defined by person loadings and representing a cluster of similarly-sorting children. The emphasis was on 'subjectivity' and "how the individual perceives things" (Brown, 1972:59). The advantage of the methodology was its ability to examine and compare children by bringing ". . . self-notions, and every manner of verbal report into the domain of singular testable propositions" (Stephenson, 1953:206).

The disadvantage of the methodology was the inability to infer from the study to the larger population as responses were based on such small numbers of individuals. This is no doubt one of the reasons why so many researchers have contented themselves with utilizing the Q-sort, which they have analyzed by means of conventional R-methodology, rather than the alternative Q-methodology suggested by Stephenson (1953) and applied here.

Q-Analysis

The analysis was carried out in two parts; the emphasis in the first part was on intra-group characteristics, and the focus in the second part on inter-group variation.

Owing to the complexity of the data (12 children and 24 sorts composed of 50 descriptors each), the first part of the analysis was carried out in stages. The sorts of two groups of children were correlated at each stage, giving two matrices of correlation, one for the actual and one for the ideal (see Table 1). Each matrix of correlations between persons was subjected to factor analysis (cf. Stephenson, 1953; Gordon, 1967; Van der Veen, 1971). Principal factoring with iterations and a varimax arthogonal rotation was used (Kerlinger, 1973); a loading of $\pm.35$ was considered significant (cf. Redburn, 1975).

In order to gain a description of the sorts of children belonging to each factor, the factor score for each of the 50 descriptors was computed on each of the factors (cf. Nie, 1975), and the descriptors rank-ordered

TABLE 1

Matrix of correlations between Actual and Ideal Sorts of Ashkenazi, Iraqi and Moroccan Children.

		Ashkenazi				Iraq				Moroccan			
		A	B	C	D	E	F	G	H	I	J	K	L
Ashkenazi	A	.72	.09	.54	.61	.26	.48	.35	.59	.35	.11	.31	.24
	B	.35	.54	.35	.46	.22	.06	-.08	.09	.52	.06	.24	.17
	C	.32	.42	.62	.52	.43	.44	.47	.50	.44	.26	.48	.42
	D	.37	.24	.42	.48	.40	.30	.10	.35	.13	.22	.09	.06
Iraq	E	.54	.19	.50	.40	.40	.22	.40	.17	.54	.41	.43	.43
	F	-.24	-.04	-.12	-.07	-.04	.30	.49	.72	.37	.54	.35	.39
	G	.31	.22	.50	-.01	.30	.07	-.02	.40	.32	.37	.21	.43
	H	.26	.09	.32	.15	.30	.05	.50	.35	.28	.48	.43	.35
Moroccan	I	.35	.11	.31	.24	.33	.44	.41	.43	.45	.58	.36	.54
	J	.52	.06	.24	.17	-.07	.20	.24	.30	.33	.26	.35	.56
	K	.44	.02	.48	.42	.20	.28	.52	.28	.31	.41	.75	.36
	L	.13	.22	.09	.06	.06	.11	.28	.22	.43	.61	.48	.46

IDEAL (column group); ACTUAL (row group)

according to their score. The five highest descriptors were selected to represent a "factor array", which is a Family Q-sort typical of a specific factor.[9] The factor analysis thus revealed clusters of children grouped according to their different modes of sorting, while the factor arrays described the typical sorts generated by the clusters of children characterizing each factor.

The second part of the analysis consisted of averaging the sorts of all twelve children in an attempt to concentrate on inter-group variation. By this method, the actual and ideal sorts of all three groups of children were averaged to create the "average" Ashkenazi, the "average" Iraqi and the "average" Moroccan, each "average" child representing all four children from his respective ethnic group. The average sorts were correlated and the degree of congruency between actual and ideal sorts both intra- and inter-ethnically was examined. The inter-relationship between the sorts of children from all three groups was further analysed by means of factor analysis of the average sorts.

Results

Part I: A comparison of the sorts of children by means of factor analysis

Ashkenazi and Iraqi children

The actual and ideal family sorts of Ashkenazi and Iraqi children were compared by means of factor analysis according to the Q-technique outlined in Section II and a two-factor solution was accepted for both sorts (see Table 2). Factor I represented the actual sorts of all the Ashkenazi children and one Iraqi child. Two Iraqi children (and one Ashkenazi child) were highly loaded on factor II; one Iraqi child had low communality and was loaded on neither factor.

In the ideal, factor I was a "mixed" factor common to both Ashkenazi and Iraqi children, while factor II was characteristic of Ashkenazi children alone and the one Iraqi child who also clustered with the Ashkenazi children in the actual.

The factor arrays (presented in Table 3) reveal that in their actual sorts Factor I, which can be labelled as "Ashkenazi Factor", is characterized by the selection of such descriptors as "My parents rely on me" (D.4)[10] and "My parents take an interest in my studies" (D.13). The descriptor

TABLE 2
Factor Solutions for Ashkenazi and Iraqi Children

Child	Actual Family Q-Sort Factor Loadings		Ideal Family Q-Sort Factor Loadings	
	Factor I	Factor II	Factor I	Factor II
Ashkenazi				
A	.67	.32	.45	.49
B	.38	.21	-.01	.39
C	.62	.51	.54	.59
D	.60	.04	.25	.85
Iraqi				
E	.58	.33	.27	.40
F	-.16	.05	.82	.07
G	.02	.89	.61	.05
H	.13	.55	.79	.17
Eigenvalue	3.05	1.15	3.65	1.32
% variance	38.2	15.7	45.6	16.6

"My parents don't pay attention to me" (D.13) is least like the families of these children. By contrast, the children loaded on Factor II emphasize joint family activities with siblings or with uncles (D.31, 49). The descriptor "My brothers and I quarrel all the time" (D.40) is considered by children loaded on Factor II to be an item that most characterizes their families; the same descriptor, however, is stated to be most unlike the families of Ashkenazi children loaded on Factor I.

The factor arrays computed for children's ideal sorts show that children highly loaded on factor I, who are both of Ashkenazi and Iraqi origin, want to be their own masters, yet they still value parental aid. The yearning for independence is manifested in the selection of such ideal descriptors as "My parents never punish me" (D.21); "My parents give me as much money as I want" (D.2), and "I go to sleep whenever I want" (D.19). The desire for continued parental cooperation is manifested in the choice of the descriptors "I go on lots of trips with my parents" (D.26) and "My parents and I have fun together" (D.44) and in the

TABLE 3
Factor Arrays of Ashkenazi and Iraqi Children[a]

	ACTUAL	
Factor Array I		*Factor Array II*
	"Most like" children's families	
D.4		D.40
D.36		D.7
D.5		D.31
D.41		D.49
D.18		D.16
	"Least like" children's families"	
D.13		D.42
D.40		D.45
D.3		D.13
D.47		D.32
D.42		D.35
	IDEAL	
Factor Array I		*Factor Array II*
	"Most like" children's families	
D.21		D.4
D.2		D.36
D.19		D.11
D.26		D.30
D.44		D.44
	"Least like" children's families	
D.3		D.13
D.42		D.33
D.35		D.42
D.45		D.47
D.47		D.2

[a]For elaboration of descriptors, see Appendix.

rejection of the descriptor "My parents promise (things) and don't keep (their promise)" (D.3), which children state is least like their ideal family.

It is interesting to note that Ashkenazi children, who are all highly loaded on the second factor, share certain extra elements in common, such as parental trust (D.4), interest in school work (D.36) and indiffer-

TABLE 4
Factor Solutions for Ashkenazi and Moroccan Children

Child		Actual Family Q-Sort Factor Loadings			Ideal Family Q-Sort Factor Loadings	
		Factor I	Factor II		Factor I	Factor II
Ashkenazi	A	.62	.14	A	.53	.43
	B	.60	.09	B	.11	.36
	C	.73	.35	C	.40	.72
	D	.44	.06	D	.54	.60
Morocco	E	.49	.39	E	.59	.51
	F	.07	.72	F	.81	.20
	G	.33	.53	G	.26	.59
	H	.16	.83	H	.57	.31
Eigenvalue		3.31	1.37		4.21	0.97
% Variance		41.4	17.1		52.6	12.1

ence to money (D.11), which also appear in the descriptions of their actual families

Ashkenazi and Moroccan Children

Factor analysis of the actual sorts of Ashkenazi and Moroccan children reveal clear differences between the two groups of children (as shown in Table 4). Factor I emerges as a distinct "Ashkenazi" factor, while Factor II emerges as a predominantly "Moroccan" factor; one Moroccan child is highly loaded on both factors. In the ideal, no clear pattern is evident suggesting that Ashkenazi and Moroccan children's ideal families are similar.

In the light of the above results, factor arrays were computed for the actual sorts only in order to examine in closer detail the descriptors which make up a "typical" sort (see Table 5). The difference between the two factor arrays, the first representing Ashkenazi children and the second representing Moroccan children, is striking. For example, in factor array I, the two descriptors that are respectively "most like" and "least like" Ashkenazi children's actual families—"My parents take an interest in my studies" (D.36) and "My parents don't pay attention to me". (D.13)— are notably absent from Moroccan children's descriptions of their families.

TABLE 5
Factor Arrays of Ashkenazi and Moroccan Children[a]

	ACTUAL	
Factor Array I		*Factor Array II*
	"Most like" children's families	
D.36		D.27
D.4		D.32
D.9		D.5
D.18		D.34
D.22		D.28
	"Least like" children's families	
D.13		D.22
D.29		D.42
D.42		D.8
D.45		D.13
D.40		D.24

[a]For elaboration of descriptors, see Appendix.

For Moroccan children, who normally eat with their parents during the week (D.28), the traditional Jewish Friday night meal (D.27) is of special significance.

One descriptor demonstrates an important difference between Ashkenazi and Moroccan families. The former turn to their elder brother instead of their parents if they have a problem, but Moroccan children do not. Indeed, follow-up interviews with children confirm that in Moroccan families the elder brother often metes out discipline instead of the father, while in Ashkenazi families he is a more approachable and less feared figure.

Iraqi and Moroccan Children

Factor analysis of the actual sorts of Iraqi and Moroccan children shows that Factor I emerges as an "all Moroccan" factor despite the facts that one Iraqi child is also loaded on this factor. Two Iraqi children and one Moroccan child are highly loaded on Factor II.

In the ideal, both factors are again mixed, indicating no variation between children of Iraqi or Moroccan origin (see Table 6). In order to discover the differences between children's perceptions, factor arrays were computed in the actual only (see Table 7).

TABLE 6
Factor Solutions for Moroccan and Iraqi Children

Child		Actual Family Q-Sort Factor Loadings		Ideal Family Q-Sort Factor Loadings	
		Factor I	Factor II	Factor I	Factor II
Morocco	A	.47	.12	.29	.77
	B	.73	.13	.42	.57
	C	.51	.48	.37	.35
	D	.81	.17	.40	.53
Iraq	E	.49	.32	.07	.65
	F	.22	.05	.86	.25
	G	.21	.76	.39	.44
	H	.08	.62	.79	.19
Eigenvalue		3.16	.122	3.9	.106
% variance		39.5	15.3	48.7	13.2

Factor array I is of particular interest for it represents the typical family sort of all four Moroccans. These children enjoy Jewish tradition on the Sabbath (D.27) and television every evening (D.5), their parents are at home most of the time (D.8) and they find their elder brother inaccessible (D.22).

The children who are highly loaded on factor II, like their counterparts who are loaded on factor I, selected the descriptors "My parents quarrel all the time" (D.42) and "My parents don't pay attention to me" (D.13) in second and third place respectively as "least like" their actual families. However, the children who are loaded on factor II chose in first place as most dissimilar to their families the descriptor "My uncles have a say in my education" (D.45), an interesting choice in light of the fact that in the summer vacation these same children go to stay with their uncles (D.49). The extended family, and particularly the male members of the family, obviously play a significant role in the lives of these children; in fact, all the descriptors that are most similar to the families of children loaded on factor II relate to masculine family members (D.40, 7, 31, 49 and 16). Whereas Moroccan children appear to be home-oriented and bound by tradition, the Iraqi children and one Moroccan child also loaded on factor II appear to be dominated by the male role.

TABLE 7
Factor Arrays of Moroccan and Iraqi Children

	ACTUAL	
Factor Array I		*Factor Array II*
	"Most like" children's families	
D.27		D.40
D.5		D.7
D.32		D.31
D.34		D.49
D.28		D.16
	"Least like" children's families	
D.22		D.45
D.42		D.42
D.13		D.13
D.8		D.35
D.24		D.12

Part II: Analysis of average sorts

The average sorts of all three groups of children under study were correlated in the tradition of Block (1969), in order to demonstrate the relationship between the Family Q-Sorts inter-ethnically. The results presented in Table 8 show that the correlation between the average actual sorts of Ashkenazi children and the average actual sorts of Iraqi and Moroccan children is .42 and .46 respectively, while the correlation between the "average" Ashkenazi child and the "average" Moroccan child is .55. The implication is that although families belonging to the broader category *edot hamizrach* are slightly more similar to one another than they are to Ashkenazi families, there is no clear dividing line between Ashkenazi families on the one hand, and the families of *edot hamizrach,* on the other. On the contrary, the results demonstrate that clear differences in perception of existing family arrangements pertain between members of all three groups who can be seen to organize their families differently.

The correlations between the average ideal sorts of children prove to be much higher than the correlations between their average actual sorts indicating a far greater agreement among children as to how their desired family should be constituted. For example, the correlation between Ashkenazi and Moroccan average ideal sorts is .77 (as opposed to .46 for their average actual sorts), and the correlation between Iraqi and Moroccan

TABLE 8
Correlations Between Average Sorts

	Ashkenazi-Actual	Ashkenazi-Ideal	Iraq-Actual	Iraq-Ideal	Morocco-Actual	Morocco-Ideal
Ashkenazi-Actual	–	–	–	–	–	–
Ashkenazi-Ideal	.77	–	–	–	–	–
Iraq-Actual	.42	.47	–	–	–	–
Iraq-Ideal	.40	.56	.30	–	–	–
Morocco-Actual	.46	.52	.55	.28	–	–
Morocco-Ideal	.60	.77	.40	.69	.64	–

average ideal sorts is .69 (as opposed to .55 for their average actual sorts). It is noteworthy that the average Iraqi ideal family is closer to the Moroccan ideal family (.69), than to the average Ashkenazi ideal family (.56); but in contrast to the situation in the actual, the correlation between the average ideal sorts of Moroccan and Ashkenazi children (.77) is higher than the correlation between the average ideal sorts of Moroccans and Iraqis (.69).

Correlation between the average sorts of children from Ashkenazi, Iraqi and Moroccan backgrounds reveals clear differences between groups with respect to the degree of congruency between actual and ideal sorts. The highest congruency exists between the actual and ideal sorts of Ashkenazi children (.77) indicating far greater satisfaction with their existing family arrangements than Iraqi children, who obtained the low actual-ideal congruency score of .30. The congruency score of Moroccan children is .64, which is closer to the congruency score of Ashkenazi than Iraqi children, demonstrating Moroccan children's relatively low desire to change actual family patterns.

When the average sorts representing children from the three different groups were factor analysed, it was discovered that all the sorts, both in the actual and in the ideal, were highly loaded on one factor which explained more than 60% of the variance (see Table 9). The family type which is loaded highest on the factor is the Ashkenazi ideal family, to which all other family types appear to be related. Since, however, Ashkenazi children are characterized by a high actual-ideal congruency score so that there was little difference between the children's desired family and the family in which they are living today, the evidence strongly suggests that the Ashkenazi ideal family, upon which the Moroccan and

TABLE 9
Factor Analysis of Average Sorts

Factor I Factor Loadings[a]	
Ashkenazi-Ideal	.90
Morocco-Ideal	.89
Ashkenazi-Actual	.74
Morocco-Actual	.66
Iraq Ideal	.61
Iraq-Actual	.55
Eigenvalue	3.66
% variance	60.9

[a]Ordered according to magnitude of load.

Iraqi actual and ideal families are also based is derived from knowledge of existing Ashkenazi family patterns.

Conclusion

The general conclusion resulting from this study is that ethnic origin continues to color perceptions of family life among Israeli children whose parents or grandparents immigrated to Israel from different countries or cultural backgrounds. In line with the theoretical bias exposed in the introduction to this paper, the study only examined the effect of ethnicity with respect to one specific arena, namely, family life. It would, of course, be interesting to examine whether ethnicity also determines perceptions of other areas of social life, such as work or school, which are less "private" domains.

This study shows that ethnicity not only persists with respect to actual family organization but that it persists intergenerationally. The children examined in this research were all born and raised in Israel, yet the ethnic origin of their parents (and in some cases their grandparents) affected children's perceptions of their family situations. This conclusion is interesting in view of the widely-held belief that ethnicity dies quickly, particularly in a country such as Israel where national ideology advocates the settling of ethnic differences in most social spheres.

The study shows that while differences exist between the family styles of children from Ashkenazi, Iraqi and Moroccan origins, there is no marked dichotomy between Ashkenazi children, on the one hand, and children from the *edot hamizrach,* on the other. From both the factor arrays computed in the actual and from the correlation of the average actual sorts, it can be seen that differences exist between children from all three ethnic groups and that perceived Iraqi and Moroccan family arrangements are only slightly more similar to each other than they are to perceived Ashkenazi family patterns.

In the ideal, there is no dividing line at all between Ashkenazi children, as members of one group, and Iraqi and Moroccan children, as members of another. In fact, as the correlation of the average ideal sort shows, Ashkenazi and Moroccan ideal families bear the greatest resemblance to each other, the correlation between these two types of ideal families being higher than the correlation between the ideal families of children from the *edot hamizrach.* From the point of view of satisfaction with existing family arrangements (the actual-ideal congruency score), Moroccan children appear to be more similar to Ashkenazi children than to their Iraqi counterparts. These findings, of course, negate preconceived notions that members of the *edot hamizrach* display greater affinity to one another than they do to Jews of European descent. It is contended, therefore, that the binary opposition between Ashkenazi Jews and Jews belonging to the category of *edot hamizrach* must be reviewed in favor of a more detailed study of ethnic dynamics when dealing with micro-analysis and the perception of on-the-ground variables.

With respect to the persistence of ethnicity in the future, the evidence suggests that the perpetuation of ethnic difference in family style will not continue unabated—and herein lies the predictive power of this Q-Study. The ideal sorts of children from all three groups—Ashkenazi, Iraqi and Moroccan—display similarities indicating common Israeli ideals concerning desired future families. The factor analysis of all the average sorts, moreover, suggests that the desired family of the future is based upon the Ashkenazi model, although the desire of children from different ethnic origins to converge upon the Ashkenazi family type is conceived at different rates. From the data presented in the text, it appears that the wish of children of Moroccan origin to assimilate to an Ashkenazi ideal is stronger than their Iraqi counterparts, and that Moroccans may thereby lose their ethnic distinctiveness at faster rate than Iraqis.

Young Israelis, though dissimilar one from another in their actual family patterns, appear to be united in their ideals. Irrespective of their ethnic affiliation and the ethnic origin of their parents, pre-adolescent Israelis basically desire the same kinds of families based on Ashkenazi standards and norms. The trend of convergence thus appears to be a common aim, even if idealization will not, and cannot, instantly transform ideals to actuality.

APPENDIX
Descriptors used in the Family Q-sort[11]

1. If I do something bad Mother tells Father.
2. My parents give me as much money as I want.
3. My parents promise (things) and don't keep (their promises).
4. My parents rely on me.
5. I watch T.V. every night for at least 2 hours.
6. When I return home from school, I help clean the house.
7. Father returns home from work late.
8. My parents are not usually home in the evening.
9. On Shabbat and Festivals we visit (our) uncles or grandfather and/or grandmother (grandparents).
10. My Mother is more irritable than my Father.
11. We're not short of money in our house.
12. I usually play with friends from the same ethnic origin (as me).
13. My parents don't pay attention to me.
14. My father tells me about his work.
15. When my parents are cross with me, they don't let me go out.
16. Father allows me to do more things than Mother.
17. When Mother is angry with me, she doesn't speak to me.
18. When I have a difficult question with my homework, my parents help me.
19. I go to sleep whenever I want.
20. When my parents are cross with me, they hit me.
21. My parents never punish me.
22. When I have a problem, I go to my big brother instead of my parents.
23. I usually go to the club or (youth) movement in the afternoon.
24. It's always noisy in my house.
25. I go to synagogue every Saturday.
26. I go on lots of trips with my parents.

27. On Friday night we eat a festive meal.
28. We eat supper together.
29. It's very crowded in our house.
30. Grandfather and grandmother (my grandparents) spoil me.
31. Sometimes all my brothers (and sisters) pool their savings to buy something together.
32. My parents are always frightened that I may have an accident.
33. My parents shout at me a lot.
34. My parents let me do whatever I want.
35. When I do badly in my studies, my parents get angry.
36. My parents take an interest in my studies.
37. When I lose or break something, my parents get angry with me.
38. I often go with my parents to the cinema.
39. I have to tell (my parents) where I'm going.
40. My brothers and I quarrel all the time.
41. I invite friends to play at my house.
42. My parents quarrel all the time.
43. On Friday evening my parents want all the family to stay together.
44. My parents and I have fun together.
45. My uncles have a say in my education.
46. I have a birthday party every year.
47. Father goes out with friends in the evening, and Mother stays home.
48. In the evening, Father tells Mother about his problems.
49. In the summer vacation, I go to stay with my uncles.
50. I help Mother make the food.

Notes

[1] The research upon which this paper is based was carried out between September 1977 and August 1978 under the sponsorship of the Research Department of the Ministry of Labour and Social Welfare, Israel (Contract No. 11025/01.) The author gratefully acknowledges the help and devotion of Mr. Rami Benvenisti, School of Social Work and Social Psychology, University of Michigan, Ann Arbor, USA, without whom this work could not have been completed.

[2] In Weil and Benvenisti (198) the Family perceptions of 138 of those pre-adolescents were analysed.

[3] For the difference between Ashkenazi and Sephardi Jews, and the nuances of meaning between *edot hamizrach*, 'Middle Eastern' Jews and so on, see Goldberg (1977).

[4] A good example is Smooha (1978), who reduces Israel's Jewish ethnic problems to the conflict between Western and Oriental Jews.

[5] These observations were made on the basis of a study of ethnicity in an 'immigrant town' in Israel from 1972-75 (Weil, 1977b).

[6] "Sephardi" can, however, also be used as a restricted category to refer to Jews of Spanish origin, who are usually Ladino-speaking.

[7] For the relative merits of 'forced' vs. 'free' distributions, see Block (1969, pp. 71-78).

[8] Stephenson (1953), for example, studies students who, on the basis of prior testing, are already recognized to be 'under' or 'over' achievers, while Kerlinger (1973) uses as subjects persons who are known to be 'conservative' or 'progressive'.

[9] This procedure was, in effect, more similar to Stephenson's (1953) proposed methodology than to Block's averaging method (1969), although computation of factor scores was done by a computer programme using matrix algebra (cf. Nie, 1975, pp. 487-488).

[10] D. denotes 'descriptor' passim.

[11] Translated from Hebrew.

References

Aldous, J. 1972. "Children's Perceptions of Adult Role Assignment: Father-Absence, Class, Race and Sex Influences", *Journal of Marriage and the Family* 34:55-65.

Bar-Yosef. 1958. "Socialization Patterns in the Kibbutz", *Megamot* 11:23-32 (in Hebrew).

———. 1969. "Role Differentiation in the Urban Family in Israel", in R. Bar-Yosef and I. Shelach (Eds.), *The Family in Israel.* Jerusalem: Academon Press (in Hebrew), pp. 167-180.

Beck, Samuel. 1972. "Differential Judgments by Social Workers: A Q-Technique Research in Families of Schizophrenic Children", in Brown and Brenner (Eds.), *Science, Psychology and Communications.*

Block, J. 1955. "The Difference Between Q and R8. *Psychological Review* 62:356-358.

———. 1969. *The Q-Sort Method in Personality Assessment.* Springfield: Charles C. Thomas.

Brenner, Donald, 1972. "Dynamics of Public Opinion on the Vietnam War", in Brown and Brenner (Eds.), *Science, Psychology and Communications.*

Brown, Steven. 1972. "A Fundamental Incommensurability Between Objectivity and Subjectivity", in Brown & Brenner (Eds.), *Science, Psychology and Communications.*

Brown, Steven, and Brenner, Donald (Eds.). 1972. *Science, Psychology and Communications: Essays Honouring William Stephenson.* New York: Teacher's College Press.

Butler, John. 1972. "Self Concept Change in Psychotherapy", in Brown and Brenner (Eds.), *Science, Psychology and Communications.*

Fiedler, Fred. 1972. "Research on Quasi-Therapeutic Relations in Small Task Groups", in Brown and Brenner (Eds.), *Science, Psychology and Communications.*

Geertz, Clifford, 1973. *The Interpretation of Cultures.* New York: Basic Books.

Goldberg, Harvey. 1977. "Introduction: Culture and Ethnicity in the Study of Israeli Society", *Ethnic Groups* 1:163:86.

Golding, T., and Wilbur, P. 1971. "Q Techniques as an Effective Measurement of Teacher Attitudes", *The Journal of Teacher Education* 12:36-42.

Gordon, L. 1967. "Q-Typing Oriental and American Youth: Initial and Clarifying Studies", *The Journal of Social Psychology* 71:185-95.

Hechter, Michael. 1975. *Internal Colonialism*. London: Routledge and Kegan Paul.

Katz, Elihu, and Zloczower, Avraham. 1961. "Ethnic Continuity in an Israeli Town", *Human Relations* 14, No. 4:293-328.

Kerlinger, Fred. 1973 (1964). *Foundations of Behavioral Research*. London: Holt, Rinehart and Winston.

Kilson, Martin. 1975. "Blacks & Neo-Ethnicity in American Political Life", in N. Glazer & D. P. Moynihan (Eds.), *Ethnicity: Theory & Experience*. Cambridge, Mass: Harvard University Press.

Kobrin, Frances, and Goldscheider, Calvin. 1978. *The Ethnic Factor in Family Structure and Mobility*. Cambridge, Mass: Ballinger.

MacKay, R. 1974. "Conceptions of Children and Models of Socialization", Roy Turner (Ed.), In *Ethnomethodology*. London: Penguin Education Series, pp. 180-193.

Metzger, D., and Williams, G. 1966. "Procedure and Results in the Study of Native Categories: Tseltal Firewood". *American Anthropologist* 65:1076-1101.

Nie, Norman. 1975. *Statistical Package for the Social Sciences,* New York: McGraw Hill.

Palgi, Phyllis. 1970. "The Adaptability and Vulnerability of Family Types in the Changing Israeli Society", in Arieh Jarus (Ed.), *Children and Families in Israel,* New York: Gordon and Breach, pp. 97-150.

Pike, Kenneth. 1954. *Language in Relation to a Unified Theory of the Structure of Human Behavior*. Glendale, California: Summer Institute of Linguistics.

Redburn, F. 1975. "Q Factor Analysis: Application to Educational Testing and Program Evaluation", *Educational and Psychological Measurement* 35:767-778.

Rogers, Carl. 1958. "The Self-Concept in Paranoid Schizophrenia", *Journal of Clinical Psychology* 14:365-366.

Rogers, Carl, and Dymond, Rosalind. 1954. *Psychotherapy and Personality Change,* Chicago: University of Chicago Press.

Schlinger, Mary Jane. 1972. "The Immediate Experience of Television Advertising", in Brown and Brenner (Eds.), *Science Psychology and Communications*.

Singer, E. 1971. "Adult Orientation of First and Late Children", *Sociometry* 34: 328-345.

Smooha, Sammy. 1978. *Israel: Pluralism and Conflict,* London: Routledge and Kegan Paul.

Sontag, M. 1968. "Attitudes Toward Education and Perception of Teacher Behaviour", *American Educational Research Journal* 5:385-402.

Spiro, Melford. 1958. *Children of the Kibbutz*. Cambridge: Harvard University Press.

Stephenson, William. 1953. *The Study of Behaviour: Q Technique and its Methodology*. Chicago: Chicago University Press.

——. 1967. *The Play Theory of Mass Communication*. Chicago: University of Chicago Press.

Talmon-Garber, Yonina. 1969. "Social Change and Family Structure", in Rivka Bar-Yosef and Ilana Shelach (Eds.), *The Family in Israel*. Jerusalem: Academon Press (in Hebrew), pp. 125-52.

——. 1972. *Family and Community in the Kibbutz*. Cambridge: Harvard University Press.

Tiger, Lionel, and Shepher, Joseph. 1975. *Women in the Kibbutz*. New York: Harcourt Brace Jovanovich.

Van der Veen, F. 1971. "Dimensions of the Family Concept in Relation to Emotional Disorder and Family Position", *Proceedings,* 79th Annual Convention, APA:451-52.

Weil, Shalva. 1977a. "Names & Identity Among the Bene Israel", *Ethnic Groups* 1, No. 3:201-219.

——. 1977b. "Ben Israel Indian Jews In Lod, Israel: A Study of the Persistence of Ethnicity & Ethnic Identity". Unpublished D.Phil. thesis submitted to the University of Sussex, England.

Weil, Shalva, and Benvenisti, Rami. 198 . "Family Perceptions Among Pre-Adolescent Children in Israel", in Floyd Martinson (Ed.), "The Child and the Family", *Journal of Comparative Family Studies*

Weingrod, Alex. 1979. "Recent Trends in Israeli Ethnicity", *Ethnic and Racial Studies* 2:55-65.

6

Ethnic Relations in an Arab Town in Israel

Majid al-Haj

Most students of ethnic relations in Israel have dealt exclusively with Jewish communities. Generally speaking, their analyses are developed from the viewpoints of "nation building" (Eisenstadt, 1973), "pluralism" (Smooha, 1978; Peres, 1982) or what may be termed the "directed discrimination" of the Oriental communities (Swirski, 1981). Few scholars have thus far dealt with the Arab sector as part of the multi-ethnic Israeli society. Whether they regarded Israeli Arabs as a group within the pluralistic structure of the society (Smooha, 1976), or as one of its three principal communities (Ashkenazim, Oriental Jews and Arabs) they have tended to use affiliation to the Jewish people and the degree of involvement in Jewish civilization as their principal analytic criteria (Peres, 1982:42). Indeed, even those few scholars who studied the communal structure of the Arab population did so without analyzing the internal dynamics of Arab inter-ethnic relations or the genesis of an Arab minority within Israeli society.

This article analyzes the patterns of inter-ethnic relations in an Arab town in Israel in which three distinct communities live together: Christians, Muslims and Druze. Relations between them will be discussed in terms of "minority and majority" patterns, and, in addition, the interactions within each community will be examined historically in the framework of the social, economic and political status of each community during the period of the British mandate as well as within the state of Israel. It should be stressed at the outset that notwithstanding the social and national characteristics that these three groups have in common, each has preserved its own ethnic identity throughout the various historical periods. How these Arab ethnic groups relate to one another within the context of rapidly changing external circumstances is the main theme of this study.[1]

Theoretical Framework

The concepts "minority" and "minority group" can be traced back to the period of nascent nationalism in 18th and 19th-century Europe when various groups began to demand national rights. The terms "majority" and "minority" were generally defined by numerical criteria, while the minority groups were divided into ethnic, national, linguistic and/or religious minorities (Fischer, 1980). In the course of time, however, the definition of "minority" was expanded and began to refer in a more comprehensive manner to the position of a particular group in the status system of a given society. In addition to numerical criteria, other characteristics, especially economic power and political hegemony, have recently been used to distinguish between "majority" and "minority" status (see Yetman and Steel, 1975). According to these characteristics, numbers alone do not necessarily imply "majority status", and in certain societies (South Africa, for example) the "minority group" actually constitutes the population majority (Gitter, 1956). In addition to these criteria, some scholars also take into account subjective factors, such as "minority sentiments" and the development of a separate set of attitudes and behavioral patterns within a group which has been defined as a minority (Wirth, 1946).

We tend toward a broader, multi-dimensional approach to the concept of "minority status". In this study we concentrate upon particular ethnic groups on the assumption that a status system deriving from minority-majority relations is a valid basis for the analysis of social relations both at the community-level and at the national level. At the same time we do not ignore the fact that certain features (for example, political domination and control, discrimination, hostility, etc.) which are the result of majority-minority relations on the national level do not necessarily exist at the community level, or if they do, they do not always have the same effect and force. Throughout this study we therefore place emphasis upon different levels, and examine in particular how the community "inter-

ethnic" status system is influenced and changes as a consequence of transformations taking place within both the region and the nation.

Our analysis is also based on three additional assumptions: First, status
patterns are not stable, but may change in the course of time. They may
in fact be reversed as the result of changes in the balance of political and
economic power; Second, the elements of a "minority status" may function in a differential manner—that is, a group may have a minority status
in one sphere, and a majority status in another; Third, the various types
of status on the regional or national level may or may not be in accordance
with those on the community level. If they conform with each other, we
speak of a "majority within a majority", or a "minority within a minority". If the status patterns do not agree, we may have "a majority within a
minority" or "a minority within a majority".

Socio-Historical Background

Shefaram, the town that is the focus of this study, is located on the western fringes of Lower Galilee, in the centre of a triangle which lies at a
distance of approximately eighteen kilometers from Acre, Haifa and Nazareth. It has an estimated population of 22,000 and is the second-largest
Arab town in Israel. During the period of Ottoman rule Shefaram served
as a district center (*modiriyah*), and it then provided services to 22 villages
in the region. Indeed, Shefaram was the first settlement in the northern
part of the country to officially be declared a town.

The fact that Shefaram was a service center attracted many immigrants
who came to settle there in various periods. An analysis of the settlement's
nucleus shows that Druze and a number of well-to-do Christian families
were among the first settlers. There was, however, considerable population
fluctuation among the Christian families, some of whom emigrated to
Lebanon but returned later during the eighteenth century. During this
same period, and in particular under the rule of Dahar al-Omar, Muslim
families began to settle in Shefaram, especially on the eastern fringes of
the built-up area. Throughout the Ottoman and British Mandatory periods
the Christian community preserved its numeric preponderance (approximately forty-five percent), while the Muslims constituted the second
largest community (approximately thirty-eight percent), and the Druze
the smallest (seventeen percent).

Following the establishment of Israel in 1948 drastic changes took
place in Shefaram's demographic and social structure. These changes were

partly the result of the massive evacuation of local families who became refugees in the neighboring Arab countries, and partly were due to the re-shuffling of populations within the Israeli border (what became known in the wake of the war as the "green line") and as the result of official government policy.

In the first months of 1948 Shefaram had a population of 4,869. Later, that year, following the war, the socio-demographic structure of the local community became radically changed. Large sections of the Muslim population, as well as a number of Christian and Druze families, left the town when they learned that the Israeli Army intended to capture it. Many fled to the east, to Sephoris, and to the north, to the Jodpata region in Galilee, while other Muslim families crossed the border into Lebanon. After the capture of Shefaram on July 14, 1948, when it became known that it was possible to return and to receive an Israeli identity card, dozens of families did return, although a smaller number went further northwards and selected to settle in Lebanon "until the situation would clear up".

During the next first three years there followed a fluctuating situation of immigration and emigration. Some families were re-united with returning relatives who settled again in Shefaram and became Israeli citizens, while other families were split because the authorities did not permit the return of their members who had left the town during the war.

It is important to point out that it was almost exclusively the Muslim families that were broken up in this manner. A comparison of the population before and after Israeli independence (1948) shows that 494 inhabitants—474 Muslims and 20 Christians—left Shefaram for the Arab countries. No Druze left the settlement permanently. Those among the Druze who had left in the beginning of the war returned immediately and none of them was refused an Israeli identity card (that is, citizenship) by the Military Government. On the other hand, there also was a population influx into Shefaram during these first three years: 548 refugees from neighboring villages which had been destroyed during the war moved to the town. In 1953 the population had become more or less stabilized and was composed as shown in Table 1.

Significant changes in the demographic structure of the town population have taken place since the early 1950s, not merely as the result of natural population increase, but also because of the migration of Beduin refugees and Druze from Hauran. The process of settlement of these "internal refugees" (that is, Palestinians whose homes were destroyed but who did not flee and remained in Israel) went through several stages,

TABLE 1
Shefaram Population by Ethnic Group

Communities Population-groups	Christians	Muslims	Druze	Total
Locals	2216	1192	958	4366
Refugees	120	428	–	548
Total	2336	1620	958	4919
Percentage of total	48	33	19	100

beginning with their search for shelter and, after a period of waiting and hoping, ending, in the late 1950s, with their permanent settlement. By that time they had given up hope that the problem of the Arab internal refugees could be solved in the context of a solution of the general Arab refugee problem. These refugees had begun to regard their case as lost, or, as one of them expressed himself: "Rahat e-seqrah va-ajat e-fegrah"– "the shock is over and thought has taken its place". They began then to prepare themselves for long-term settlement; some bought plots of land and built small, temporary houses, or purchased existing homes from the local residents, and gradually they became integrated into the local community.

During this time, refugee families and clans that had been dispersed between various towns and villages, began to be re-united. Generally speaking, they tended to concentrate in those places where family members had succeeded in settling. In Shefaram, the refugees constitute twenty-two percent of the total population–thirty-six percent of the Muslim community, and eight percent of the Christians.

150 years earlier there already were Beduin in the fields of Shefaram. Members of the large Beduin tribes, such as the Turkaman, Sua'ad and Hurjirat, then used the grazing lands of Shefaram. Permenent Beduin settlement on Shefaram land began in the early years of the twentieth century. According to a report of 1917, 89 Beduin families lived there in that year; they were granted the status of permanent residents and, consequently, the right to vote for the council of the Turkish regional administration.

Although the Beduin had maintained close contacts with Shefaram for

E

several decades, their permanent settlement in the town did not begin until the 1950s. The migration waves came from two directions: the first was a gradual and slow influx of Beduin from the immediately surrounding region, while the second was an influx of Beduin families from distant regions in the north. The first wave of Beduin settlers came in 1954 and consisted of 100 persons; most settled in the southern part of the town, the others in the eastern part. The second wave took place in 1958. According to municipal reports 34 families, numbering 241 persons, came in that year to Shefaram: 30 families belonging to the Sua'ad tribe, two to the Ka'abiyeh and two to the Hujirat tribes respectively.

These Beduin tended to settle on the fringes of the town and were not formally under the municipality's jurisdiction; for this reason they were neither granted voting rights in municipal elections, nor were they entitled to municipal services such as water and electricity. However, in 1967 the Beduin settlement came under the municipal jurisdiction of Shefaram. Since then additional Beduin families have come to join their relatives who have lived there since the 1950's. The Beduin presently account for 6.5% of the total population, and 13% of the Muslim community.

The second main group if in-migrants are Druze. "Druze e-Jebel" or "el-Haurana" as the local Druze call them, originally came as soldiers with Sakhib Aluhab, the Syrian commander who lead Arab armies in the Galilee during the 1948 war. On May 24, 1948, Sakhib Aluhab returned to Syria with most of his soldiers. However, approximately 100 soldiers, almost of all them Druze, stayed behind. At the end of the war they volunteered for service in the Israeli Army, within the framework of the Mahal ("Volunteers from abroad"). Most of them subsequently married and settled in various places throughout Israel. In 1957, thirty of these Druze families settled in Shefaram. They concentrated in a special neighborhood for released soldiers that was built by the Defense Ministry in 1958.

Since that time they have been called by the local inhabitants "el-Haurana", because of their origin in the Hauran, although they call themselves "Druze e-Jebel". The difference between these two names is not semantic, but is rather an expression of the delicate relations between them and the other inhabitants, and in particular the members of the Druze community.

The addition of the groups of immigrants we have just described brought about a drastic change in the ethnic balance of power in Shefaram, not only in the numerical sense but also socio-politically. The Muslim community, to which most of these immigrants belong, was affected more than the others. Whereas during the 1950's the Muslims were the second largest community with 33% of the population as against 48% Christians, by the 1970's they had reached the same number as the Christians (40%), and today they constitute the population majority (45% as against 37% Christians and 18% Druze).

This brief socio-historical analysis justifies the conclusion that present-day Shefaram can provide us with a representative sample of the various sectors of the Israeli Arab population. The town population includes Muslims, Druze and Christians of various denominations; Beduin and fella-him; refugees and locals; local Druze and Druze e-Jebel; and groups originating in the village as well as in-migrating groups.

Economic Structure

Until the last years of the British Mandate Shefaram was an agricultural settlement—90% of the Druze families, 80% of the Muslims and 70% of the Christians were engaged in agriculture. 65% of the farmers worked their own land, 19% were compelled to work as hired labor in addition to working their own land, while 11% had no land of their own and made their living mainly as employed agricultural workers. Among the last-mentioned were farmhands, shepherds and casual workers. In addition to working as hired laborers they often also tilled a small plot of land they had received or leased from their employer. Five percent were employed as camel drivers and transported the agricultural products from the fields to the threshing floor.

In an agrarian society the control of land, and in particular of agricultural land, is not only a means of existence, but also a status symbol and an instrument of power in other spheres. It is therefore important to understand how the land was divided among and within the various ethnic groups. Until the land registration introduced by the mandatory government in 1933, the population of Shefaram had approximately 125,000 dunam of land at its disposal. Following the land registration about 30,000 dunam were declared government land, allegedly because they consisted of uncultivated hill country, while 7,000 dunam were sold to Jews by Salah Effendi, a wealthy landowner from Acre. One of the immediate results of the registration was the breakdown of the communal land, or "musha'a" system, as had happened in other parts of Palestine as well

TABLE 2

Division of Land in Shefaram by Ethnic Group (1935)[a]

% of land per community Fadanim per family	Druze	Christians	Muslims
Less than 1 fadan	40	47	78
1–2 fadanim	22	17	18
2 or more fadanim	38	36	4
Total	100	100	100

[a]Abramovitch and Gilfat (1940) write that the Palestinian fadan is not a fixed surface unit, but varies from region to region. It is always and everywhere a plot large enough to sustain an average fellah family under the specific conditions prevailing in the region. In Shefaram one fedan is 250 dunam.

(Veshitz, 1947). Most of the remaining land became "neutral", privately-owned land. Approximately 32,000 dunam of this area consisted of cultivated agricultural land.

From Table 2 we may draw a number of important conclusions:

1. The percentage of families able to subsist by cultivating their own land without additional employment was high among the Druze and the Christians and low among the Muslims (53%, 60% and 22%, respectively).

2. Two broad categories can be clearly distinguished among the local population: those with and those without land. Only a relatively thin layer of the population belongs to a third category, the middle class: 22% of the Druze, 17% of the Christians and 18% of the Muslims. The families belonging to this latter category were generally able to sustain themselves without the help of hired labor, except occasionally during the harvest.

3. Class and ethnic boundaries are not symmetrical—each ethnic group is not a class, but instead comprises several classes. As in Lebanon and other Middle Eastern countries class division and ethnicity do not coincide.

When we analyze each ethnic group and its control of the land it becomes clear that the Christians were the dominant community. They possessed 50% of the land, although they accounted for only 45% of the population. The Druze had the largest portion of land in proportion to their numbers: 17% of the population with 38% of the land. The Muslims were at the bottom of the scale: they controlled only 12% of the cultivated land, although they constituted 38% of the population.

In the other economic spheres the Christians also held a dominant position. Trade and industry were important branches in the employment structure of Shefaram; towards the end of the Ottoman period 15% of the families made a living in these two branches. During the British mandate there was a minor recession in industry and crafts, but trade retained its stability. An analysis of the employment structure in 1940 shows that 13% of the population were engaged in these two branches: 21% of the Christians, 8% of the Muslims and only 4% of the Druze.

The central economic position of Shefaram among the surrounding villages and its function as supplier of services made the control of trade and industry an extremely important asset. Not only the local population, but also the surrounding villages were therefore dependent on the Christians who controlled these two branches.

In Shefaram, the process of proletarization was rather slow compared with the rest of Palestine. Until the late 1930's only a few Shefaram residents worked as employed laborers in other than agricultural work. Towards the end of the 1930's and in the early 1940's the first signs of this process began to appear; on the basis of municipal reports and interviews we estimate that 10% of the wage-earners were then employed in non-agricultural work. The majority of this labor force was recruited from among the Muslim community, which was already at that early date becoming a reservoir of hired labor.

The employment structure and the possession of land during the period prior to the rise of the state of Israel indicate that there were four main socio-economic strata, each linked to an ethnic group. The merchants and business owners were nearly all Christians; the large land-owners were mainly Christians and Druze; small farmers were found among all three communities; while the overwhelming majority of the poor fellahim and hired workers were Muslims. This economic structure suggests two patterns of dependence. On the local level Druze and Christians held the central positions, the former in agriculture, the latter both in agriculture and trade and industry. The Muslims lived along the periphery and were economically dependent on the other two groups. They supplied the unskilled labor force, and only a small percentage of Muslim families could subsist from privately-owned independent farms. On the regional level, the surrounding Arab villages were also dependent on Shefaram, which provided the village population with seasonal agricultural work, maintained trade relations with them and supplied various services to the fellahim. In this respect the Christian community was the dominant group.

The radical political changes that took place after the establishment of Israel did not immediately bring about economic changes. On the contrary, during the 1950's the existing economic structure was preserved. The local economy continued to function, for the lack of an alternative, as the main employer of local labor; land remained the main source of livelihood, as well as a key status symbol and an important element in the intercommunal power structure.

However, in contrast with the pre-1948 period, Shefaram lost its central economic position among the surrounding villages. A number of objective reasons may be adduced regarding this change. First, the new Israeli government instituted severe regulations which restricted the movement of the population and consequently of labor and trade. In addition, the destruction of some of the surrounding villages also severely affected trade relations. Finally, the people from these villages who migrated to Shefaram as "internal refugees" possessed neither land nor other assets, and therefore they became a dependent labor force willing to accept every type of work and competing with the local population for the few remaining sources of livelihood.

As a result, at the end of the 1950's and in the early 1960's the pressures that had been building up became visible. The reservoir of available local workers moved out from the settlement to become part of the great Arab labor force in search of casual, unskilled work. Local farmhands were increasingly scarce, and agriculture became a marginal source of subsistence. As a result, land gradually lost its significance as a major asset, and this in turn drastically altered the local status system.

The dependence of the local labor force on the outside labor market increased from year to year. Changes in the national Israeli economy have had immediate repercussions for the town economy since they led to fluctuations in the demand for hired labor, depending upon the situation in the dominant Jewish economy: a boom until the mid-fifties, recession in 1966 and 1967, and again later, proletarization and dependence.

While Shefaram was deprived of its traditional economic basis—agriculture, trade and crafts—no alternative economic basis (industry and trade, for example) was created. Even the rise in the standard of living did not free the local labor force from its dependence on outside jobs.

On the contrary, dependence increased in proportion to the rise in the standard of living, since the workers worked more, or sold plots of land and converted them into other assets, in order to reach the coveted standard of living or to preserve their existing living standards.

Today the employment structure of Shefaram is not different from that typical of the other large Arab villages in Israel: local labor is largely dependent on employment in the Jewish center; the majority is employed in construction and services (private and public), while only 10% are employed in agriculture and small cattle breeding (see Table 3).

An examination of the current employment structure among the three ethnic groups shows that there is no substantial difference between them, with the exception that 76% of the Druze still work in agriculture. This can be explained by the fact that less Druze land was confiscated, as well as by the strong Druze agricultural and family traditions.

In summary, after the first decade of Israeli statehood the focus of dependence rapidly moved outside the settlement to such a degree that local inter-ethnic economic dependence was greatly reduced or even eliminated. Economic dependence became one-sided—the communities and groups in Shefaram became dependent on employment in the dominant

TABLE 3
Number of Employed in Shefaram in 1981 (age 15 and older)

Branch of Employment	Number	%
Locally employed		employed
Agriculture and small cattle	383	9.5
Public and financial institutions	215	5.0
Education	245	5.7
Trade and business	490	11.5
Construction	120	2.8
Industry	175	4.1
Employed outside		
Construction	780	18.2
Industry	638	15.0
Transport and storage	340	8.1
Various private services	—	—
Various automobile services	894	20.1
Total	4280	100.0

Jewish economy. The new immigrants of the early 1950's—internal refugees, Beduin and Druze e-Jebel—have also been absorbed in the larger employment structure and have become part of this dependent labor force rather than becoming a population group on the periphery.

Political Hegemony

Shefaram was one of the first settlements in the north to be granted city rights and to be administered by an elected city council. Control of local administration became the touchstone of the power balance between the various local communities and groups. The first city council was appointed in 1911 by the regional governor (the Ottoman "mudir"); it was composed of five Christian members (one of whom was the mayor) and one Druze. No Muslim member was appointed. This composition clearly demonstrated the great differentiation in the economic position of the various communities—membership in the city council was the exclusive right of landowners and tax-payers, both during the Ottoman period and, later, under the British mandate (Maoz, 1962:233).

Following a transitional period of four years the first municipal elections were held in March, 1915. Thirty-three citizens had put up their candidacy: five Druze, eight Muslims and twenty Christians. The elections were held over a period of three days in order to enable all franchized citizens who wished to cast their vote to reach the polls in time. The right to vote was, however, granted only to citizens 25 years' and older who paid the minimum amount of municipal taxes. The latter condition deprived the low-income classes—in this case the Muslim community—of the right to vote. In the course of these three days 64 persons cast their ballot: 38 Christians, 14 Druze and only twelve Muslims. Seven candidates were elected: one Druze, one Muslim and five Christians. The district governor then appointed the mayor from among the elected members.

The composition of the city council was a clear reflection of the inter-ethnic power balance and of the dominance of the Christians. This situation continued during the mandatory period, but the end of the first mayor's term of office in 1933 revealed the conflicts within the Christian community itself. Two candidates contested for the office of mayor, one of them the son of the *mukhtar* of the Catholic community, the other a well-known Maronite who had been a member of the council since the first elections. The Catholic candidate won the context. It should be noted that these were the only elections held in Shefaram during the entire pre-

Israel period. After the first elections the members of the council, including the chairman, were re-appointed by general agreement of the communities (*tazkiyeh*).

In the wake of the 1948 war the city council of Shefaram ceased to function; for the next three years the mayor dealt with the affairs of the town from his home. In 1951 a new city council, consisting of seven members in addition to the mayor, was appointed; three Christians, three Druze and two Muslims. This development had three notable aspects.

First, the composition of the council was in a way a continuation of the situation in the pre-state days, with representation along communal lines. The Christians retained their dominance and continued to hold the post of mayor. The strengthening of the position of the Druze after the formation of Israel was immediately reflected in their representation in the council. For the first time in Shefaram's history this community was represented by three members, almost one third of the council's membership, although the community itself accounted for only twenty percent of the population. The Muslims remained in their marginal position, and their two representatives in the council had no influence whatsoever on the municipal procedures.

Second, the members of the appointed council belonged to rich families of landowners who had always been represented in the council. Thus the traditional status quo in the council was preserved until the end of the first decade of statehood, with communal affiliation and landed property as the principal keys to the town's administration.

Third, the economic and socio-demographic changes which had occurred during the first decade found their expression later during the second decade and drastically influenced the power struggles between the communities and clans in the council. The changes in the economic structure ultimately led to a change in the status system at the expense of the Christians. The Muslim community which had always been at the bottom of the social ladder became stronger, not only because of its growing numbers, but also because of its ability to close ranks, two factors which counterbalanced its economic weakness. In the mid-sixties the internal refugees, who had been an important factor in the change in the demographic, inter-ethnic balance, began to demand their rightful place in the power structure of the Muslim community. Indeed, towards the end of the second decade a political upheaval occurred: for the first time the Muslims seized the post of mayor. This upheaval was the result of factors we have mentioned earlier, as well as of the fact that for the first time in the town's history the Muslims had obtained population equality with the Christians.

The closing of the ranks of the Muslim community provoked a similar move among the Christians and the Druze, each of whom presented outspokenly communal lists in the elections of 1973. But this communal unity did not last: it disintegrated before the next elections, four years later, because of fierce internal conflicts between the clans that composed the Christian and Druze communities. Paradoxically, the Muslim communal list succeeded in maintaining its solidarity for the opposite reason. The weakening of the Muslim clans and the considerable strenthening of the Druze and Christian clans was due to the same socio-demographic factors which were discussed earlier. First, the central position of the Muslim clans was weakened because of the departure of large numbers of Muslim families who had settled in the Arab countries. Secondly, the influx of internal refugees (almost all of them Muslims), who had come as single families or as sections of clans, did much to strengthen the collective character of the Muslim community at the expense of its clan character. These refugees pressed for communal unity because such unity would increase their chances to influence, as a group, the general social structure of the settlement, while a division into clans would likely diminish their power to advance their own interests.

In effect, the priorities within the ethnic groups were reversed. Whereas among the Christians and the Druze the transition was from loyalty to the community to loyalty to the neighborhood and the clan, a reverse tendency prevailed among the Muslims: from clan and neighborhood to loyalty to the community.

The inter-ethnic political agreements and covenants also assumed a different character. From the establishment of the first city council until the end of the first decade after the rise of Israel, the Druze had kept their agreement with the Christians and thus helped to preserve the balance in the settlement in which the Christians had both political hegemony and economic power. The mid-sixties saw the first signs of a change and a rapprochement between the Druze and Muslim. This process reached its climax in the late 1960's with the political upheaval that became possible because of the unity of the Muslim community and its coalition with the Druze, a coalition which has persisted till the present day. For example, in the recent 1983 municipal elections a Christian list, representing virtually the entire local Christian community, joined the Muslim-Druze coalition. The new coalition thus comprises all of the ethnic groups; it is headed by a Muslim mayor who has two Druze deputies and a Christian acting mayor. This coalition was formed on the basis of the "communal balance" and is acceptable to the overwhelming majority of the local population, as it consists of eight of the council's eleven members.

The recent elections confirmed an interesting development: the focus of inter-communal strife has shifted to the sphere of the clans and sectors within each of the ethnic groups, and the principal contests were held between lists within each of them. Among the Muslims, for example, two lists competed with each other: a major list representing the community at large and a new list made up of clans and neighborhoods. The Christians also had two lists: the traditional one which claims to represent the community, and a new list which defeated the former and subsequently joined the existing coalition. The Druze, too, campaigned with two lists, the traditional one representing the entire community, and a new list of young people from all the clans. The latter, however, did not obtain the required quota. These contests within the communities will in the future doubtless have far-reaching repercussions for the division of power in the town.

The final point that deserves to be mentioned is the linkage between economic dominance and political hegemony. Prior to the rise of the state the linkage between the two spheres had been extremely strong, and the economic inter-dependence of the communities was a restraining factor on inter-ethnic conflicts. Following the birth of the state, and in particular in the first decade when Shefaram became economically dependent upon the outside world, internal economic inter-dependence lost its significance; as a result the conflicts became aggravated and groups which had hitherto been at the periphery began moving towards the center and participating in the struggle for political control. This development is reflected in the dynamics of change in the inter-ethnic power balance. More particularly, the Muslims who had been at the periphery because of their economic dependence on the Christians at first showed no inclination whatsoever to contest over local political control. It was only in the middle 1960's, after the economic foundations of the system of social status had crumbled, that the Muslims began to reveal signs of communal consolidation in their struggle for the mayoralty, and towards the end of that decade they reached their goal.

Regional Status and External Aid

On March 31, 1947 there were 1,253,000 Arabs in Palestine, of whom 1,091,000 were Muslims (86.3%), 146,000 Christians (11.7%) and 16,000 Druze and others (2%) (Government of Palestine, 1947). From these figures it is clear that the Muslims constituted the overwhelming majority, a fact reflected in their control of the national economic resources and of the political and social elite among the Palestinian Arabs. This was also the situation in the Shefaram region, and this regional pattern deeply affected communal relations in the town.

The weakness of the central government in the pre-state period caused the individual citizen to feel insecure and to live in permanent fear for his life, family and property. He was therefore compelled to seek security by affiliating to a group which was as large as possible and in which the binding elements were stronger than the dividing ones (clan, neighborhood, sect, community); such groups were not only reinforced from within, but also from the outside, in particular by groups or settlements with whom they had close ties, preferably based upon blood ties or common descent. These external relations, and their potential or actual aid in case of need, were extremely important for members of every community.

The networks of relationship of ethnic group members in Shefaram was very wide. In many cases these links were of an individual kind and found expression in trade, work, reciprocal visits, participation in various social events, and so forth. However, in addition to these kinds of ties, each group had its own special external orientation of a communal nature.

The Muslims chiefly maintained relations with the surrounding villages which had a clear Muslim majority. Among the 22 villages which constituted the Shefaram district, eighteen were Muslim villages and four had a mixed Muslim-Christian population. There were no Druze villages in the district. The Muslim community of Shefaram therefore enjoyed the position of a community belonging to the regional majority, a status which positively affected their relations with others since they could count on immediate help from the surrounding villages in cases of a blood feud or other conflicts. Groups from outside the settlement frequently interfered in individual disputes and even exploited the chaos created by divisions in order to steal or to extort, sometimes against the wish of the local Muslims.

The Druze maintained strong ties with the villages in the Golan Heights,

Lebanon and Jebel al-Arab in Syria. In the memoirs of one of the Druze Sheikhs we found reports of frequent reciprocal visits of the Druze in Shefaram to their co-religionists in these villages, and vice cersa. We also found an extensive correspondence between them. The Druze in Lebanon and Syria maintained a deep interest in the vicissitudes of their brethren in Shefaram. For example, in 1937 one of the Druze notables from Jebel al-Arab sent a letter to the manager of the Arab bank in Haifa requesting him to intervene personally with the Muslims in Shefaram in order to improve their relations with their Druze neighbors. Among other things he wrote:

> ... we know that the affair started as an incident between two people, and that fate hit one of them: the government arrested the suspect and he will be brought to trial. The question is whether it was just that the surrounding villages attacked the Druze, committed acts of destruction, frightened women and children and offended the men's honor. The same thing could have happened when Salah Effendi was killed, and were it not for the mercy of God, who revealed the real murderer, acts of violence would have been committed of which no-one would know the end.
>
> Brothers, the Druze e-Jebel know what happened and in the name of our brotherhood in religion, language and country we try to do all in our might to ensure the peace of the Druze in Shefaram and to preserve the good relations between you and your brethren, the Druze of el-Arab and of Mount Lebanon who have spared no effort to support every Arab cause and in particular the Palestinian cause. I beg to remark that you shall shortly receive similar letters from Sultan Basha al-Atrash and other Druze notables. . . .

In the rioting between Druze and Muslims in 1939 the Druze of Jebel el-Arab also intervened. We found a report dated January 31, 1939, about a Druze delegation from Jebel-el-Arab which had come especially to reach a compromise between the communities and to restore peace.

Although this external aid was important for the local Druze community, it nonetheless was not sufficient to ensure their safety. This was due to two reasons—first, because of the geographical distance, and second, since the Druze from these outside areas did not intervene physically, but instead played the part of mediators between the two "Muslim branches", a reference to the fact that they regarded the Druze and Muslims as two branches of the same religion.

For their part, the Christians of Shefaram maintained an urban orientation in their relations with the outside world. Their principal ties were with the urban Christian communities of Haifa, Acre, Jaffa, and even Beirut. These relations became closer in the course of time and led to the migration of Christian families from Shefaram to these places. Some informants reported that well-to-do Christians used to spend most of their time in Beirut. These relations, however, were not translated into actual assistance of the Christians in Shefaram and had little influence on their relations with the other communities. It may be assumed that during the mandatory period there was no need for such assistance since the political and social elite of the town consisted mainly of Christian notables whose close relations with the British authorities bolstered their position both within and outside the settlement.

The formal aid the local communities, and in particular the Muslims, had received from their co-religionists prior to the formation of Israel, lost much of its practical significance after 1948. Following the 1948 war only 160,000 of the 700,000 Arabs who had lived in the territory which became Israel, remained in the country. Of these, 68.7% were Muslims, 21.2% Christians and 9.1% Druze (Ben-Amram, 1965). Since the establishment of the state the Arab population has expanded at a fast rate because of its high birth rate, but not as the result of immigration. The proportional division of the communities has not changed much, although the Muslim population has slightly increased in relation to the other communities since its birth rate has been higher.

Immediately after 1948 relations with the Arab countries were cut off, the borders were closed and the links between the Israeli Arab population and their co-religionists beyond the "green line" were cut off. Relationships outside their own settlement but within the borders were also drastically reduced. Many of the surrounding settlements with whom fruitful relations had existed in the past were destroyed: of the 22 villages in the Shefaram region eight were destroyed; six of these had been Muslim villages, two had a mixed Muslim-Christian population. Moreover, a military government was installed in large areas with an Arab population, including the Western Galilee where Shefaram is located. The military government (which continued until 1966) restricted the movement of the local population who had to equip themselves with special permits for entering or leaving the region for a limited period of time.

An additional reason for the changing social relations with other Arab settlements was the weakening of economic inter-dependence. As was pointed out earlier, the transformation of the enjoyment structure in the Arab sector led to the same pattern in all the Arab settlements: almost total dependence on wage-labor in the Jewish centers, and the simultaneous reduction or elimination of the economic inter-dependence of the Arab settlements. This development deeply affected the social relations between these settlements and reduced the possibilities of mutual influence. In addition to these factors, the restraining element of a strong central government which imposed law and order must also be added. The development of the judicial system and the presence of the police was felt in every settlement, and this greatly reduced the possibility of spontaneous action such as vengeance and the exploitation of individual conflicts to stir up inter-communal tension.

Partly as a result of the loss of these "informal" regional supports, the government's formal powers became the decisive element. One of the striking features of the policy conducted by the Israeli Government among the Arab minority since the beginning of statehood, was its attempt to turn it into a "mixture of minorities" with the goal of splitting the population into a great number of tiny minorities (Smooha, 1980:17). For example, the Druze were granted the status of a separate community, and in 1957 the Minister of Religious Affairs issued regulations which recognized the Druze as a religious community. Four years later, in October 1961, the religious leadership of the Druze was recognized as a "Religious Council" headed by Sheikh Amin Tarif, while in 1962 the Knesset completed the process by approving the Law on Druze Religious Courts (Falah, 1974; Standel, 1972). The most important move in this regard was the application of the Law on Compulsory Army Service to the Druze in 1956; since that time Druze males have been conscripted into the Israeli Army. The fostering of the Druze community as a separate religious and political entity found further expression in the change of the "nationality paragraph" in their identity cards from "Arab" to "Druze", and, finally, in the recognition of separate Druze education and the establishment of a Druze Education Committee in 1976.

The Beduin also received special treatment in the attempt to turn them into a separate community. This policy found its expression at several occasions, the most recent being Prime Minister Shamir's separate meetings with representatives of the Arabs and the Beduin in the framework of a series of meetings with the minorities in Israel.

A similar attempt was made to emphasize the special character of the Christian community. A recommendation in this spirit may be found in a

Labour Party document: "A special status should be given to the Christian communities and their special character should be stressed in order to distinguish them from the Muslim majority, so as to prevent Arab organization on a national level in which Muslim, nationalistic tendencies often dictate the forms of action" (Smooha, 1980:17).

These differentiating tendencies have also been apparent in the attitude of the government towards the various communities in Shefaram. Since the first days of Israeli statehood the leadership of the Druze community has become increasingly powerful and it has strengthened its influence on the other local communities. One of the main Druze leaders, Sheikh Salah Khanifes, was a Knesset Member until 1959, and he is still regarded as one of the outstanding personalities in the region. During the 1950's he was the link between the population of Shefaram and the neighboring villages and the government. Many individual as well as clan interests could be furthered through his mediation, which was especially important when the local population was ruled by the military government.

The Druze have also held a pivotal position in the Shefaram city council and have participated in each coalition. Consequently, the Druze community has become the central factor in the shaping of the internal politics and the division of power and economic resources. It should be added, however, that the religious and political participation of the Druze is less conspicuous in Shefaram than in the villages with a homogenous Druze population. The fact that the Druze in Shefaram reside in a mixed town, side by side with two other groups who constitute an overwhelming majority, prevented them from becoming entirely absorbed by the trend towards Druze particularism which generally characterizes the Druze community in Israel (Druze children in Shefaram attend local Arab schools which are not supervised by the Druze Educational Committee).

The development towards particularism of the Muslim Beduin is less striking, but it too merits attention. Many Beduin families settled in Shefaram in the framework of the program for Beduin population concentrations. A few young Beduin serve in the Israeli Army on a voluntary basis. Some Beduin concerns are dealt with by the Commission for Beduin Affairs which was established by the Prime Minister's Adviser for Arab Affairs, but there is as yet no deep separatism.

Christian particularism has been unsuccessful on the local and the national level alike. Although some signs in this direction can currently be seen, there is no indication that the tendency is developing. This may be due to the influence of Rakah, and anti-establishment party, whose Arab leadership is mainly recruited from among the Christian ranks.

Minority Feelings

Minority feelings are subjective and it is therefore difficult to determine their dimensions and scope. This becomes even more difficult when we try to analyse a system of relations in a period which belongs to the past, even if it is not a remote past. Moreover, when one attempts to understand these past "feelings" through interviews with people who lived during a previous time-period, the risk is great of judging the past by the standards of the present and being prejudiced by changes that have occurred since then. In order to remain consistent in our analysis of the two periods –before and after the establishment of Israel–we shall try to understand the "minority feelings" of the various ethnic communities by analyzing behavioral elements reflected in various events, and in the regional and social composition of the settlement.

In the pre-state period "minority feelings" were especially strong among the Druze. They were physically threatened by the Muslims who were then the most powerful group in the region. This threat became real when, for example, a number of Muslim families without land seized Druze lands and arrogated to themselves the right to cultivate them, all the time ignoring the protests of the original owners. The Druze victims were unable to regain their land, and according to some informants they were afraid to submit a complaint to the authorities. They appealed therefore for help to Salah Effendi, a rich Muslim from Kafr Makhar, who was a powerful and influential man among the Muslims of the region.

The Druze initially sought unofficial guarantees for their safety; they tried, for example, to recruit the support of leading personalities who held positions of power. But when such guarantees could not be found they began to look for an alternative, and turned to the official authorities, such as the British mandatory government. Yet their contacts with the government merely aggravated their conflict with the Muslims, and this in turn led to the reinforcement of their particularistic tendency and to a closing of the ranks. In the diary of a member of the Druze community we read that "in the night of 13 August 1939, the 'rebels' attacked the Druze in Shefaram because they refused to cooperate with them. Three Druze were killed, and the relations with the Muslims deteriorated even further when several houses belonging to Muslims were destroyed by the British authorities in the wake of a complaint by the Druze about the incident".

The Arab revolt of 1939 and the ensuing danger for the Druze who were harassed by the rebels greatly intensified their "minority feelings".

The revolt was thus a turning point for the Druze on the way to the development and consolidation of a particularistic Druze identity in Palestine, and, consequently, their rapprochement with the Israeli establishment. This development can be clearly traced in several Druze settlements. During March 1939, for example, 65 Druze leaders from Osfiyeh sent a letter to the British commander in Haifa, in which they wrote, inter alia: "We, the notables and elders of Osfiyeh, herewith express our deep gratitude to the mandatory government which has done much to preserve the safety in the village by handing over 19 rifles to the local guards. Since these rifles were delivered we feel that order has been restored, and the rebels no longer dare to enter the settlement. . . ." A further example of the Druze minority feelings is provided by an analysis of the composition of the social areas with a Druze population. As mentioned above, the Druze were among the first to settle in the new Shefaram. They founded two important neighborhoods, one in the settlement's nucleus, and the second to the east of it. When in the eighteenth century Muslim families settled in Shefaram, the eastern neighborhood became a mixed Druze-Muslim district as some of these families settled around the existing Druze. The fact that the Druze lived in a mixed neighborhood doubtless enhanced their minority feelings and their feeling of being permanently threatened. Consequently, when tempers became heated in the 1939 riots and the Druze felt that their lives and families were in danger, they left their houses and moved to the fringes of the homogeneous Druze district in the town's nucleus. The Druze residential neighborhoods have since then become increasingly homogeneous ethnically.

Minority feelings were expressed by the Christians as well, though to a much lesser degree than among the Druze. They constituted the political and social elite of the settlement, and their position was strengthened by their relations with the British authorities. The one-sided economic dependence on them by the local Muslim population also enhanced their feelings of social security. Yet in spite of this, their minority feelings never disappeared entirely and were forcefully awakened in times of tension or rioting. A typical example was presented by the riots of 1907. In one of the notebooks that we examined we find that on May 13, 1907, a Christian named Ibn Khamisi killed two Muslims from Shefaram, Ibn Sefori Khamudi and Ibn Hassan Nasser, who had ambushed him when he returned home from Acre. This incident became the cause of a blood feud. For three months the Christians were harassed: their possessions were confiscated or stolen and their houses burnt. The attackers were chiefly Muslims from the neighboring villages. The riots continued until a *"sulhah"* (Council of Peace) was organized and the family of the murderer paid 200 Turkish reals. The total damage caused by the riots was estimated at 400 reals.

The Muslims of Shefaram, on the other hand, in the past had "majority feelings" as the result of their strong position in the region and the support they could count on from the Muslims in the near-by villages. These "majority feelings" found an outlet in many behavioral patterns, of which we have mentioned a few in our description of the violence between Muslims and members of other communities.

As to the "minority feelings" following the establishment of Israel, we must distinguish between the local, "internal level" and the national, "external level". With the proclamation of Israeli independence the concept of "minority status" assumed an entirely different meaning since all of the Arab communities suddenly belonged to the non-Jewish minority. Minority feelings on the national level have never disappeared, even though Israeli Arabs are a part of the regional majority in the Arab society of the Middle East. Indeed, the Israeli-Arab conflict and the recurring wars turned the Israeli Arabs into a "hostile minority" (Smooha, 1976). The economic, social and political changes which the Arab population experienced, and the special relations of Jews and Arabs in Israel, enhanced the latter's minority status in the national sphere. The various Arab communities and groups in Shefaram, like elsewhere in Israel, strongly felt that they belong to the non-Jewish minority. During the first decade of Israeli statehood these minority feelings on the local level were especially pronounced for the Muslim community of Shefaram. Many Muslim families had become separated, and some had left for the Arab countries, especially Lebanon; those who later returned from Lebanon and decided to remain in Shefaram lived with the persistent fear that they would not be granted Israeli citizenship because they had left the settlement during the war and were regarded as 'deserters'. The Muslim community had lost its sense of regional majority which it had fostered for hundreds of years, and had instead become part of the Arab minority in Israel. Moreover, the Muslims were not part of the government's "particularistic" approach, and they therefore did not enjoy the sense of security which government support might have given them. The influx of internal refugees, almost all of them Muslims, intensified the feeling of having a "minority status", for these refugees were a group of broken have-nots.

In the course of time the Muslims began to derive inner strength from the growing number of Muslim immigrants and from the change in the social structure of the settlement resulting from the large-scale economic changes. These, in turn, led to a radical change in the social status structure which made it possible for them to control the positions of local power.

Minority feelings were also felt by the Muslim immigrants, the Beduin and the internal refugees, who had the status of a "jarib" (stranger) who had come to the town empty-handed and were forced to compete for the existing resources which were in the hands of the local population. Among members of these groups a strong feeling developed of belonging to a minority which, on the one hand, wished to defend itself, but, on the other, wanted to become integrated into the majority. These feelings were clearly reflected in their housing patterns and the composition of their neighborhoods. They lived close to one another in crowded buildings, and in the course of time they created sub-districts within the heterogeneous districts of the town. In my interviews with many of these immigrants their minority feelings could be easily distinguished, and it was also clear that these feelings lead them to demonstrate their strength in various ways, in particular voting during municipal elections.

The minority feelings among the Christians after 1948 were much weaker than those of the Muslims, since they had always been a minority. Their minority status did not make them feel weak; they continued to be the dominant economic and political group in the town until the late 1960's when, as we have seen, the Muslims again became the major community. Even though they had lost their political power, it took the Christians many years to resign themselves to the new balance of power.

The changes experienced by the Druze are of special interest. This ethnic group passed in a very short period of time from a persecuted minority to "feelings of strength". The process of ethnic particularization which had already begun in the pre-state days was accelerated and consolidated after the rise of Israel. Dozens of young Druze volunteered for the Israeli Army, particularly for the border police units. In 1956 the compulsory army draft was applied to the young Druze of Shefaram with the approval and encouragement of the community's elders (Standael, 1972).

The feelings of strength among the Druze are also reflected in the reversal of the process of outside assistance: whereas before 1948 the local Druze needed the help of their brethren from Jebel el-Arab in Syria and Mount Lebanon, more recently the Druze have closed ranks to help their co-religionists beyond the borders. This was demonstrated recently, for example, by their solidarity with the Druze in the Golan Heights when the government imposed a curfew on the Druze villages because of their refusal to accept Israeli Law.

During the recent Lebanese War the Druze openly sided with their community in the Shuf Mountains and tried to help them in various ways: they requested permission to volunteer for their militia, collected money, and also organized within Israel as a political pressure group. The Druze of Shefaram actively participated in these activities. They organized a meeting in the "Hilveh", the Druze house of prayer, during August 1983; the speakers stressed that Israel had a commitment towards the Druze in Lebanon because of the contribution of the Israel Druze to the state.

> The Druze in Israel are the most loyal allies of the State of Israel. They have sacrificed the best of their sons who participated in the wars of Israel, as is witnessed by the 290 Druze soldiers who have fallen since the birth of the State. This is a large number in relation to the number of Druze in Israel which does not exceed 50,000. Our morale is evidently very high, we have done the government great favors and we don't think that they will deny this ("El Anba", 7 August 1983)

These feelings of strength or "feelings of security", are also reflected in new patterns of residence. The Druze passed from the agglomerate model to the "dispersed residential area" model: today many scattered Druze houses can be seen far from the densely populated town areas, which serve as a kind of incentive for the municipal council to expand its jurisdiction and, consequently, the town's building zone.

Nevertheless, even in the Druze community a group exists that expresses "minority feelings". This is the "Druze el-Jebel" group who compose a small minority. Their relations with the other sections of the Druze community are formal, and there is almost no intermarriage among them; since the proclamation of the state only two young men from Druze el-Jebel have married local Druze girls. They maintain relations mainly with members of their own group in Daliat e-Karmel and Osfiyeh. One of the interviewees from Druze el-Jebel expressed himself sharply:

> We feel as if we are a minority within a minority. We feel that we are an alientated minority within the Druze community which itself is part of the Arab minority in Israel. The local Druze still regard us

as refugees and every achievement by one of our group arouses
their envy and hatred. I feel more at home, in speech, visits and
recreation, with the Druze el-Jebel families in Osfiyeh and Daliat
e-Karmel than with the local Druze.

Conclusions

Our analysis of inter-ethnic relations in Shefaram is based on the multi-
dimensional approach to the concept of "minority status". Examining
the elements that together compose a minority status reveals a number
of major features. The first among these is the importance of outside
influence as reflected in regional status and official and unofficial aid
from external sources. This emphasizes the fact that a system of inter-
ethnic relations within a given society is not isolated from contacts with
related groups outside the defined borders of the social unit in question.
These outside groups typically function as a potential source of help,
which is sometimes realized, but these contacts often remain potential
without losing their ability to intensify the feelings of belonging to a
larger and stronger group.

Our hypothesis that status elements operate in a differential manner
was confirmed for both the pre-state and the post-state period. During
the mandatory period the Muslims were the regional majority, but with
respect to the factors of economic dominance and political control they
were a minority. The Druze were a majority from the viewpoint of economic dominance, but in all other respects a minority. The Christians
were a minority with respect to their regional postion, but a majority
with respect to the other elements of status.

Our examination of "minority status" feelings also shows that the
type of subjective status feelings are not dichotomous. That is, a given
group can find itself somewhere between "majority" and "minority"
feelings. This was the pattern for the Christian community during the
pre-state period when it did not have majority or power feelings in an
unambiguous manner, because of its status as a regional minority which
from time to time was subject to outside threats. These ambivalent feelings continued to exist after the rise of the state. The Druze, on the
other hand, moved from strong minority feelings in the mandatory period
to a sense of strength after Israeli independence. The feelings of the Muslim community also passed through various stages: before 1948 Muslims

had a majority position because they were a regional majority; later, following the 1948 war, their sense of weakness and crisis was 'sharp', while in the 1960's there was swift transition to majority feelings as a result of changes in the internal status system.

A comparison of the objective and the subjective elements of status feelings shows that there is no necessary positive correlation between them. A given group can have a minority status in accordance with objective factors, and nevertheless have subjective majority feelings; on the other hand, a group can also have most of the important factors of a majority status and at the same time have strong minority feelings. The social and political security of a group is what in the last analysis determines its status feelings. It should be added that majority feelings which are not founded on an objective reality are bound, paradoxically, to strengthen the objective elements of a minority status, just as minority feelings may lead to the attempt to strengthen the objective elements of the majority status. The sense of belonging to a regional majority gave the Muslims a sense of security during the pre-state period, and at the same time this reduced their desire to seek this security in the other status elements (economic, political). The minority feelings of the Druze community, on the other hand, induced it to seek security in a strengthened economic position and to close their ranks internally.

Our analysis of the inter-ethnic political structure in Shefaram shows that stability was maintained during a long period of time. Throughout the mandatory period this stability was the result of the inter-ethnic balance based upon the hegemony of the Christian community and the economic inter-dependence of all of the ethnic groups. After 1948, in the wake of the elimination of this inter-dependence and the Christian hegemony, inter-communal conflicts arose which over time became increasingly fierce. The recent establishment of Muslim hegemony heralded a new era of continuous stability. Indeed, we may hypothesize that in multi-ethnic communities stability between various groups is achieved as the result of the hegemony of a single strong group on which the other groups become dependent. If this hegemony is undermined, and it becomes unclear where the focus of power is, the situation becomes unstable and fierce struggles break out to restore stability in accordance with the ambitions of each group. Subsequent restoration of stability depends on the ability of one group to gain the upper hand and to seize exclusive control of the center of power.

Notes

[1] The material presented in this article is based mainly upon my doctoral dissertation which deals with styles of family life in an Israeli Arab town. The fieldwork combined both anthropological and sociological methods of data collection.

References

Abromovitz, Z., and Gilfat, I. 1940. *The Arab Economy in Palestine and the Middle East* (in Hebrew). Tel Aviv: Kibbutz Meuchad.

Ben-Amram, E. 1965. "The Arab Population in Israel–A Demographic Analysis" (in Hebrew), *Mizrakh HaChadash,* No. 1-2, 7-24.

Chevallier, D. 1971. *La Societé du Mond Liban.* Paris: Librairie Orientaliste Paul Geuthner.

Eisenstadt, S. N. 1973. *Israeli Society* (in Hebrew). Jerusalem: Magnes Press.

Falah, S. 1974. *History of the Druze in Israel* (in Hebrew). Jerusalem: Prime Minister's Office.

Fischer, E. 1980. *Minorities and Minority Problems.* New York: Vantage Press.

Gittler, J. 1956. *Understanding Minority Groups.* New York: John Wiley and Sons.

Government of Palestine, Department of Statistics. 1947. *General Monthly Bulletin of Current Statistics,* Vol. 7, No. 2.

Maoz, M. 1962. "Local Relations in Israeli Arab Communities" (in Hebrew), *Mizrakh HaChadash,* Vol. 2, 233-240.

Peretz, D. 1969. *The Palestine Arab Refugee Problem.* Santa Monica: The Rand Corporation.

Pinner, W. 1960. *How Many Arab Refugees?* London: Landman MacKibben.

Peres, Y. 1982. *Ethnic Relations in Israel* (in Hebrew). Tel Aviv: Sifriat Poalim.

Smooha, S. 1976. "Arabs and Jews in Israel–Minority-Majority Relations" (in Hebrew), *Megamoth,* Vol. 4, 397-423.

——. 1978. *Israel: Pluralism and Conflict.* Berkeley: University of California Press.

——. 1980. "Alternative Policies Towards the Arabs in Israel", *Megamoth,* Vol. 1, 7-36.

Swirski, S. 1981. *The Exploited* (in Hebrew). Haifa: Notebooks of Research and Critique.

Standel, O. 1972. *The Minorities in Israel* (in Hebrew). Jerusalem: The Government Information Office.

Veshitz, J. 1947. *The Arabs in Palestine* (in Hebrew). Merchavia: Sifriat Poalim.

Wirth, L. 1946. "The Problem of Minority Groups" in R. Linton (Ed.), *The Science of Man in the World Crisis.* New York: Columbia University Press, pp. 347-372.

Yetman, B. and Steel, R. 1975. *Majority and Minority.* Boston: Allyn and Bacon.

7

Phantom Ethnicity: "Oriental Jews" in Israeli Society

Arnold Lewis

As various collectivities have harnessed ethnic symbolism to political ends, the ethnic unit, long a primary concern of anthropologists, has blossomed into a phenomena of general interest. In Israel, where the coming together of culturally diverse immigrants at Independence in 1948 was a salient social occurrence (Eisenstadt, 1954; Patai, 1970; Shuval, 1963), the ethnic factor has been prominent in folk and sociological models of society. According to this perspective, the Jewish population of Israel divides into two major ethnic categories—"Ashkenazim" of European and American descent and "Eastern" or "Oriental Jews" of North African and Near Eastern origins.[1] The Ashkenazim, including among their numbers the pre-State Zionist "pioneers,"[2] comprise most of the middle-class and dominate elite positions in society. In contrast, the Oriental Jews generally hold working-class jobs, have relatively poor educational credentials and low per capita incomes (Eisenstadt, 1967; Lissak, 1969; Matras and Weintraub, 1977; Smooha, 1978). While accounting for more than half the Jewish population of contemporary Israel, they control relatively few economic, political and social resources. Whereas high-status Israeli communities are populated predominantly by Ashkenazim, residents of development towns[3] and urban slums are mostly Oriental Jews. To pundits, the "social gap" between these populations is a central problem in present day Israeli society. It is assumed that at the root of the "social gap" are

133

fundamental differences between culturally disadvantaged Jews of the East
and their more advanced compatriots of Western origins (Curtis and Chertoff, 1973; Eisenstadt *et al.,* 1970).

In 1975, hoping to learn why Oriental Jews underperform at school
(Lewy and Chen, 1974), I set out for Israel. Working from assumptions in
the literature (Minkovich, 1969; Smilansky and Smilansky, 1967), I hypothesized that cultural differences inplicit in the ethnic structure of Israeli society inhibit the educational efforts of Oriental Jewish youth. Following the anthropological instinct, I looked for an appropriate community in which to develop holistic insight into the problem at hand. Helpful
informants, knowledgeable about Oriental Jews, who they are and where
they live, were quick to suggest appropriate field settings. A typical candidate was Sharonia, a town of 3,500 working-class Israelis of North African and Near Eastern origins.[4] From afar, Sharonia clearly fit the classic
profile of a low-status Oriental Jewish community. Large families, poor
incomes and low-status educational credentials were the rule. To government officials and community workers, Sharonia consisted of residents
"in need of fostering."[5] To middle-class residents of Seaview, a nearby
urban center, Sharonia was a poor satellite town. It was a good source
of workmen and domestics. Its inhabitants were seen as culturally disadvantaged Oriental Jews (Lewis, 1979a).

With the onset of field work, preconceived assumptions were quickly
confounded by the "reality" of everyday life. Although townspeople
were of North African and Near Eastern ancestry, the anthropologist was
hard pressed to distinguish local cultural traits from those of compatriots of European heritage. Among younger residents raised in the town,
language, religious practice, national identity, styles of entertainment,
aspirations for the future and social expectations were similar to higher
status countrymen. Discernible cultural differences between Sharonians
and middle-class Israelis appeared to be more a function of socioeconomic
possibilities than of primordial cultural characteristics. Although cognizant
of their Kurdistani, Tripolitanian or Tunisian origins, residents consistently
characterized themselves as "Israeli in all matters" (Lewis, 1979a). To
these citizens, the ethnic category of Oriental Jews had little relevance.

These social facts contradict images of townspeople held by outsiders
and implied in the literature. Thus the question is raised, "Who are the Oriental Jews?" or, more accurately, "What is the sociological meaning of
the ethnic category Oriental Jews?"

Ethnic Models and Ethnographic Facts

Field work, the foundation of the anthropological enterprise, implies cultural confrontation between anthropologist and native. Yet the "thick description" (Geertz, 1973) we covet must be more than the product of idiosyncratic encounter. Separating anthropologist from erudite traveler is a tool kit of methods and models by which field material is collected and organized. What can the anthropologist draw from his professional knapsack in order to sort out contradictory information on ethnicity in Sharonia?

To begin with, what do anthropologists generally mean when employing the concept of ethnicity? Human beings create social meaning by assimilating disparate sensory stimuli into cognitive categories of things similar and different. To account for human differences, a myriad of principles by which to contrast and compare have been mobilized. Popular principles in the ethnographic literature include differentiation by sex, kinship ties, age, sets, relationships to the means of production and ethnicity. The concept of ethnicity suggests the division of a given population into socially meaningful categories according to actor or observer evaluation of cultural differences.

Anthropological studies of ethnic phenomena tend to stress what has been characterized as cultural ethnicity or political ethnicity (Bennett, 1975; Deshen, 1974). The primary focus of study in cultural ethnicity is the culture bearing unit, a collectivity of people who share a unique set of cultural traits that exhibit underlying consistency over time (Naroll, 1964). This is the ethnicity of the folklore specialist. It suggests that we view social behavior against the backdrop of a typology of cultural traits, which the anthropologist can distinguish from one another. Studies of acculturation and ethnic relations in complex societies that view the social behavior of a given population in reference to a primordial set of cultural traits adopt this perspective (Gans, 1979; Sandberg, 1974).

In contrast, political ethnicity switches the focus of study from the ethnic unit as a vessel in which cultural content is preserved to a social group that manipulates cultural symbols in a collective struggle for scarce resources in complex societies (Barth, 1969; Cohen, 1969; Despres, 1975). As Fredrik Barth has postulated, this view emphasizes the social boundaries that define group competition, not the cultural stuff that boundaries enclose (Barth, 1969). Thus, an ethnic unit becomes any social group that manipulates cultural symbols for political and social ends (Aronson, 1976).

In what way can the concepts of cultural and political ethnicity assist in organizing ethnographic facts relating to Sharonia? Unfortunately, analysis proceeding directly from either perspective tends to obscure rather than to illuminate. In social situations where ecological and socioeconomic boundaries clearly delineate one cultural group from another, the cultural ethnicity perspective has proved of high utility (Driver, 1973). Researchers examining social processes in complex societies, however, have found this approach increasingly inadequate (Barth, 1969; Cohen, 1969; Yancey *et al.*, 1976). Indeed, the political ethnicity formulation has developed in reaction to the explicit failure of the cultural approach to sufficiently account for the persistence and reassertion of ethnic expression in societies in which acculturation among social groups of divergent cultural traditions is well advanced (Glazer and Moynihan, 1963; Van Den Berghe, 1973).

An attempt to view the contemporary life style of Sharonians from a cultural ethnicity perspective generates inconclusive results. During thirty years of social life in Israel, townspeople have undergone rapid cultural change, assimilating a life style markedly similar to urban Israelis of European origins (Lewis, 1979a). Studies of other Israelis of North African and Near Eastern origins generally support this finding.[6] When cultural continuity with a pre-Israeli way of life has been identified, it has generally been associated with religious activity (Deshen, 1976), a relatively marginal factor among the secularized residents of Sharonia. Although Sharonians continue to flavor their lives with ethnic foods and folk music, these artifacts of a cultural past are tangential to the dominant cultural thrust in everyday life. Pre-Israeli cultural characteristics explain little of life in present day Sharonia.

The major contribution of the cultural ethnicity approach in exploring data from Sharonia is that it tells us where not to look for answers. Information organized from this perspective strongly suggests that the ethnic category Oriental Jews has little objective association with the pre-Israeli cultural characteristics of townspeople. Why then do middle-class Israelis insist that Sharonians, who are seen as Oriental Jews, are culturally different from other Israelis-in ways that resemble a primeval cultural heritage?

In exploring this question, the anthropologist might logically be expected to turn to the second model in the knapsack, political ethnicity. At first glance, this perspective appears to be a most promising one. After all, hasn't political ethnicity been conceptualized to deal with problems of ethnic categorization in complex, culturally fluid situations? Yet, before this approach can bear fruit, another ethnographic fact must be confronted. The political ethnicity formulation suggests that analysis should be based on a group of persons who identify and manipulate salient ethnic symbols in pursuit of political, economic and social ends. Hence, the anthropologist is encouraged to seek out persons who view themselves as Oriental Jews in certain situations and to examine the social import of consequent behavior. Yet, it is rare that Sharonians identify themselves as Oriental Jews in political contexts. In some social situations, ethnic categories such as Kurdistani, Tunisian and Tripolitanian help Sharonians to differentiate themselves from others, but the category Oriental Jews is rarely used by local residents. When articulated, it refers to low-status Israelis, usually excluding the speaker, in much the same way that this image is projected by non-residents when referring to Sharonians.

The negative attitude of townspeople to the ethnic category Oriental Jews is best illustrated in their response to the Israeli Black Panthers. The panthers, a group of young Israelis from Jerusalem, attempted to mobilize collective political action in the early 1970s by manipulating symbols associated with the ethnic category Oriental Jews (Smooha, 1972). The activities of this group, while causing much alarm in the Ashkenazi dominated national polity, gained little support in Sharonia and other low-status communities (Cohen, 1972; Etzioni-Halevy, 1975). Sharonians, with few exceptions, talk of the Panthers with great disdain. To the present, townspeople symbolically distance themselves from this movement of persons they define as "good for nothings."

Who then are the Oriental Jews? To this end, it has been argued that a suitable answer will not be found in Sharonia. From the inside looking out, Sharonians are not Oriental Jews in either cultural or political terms. Yet, outsiders looking in on Sharonians are convinced that they are viewing Oriental Jews. Where should one look for a solution to this paradox? Might a sociological explanation of the ethnic category Oriental Jews be found through an analysis of the ideology of those who use the term? This possibility will be explored throughout the remainder of the paper.

Analysis will proceed in three stages. First, the Zionist idea, the ideological underpinning of Israeli society, will be described. Second, the genesis of ethnic symbolism since Statehood and situational use of ethnic stereotypes in everyday life will be examined. Third, the sociological meaning of ethnic symbolism in contemporary Israel will be discussed.

The Zionist Idea

The impact of collective beliefs on social behavior has long been a central theoretical concern of anthropolotists (Benedict, 1934; Geertz, 1964; Leach, 1954; Redfield, 1953). This suggests that a discernible compendium of beliefs in the public domain structures the meaning that people give to behaviors and events in everyday life. Often expressed in myth and folklore, these root paradigms, to borrow a phrase from Victor Turner (1974: 67), "affect the form, timing and style of the behavior of those who bear them." In other words, root paradigms are collective cultural recipes for the construction of social meaning.

What root paradigm structures the meaning of ethnicity in Israeli society? To explore this question, one must turn to an analysis of Zionism, the national ideology by which most Israeli Jews evaluate their places in history, relationships to one another and associations with salient others (Levy and Gutman, 1976; Arian, 1970). Explanations or pertinent social facts and the collective social consciousness of Israeli society are constructed in Zionist imagery.

In a classic discussion, H. G. Barnett has identified cultural innovation, the fusion of two or more elements into a qualitatively distinct whole, as a central mechanism in the process of social change (Barnett, 1953). Zionism, as conceived in collective sociopolitical action in Europe and Palestine, is an innovative Jewish ideology. Synthesizing the Messianic image of Zion in traditional Judaism with 19th century European nationalism, Zionism posited the concept of a Jewish national homeland in Palestine, the Biblical abode of the Jewish people.[7] To numerous European Jews caught in deadly social crosscurrents of assimilation and anti-Semitism, the Zionist innovation offered existential safety on a distant shore. To the tens of thousands who journeyed to Palestine after 1880, the Zionist idea was a tangible call to action. These "pioneers" constituted the human vessels in which the Zionist idea was transported from Europe to Palestine. They became the nucleus of a new society, which gained nationhood in 1948.[8] In this, the immediate goal of Zionism came to fruition.

Yet, the Zionist idea suggested more than the concept of a Jewish State. It also offered adherents a model of the society they were leaving as well as a vision of the commonwealth that lay ahead. The meaning of ethnicity in Israeli society is anchored in these images.

Zionism was invented to explain social facts relating to the Jewish condition in modern Europe. Its prescription for social action is based on

European nationalistic principles, but its existential thrust is deeply rooted in the ethno-history of the Jewish people. In this, it adopts a conception of time implicit in the Bible, a view that suggests that the meaning of the Jewish people is intimately bound up with the working out of Jewish history.

The centrality of time in Zionist imagery is vividly expressed in the Museum of the Jewish Diaspora.[9] Ostensibly, the purpose of this impressive multimedia display is to commemorate Jewish existence before the reemergence of national independence. To half a million annual visitors, the Diaspora Museum is a profound statement of salient aspects of the Zionist vision.

The permanent exhibit, consisting of slide shows, minicinemas, music, pictures, sculptures, visual projections, artifacts and the written word, creates images of Jewish existence in the many places where communal life was sustained over the past two millennia. In sections of family and community, and martyrdom and faith, symbolic continuity in divergent experience is suggested. Through diverse stimuli, the visitor learns how a people divided in social space preserved psychic unity through symbolic commitment to a common temporal vision, past and future. This is established as a dominant message in entrance and exit exhibits as well as in the context of various displays throughout the museum. Indeed, two millenia of Jewish life are portrayed as a single epoch bounded by contrasting social processes, exile and return.

In various contexts, the fundamental importance of heritage, collective purpose, remembering the past and longing for future communal fulfillment are stressed. One is told that these values were nurtured through communal life, both spiritual and secular. Hence, "A tree may be alone in a field, a man alone in the world, but no Jew is alone on his holy days."

The visitor is able to reflect on these themes through a synergism of stimuli. For example, one display projects mezuzot,[10] candlesticks, Hannukkah lamp and prayer book, core spiritual artifacts, against a backdrop of changing interior settings. In all, ten interiors from different Jewish communities are portrayed, each emphasizing the fashion prominent in the non-Jewish environment in which they are immersed. Herein, symbolic constancy is contrasted with transient life styles adopted from non-Jewish neighbors. In another section, twenty-one exquisite model synagogues are displayed. Although each reflects the architectural style of host peoples, the symbolic content remains fixed in time.

The visit ends with the return. Here, one is exposed to three related themes: Jewish yearning throughout the ages for a paradise lost, Zionist pioneers reestablishing the Jewish commonwealth, and the ingathering of the exiles. The final image expresses a moral imperative "To remember the past, To live the present, To trust the future." Whereas the subject matter of the Museum of the Jewish Diaspora focuses on the quality of Jewish existence from exile to return, Zionist thought is equally concerned with social and spiritual contours of the future. During its formative years, the Zionist revolution bifurcated into religious and secular, socialist and non-socialist camps (Fisch, 1978; Heller, 1974; Sachar, 1976). It was further divided by "political" and "cultural" schools of thought (Buber, 1952). In polemic among adherents of each camp, the structure of the Zionist innovation was constructed. Through an examination of the dialogue among Zionist spokesmen, common underlying assumptions can be discerned.[11]

The Zionist vision of Jewish history (Figure 1) postulates four historical periods in development sequence: pristine paradise, diaspora, statehood, utopia, mediated by three social processes, exile, return, redemption.

Vigorous debate among Zionist adherents on the social content of each historical epoch and the transforming quality of mediating social processes is predicated on the fundamental acceptance of the underlying model. Concerned with European Jewry, Zionist thought focused particular atten-

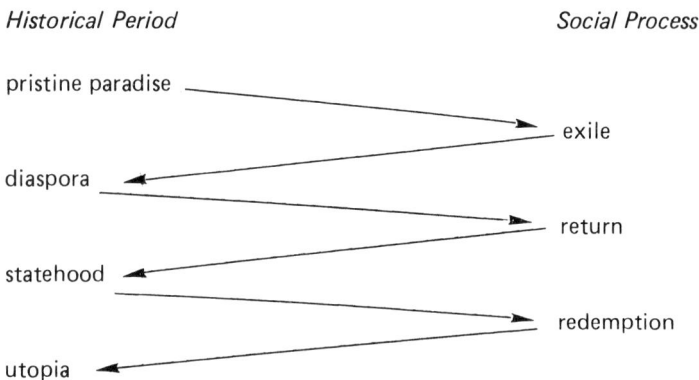

Figure 1. The Zionist Model of Jewish History.

tion on the maladies of diaspora, a historical period in which Jews were scattered among other peoples. From a Zionist viewpoint, diaspora is an unnatural condition, a negation of utopia, pristine and future. Thus, Max Nordau, an important political Zionist, bemoaned "twenty centuries of unutterable sufferings of millions of highly gifted human beings, artificially kept down in a low state of development" (Nordau, 1916). Rabbi Kook, a spiritual founder of religious Zionism, lamented the "destruction of the nation's life in its severance from its own place" (Kook, 1975), and Achad Ha'Am, the creator of cultural Zionism, postulated a need to "wipe out the spiritual taint of galuth (exile)" (Achad Ha'Am, 1916).

Living in unnatural conditions, Jews of the diaspora were viewed as suffering a multitude of cultural and spiritual ills. To Zionist thinkers, the primary cause of cultural degeneration is the detachment of individual Jews from proper (Zionist) historical perspective and collective purpose, i.e., the loss of temporal vision. This is succinctly expressed by Bertram Benas, a Jewish nationalist writing at the turn of the century. "Ghetto idealism derived its inspiration from a living present based on the future, but unhistoric assimilation, which has detached itself from the past and looks but to an amorphous future, deprives itself of the force necessary for a current vitality" (Benas, 1969).

This theme is widely and consistently expressed in Zionist literature. Hence, Rabbi Kook argued that "Jewry in the Diaspora has no real foundation and lives only by the power of vision and by the memory of our glory, i.e., the past and the future" (Zionist Library, 1972). Leon Simon, a disciple of Achad Ha'Am, described the absence of "the normal relation of a people to its past and its future" (Simon, 1916), and Louis Brandeis, the eminent American Zionist, worried over "a new generation left without necessary moral and spiritual support" (Brandeis, 1916).

The Zionist solution to problems posed by diaspora was to instigate, through sociopolitical action, a return to Palestine and the establishment of the Third Commonwealth. It was reasoned that national independence would offer the Jewish people shelter from persecution, a hallmark of diaspora existence. Yet statehood was not viewed as a final goal, but rather as a means to foster a historic end, the creation of a Jewish utopia. Thus, the moral legacy of the Zionist revolution was to be a society in which every Jew would be able to sustain a full spiritual and material life. This is expressed in the insistence of David Ben Gurion, the first Prime Minister, that Israel must become "a model people and a model state" (Ben-Gurion, 1963). How could utopia be achieved? Rabbi Bar Ilan, a religious Zionist leader, points to the Zionist answer, suggesting that "our

F

immediate preoccupation is with national redemption, with physical and spiritual deliverance" (Bar-Ilan, 1975). Similar sentiments are expressed in the Israeli Declaration of Independence. "We call upon Jewish people throughout the Diaspora to join forces with us in immigration and construction, and to be at our right hand in the great endeavor to fulfill the age-old longing for the redemption of Israel" (Ben-Gurion, 1971).

The centrality of the quest for cultural regeneration is symbolized in the life and spirit of Aaron Gordon. Referred to as the "high priest of the 'religion of Labor'" (Levenberg, 1945), Gordon was the prototype "pioneer." Leaving Russia in 1903 at the age of 48, he came to Palestine to build a new life and renew the Jewish people. Although frail and often ill, Gordon relished in hard field labor, exemplifying in deed the social Zionist vision of redemption. The emphasis in Zionist thought on cultural revival as both an individual and collective quest is vividly expressed in Gordon's erudite words: "You will build the house of Israel; you will find the road on which we set our hearts, on which all the Jews have set their hearts from time immemorial, along which they will desire to go in the days to come. You will live the life of all Jews, and this life will be like an ever-deepening and overflowing spring. And your life will be renewed. This new life, like a tidal river, will go on, will renew itself, and flow onward, onward, onward. . . . " (Levenberg, 1945).

Indeed, from a Zionist view, redemption is a moral imperative. Although divergent utopian visions have been promulgated, central to each is the assumption that the just society must be preceded by the creation of righteous men. Social perfection is thought to be a natural product of cultural revival. This is explicit in the temporal structure of the Zionist paradigm, which postulates the relationship between redemption and utopia as one of cause and effect.

To this juncture, three central themes in Zionist ideology have been described: negative images of diaspora Jewry, the moral imperative to create a Jewish utopia and the saliency of redemption, cultural and spiritual, as a means to accomplish cherished ends. Embedded in Jewish history, these principles are posited in casual relationships to one another. Subsequently, I shall argue the the ethnic category "Oriental Jews" organizes central social facts in reference to these key assumptions.

Oriental Jews

In contemporary Israel, a society born of the Zionist revolution, Zionist ideology remains a moral measuring stick, a road map to collective

salvation. Through ritual and public debate, Israelis evaluate social progress in relation to national vision, past and future. To explain social facts
bearing on collective identity and moral vitality, the Zionist paradigm is
mobilized as a guide. From this perspective, a worrisome social problem
is the issue of the geographic origin of immigrants and descendants in the
socioeconomic stratification of society. Whereas persons of European and
American descent dominate high-status position, compatriots of low status
are invariably North African and Near Eastern origins (Lissak, 1969;
Smooha and Peres, 1975).

Characterized in public discussion as the "social gap," this obtrusive
social fact contradicts the moral imperative that the Jewish commonwealth must maximize the spiritual and material well-being of each Jewish
citizen. Yet, if the contours of social issues are conceptualized in root cultural paradigms, so are their explanations. An examination of the literature
suggest a collection of folk concepts[12] that have been generated toward
this end.

The first Zionist "pioneers" entered a Palestine inhabited in part by
an indigenous non-European Jewish population. These communities were
composed of Jews from North Africa and the Near East, and operated
from cultural premises alien to the European bearers of the Zionist idea.
In European eyes, the language, attitudes and actions of this population resembled those of the Arabs among whom they lived. As a result of social
contact between settlers and indigenous Jews, the ethnic term "Oriental
Jews" was used by ethnocentric Europeans and filled with negative cultural images (Eisenstadt, 1954). Although eligible as Jews to join the Zionist
experiment, this population was seen to require radical cultural transformation. However, the problems associated with Oriental Jews remained
tangential to the central thrust of the Zionist revolution until independence.

With independence, the role of North African and Near Eastern Jewry
in the Zionist revolution changed dramatically. In the period between
1948 and 1953, the Jewish population of Israel more than doubled from
650,000 to 1,450,000 inhabitants (Patai, 1970:74-75). Of the new arrivals,
half were of North African and Near Eastern descent. To the veteran Zionists, mass immigration suggested both promise and problem. In each newcomer, the historic process of return was enacted, the prospect of individual and collective redemption enhanced. Yet, the new immigrants were
tarnished by diaspora experience.

From the view point of the European elite, cultural imperfection was especially pronounced among immigrants from North Africa and the Near East. Like the native Jewish population they resembled, these immigrants were seen as lacking in basic social and psychological skills (Frankenstein, 1953b; Ortar, 1953). Examining ethnic imagery in leading Israeli newspapers in the early 1950s, Raphael Patai has catalogued a host of negative stereotypes associated with the ethnic category "Oriental Jews." These include instability, emotionalism, impulsiveness, unreliability, incompetence, habitual lying, cheating, laziness, boastfulness, inclination to violence, uncontrolled temper, superstitiousness, childishness and lack of cleanliness (Patai, 1970:314). This array of negative characteristics are summarized in the folk concepts of "primitivity," implying cultural inferiority and "lacking culture" (Patai, 1970:314), suggesting an absence of social characteristics positively associated with being civilized. (On ethnic stereotyping in Israeli society: Peres, 1971; Shumsky, 1955:5-7; Tamarin, 1971; Zenner, 1965:297-306).

It would, however, be analytically incorrect to conclude that prejudicial stereotypes of immigrants from North Africa and the Near East are a product of a Zionist world view. Spawned by veteran settlers and European immigrants, prejudicial ethnic imagery is a function of European ethnocentrism, not Zionist ideology. In light of the Zionist idea, the social meaning of culturally different newcomers was translated into a moral imperative for cultural change and social integration. Thus, the Zionist paradigm fostered ambivalence toward new immigrants who were otherwise seen as utterly repulsive. This is well expressed in the folk concept "Generation of the Desert," an allusion to culturally tainted Jews led by Moses at God's behest to wander about the wilderness until a new generation of culturally purified offspring were ready to inherit the Land of Israel (Friendly, n.d.:5-6; Marx, 1979:X).

Through this and similar analogies, social facts relating to culturally different and abhorrent immigrants were recast in terms of the Zionist paradigm. If the adult generation of Oriental Jews was beyond redemption, this was a lamentable, but anticipated consequence of diaspora life and yet, as diaspora is a transitory phase in Jewish history, so are the negative cultural traits of diaspora Jewry, no matter how uncouth. In the act of return, immigrants had proceeded to a more advanced stage of Jewish existence. This was to be followed by redemption, the socialization of progeny into new Israeli men and women. The veteran Zionist population was to guide this collective cultural quest. Every effort was to be made to recreate these children in the image of their benefactors, not in that of their parents.[13] From the Zionist perspective, social progress required successful fulfillment of this mission. Pitfalls inherent in failure were vividly expressed in the folk concept "Levantinization" (Patai, 1970: 320-323; Zenner, 1965:323-324), the fear that cultural deficiencies of North African and Near Eastern Jews, if not eradicated, would stymie the utopian future postulated in the Zionist paradigm.

Contemporary Ethnic Images

In contemporary Sharonia, the meaning of the ethnic category "Oriental Jews" is derived from folk concepts that originated in the 1950s. These have been updated to explain subsequent facts. Sharonia is a community of relatively poor residents of North African and Near Eastern origins. Its undereducated inhabitants have relatively large families, relatively little living space, and they finance their life styles on half the per capita resources of the average urban dweller (Lewis, 1979a:21-22). Nearly thirty years after their arrival in Israel, Sharonians remain on the socioeconomic edge of middle-class Israeli society. Thus, Sharonia and its residents, in light of the Zionist paradigm, is an ideological sore spot, a social occurrence in need of explanation and amelioration.

Toward this end, outsiders often conceptualize Sharonia as a community of the "Second Israel." First hinted at in the early 1950s (Shumsky, 1955:6), the image of a Second Israel has become a prominent means of expressing consequences of persistent ethnic stratification in Israeli society (Heller, 1973; Selzer, 1967:51-86; Toledano, 1973). In the public eye, the Second Israel is a stigma, an undesirable place to live that is inhabited by culturally deficient Oriental Jews. Yet, it is also an indictment of the elite of the wider society for not fulfilling Zionist destiny.

How has the ideologically embarrassing Second Israel come about? In light of the Zionist paradigm, two logically consistent answers can be postulated. These are the culturally disadvantaged and institutional discrimination perspectives. The culturally disadvantaged argument suggests that socioeconomic inequality in Israeli society is primarily a result of persistent cultural differences between Jews of European and North African and Near Eastern heritages. This view, strongly supported by prevailing folk images, implies that national institutions generally operate in accordance with an egalitarian creed, but that Oriental Jews, as a category of persons, remain culturally distinct in ways that violate norms valued in the wider society. Thus, Oriental Jews are in need of resocialization, which must be accomplished before they can assume their rightful place as full citizens, contributors and benefactors, of the developing Jewish commonwealth. From this viewpoint, responsibility for negative social progress is seen to rest in the lifeways of relatively poor citizens of North African and Near Eastern descent.

The alternative institutional discrimination model also builds on the Zionist paradigm, but interprets social facts differently. It assumes that immigrants and progeny of North African and Near Eastern origins have undergone prescribed cultural transformations and are presently similar to Israelis of European background. Thus, persistent social inequality is an end product of discriminatory practices on the part of public institutions. This line of reasoning projects fault for ideologically unacceptable social inequality at the wealthy and powerful in Israeli society.

The culturally disadvantaged model is the predominant explanation by which relevant social facts are organized in Sharonia. Frequently used by the national elite and in the media, it draws on folk images, which give a history to the rationalizations inherent in the argument. In contrast, the institutional discrimination model is rarely applied to Sharonia. Efforts by townspeople and others (such as the anthropologist) to advance this argument are looked at askance by government officials, civil servants, educators and middle-class observers of local social life. Indeed, such interpretations are invariably refuted by the reorganization of relevant social facts in reference to the culturally disadvantaged argument. The only consistent use of the institutional discrimination argument on the part of the Sharonians are the complaints of individuals claiming prejudice when turned away unsatisfied by authorities. Yet, to the present, such incidents have not been translated into a collective expression of institutional discrimination by the townspeople.

The potency of the culturally disadvantaged perspective in organizing social facts in contemporary Sharonia is evident in its frequent use by civil servants, educators and townspeople in various social contexts. When budgeting resources for Sharonia, social planners and bureaucrats of various government ministries operate from the assumption that residents remain insufficiently socialized to the life ways of the wider society. For example, a trailer camp was established in town in order to afford temporary abode to large numbers of new immigrants expected to arrive from the Soviet Union. Making little contribution to the community, the Immigrant Absorption Center was seen by townspeople as an unwarranted intrusion into their affairs. When asked by residents or anthropologist to justify this project, officials invariably talked of the need to bring "new blood" to the town.

Folk concepts such as "primitives" and "lacking culture" are often used by civil servants to rationalize personal failings as well as to deflect social pressures emanating from townspeople and outsiders. The relationship between the local rabbi and congregants illustrates this point. The rabbi, a young man of European background, was assigned to Sharonia by the Ministry of Religion immediately after finishing his studies. Uncompromising in religious matters, he was poorly suited to serve the spiritual needs of "traditional,"[14] but not strictly religious, Sharonians. Many townspeople, finding the young rabbi too demanding, took a negative view of events organized under his auspices. To explain the behavior of uncooperative congregants, the rabbi pointed to what he characterized as the "primitive" religious traditions of Oriental Jews. In contrast to his European Jewish heritage, the rabbi felt that the cultural background of Sharonians was deficient. Thus, they had become morally degenerate. Ironically, nonreligious civil servants, when complaining that residents remain relatively "primitive," often refer to what they see as a religious orientation in the townspeople.

Situational use of the culturally disadvantaged argument is perhaps best exemplified in the symbolic actions of educators. In light of the Zionist paradigm, education assumes a pivotal role in enhancing social justice. Through successful participation in extensive educational programs, youth of the "Generation of the Desert" were to be recast into new Jewish Israeli men and women. Thus, one of the first actions of the fledgling government after independence was to enact a compulsory education law. Today, youth are required to attend a minimum of one year of kindergarten and ten years of formal schooling. Sharonians accept this concept of cultural renewal and want their children to complete their educations. Truancy is a rare occurrence.

In dealing with youth from Sharonia and other low-status communities, the Ministry of Education has invented to concept of "those in need of fostering." Officially, this designation, based on socioeconomic characteristics, has been promulgated to enable the educational bureaucracy to target additional funds and special curricula to schools serving low-status Oriental Jewish communities. As used by teachers, this notion has become a euphemism for more provocative folk concepts such as "primitive" and "lacking culture" (Halper, 1978:270-278; Lewis, 1979a:88-89). Pedagogues entrusted with the task of educating Sharonian youth constantly refer to their charges as "those in need of fostering." Decisions on pedagogic methods, curricular content, grading policy and other important educational matters are made in accordance with this perception (Lewis, 1979a:91-114).

Given the ideological importance of education in Israeli society, educators are constantly pressured to explain the poor achievements of low-status youth of North African and Near Eastern origins. Toward this end, teachers in Sharonia respond by arranging relevant facts in reference to the culturally disadvantaged perspective. Specifically, they argue that learning or behavior difficulties at school are a function of negative home and community environments. This explanation is strengthened in gossip sessions in which teachers exchange anecdotes on the "primitive" ways of pupils and parents (Lewis, 1979a:104-105; 117-137). Teachers view the official designation of Sharonia as an area populated by "those in need of fostering" as validation of the culturally disadvantaged contention (Lewis, 1979a:104-105).

Townspeople also use the culturally disadvantaged argument to advance and defend personal interest in certain social situations. In maneuvering to gain additional resources from national institutions, local politicians and community spokesmen often argue that greater efforts are needed to compensate for culturally backward elements in the local population. This stance is particularly useful in efforts by residents to gain further educational and welfare services. Individuals seeking aid from the local welfare office employ a similar symbolic strategy. In these circumstances, the symbolic perspectives of civil servants and clientele complement one another.

In another context, townspeople advance the culturally disadvantaged perspective in order to distinguish themselves from lower status neighbors. In this, they emulate the posture that middle class compatriots have adopted towards them. For example, in the early 1970s, the government constructed a new housing project for destitute persons. Over the years, families from various parts of Sharonia and adjacent communities have been settled in this complex. In order to distance themselves from the social implications of the project, townspeople have named it the "Refugee Camp," implying temporary abode for person who have yet to gain full entry into Israeli society. Residents portray persons living in this section of town as "primitive" Oriental Jews.

In the frequent use of the culturally disadvantaged argument to organize social facts in Sharonia, Oriental Jews as a category of people are constantly denigrated. In daily competition for economic and social rewards, a host of ethnically related folk concepts become symbolic weapons that individuals and groups can use to advance and defend their interests. The cumulative impact of these symbolic exchanges places Israelis of North African and Near Eastern origins at a disadvantage when interacting with others in everyday life.

Phantom Ethnicity

Who then are the Oriental Jews? Implicit in the presentation of the data is a model suggesting that social meaning is synthesized through dialectical interaction between a root cultural paradigm and subsequent social facts. Specifically, it is argued that the meaning of ethnicity in contemporary Israeli society emerges from confrontation of the Zionist idea with two salient social developments: large numbers of North African and Near Eastern Jewish immigrants who were deprecated by ethnocentric veteran and new immigrant European Jews, and division of society into social classes on the basis of primordial sociogeographic origins. In diachronic analysis of this process, sociological explanation of the ethnic category Oriental Jews is generated.

The meaning of ethnicity in Israeli society is structured by basic Zionist tenets. Spiritual unity of the Jewish people is recognized as a highest principle. Unity is expressed in two ways: shared vision of social time, past and future, and mutual commitment to sociocultural oneness through redemption and cultural renewal. Yet sociocultural differences among Jews in an imperfect present are also recognized and viewed as a legacy of diaspora existence. In this, an interesting paradox emerges. Although ethnicity is denied as a legitimate category by which to distinguish Jew from Jew in a utopian future, ethnic differences among Jews in the present are highlighted. Ethnicity is rejected as an ultimate principle, but acknowledged as a contemporary social fact.

With the arrival of massive numbers of Jewish refugees from Moslem areas of North Africa and the Near East, ethnic differentiation became a central issue in Israeli society. Articulated in the folk concepts "primitive" and "lacking culture," the ethnic category of Oriental Jews was created and filled with negative cultural connotations. Nevertheless the belief in the spiritual unity of the Jewish people bridged the social distance between the European elite and low-status newcomers from North Africa and the Near East. Through cultural fusion, progeny of social strangers were to create the desired Jewish commonwealth.

In contemporary Israel, partial congruence between socioeconomic inequality and primordial sociogeographic origins contradicts idealistic egalitarian expectations. Nevertheless, these divisions have become a prominent feature of everyday life. How can this morally unjustifiable development be rationalized? Israelis have thought their way out of the dilemna through the use of the concept of the Oriental Jew. In this imagery, the division of society by social class is recast into social division by cultural characteristics. Thus, socioeconomic inequality, a stable sociological feature of Israeli society (Hartman and Eilon, 1975; Lissak, 1969; Smooha and Peres, 1975), is transformed into a transient quality, a negative development, which can be set right by further cultural change among low status citizens of North African and Near Eastern origins.

Yet, the ethnic category Oriental Jews is not rooted in the cultural tradition and life ways of concrete, living people. It has no tangible ethno-history, rarely delineates an existentially meaningful identity, and lacks vigorous defenders. The anthropologist can identify and study cultural continuity and change among Moroccan and Tunisian immigrants (Deshen and Shokeid, 1974), Jews of Tripolitanian descent (Goldberg, 1972), Syrian Jews (Zenner, 1965), Yemenite women (Katzir, 1976), and working class Israelis (Weingrod, 1979). As I learned in Sharonia, however, Oriental Jews are difficult, if not impossible, to find, even if most Israelis are confident that they can point the way. Indeed, analysis has revealed that the ethnic category Oriental Jews is a phantom, a figment of collective Israeli imagination, a symbolic vehicle by which cultural differences capable of masking socioeconomic inequality are explained.

The elastic cultural content of phantom ethnicity is well illustrated in the folk etiology of lice. From time to time, elementary school children in Sharonia have been known to come to school with lice infested hair. How are such occurences explained? To teachers, lice are viewed as concrete manifestations of the primitive, lacking culture lifeways of townspeople. Educators often argue that lice and academic underachievement in Sharonia are tangible effects of a single underlying cause, the "in need of fostering" social milieu of low-status Oriental Jews.

Recently, a feature expose on a popular television news program reported a surprising discovery, an epidemic of lice in fashionable, upper middle class neighborhoods of Tel Aviv and Haifa. On camera, one educator wondered aloud how lice had come to a school attended by youth from good families. In the course of the program, an answer to this query was suggested: lice in high status communities are a biological, not a cultural, phenomenon. In this, the social meaning of lice has been situationally defined. Lice in Sharonia and other low-status communities are viewed as evidence of the culturally disadvantaged background of Oriental Jews, while explanation of similar manifestations in high-status neighborhoods eschews assumptions concerning cultural characteristics of the infected.

The situational etiology of lice is a vivid example of the spurious cultural content of the ethnic category Oriental Jews. Likewise, an endless assortment of undesirable events can and are explained by invoking phantom ethnic imagery. In these symbolic actions Oriental Jews, as a category of people, are continuously characterized as culturally tainted. In light of the Zionist paradigm, they remain in need of cultural renewal, an ideological prerequisite for social justice, a hope for the future. Yet, in the elastic cultural content of phantom ethnicity, perception of cultural change is perpetually blunted, realization of cultural renewal consistently postponed. Hence, vision of existential unity is sustained in the face of socioeconomic differentiation. Contradiction between the moral imperative of ultimate social justice and mundane political and economic interests in everyday life is dissolved.

Notes

[1] Oriental Jews is the accepted English equivalent of the Hebrew term "Edot Hamizrach" (see Deshen, 1970:10). The term "Sephardim," although occasionally used to label Jews of North African and Near Eastern origins, refers specifically to Jews of Spanish and North Mediterranean descent.

[2] The term pioneer (chalutz) recognized in formative years of the Zionist revolution, refers to persons who came to Palestine in order to actualize the Zionist idea. Pioneers and their progeny dominate elite positions in contemporary Israeli society. On the composition of Israeli elites see Weingrod and Gurevitch (1977). On the pioneers and their descendants see Elon (1971).

[3] Development towns are immigrant communities planned from inception by the national government. They are constructed and maintained with public funds. See Cohen (1970, 1972); Aronoff (1973).

[4] Sharonia is a pseudonym for a town where I conducted field work from September 1975 to January 1977.

[5]The term "in need of fostering" (teounay tipouach), invented by the Ministry of Education to designate low status clientele of North African and Near Eastern descent, is used by educators and others as a euphemism for persons viewed as culturally deficient. See Adler (1970:301); Halper (1978:270-78).

[6]A myriad of studies have examined cultural change among Israelis of North African and Near Eastern descent. Prominent examples of this work include: Deshen (1970); Deshen and Shokeid (1974); Goldberg (1972, 1973); Matras (1965); Shokeid (1971); Weingrod (1965); Weintraub and Associates (1971); Zenner (1965). Although there has been some debate in the literature regarding the pace and process of cultural change (compare Ben-David, 1953 to Deshen and Shokeid, 1974), I am unaware of any work that would contradict the assertion that rapid cultural change has been the dominant trend among immigrants and their offspring.

[7]For a general discussion of Zionism, the idea and the social movement, see Laqueur (1972); Vital (1975).

[8]On the sociopolitical structure of the Jewish community in British Mandatory Palestine see Eisenstadt (1967); Horowitz and Lissak (1978); Shapiro (1976).

[9]Located on the campus of Tel Aviv University, the Museum of the Jewish Diaspora is a multimillion dollar exhibit of Jewish life over the past 2,000 years. The project was conceived and is sponsored by the World Jewish Congress.

[10]A *mezuza* is a religious artifact customarily placed on the doorpost of a Jewish abode.

[11]My discussion of formative Zionist polemic is based primarily on the following anthologies and interpretive essays: Buber (1952); Fisch (1978); Goodman and and Lewis (1916); Hertzberg (1959); Heller (1949); Levenberg (1945); Tirosh (1975).

[12]As used in this paper, folk concepts refer to informant generated (emic), as distinct from observer generated (etic) summaries of relevant cognitive stimuli. On the epistemological distinction between emic and etic constructions of social reality, see Harris (1968).

[13]On government attempts to actualize this ideological imperative see Deshen (1970); Shokeid (1971); Weingrod (1965); Willner (1969). On the role of educational services in efforts at cultural transformation see Frankenstein (1953a). Kleinberger (1969); Kashti (1979); Lewis (1979b).

[14]Most Sharonians characterize themselves as traditional but not strictly religious in spritiual matters. In expressing this contention, they distinguish between religious sentiment and religious practice in everyday life.

References

Achad Ha'Am. 1916. "A Spiritual Centre," in Paul Goodman and Arthur D. Lewis (Eds.), *Zionism: Problems and Views*. London: T. Visher Unqin Ltd., 48-59.

Adler, Chaim. 1970. "The Israeli School as a Selective Institution," in S. N. Eisenstadt *et al.* (Eds.), *Integration and Development in Israel*. New York: Praeger, 287-301.

Arian, Asher. 1970. "Consensus and Community in Israel, *Jewish Journal of Sociology,* Vol. XII, 39-53.

Aronoff, Myron J. 1973. "Development Towns in Israel," in Michael Curtis and Mordechai S. Chertoff (Eds.), *Israel: Social Structure and Change.* New Brunswick: Transaction Books, 27-46.

Aronson, Dan R. 1976. "Ethnicity as a Cultural System," in Frances Henry (Eds.), *Ethnicity in the Americas.* The Hague-Paris: Mouton, 9-19.

Barnett, H. G. 1953. *Innovation: The Basis of Cultural Change.* New York: McGraw-Hill.

Bar-Ilan, Rabbi Meir. 1975. "Achievements and Aspirations" in Yosef Tirosh (Ed.), *Religious Zionism: An Anthology.* Jerusalem: World Zionist Organization.

Barth, Fredrik. 1969. *Ethnic Groups and Boundaries.* Boston: Little, Brown and Company.

Ben-David, Joseph. 1953. "Ethnic Differences or Social Change?" in Carl Frankenstein (Ed.), *Between Past and Future: Essays and Studies on Aspects of Immigrant Absorption in Israel.* Jerusalem: Henrietta Szold Foundation, 33-52.

Ben-Gurion, David. 1963. "Vision and Redemption," in Jacob Baal-Teshuva (Ed.), *The Mission of Israel.* New York: Robert Speller and Sons, 218-245.

——. 1971. Israel: *A Personal History.* Tel Aviv: American Israel Publishing Co.

Benas, Bertram B. 1969. "The Renascence of Jewish Aesthetics," in Paul Goodman and Arthur D. Lewis (Eds.), *Zionism: Problems and Views.* London: T. Fischer Unwin, Ltd., 69-84.

Benedict, Ruth. 1934. *Patterns of Culture.* Boston: Houghton and Mifflin Co.

Bennett, John W. 1975. *The New Ethnicity: Perspective from Ethnology.* St. Paul: West Publishing Co.

Brandeis, Louis D. (Ed.). 1916. *Zionism: Problems and Views.* London: T. Fischer Unwin, Ltd., 93-114.

Buber, Martin. 1952. *Israel and Palestine.* London: Horovitz Pub. Ltd.

Cohen, Abner. 1969. *Custom and Politics in Urban Africa.* Berkeley and Los Angeles: University of California Press.

Cohen, Erik. 1970. "Development Towns: The Social Dynamics of 'Planted' Urban Communities in Israel," in S. N. Eisenstadt *et al* (Eds.), *Integration and Development in Israel.* New York: Frederick A. Praeger, Inc., 586-617.

——. 1972. "The Black Panthers and Israeli Society," *Jewish Journal of Sociology.* Vol. 14, 93-109.

Curtis, Michael, and Chertoff, Mordechai S. 1973. *Israel: Social Structure and Change.* New Brunswick: Transaction Books.

Despres, Leo A. 1975. *Ethnicity and Resource Competition in Plural Societies.* The Hague-Paris: Mouton.

Deshen, Shlomo. 1970. *Immigrant Voters in Israel: Parties and Congregations in a Local Election Campaign.* Manchester: Manchester University Press.

——. 1974. "Political Ethnicity and Cultural Ethnicity in Israel during the 1960s," in Abner Cohen (Ed.), *Urban Ethnicity: ASA Monograph 12.* London: Tavistock.

——. 1976. "Ethnicity and Cultural Paradigms among Southern Tunisian Immigrants' *Ethos,* Vol. IV, 271-294.

——, and Shokeid, Moshe. 1974. *The Predicament of Homecoming: Cultural and Social Life of North African Immigrants in Israel*. Ithaca and London: Cornell University Press.

Driver, Harold, E. 1973. "Cross-Cultural Studies," in John J. Honigmann (Ed.), *Handbook of Social and Cultural Anthropology*. Chicago: Rand McNally College Pub. Co., 327-368.

Eisenstadt, S. N. 1954. *The Absorption of Immigrants: A Comparative Study Based Mainly on the Jewish Community in Palestine and the State of Israel*. London: Routledge and Kegan Paul, Ltd.

——. 1967. *Israeli Society*. New York: Basic Books.

——, S. N. Bar-Yosef, R. Adler, C. (Eds.). 1970. *Integration and Development in Israel*. New York: Praeger.

Elon, Amos. 1971. *The Israelis: Founders and Sons*. London: Weidenfeld and Nicolson.

Etzioni-Halevy, Eva. 1975. "Patterns of Conflict Generation and Conflict Absorption: The Case of Israeli Labour and Ethnic Relations," *Journal of Conflict Resolution*, Vol. 19, 286-309.

Fisch, Harold. 1978. *The Zionist Revolution*. London: Weidenfeld and Nicolson.

Frankenstein, Carl. 1953a. *Between Past and Future: Essays and Studies on Aspects of Immigrant Absorption in Israel*. Jerusalem: Henrietta Szold Foundation.

——. 1953b. "The Problem of Ethnic Differences in the Absorption of Immigrants," in Carl Frankenstein (Ed.), *Between Past and Future: Essays and Aspects of Immigrant Absorption in Israel*. Jerusalem: Henrietta Szold Foundation, 13-32.

Friendly, Alfred. (n.d.). *Israel's Oriental Immigrants and Druzes*. London: Minority Rights Group.

Gans, Herbert. 1979. "Symbolic Ethnicity: The Future of Ethnic Groups and Cultures in America," *Ethnic and Radical Studies*, Vol. 2, 1-20.

Geertz, Clifford. 1964. "Ideology as a Cultural System," in David Apter (Ed.), *Ideology and Discontent*. New York: Free Press, 47-56.

——. 1973. "Theory of Culture," in *The Interpretation of Culture*. New York: Basic Books, 3-32.

Glazer, Nathan, and Moynihan, Daniel Patrick. 1963. *Beyond the Melting Pot: The Negroes, Puerto Ricans, Jews, Italians and Irish of New York City*. Cambridge, Mass.: The M.I.T. Press.

Goldberg, Harvey. 1972. *Cave Dwellers and Citrus Growers: A Jewish Community in Libya and Israel*. Cambridge: Cambridge University Press.

——. 1973. "Culture Change in an Israeli Village: How the Twist Came to Even Yosef," *Middle Eastern Studies*, Vol. 9, 73-80.

Goodman, Paul, and Lewis, Arthur D. 1916. *Zionism: Problems and Views*. London: T. Fisher, Unwin, Ltd.

Halper, Jeffrey. 1978. *Ethnicity and Education: The Schooling of Afro-Asian Children in a Jerusalem Locality*. Ann Arbor: University Microfilms.

Harris, Marvin. 1968. "'Emics,' 'Etics,' and the 'New Ethnography,'" in Morton H. Fried (Ed.), *Readings in Anthropology*. New York: Thomas Y. Crowell Co., 102-134.

Hartman, M., and Eilon, H. 1975. "Ethnicity and Class in Israel" (in Hebrew), *Megamot,* Vol. 21, 129-139.

Heller, Celia S. 1973. "The Emerging Consciousness of the Ethnic Problem Among Jews in Israel," in Michael Curtis and Mordechai S. Chertoff (Eds.), *Israel: Social Structure and Change.* New Brunswick: Transaction Books, 313-332.

Heller, Joseph. 1949. *The Zionist Idea.* New York: Schocken Books.

Hertzberg, Arthur. 1959. *The Zionist Idea.* New York: Atheneum Press.

Horowitz, Dan, and Lissak, Moshe. 1978. *Origins of the Israeli Polity.* Chicago and London: University of Chicago Press.

Kashti, Yitzhak. 1979. *The Socializing Community: Disadvantaged Adolescents in Israeli Youth Villages.* Tel Aviv: School of Education, Tel Aviv University.

Katzir, Yael. 1976. *The Effects of Resettlement on the Status and Role of Yemeni Women, The Case of Ramat Oranim, Israel.* unpublished Ph.D. dissertation, University of California at Berkeley.

Kleinberger, A. F. 1969. *Society, Schools and Progress in Israel.* London: Pergamon Press.

Kook, Rabbi Zvi Yehuda Hacohen. 1975. "Zionism and Biblical Prophecy," in Yosef Tiroch (Ed.), *Religious Zionism: An Anthology.* Jerusalem: World Zionist Organization, 167-179.

Laquer, Walter. 1972. *A History of Zionism.* London: Weidenfeld and Nicholson.

Leach, E. R. 1954. *Political Systems of Highland Burma.* Boston: Beacon Press.

Levenberg, S. 1945. *The Jews and Palestine: A Study in Labor Zionism.* London: Poale Zion-Jewish Socialist Party.

Levy, Shlomit, and Guttman, Louis. 1976. "Zionism and Jewishness of Israelis," *Forum,* Vol. 1, 39-50.

Lewis, Arnold. 1979a. *Power, Poverty and Education: An Ethnography of Schooling in an Israeli Town.* Ramat Gan, Israel, Turtledove Publishing.

——. 1979b. "Educational Policy and Social Inequality in Israel," *Jerusalem Quarterly,* 101-111.

Lewy, Arieh, and Chen, Michael. 1974. *Closing or Widening of the Achievement Gap: A Comparison Over Time of Ethnic Group Achievement in the Israeli Elementary School.* Tel Aviv: School of Education, Tel Aviv University.

Lissak, Moshe. 1969. *Social Mobility in Israeli Society.* Jerusalem: Israel Universities Press.

Marx, Emanuel. 1979. "Foreword" to Arnold Lewis, *Power, Poverty and Education: An Ethnography of Schooling in an Israeli Town.* Ramat Gan, Israel: Turtledove Pub.

Matras, Judah. 1965. *Social Change in Israel.* Chicago: Aldine Publishing Co.

——, and Weintraub, Dov. 1977. "Ethnic and Other Primordial Differentials in Intergenerational Mobility in Israel." Jerusalem: Brookdale Institute.

Minkovich, A. 1969. *The Disadvantaged Child.* Jerusalem: Hebrew University and the Ministry of Education. (In Hebrew.)

Naroll, Raoul. 1964. "On Ethnic Unit Classification," *Current Anthropology.* Vol. 5, 283-312.

Nordau, Max. 1916. "Introduction," to Paul Goodman and Arthur D. Lewis (Eds.), *Zionism: Problems and Views.* London: T. Fisher, Unwin, Ltd.

Ortar, Gina. 1953. "A Comparative Analysis of the Structure of Intelligence in Various Ethnic Groups," in Carl Frankenstein (Ed.), *Between Past and Future: Essays and Studies on Aspects of Immigrant Absorption in Israel*. Jerusalem: Henrietta Szold Foundation, 267-290.

Patai, Raphael. 1970. *Israel: Between East and West*. Westport: Greenwood Publishing.

Peres, Yochanan. 1971. "Ethnic Relations in Israel," *American Journal of Sociology*, Vol. 76, 1021-1047.

Redfield, Robert. 1953. *The Primitive World and its Transformations*. Ithaca: Cornell University Press.

Sachar, Howard M. 1976. *A History of Israel: From the Rise of Zionism to Our Time*. New York: Alfred A. Knopf.

Sandberg, Neil C. 1974. *Ethnic Identity and Assimilation: The Polish-American Community*. New York: Praeger.

Selzer, Michael. 1967. *The Aryanization of the Jewish State*. New York: Black Star Publishing Co.

Shapiro, Yonathan. 1976. *The Formative Years of the Israeli Labor Party*. London-Beverly Hills: Sage Pub. Ltd.

Shokeid, Moshe. 1971. *The Dual Heritage: Immigrants from the Atlas Mountains in an Israeli Village*. Manchester: Manchester University Press.

Shumsky, Abraham. 1955. *The Clash of Cultures in Israel: A Problem for Education*. New York: Teachers College Press.

Shuval, Judith T. 1963. *Immigrants on the Threshold*. New York: Prentice Hall.

Simon, Leon. 1916. "Modern Hebrew Literature," in Paul Goodman and Arthur D. Lewis (Eds.), *Zionism: Problems and Views*. London: T. Fisher Unwin, Ltd., 205-213.

Smilansky, Moshe, and Smilansky, Sarah. 1967. "Intellectual Advancement of Culturally Disadvantaged Children: An Israeli Approach for Research and Action," *International Review of Education*, Vol. 13, 410-429.

Smooha, Sammy. 1972. "Israel and its Third World Jews: Black Panthers—the Ethnic Dilemma," *Society*, Vol. 9, 31-36.

——. 1978. *Israel: Pluralism and Conflict*. Berkeley and Los Angeles: University of California Press.

——, and Peres, Yochanan. 1975. "The Dynamics of Ethnic Inequalities: The Case of Israel" *Social Dynamics* 1, 63-79.

Tamarin, Georges R. 1971. *The Israeli Ethnic Landscape*. Givatayim, Israel: Monographs of the Institute of Socio-Psychological Research, Volume III/IV.

Tirosh, Yosef. 1975. *Religious Zionism: An Anthropology*. Jerusalem: World Zionist Organization.

Toledano, Henry. 1973. "Time to Stir the Melting Pot," in Michael Curtis and Mordechai Chertoff (Eds.), *Israel: Social Structure and Change*. New Brunswick: Transaction Books.

Turner, Victor W. 1974. "Religious Paradigms and Political Action: Thomas Becket at the Council of Northampton," in *Dramas, Fields and Metaphors: Symbolic Action in Human Society*. Ithaca and London: Cornell University Press, 60-97.

Van Den Berghe, Pierre L. 1973. "Pluralism," in John J. Honigmann (Ed.), *Handbook of Social and Cultural Anthropology*. Chicago: Rand McNally, 959-978.

Vital, David. 1975. *The Origins of Zionism*. Oxford: Oxford University Press.

Weingrod, Alex. 1965. *Israel: Group Relations in a New Society*. London: Pall Mall Press.

———. 1979. "Recent Trends in Israeli Ethnicity," *Ethnic and Racial Studies*, Vol. 2, 55-65.

———, and Gurevitch, Michael. 1977. "Who are the Israeli Elites?" *Jewish Journal of Sociology*, Vol. XIX, 66-77.

Weintraub, Dov. 1971. *Immigration and Social Change*. Manchester: Manchester University Press.

Willner, Dorothy. 1969. *National Building and Community in Israel*. Princeton: Princeton University Press.

Yancey, William L., E. P. Erickson, R. N. Juliani. 1976. "Emergent Ethnicity: A Review and a Reformulation," *American Sociological Review*, Vol. 41, 391-403.

Zenner, Walter. 1965. *Syrian Jewish Identification in Israel*. Ann Arbor, Michigan: University Microfilms.

Zionist Library. 1972. *The Voices of Jewish Emancipation*. Jerusalem: The Zionist Library.

8

Ethnicity as a Negotiated Issue in the Israeli Political Order: The "Ethnic Lists" to the Delegates' Assembly and the Knesset (1920-1977)[1]

Hanna Herzog

The aim of this study is to examine the development of political ethnicity in Israel as expressed in "ethnic lists" organized for national elections. Expressions of political ethnicity can also be found in ethnic lists at the local level (Deshen, 1970, 1974); in ethnic divisions within ordinary political parties (Cohen, *et al*, 1962), and in various other organizations that are not formally defined as political. These other forms of political ethnicity are important subjects for study, but they will not be dealt with here.

What is meant by the term "ethnic lists"? In Israel, "ethnic" has been applied almost exclusively to persons of "Oriental" origin,[2] and rarely to those coming from Europe and America.[3] In this sense, "ethnic" refers to minority groups or to those who are thought to be "weak", while the dominant group has become representative of "society" ("the Israelis"). The label "ethnic lists" derives from this broad classification: the term has been applied to those groups of Oriental origin who organized in order to present election lists to national representative legislatures.

Several general facts should be noted regarding the ethnic lists on the political and electoral map of Israel. First, ethnic groups took part in all thirteen election campaigns beginning with the first *Asefat Nivcharim* (Delegates Assembly) (1920), and in all of them, except for the 7th *Knesset* (1969), more than one ethnic party was involved. Secondly, since elections to the Fourth *Asefat Nivcharim* (1944), there has been a drastic decrease in the electoral strength of the ethnic lists. Finally, since elections to the 3rd *Knesset* (1955) no ethnic list has obtained even a single mandate.

A number of previous studies have attempted to explain the reasons for the failure of these ethnic lists. Among the main theories proposed were the lack of financial resources, organizational problems, the neutralization of feelings of deprivation, and the existence of "cross-cutting ties", which prevent the crystallization of ethnic consciousness (Lissak, 1972; Peres, 1976; Cohen, 1972; Smooha, 1978; Bernstein, 1976, 1979).

These explanations typically assume the existence of an ethnic entity that is identified with all persons of Oriental origin. Given this assumption, the decline of the ethnic lists during the pre-state period was explained as resulting from the decline of the proportion of Orientals in the population as a consequence of the growing immigration from Eastern and Central Europe (Rubenstein, 1976). However, the continued decline after the establishment of the State is not amenable to this explanation; statistics show that there has been a continuous growth in the proportion of Orientals in the population in recent years (from about twenty percent in 1944 to fifty-five percent in 1977). Moreover, scholars have pointed to the existence of various factors that should have encouraged ethnic organization—for example, the persistent inequality between ethnic groups in the allocation of social resources such as income, property, education, power and prestige (Smooha and Peres, 1975; Smooha, 1978). The failure of the ethnic lists following the establishment of the State might therefore be greeted with surprise.

Taking a different direction, other explanations attribute the failure to attain power to shortcomings within the group, e.g. the absence of organizational ability, inadequate leadership, etc. However, explanations along these lines do not account for repeated reorganization despite electoral failure, or for splintering instead of uniting among the ethnic lists. Should we attribute these failures to political naivete, unfamiliarity with the rules of the political game, or even general political ineptitude? In my view the explanation should be sought in other directions.

Two overall theoretical approaches have guided this research. The first approach entails a redefinition of ethnicity as a situational phenomenon that emerges in interaction between groups (Barth, 1969; Despres, 1975; Cohen, 1974a; Yancey *et al.*, 1976; Deshen, 1976b). A series of research questions derive from this approach. For example, did (or do) people see their ethnic origin as a basis for political organization? Who were those persons? What was their aim and what meaning did they apply to their origin when they made use of it as a political resource? The second theoretical approach emphasizes the analysis of the interaction process among groups active in the arena of politics (Hall, 1972). On the face of it, all those who deal with political power belong to this school. Nonetheless, there is a tendency in many studies to present differential power as a fact, or to define the sources of power without reference to the processes by which it was attained. Often ignored is the process of negotiation itself, a process in which decisions are made regarding the source of relevant resources and their rates of exchange, while at the same time organizational frameworks are formed and political support enlisted.

In this study, I maintain that ethnic identity is not in itself a political resource unless defined as such in the process of political negotiation. The manner of its enlistment as a resource, and its use in organization, are defined in the process of interaction with other contestants. In other words, ethnic political organization is analyzed in terms of negotiations over the definition of the political order among groups which participate in the political contest.

This approach appears to fit well with organizational theories, which emphasize that organizations should not be studied as autonomous units, since they affect their environment and are affected by it. Various researchers claim that developments in organizations are not the result of their size, efficiency and rationality, but rather as a consequence of a constant process of interaction between the organization and its environment (Blau and Scott, 1963; Perrow, 1979; Benson, 1977). This viewpoint does not only focus on control of resources or efficient functioning, but deals as well with the organization's success in gaining legitimization (Meyer and Rower, 1977; Perrow, 1979). This concept holds for political organizations as well.

With these theoretical perspectives in mind, this study has sought to test three hypotheses. They may briefly be stated as follows:

1. Political ethnicity is a new phenomenon in Israel, and it has increased in scope as a result of conditions in Israel and in interaction
   with different political groups.
2. The value of ethnicity as a resource in political contests has been
   changing.
3. There was in the past and still continues to be a struggle regarding
   the proper definition of political ethnicity.

Method and Data Collection

This study is both sociological and historical. All the ethnic lists that campaigned in elections, from the first *Asefat Hanivcharim* (1920) to the
elections for the Ninth *Knesset* (1977), have been examined. A total of
forty-four lists, some of which were identified with the same organization,
were included.

The research method combines content analysis of documents, and
prosophographical analysis of biographical documents. The prosophographical analysis deals with the life histories of groups by means of a
collective analysis of biographies. Its basic premise is that human experience molds and influences the various possibilities open to politically active individuals (Stone, 1971). The point of departure of the study was the
location of a concrete population of activists, and the unveiling of the figures behind the "ethnic lists". The content analysis of written documents
follows the Weberian tradition in which the motives of the actor and the
meaning he attaches to his action must be understood. For this purpose,
documents written as close as possible to the period studied are of the
greatest importance. The data include documents from archives, newspaper articles, biographical and autobiographical material by and about
the activists of the lists, and earlier studies.

Political Ethnicity as a New Phenomenon

My findings show that the Yemenite organizations were founded as a result of encouragement by others. *Tseirei Hamizrach* (Young Orientals),
a party that participated in the elections to the first *Asefat Hanivcharim*
(1920), was an organization of young people of Yemenite origin that was
begun by *Hapoel Hatsair* (The Young Worker, one of the labor parties)
in 1911. The *Tseirei Hamizrach* showed a strong orientation toward social

integration; for example, they adopted the behavior patterns of the workers' organizations, such as abandoning religious observance (Tsadok, 1967: 236; Yeshayahu and Gridi, 1938:42), or joining the new agricultural settlements (Nini, 1976:395-429; Greitzer, 1980). There were also attempts made to integrate them into the Labor Party and into the *Histadrut* (General Federation of Labor) (Gluska, 1974:112-113; Tabib, 1943:2-8). Gluska, for many years chairman of *Hitachduth Hateimanim* (Yemenites' Association), was recruited to *Tseirei Hamizrach* by Yosef Shprintzak (one of the leaders of *Hapoel Hatsair* (Gluska, 1974:97). Shprintzak was Gluska's Hebrew teacher, and he employed Gluska's mother for various domestic tasks (ibid. 17). In his book, Gluska admits that, in essence, he only began to become interested in the Yemenite problem when he became vice-chairman of *Tseirei Hamizrach* (ibid. 102).

The initiative for the founding of the second group, *Hitachduth Hateimanim,* came from the Israel Office of the World Zionist Organization, which grew "tired of individual Yemenite requests for help" (Announcements of the Central Committee of *Hitachduth Hateimanim,* 1923-6:3-4; Gridi, 1943:19-20). The founders of *Hitachduth Hateimanim* were members of various parties (Tsarum, a member of *Mizrachi,* the religious party; Gluska, *Hapoel Hatsair,* Tabib and Cohen-Maramati, *Achdut Haavodah,* the biggest labor party at that time). These frameworks were for them classrooms for learning the rules of the political game. In these organizations they were perceived as representative of their group of origin. The funds making it possible for the first *Vaad Hateimanim* (Yementies' Committee) to meet were provided by the Zionist Executive (Announcements of the Central Committee of *Hitachduth Hateimanim,* 1923-6:3-5).

Hitachduth Hateimanim, as a political organization of Yemenite Jews, was a new phenomenon in their previously traditional public life. Its innovating aspects may be described as follows:

a. It was an effort to form one general framework for all Yemenites in Israel. Public and community life in Yemen had been characterized by disunity and separate local organizations (Goitein, 1953).

b. The initiators of the organization were of a different social profile from the traditional Jewish leadership in Yemen. They were all relatively young, almost from the same age group; this new elite had immigrated to Israel as youngsters together with their families. They came from rural areas of Yemen, and not from the capital, Saan'a, which was considered the center of spiritual leadership for Yemenite Jewry. Before their emigration they had no experience in public and political life. Their political and social involvement began in Israel. Their first encounter with Israeli conditions was in agricultural settlements. Most of them were active in various political parties before the establishment of *Hitachduth Hateimanim*. Their political coming of age was experienced against a background of similar conditions: immigration to Palestine, the encounter with immigrants from other countries, the confrontation with the "new *Yishuv*" in the settlements, and the political reality in the parties.

c. The founders of the *Hitachduth Hateimanim* used ethnic origin as the basis for their claim to representation and to a share in the allocation of resources, but these claims were not followed by demands for the encouragement of Yemenite culture and tradition. Although some demands that could be defined as cultural were made—such as the allocation of budgets for education, or positions for ritual slaughterers, Rabbis, and supervisors of dietary laws—the emphasis in these claims was always political.

From these data we may conclude that the new ethnic organization was not the expression of a tradition of "ethnic isolation" brought from abroad, and not even the adaptation of a traditional organization to conditions in Israel. On the contrary, it was the outcome of the lessons these young people of Yemenite origin learned in their encounters with the new environment.

This finding agrees with Zamir's (1966) description of ethnic organizations in Beer Sheva in the late 1950's, and also with Cohen's analysis of politics in a development town in the 1960's (Cohen et al., 1962). These studies show that the parties emphasized ethnic divisions by organizing members in ethnic cells. While Cohen and Zamir stress the exploitation of the traditional leadership by the regular parties, my findings show that the new ethnic lists were products of the enterprise of new political initiators who grew up in Israel, and not of the traditional elite of those ethnic groups.

Most of the leaders of the ethnic lists grew up in Israel and/or were educated there. A large number of them gained experience in earlier political activity within other party frameworks. With the exception of the *Likud Yotsei Tsfon Afrika* (Union of North Africans) which was a protest movement in the fifties, and the Black Panthers in the seventies, most of the leaders came from the upwardly mobile strata of Oriental Jews. It appears that they emerged from groups that maintained closer and more intensive reciprocal contact with other groups in society. They shaped their political identity in this new context, and not from cleaving to the tradition of the past.

The social and economic distress of the leaders of *Likud Yotsei Tsfon Afrika* and the Black Panthers was defined against the background of existential conditions and reference groups they encountered within Israeli society. Like the initiators of other ethnic lists, the organizers of the protest movements did not come from the traditional ruling elite of their communities.

The only attempt to translate positions of former social elitism into an organized political effort was made by leaders of the Sephardic community. A study of the processes that took place in the Sephardic lists, which were originally based on community councils, shows that here, too, those who became dominant were not the veteran leaders of the community. For example, in the lists for the *Asefat Hanivcharim* and the *Knesset,* the strength of the Tel Aviv committee of the Separdic community grew constantly, despite the fact that by tradition authority was lodged in the Jerusalem committee.

During the forties, the Tel Aviv committee had among its active members Sephardis who had arrived in the preceeding decade (such as Recanati) and also native sons, not necessarily from the prestigious or veteran families of the Jaffa community (e.g. Toledano, later Chief Rabbi of Tel Aviv and Minister of Religion, and Shitreet, later and until his death Minister of Police). The status and prestige of the Tel Aviv activists were not anchored in the traditional models of community organization, but in the general economic and political system of the Jewish community as a whole, and in particular, the Mandatory Government. With the establishment of the State, the Tel Aviv committee achieved a dominant position in the Sephardic list. Because of Shitreet's links with the leaders of *Mapai* (Israel Labor Party), he was appointed the representative of the Sephardis in the provisional government, despite the objections of the Jerusalem Sephardi representatives. These links made it possible for the Sephardic list to become part of the government coalition after the elections to the first Knesset (1949). The rival activists in Jerusalem were also not entirely from the ranks of the traditional leadership, but were supported mainly by young people who were not necessarily members of traditionally leading families.

In conclusion, it can be said that the roots of political ethnicity are not anchored in tradition or in the past of the group of origin. Ethnicity grew with the encouragement of the surrounding society. It developed among those people who were already more involved and who aspired to greater integration into the society. These were young, upwardly mobile persons who were interested in getting their share of social, economic and political resources and prestige in accordance with standards that had crystallized in Israel. This conclusion supports theories of emergent ethnicity, and emphasizes the importance of political competition in this process.

The Changing Value of Ethnicity

Ethnicity as a resource not only grew in political negotiations, it also changed its value through those negotiations. In the course of negotiations on the definition of the political order, each side tried to convince the other of the strength of its various power bases and the extent of its control over them. Each side sought to maneuver so as to gain maximum advantage for itself. In order to understand the political power of ethnicity one must examine the course of the negotiations that took place in the political arena.

The success of the Yemenite list in the election for the second *Asefat Nivcharim* (1925) can serve as an example of the changing value of ethnicity. The twenty mandates won were largely the result of the insistence of the leaders that a special election day be alloted to them. Just before the elections, the *Hitachduth Hateimanim* leaders demanded that voting be deferred. Their argument was that the list of Yemenite voters was incomplete. They explained the failure of people to register as "the fear that the Jerusalem public always has of such lists" (Central Commitee of *Hitachduth Hateimanim,* Central Elections Committee, 11.11.1924; 125, Zionist Archives 51/1740a), the reference being to lists for military service or tax assessments, which were customary during Ottoman rule. In addition, they claimed that the voters' cards had not reached their destination, for their distribution was given to "people from the west who only came to Palestine a short time ago. Yemenite names were strange to them and they were not familiar with addresses" (ibid. 8.12.1925). And finally, it appeared that a no less important reason for postponing the elections was the difficulty *Hitachduth Hateimanim* was having in making up its list of candiates (Tsarum to Yellin, President of the *Vaad Leumi,* ibid, 14.12.1924).

The *Vaad Leumi* (the National Council) was prepared to take this difficulty into consideration and to receive the list at the last moment, (*Vaad Leumi* to the General Committee of *Hitachduth Hateimanim,* 14. 12.1924, ibid). This readiness to make allowances encouraged the Yemenite representatives to present an ultimatum: they were prepared to take part in the election only if voters' cards were also given to all those whose names did not appear on the lists. Their ultimatum was rejected. Sabbath services were then utilized by Yemenite leaders to urge a boycott of the elections. All last-minute efforts to have them take part failed, and after the regular election day passed the Central Elections Committee agreed to allow the Yemenites to hold special elections. All Yemenites who had not voted on the regular election day were permitted to vote, and all the parties presented their candidate.

Hitachduth Hateimanim received 2,845 votes, eight and eight-tenths percent of the total, giving them twenty delegates to the Second *Asefat Hanivcharim,* as compared with five-and-eight-tenths percent achieved in the First and three percent in the Third election campaigns. In the special election they received more seats than the Sephardis (who got 19) despite the fact that the latter made up a larger proportion of the population. The interest that the leaders of *Hitachduth Hateinmanim* aroused among Yemenite voters caused them to close ranks and achieve a peak turnout that they never reached again.

The changing power of ethnicity as a political resource is clearly shown in a second example: Sephardi demands for separate polling stations, or the Curia system. This demand was accepted in 1931, but rejected in 1944. The change was not due to the organizational success of the lists nor to the consolidation of ethnic identity, but rather to the changing value of the resource of ethnicity. In 1931 the *Vaad Leumi* was interested in massive participation in elections because it was the first implementation of Jewish community regulations; consequently it yielded to the Sephardi threat to boycott the elections. In 1944, however, the organized *Yishuv* was an established fact, and the struggle then centered on internal power relations, so that the threat of boycotting the elections no longer had any effect. In the two election campaigns the rhetoric used by the Sephardis was identical: they demanded representation because of, rather than despite, their social and organizational weaknesses. The exchange value of these weaknesses were altered as the terms of negotiation themselves became transformed.

The power of ethnicity as a political resource must be measured not only by means of the electoral success of the ethnic list. The appearance of independent ethnic lists was ill-received even in the pre-state period. Yet at the same time, there were continued attempts to organize those from Eastern countries into ethnic frameworks controlled by the general parties (Zamir, 1966, Cohen *et al.*, 1962).

Political ethnicity was supported by various organizational arrangements (financial support, cooptation, favors, etc.), but at the same time faced continual attempts to weaken its legitimacy. These attempts were varied: within a party, or in a satellite party (like the Sephardic list attached to the General Zionists in the elections to the 2nd and 3rd *Knesset*), ethnicity was considered legitimate, but as a resource in the hands of an independent body, it was taboo.

In the early years of the State, parties tended to support ethnic lists as auxilliary or subsidiary lists (e.g. in the 1st *Knesset, Mapai* supported the Sephardic list, and the General Zionists, *Hitachduth Hateimanim*). This model of supporting pseudo-independent bodies was gradually replaced by coopting the leaders of the independent lists. Many examples can be cited; *Mapai* absorbed Shitreet, the General Zionists, Sasson, the Liberals, Shlomo Cohen-Tzidon, who headed an Oriental list in the 4th *Knesset,* and the United Religious Party, Sciaky, who also initiated an ethnic list for that election. All of these notables obtained "safe places" on the absorbing party's list.

This practice of coopting the heads of independent lists and providing them with safe seats later waned, and was replaced by attempts to organize persons of Oriental origin within existing party frameworks (that is, to increase the number of ethnics in the party, but not necessarily those from independent organizations). The heads of the independent lists became a matter of interest to the smaller parties, usually those described as radical. Thus, the Black Panthers cooperated with Shalom Cohen (initiator of a party called Israeli Democrats) in the 8th *Knesset* (1973) and with the Communist Party and *Sheli* (a left-wing Zionist party) in the 9th *Knesset* (1977). These facts attest to the changing power of independent ethnicity. The changes in negotiating strength did not take place because of the organizational ability of the ethnic lists, but are, to a large extent, the result of internal considerations and interests of the parties.

The Meaning of Political Ethnicity

Two contradictory trends have existed side by side in Israeli society. On the one hand, there was a tendency to classify the population and enlist it politically on the basis of its ethnic origin; on the other hand, there was a denial of the ethnic basis in the name of the "integration of exiles". These contradictory tendencies influenced the definitions of the meaning of political ethnicity. The democracy of the *Yishuv,* on which Israeli democracy is based, of necessity encouraged the participation of all groups and bodies. It granted legitimization to a wide variety of political organizations, including ethnic ones. At certain periods these bodies even obtained unusual privileges as a result of unique arrangements, as we have seen in the special voting day for the Yemenites (1925) or the arrangement for voting in ethnic polling places (1931).

In the *Yishuv* and in the State, ethnic classification and categorization gained a good deal of acceptance within general frameworks, such as the recognized political parties, but there was a tendency to reject and even condemn them when they had the character of independent organization. On the level of social action, there existed conditions that encouraged *de facto* recognition of ethnicity as a legitimate political resource. This is the only possible way to interpret the readiness of the parties to give in to the demands of ethnic political entrepreneurs. Only in this way can we interpret the system of favors and cooptation that developed, while at the same time on the ideological level all of them denied the legitimacy of political ethnicity.

The basic technique for countering the legitimacy of ethnicity in politics was stigmatization. This occurred in two ways: first, ethnicity was represented as separatism, a betrayal of the ideal of the melting pot, or the integration of exiles (*mizug galuyot*); second, individuals included in the ethnic lists were defamed. These tactics began during the *Yishuv* period and continued, with variations, until the elections of 1977. A number of examples of "personal stigmatization" can be cited.

In 1942, public committees to encourage enlistment in the British Army were formed. The request of the Sephardis to include their representatives on the committees was refused. The refusal was not couched in political terms, although the committees' composition was apparently determined according to a party key (cf. *Hamizrach,* 7, August 1942:2, 16). A poster published at the time highlights the justification which stigmatized the Sephardi leaders. The poster, whose heading was "And neither did they know shame", declares: . . . "the Sephardi leaders are angry at not being included in the enlistment committees and they know no shame. Are they really and truly interested in enlistment? Who are these interested parties and what are their actions?" Below were listed the leaders of the Sephardic community, Rabbi Uziel, Meir Gineo, Abraham Franco, Eliahu Elyashar, as well as the names of their young unmarried male relatives who had not enlisted. "Under what guise", asks the poster, "do they want to approach the public and demand enlistment? Who has enlisted from among the Sephardis? The answer is known. The members of poor and laboring families and of "Oriental"[4] Jews (the son of Alma- liah who enlisted is not a Sephardi but a Moroccan), the Sephardi and Oriental public and especially those from the ranks of the workers and laborers reject the leadership of the honored notables and hold them in contempt. Shame to the hypocrites and honor seekers wherever they may be. Go into the caves of the rocks and the holes of the earth because of the hatred of the people that hate you" (Zionist Archives, S25, 5903).

The sharp tone of the poster should be judged in comparison with the political style of the period, and from this standpoint it seems to me that it is not unusual. As to content, it should be noted that it does not deny the right in principle of the Sephardis (or any other group) to demand representation. Such a demand was considered legitimate in the political system which had evolved, and therefore the tactics of stigmatization were used: justification of non-inclusion of the Sephardis by personal vilification of their leaders.

Other examples may be cited. In the dispute over the demand for a change in the voting system for the 4th *Asefat Nivcharim,* the groups opposing it increasingly used tactics of stigmatization. Leaders of the Sephardic community were called "gravediggers" (because of the fact that some of the committee's income came from the burial society), "effendis", "sextons", "reactionaries", and the most usual epithets were "senores" and "wardens" (of synagogues) (*Hed Hamizrach,* 3, 34.6. 44:7; *Davar,* 19.10.42). These expressions were not relevant to the argu- ment. They are characteristic of the tactics of stigmatization, which trans- fers modes of character and behavior from one area of an individual's (or group's) life and stamps them as a stigma on all others areas of be- havior (Erikson, 1967; Goffman, 1963).

Labels were the lot of many ethnic lists. The Black Panthers were stigmatized from many sides. They were called "not nice" by Prime Minister Golda Meir, described as marginal youth (*Haaretz,* 28.1.71) and criminals (Haaretz 3.3.71); their violent activities were described as a danger to democracy (*Lamerchav,* 28.5.71), and their action was said to be connected with the extreme left and foreign elements (*Maariv,* 20.1.71), including the P.L.O. (*Haaretz,* 7,4,75; *Yediot Aharonot,* 12.12. 75).

An examination of the demands of all the ethnic lists reveals a consistent trend in the ways that they presented themselves. None of the lists, including the Sephardi one during the period of the *Yishuv* and the Black Panthers during the 1970's, had a separatist ideology. The conflict was conceived by them as a conflict over allocation of resources, as a re-division of economic, political and prestige assets, but not as a conflict over the essence of the social order. They did not oppose the idea of the melting pot, which was interpreted as assimilation (Deshen, 1976). Eric Cohen (1972) noted this in his analysis of the Black Panther phe-nomenon, and my findings corroborate this in the other lists as well (for examples see *Maariv,* 21.8.59; *Haaretz,* 23.10.59, 3.4.72).

The term "ethnicity" carried a stigma which the initiators of the lists tried to eliminate. In the fifties, the initiators of the ethnic lists gave them names which indicated national origin and hint at political eth-nicity as a resource, e.g. The National Sephardic Party, or The Sephardic Union founded by Sephardic and Oriental Communities List, or The Union of North-African Immigrants. Beginning with the sixties, how-ever, there was a tendency to avoid identifying with ethnicity, since this had been stigmatized. Continuous efforts were made to include Ashkenazis in the lists of candidates; the names chosen, such as Young Israel, Brother-hood, Popular Movement, symbolize the goal of integration of exiles. These attempts have not been successful: lists whose initiators were of Oriental origin were immediately labelled as ethnic. This was the fate of Ben Porath's (a former member of the Labor Party) list for the 9th *Knesset,* the Zionist Movement for Social Renewal, for, although this party did not make the social gap the central problem of its program, most of the initiators were of Eastern origin.

The Black Panthers, whose name appealed symbolically to Orientals (who are sometimes called "black"), attempted to broaden their appeal to represent all deprived people and the entire working class. In her anal-ysis of the Black Panther phenomenon, Bernstein claims that the explana-tion for social conflict they gave was not an ethnic explanation *per se.* Their cry "Where is the pride of the Sephardis?" was not meant to en-courage ethnic identity or separation. On the contrary, at a convention of immigrants from Morocco-North Africa, Eddie Malcha, one of the Black Panther leaders, came out against a return to the Oriental tradition (*Haar-etz,* 3.4.72). The issue of the pride of the Sephardis is interpreted by Bernstein (1976:203) as the intention to change the prestige alloted to ethnicity. This was auxiliary to the central demand for a just allocation of resources; the basic demand was for participation (ibid. 315). The public image of the Black Panthers as advocating ethnicity and separatism arose because they were labelled as such, as part of the attempt to reduce their power in the political negotiation process.

The attempts to push the Black Panthers outside normative limits by labelling affected the extent and style of protest, from which, in fact, their principal power came. Their activist style caused the problem of deprivation to make headlines. Yet, the fact is that they did not present an opposing ideology, and they did not create a new myth; on the contrary, as a result of stigmatization they retreated to defensive positions.

The effort to escape stigmatization is apparent in the circumstances of the Black Panther's split. In the struggle among the leaders which brought about the split there was also a conflict about links with the left. The group that withdrew, headed by Eddie Malcha, opposed ties with the far left (*Haaretz,* 14.7.71). The name Eddie Malcha chose, Blue-White Panthers, attests to the deisre to be included within the normative borders of society, and emphasizes the connection to the State and to Zionism. The name Zionist Panthers, chosen by the group headed by Victor Tayar, may be interpreted in the same way. These and other examples show the struggle of the ethnic lists to gain recognition and avoid being labelled as opponents of the Zionist idea or the integration of exiles ideology. The recurrent definition of ethnicity as opposed to the fundamental values of Israeli society brought many of the leaders of the lists to offer apologies and state reservations. This fact, without doubt, attenuated the force of their claims and diffused their message.

While the independent ethnic political lists and their activists were pushed to the margins of Israeli politics, ethnicity itself continued to be a political resource. This is illustrated by the election propaganda for the 9th Knesset (1977). The so-called ethnic lists did not make a direct appeal to Oriental Jews, but the other parties placed great emphasis on such an appeal. *Hazit Poalim v'Shchunot* (Workers' and Neighborhoods' Front), an "ethnic party" headed by Shalom Cohen, discarded an election poster putting the matter of representation in black-white terms. On the other hand, posters formulating demands in terms of class were distributed. Victor Tayar, of the Zionist Panthers, said, when speaking on the radio: "There is no one to represent the wage-earner, the housewife whose allowance doesn't last till the end of the month, the discharged soldier, young couples, the ordinary man, the silent man". Only once during the broadcast did Tayar mention the word "Orientals" (Election Broadcast, *Kol Yisrael,* 29.4.77). In contrast, the election broadcast of the Independent

Liberals began this way: "The words of an Oriental Jew on Oriental communities. . . . All parties talk about closing the gap; . . . the Independent Liberals have placed two representatives of the Oriental communities in sure places" (Election Broadcast, Kol Yisrael, 10.5.77).

It would not be accurate to claim that representatives of the ethnic lists to the 9th *Knesset* waived the use of ethnicity as a political resource entirely, but they did tone it down in view of the stigma attached to ethnic organizations. They chose to make use of ethnicity in covert fashion, in contrast to what had been customary up until 1977. This was a result of the stigma applied by society to the ethnic organization as being opposed to the integration of exiles.

In contrast to the avoidance of the expression of the social gap in ethnic terms and its formulation in terms of social class or special groups (such as young couples, neighborhoods, development towns), we can also discern an attempt to change the meaning of political ethnicity: the introduction of cultural elements. Previously the point was made that the ethnic lists formulated their demands in terms of allocation of resources, while refraining from cultural demands. In the elections to the 9th *Knesset* we can see a reversal in this area in the propaganda of the Yemenite list. *Beit Yisrael* (House of Israel) conducted its election campaign under the slogan "Spiritual, Social and Cultural Revival". The purposes of the organization were defined as social, cultural, and assistance to all who apply (*Afikim,* 12(63) January 1977:12). In the words of its leaders, "The matters we are concerned with are purely social and cultural, and we do not deal with political matters. We decided to field a list for the *Knesset* and the Histadruth not because we have become a political organization but as a means of furthering the aims of our movement. . . ." (*Afikim,* 13(65) September 1977:12). This social-cultural justification for political organization is new. It is a striking innovation when compared with the other ethnic lists and the former approach of the Yemenites themselves.

An explanation for the new meaning for political ethnicity which is being tried out must again be sought in the interaction between the ethnic leaders and the surrounding society. If we describe this system of relations in broad strokes, we shall be able to note the changes that have occurred.

The fifties were characterized by the denial of Oriental culture, a denial that was common to almost all the parties. In this rejection one can perhaps discern a hint of fear by the dominant group of being overruled by the "burgeoning masses". "Quality, not quantity, or progress, not levantinization", were the points so often stressed (cf. *Mishmar,* 6.4.66;

Haboker, 26.5.50; *Davar*, 4.7.50; *Molad*, 26.5.50:69; Zeira, 1950). The absorption of immigrants was perceived as a process of modernization which was defined as the abandonment of traditional ways of life. Within the reality of Israel, this was interpreted as the acceptance of European, or more accurately, Eastern European behavior models[5] (Deshen, 1978). Ethnic cultural activities were deemed socially and culturally negative, while the "integration of exiles" ideology aspired to transform Orientals into Israelis (Weingrod, 1965, 1979). These attitudes were to a great extent adopted by people of non-European origin themselves (Peres, 1976; Smooha, 1978).

Beginning with the end of the sixties, the first signs of cultural awakening among Orientals begin to appear (Deshen, 1974). This awakening was supported and to a large extent encouraged by the establishment (Goldberg, 1977); for example, curriculum programs focusing upon the heritage of Oriental and Sephardic Jews were introduced into the schools, funds were allocated for research in the field of Oriental Jewish tradition, support was given to various ethnic folk festivals, etc. These activities arose out of the conviction that the methods of social and cultural absorption used in the past were grossly unfair to immigrants of Eastern origin. Political factors were also involved. Weingrod (1979:61) points out that festivals like the *Mimouna* (an annual picnic get-together of Moroccan Jews) give ethnic political activists an opportunity to increase their influence within the community, to renew old ties and create new ones with various national leaders, and to demonstrate the electoral strength of the Oriental voters. During the fifties it was impossible to make use of culture as a factor in political life; by the end of the seventies, there is nothing more legitimate than to speak about and in the name of the Sephardic and Oriental Jewish cultural heritage.

Conclusion

We claim that ethnicity as a basis of power is not a given or an independent factor: in the process of negotiations over the political order, the "weight" and meaning of ethnicity is established. The fact of coming from a particular country and/or belonging to a particular culture is not automatically transformed into political ethnicity. The ethnic lists which arose during the period of the *Yishuv* and the State were new organizational frameworks which developed in Israel in the context of particular social conditions; they were neither the heritage of the past nor were political parties or mechanisms transferred wholesale. Although ethnic identity is connected with the definition of a common origin, it received and continues to receive its content and organizational expression in the conditions existing in the *Yishuv* and the State.

The ethnic list as a conflict group in the political arena developed as a result of interaction between aspiring ethnic politicians and representatives of parties and other political organizations. The meanings given to ethnicity developed and changed in the course of this interaction. A series of questions arise regarding the future of political ethnicity: Will ethnic identity become a permanent resource in political negotiations? Will it be a resource of the Orientals, or of the dominant group? Will it exacerbate the ethnic conflicts or, on the contrary, resolve ethnic tensions? Further research will be needed in order to explore these key issues.

Notes

[1] The term "lists" suits these political organizations better than the term "party". Most of the ethnic lists never reached the stage of a crystallized political organization. In many cases they were a merger of political initiators who cooperated in order to be able to take part in elections. I argue that this organizational model and the reasons for its perserverance were not accidental, but are connected to the type of interaction developed between ethnic political activists and representatives of other parties. This problem is discussed in my doctoral dissertation.

[2] "Orientals" is the common term used to refer to Jews that came from Asia, Africa and some European Ladino-speaking communities.

[3] Lists termed "ethnic" but not of the Oriental community are usually to be found on the local level, in elections for municipal authorities, mainly lists of Romania immigrants. Only one such list took part in national elections, the *Aliyah Chadasha* (New Immigration) list made up of newcomers from Germany, which participated in the elections to the 4th *Asefat Nivcharim* (1944) (Rubenstein, 1976: 263; also Ben-Avram, 1973: 155-156; Guttman and Lissak, 1977: 157).

[4] Oriental Jews make a distinction between Ladino-speaking Jews who are considered "Sephardic" and Arabic-speaking Jews from other eastern communities.

[5] Miriam Geter describes the pressures and difficulties faced by immigrants from Germany in the thirties to assimilate into the "veterans", who came from Eastern Europe (Geter, 1979).

References

Documentary Material
Zionist Archives—Jerusalem
Committee of the Separdic Community Archives—Jerusalem

Newspapers and Magazines
Afikim
Davar
Haaretz
Haboker
Hamizrach
Hed-Hamizrach
Kuntress
Lamerchav
Maariv
Mishmar
Molad
Yediot Aharonot
Yisrael Hatzeira

Published Reports, Books and Articles
Barth, F. (Ed.). 1969. *Ethnic Groups and Boundaries.* Boston: Little Brown and Company.

Ben-Avram, B. 1973. *Political Parties and Organizations During the British Mandate for Palestine, 1918-1948.* Jerusalem: The Historical Society of Israel, The Zalman Shazar Centre for Furtherance of the Study of Jewish History. (In Hebrew).

Benson, Y. K. 1977. "Innovation and Crisis in Organizational Analysis", *The Sociological Quarterly,* 18:3-16.

Berger, P., and Luckman, T. 1966. *The Social Construction of Reality.* Garden City, New York: Doubleday and Co.

Bernstein, D. 1976. *The Black Panthers of Israel 1971-1972. Contradictions and Protest in the Process of Nation-Building.* Unpublished Ph.D. Thesis, University of Sussex.

——. 1979. "The Black Panthers: Conflict and Protest in Israeli Society", *Megamot* 25:79-65 (In Hebrew).

Blau, P. 1964. *Exchange and Power in Social Life.* New York: John Wiley.

——, and Scott, W. R. 1963. *Formal Organizations—A Comparative Approach.* London: Routledge and Kegan Paul.

Central Bureau of Statistics. 1951-1977. *Results of the Elections to the Knesset—Special Series.* Jerusalem. (In Hebrew.)

Cohen, A. (Ed.). 1974a. *Urban Ethnicity* (A.S.A. Monographs). London: Tavistock Publications.

——. 1974b. *Two Dimensional Man. An Essay on the Anthropology of Power and Symbolism in Complex Society.* Berkeley and Los Angeles: University of California Press.

Cohen, E. 1972. "The Black Panthers and Israeli Society", *Jewish Journal of Sociology*, Vol. XIV:93-109.
——, Shamgar, L., and Levi, Y. 1962. *Summary Report: Immigrant Absorption in a Development Town*. Jerusalem: Hebrew University (Hebrew).
Dahl, R. A. 1957. "The Concept of Power", *Behavioral Science*, Vol. II: 201-215.
Deshen, S. A. 1970. *Immigrant Voters in Israel*. Manchester: Manchester University Press.
——. 1972. "The Business of Ethnicity is Finished? The Ethnic Factor in a Local Election Campaign" in A. Arian (Ed.), *The Elections in Israel–1969*. Jerusalem: Academic Press, 278-302.
——. 1974. "Political Ethnicity and Cultural Ethnicity in Israel During the 1960's" in A. Cohen (Ed.), *Urban Ethnicity*. London: Rabistock Publications, 281-310.
——. 1976. "Ethnic Boundaries and Cultural Paradigms: The Case of Southern Tunisian Immigrants in Israel", *Ethos*, 4:271-294.
——. 1976. "Of Signs and Symbols: The Transformation of Designations in Israeli Electioneering", *Political Anthropologist*, 1 (3/4):83-100.
——. 1978. "Israeli Judaism: An Introduction to the Major Patterns", *International Journal of Middle Eastern Studies*, Vol. 9:141-169.
Despres, L. A. (Ed.). 1975. *Ethnicity and Resource Competition in Plural Societies*. The Hague, Paris: Mouton Publishers.
Erikson, K. Y. 1967. "Notes on the Sociology of Deviance" in Becker H. S. (Ed.), *The Other Side*. New York: The Free Press, 9-21.
Getter, M. 1979. "Immigration from Germany in 1933-1939", *Cathedra* 12:125-147. (In Hebrew.)
Gluska, Z. 1974. S. Gridi (Ed.), *On Behalf of Yemenite Jews*. Jerusalem: Ya'akov Ben David Gluska (Hebrew).
Goffman, E. 1963. *Stigma-Notes on The Management of Spoiled Identity*. Englewood Cliffs.: Prentice-Hall
Goitein, S. D. 1953. "Jewish Communal Life in Yemen", in *Mordechai M. Kaplan Jubilee Volume*. New York: The Jewish Theological Seminary of America, 43-61. (In Hebrew.)
Goldberg, H. 1977. "Culture and Ethnicity in the Study of Israeli Society", *Ethnic Groups* 1:163-186.
Greitzer, D. 1980. "The Settlement of Yemenite Immigrants at Kefar Marmorek – Between Separation and Integration", *Cathedra* 14 (January), 121-152. (In Hebrew.)
Gridi, S. 1943. *Yemenite Association Center in Palestine, 1923-1943*. Tel Aviv (Hebrew).
Guttman, E., and Lissak, M. (Eds.). 1977. *The Israeli Political System*. Tel Aviv: Am Oved Publishers Ltd., 122-170. (In Hebrew.)
Hall, Peter M. 1972. "A Symbolic Interactionist Analysis of Politics" in Andrew Effrat (Ed.), *Perspectives in Political Sociology*. New York: Bobbs-Merrill, 35-76.
Horowitz, D., and Lissak, M. 1978. *Origins of the Israeli Polity, Palestine under the Mandate*. Chicago and London: University of Chicago Press.
Lissak, M. 1972. "Continuity and Change in the Voting Patterns of Oriental Jews", in Arian Alan (Ed.), *The Elections In Israel–1969*. Jerusalem: Academic Press, 264-277.

178   HERZOG

Meyer, J. W., and Rowan, B. 1977. "Institutionalized Organizations: Formal Structures as Myth and Ceremony", *A.J.S.*, 83:440-463.
Nini, Y. 1976. *The Jewish Community in the Yemen in the 19th Century and the Immigration to Palestine until 1914*. Unpublished Ph.D. Thesis, Tel Aviv. (In Hebrew).
Peres, Y. 1976. *Ethnic Relations in Israel*. Tel Aviv: Sifriat Hapoalim. (In Hebrew.)
Perrow, C. 1979. *Complex Organizations: A Critical Essay*. Glenview: Scott, Foresman and Company.
Rubenstein, E. 1976. "From a Community to a State: Institutions and Parties", in B. Eliav (Ed.), *The Jewish National Home From the Balfour Declaration to Indepencence*. Jerusalem: Keter Publishing House. (In Hebrew.)
Sartori, G. 1969. "From the Sociology of Politics to Political Sociology" in S. M. Lipset (Ed.), *Politics and the Social Science*. Oxford: Oxford University Press, 65-100.
Shapiro, Y. 1976. *The Formative Years of the Israeli Labour Party: The Organization of Power, 1919-1930*. Beverly Hills and London: Sage.
——. 1977. *Democracy in Israel*. Ramat Gan: Massada. (In Hebrew.)
Smooha, S. 1978. *Israel: Pluralism and Conflict*. London: Routledge and Kegan Paul.
——, and Peres, Y. 1975. "The Dynamics of Ethnic Inequalities: The Case of Israel", *Social Dynamics* 1 (1) (June): 63-79.
Stone, L. 1971. "Prosopography", *Daedalus*, Winter, 46-79.
Strauss, A. 1963. "The Hospital and its Negotiated Order" in Eliot Friedson (Ed.), *The Hospital in Modern Society*. New York: The Free Press.
——. 1978. *Negotiations–Varieties, Contexts, Processes and Social Order*. San Francisco, Washington, London: Jossey-Bass Publishers.
Tabib, A. 1943. *Immigration and Settlement of the Jews of Yemen in Palestine*. (Unpublished paper), Tel Aviv (In Hebrew.)
Tsadok, M. 1967. *Yemenite Jews–Their History and Ways of Life*. Tel Aviv: Am Oved. (In Hebrew.)
Weingrod, A. 1965. *Israel–Group Relations in a New Society*. London: Pall Mall Press.
––. 1979. "Recent Trends in Israeli Ethnicity", *Ethnic and Racial Studies* 2:55-65.
Yancey, W. L., Ericksen, E. P., and Juliani, R. N. 1976. "Emergent Ethnicity: A Review and Preformulation", *A.S.R.*, 41:391-403.
Yeshayahu, Y., and Gridi, S. (Eds.). 1938. *From Yemen to Zion*. Tel Aviv: Massada, (In Hebrew).
Zamir, R. 1966. "Beersheba 1958-59: Social Processes in a Development Town" in S. N. Eisenstadt *et al., The Social Structure of Israel*. Jerusalem: Academon. (In Hebrew.)
Zeira, D. 1950. *Orient vs. Progress*. Tel Aviv: Cultural Center of Hapoel Hamizrachi. (In Hebrew.)

9

Historical and Cultural Dimensions of Ethnic Phenomena in Israel

Harvey E. Goldberg

One of the complex conceputal problems regarding ethnicity in Israel is the relationship of history to ethnic phenomena. It is well known that the history of ethnic groups was given minimum attention in the sociological study of the mass immigration of the early 1950s (Goldberg, 1977). Content to sociologize history, the immigrants were categorized into those who came from "traditional," "modern" or "transitional" backgrounds by social scientists whose main focus was on the (then) contemporary development of the society and its institutions. Their argument (Ben-David, 1953) was that it would be mistaken to treat each immigrant group as if it were an island tribe, focusing on its particular history and culture and thus ignoring the pervasive political and economic frameworks within which the absorption of all the groups was taking place. In addition, it was claimed that the newcomers had little interest in maintaining their original cultures—being oriented toward rapid and successful integration into the new society. Thus, aside from a general understanding of background and cultural dispositions, these two factors made detailed historical study irrelevant to the question of "the absorption of immigrants." Studies from that period characteristically ignored the opportunity to collect in-depth information on social and cultural forms in the countries of origin of the immigrants.

Ostensibly, this stance with regard to history and culture had much to recommend it. In terms of material culture, most of the former belongings of the immigrants were quickly sloughed off, the immigrants wearing clothes appropriate to the new society and discarding tools that had no use in an industrial economy. Many came with no capital, even those who might have been relatively well off by the standards of their pre-immigration situation. Formal communal institutions to which the immigrants had been attached immediately became irrelevant, and the demands of nuclear family organization, rather than some sort of extended arrangement (to the extent that these had existed in the past), were apparent. It is thus understandable that the immigrants were assumed to be close to a *tabula rasa* in respect to the expectation that they would adjust to the new environment. Concrete expressions of continuity in cultural form were not immediately apparent except in the customs and dress of older people and in "mistaken" perceptions of the new social forms (see discussion of religion below). Often, when the impress of the past was invoked in reference to current behavior, the focus was one-sided, stressing problematic aspects of the absorption process. If we wish to explore the historical and cultural dimensions of the absorption process systematically, a more adequate formulation of the nature of culture and its dynamics in relation to immigrant adjustment is called for. The vantage point of close to 30 years of hindsight allows us to point to events and empirical trends that might have been better understood had greater attention been paid to the concept of culture. In addition, it allows us to bring to bear theoretical perspectives in the study of cultures that have developed during that same period.

We have used the terms culture and history in an almost interchangeable fashion, and it is time to clarify the intention of this usage. By culture, we refer to learned systems of meaning, embodied in symbolic forms, which both define and express human action. It is culture, unique in its complexity to human beings, which makes history possible. It is through the transmission of symbols that events and experiences directly affecting one set of human beings become relevant to other human beings, regardless of whether or not that second set of individuals have undergone the specific experience. Without culture, history is inconceivable. Culture, by the same token, is a historical product, constantly in flux, but reflecting the accumulated (and discarded) culturally coded experiences of others, and thereby continually shaping further reactions and interpretations. This perspective on culture is taken for granted by many scholars as the "frame-

work" for understanding social action and, therefore, is not considered
illuminating with regard to any specific sequence of social events. It is our
claim, however, that precisely because we tend to take human beings' cul-
ture-bearing capacities for granted, that we tend to overlook the cultural
dimensions of certain social events and developments. An example, I believe, is the very fact that the mass migration to Israel by hundreds of
thousands of people from dozens of different countries, is often taken for
granted as the starting point for analysis, while the event itself is not subject to cultural scrutiny.

To elaborate on this point, let us summon the anthropologist's ubiquit-
ous helper, a man from Mars. Envision our Martian descending to earth in
the years 1948-1952, and observing the migration of people from diverse
points of the globe, who superficially are quite different from one another
and who were economically and socially enmeshed in their original societies, to a small country whose existence seems, as best, precarious. While
in each instance the migration might be explained in a different manner
(in terms of economic factors here or political factors there), the phenomenon as a whole can only be explained by taking into account the
meanings associated with the term Jew, Jewish, and the history(ies) shaping those varied (and even contradictory) meanings. Moreover, it is suggested that certain aspects of the absorption process and the nation-
building that followed can only be understood by paying more explicit
attention to the significance of the cultural notion than has been given in
the past. That the Jewishness of the new state immediately came to be
taken for granted does not make the notion any less important. On the
contrary, one can argue that the switch from being a marked to an unmarked category (as encapsulated in the phrase: "In Morocco I was a
Jew, here I am a Moroccan"), gave the various forms of the now unmarked Jewish identification even greater potency as a cultural focus for
unchallenged loyalty. If this brief example holds any validity, it shows
that a more sophisticated and dynamic notion of culture is called for than
that employed by social analysis at the time.

There are further implications to the explicit recognition of Jewishness
as a cultural category. The Jewishness of the immigrants must be seen as
something that was carried in each individual's "mind." While not deny-
ing the socialized nature of human cognition, the migration situation in
which individuals are uprooted from their original settings highlights the
fact that culture is something that people carry about within them "in
their heads." Even taking into account "non-mental" indications of

Jewishness, such as circumcision, it must be appreciated that this sign of identification takes on significance only when interpreted according to conventional understandings. We are thus forced to face the fact that culture is made up of meanings, processed by human beings' special mental capacities, even while these meanings are made manifest in the public sphere of the spoken word, social interaction, or material objects. Thus, if evidence of the impact of culture in its older ethnographic sense was apparent to only a limited degree in the absorption process, this should not detract our attention from culture as a real (even if "intangible") factor capable of giving meaning to the experience of absorption (or lack thereof) into the new society, and thereby shaping the historical course of different absorption trajectories.

Thus far we have tried to show that a concept of culture, as an ever-changing distillate of history, was required from the very outset in the study of the mass immigration, even though the sociology of that period developed analytic tools that de-emphasized the culture concept. Moreover, the experience of the past thirty years has shown us clearly that the process of absorption, with respect to the question of ethnicity, is much more complex than originally thought. While the central institutions of the absorbing society (political parties, Histadrut, school, army) have had a major effect on all the ethnic groups, the overall outcome cannot be reduced to a simple model in which there is a continuing shedding of ethnic baggage, along with an evermore close approximation to a model of homogeneous and ethnicity-free "Israeli society." The reawakening of ethnicity that has been in evidence for more than a decade cannot be viewed as the simple inertia of culture traits—a survival that is ultimately doomed. While these phenomena certainly have to be understood in terms of current social developments within the society, their interpretation also demands an adequate cultural theory of how cultural forms from the past relate to changing realities in new social situations. I do not believe that the social science disciplines have such an overreaching theory, but I shall attempt to point to some of the empirical phenomena in Israeli society and the conceptual issues related to these phenomena, that such a theory will have to take into account.

Before turning to these specific examples, it is perhaps worth discussing some of the features of modern culture theory to which we refer. Although these theoretical points were not completely unknown thirty years ago, I think it is fair to say that they have become much more central in the analysis of social forms and processes since that time. The examples that we shall soon present will indicate how these perspectives might have enriched the analysis of ethnic phenomena.

It is now generally accepted that culture, while carrying the weight of history, can be manipulated by individuals (and groups) so that it is not to be viewed as a monolithic force from the past, but as a set of potentialities seized upon by actors in dynamic social contexts. The manipulability of culture should not make us forget the other side of the coin, that culture is worth manipulating precisely because these symbols from the past are effective in shaping contemporary behavior. It should be recognized (Deshen, 1974) that one of the objects of human striving is meaning, most generally religious meaning, so that cultural symbols can be manipulated in the drive toward salvation, and not only toward economic and political goals, even though these may be closely intertwined.

It is now apparent that culture is a complex, ever changing, and multi-leveled phenomenon. Simple terms like "continuity" and "change" are hardly adequate to specify the impact of a cultural heritage on the present. The work of Levi-Strauss, Turner, Schneider and others have shown how symbols can be inverted, camouflaged, situationally emphasized, ignored, or taken for granted so that the task of specifying the impact of these bundles or meaning from the past on the present is enormously challenging. The answer to this challenge, however, is not to throw up one's hands and claim that the clue to people's actions lies solely in their present situation and goals. This is because the very definition of that situation, and the goals that people cherish, partake, inexorably, of cultural forms which took shape in a historical process.

With these general thoughts in mind, we may briefly discuss several topics in the realm of ethnicity in Israel, which may be advanced when seen through the lenses of more recent cultural theory. These topics are: the immigration process, demography, social relations, ethnic boundaries, ethnic stereotypes, and religion.

The Immigration Process

Understandably we have little systematic data of a social anthropological nature about the events of immigration and the most immediate reactions of immigrants upon arrival in Israel. Theoretical statements relating to this phase of migration are usually negative—stating what is absent rather than suggesting substantive content to the process. We refer to Eisenstadt's formulation (1953) of the shrinking of social ties and networks and the development by Bar-Yosef of the notion of desocialization and resocialization (1968). There is no doubt that the movement from one country to another cuts the individual off from a set of social ties and routinized expectations, but are individuals and groups undergoing this process to be characterized only by what is missing in comparison to the former situation? In *The Ritual Process*, Turner (1969) emphasized that the simplification of structure in the sociological sense is often accompanied by the elaboration of structure in the Levi-Straussian (symbolic) sense. Is there any way of recovering, from novels, memoirs, or oral history, the impressions, visions, hopes and fears, which undoubtedly shifted with great rapidity, of immigrants during the process of immigration and immediate contact with the new society? These highly personalized documents will show cultural imprints, both of the past and of an envisioned future, which at first is largely conceptualized on the basis of past (cultural) experiences. Assuming that such data can be recovered and organized, is there any way of relating them to the more regularized and routinized responses that later came to characterize the various paths of absorption?

In her paper on *Desocialization and Resocialization,* Bar-Yosef (1968) states that little attention has been paid to the material environment in relation to the process of absorption. This remains the case today. Some anecdotal data with regard to physical matters, however, may give clues as to how the new present was viewed in terms of the past and how images of each may be assimilated to one another. The Jews of Libya arrived in the country *en masse* from 1949-1951. After initial processing at *Sha'ar ha Aliyah* (Near the Haifa port), many were directed to the *ma'abarah* (transit camp) at Bet Lid. Today, Netanya (near Bet Lid) is one of the centers of Libyan Jews in the country. It thus appears that the immigrant had little choice but to accept the *ma'abarah* selected by the Jewish Agency, and then settle down in a nearby town. Casual conversations with informants, however, reveal that the situation was not completely one-sided. The first Tripolitanian arrivals at Bet Lid often sent letters back to Tripoli to tell their relatives to request the Bet Lid camp upon arrival. One of the leaders of the Libyan community in the camp was Rabbi Frija Zuaretz, later a member of the Knesset fo the Mafdal (National Religious Party). Born in Tripoli, Zuaretz spent most of his life as a rabbi in a small town east of the capital named Khoms. Khoms is a coastal city, surrounded by sands. Zuaretz told me that when he first saw Netanya he said to himself "this is Khoms." Immigrants from Tripoli, also a coastal town, have told me the same. We are not proposing a new theory of factors making for successful absorption, but what is suggested is that much more can be learned about the way that people take stressful, unclear and changing situations and make them more meaningful by linking them to the past.

In a similar vein, I have sometimes noticed that people in *moshavim* in the 1960s (cooperative villages) grew plants in their gardens that were not fitted to the region in terms of Israeli agriculture. In Mesillat Zion in the Judean Hills, for example, one could find banana trees in many yards. In Porat, in the Sharon, many people attempted to grow grapes on a trellis attached to their homes. Upon questioning one finds that the growing of grape vines was common in the region of Tripolitania from which the Poratniks came, and that the Cochinis of Mesillat Zion hailed from a banana-growing region, even though they themselves did not work at cultivating the plant. Is it not possible to see in these seemingly peripheral activities an attempt to reconstruct a past which, despite the problems of minority status, marginality, and even outright persecution was still regarded as "home?" And is it not further possible that the ability to selectively indulge one's nostalgia by giving it cultural expression is significant in gaining strength to cope with current exigencies? If such a process is at work in the making and interpreting of the material world, may it not be at work with regard to the social world as well?

Demography

The influence of the past, and the attempt to remake the present in its (selectively remembered) image can be found in many aspects of social life, including such a weighty topic as demography. Among the Jews of Libya, there is a clear connection between those who formally lived in market towns in the Tripolitanian countryside and present day moshav dwellers on the one hand (Goldberg, 1972), and between former Tripolitans (from the city of Tripoli) and those who are found in the urban concentrations of Netanya, Bat Yam and Ashkelon, on the other. Of course, there are examples of former "villagers" who live here in urban centers and, to a much lesser extent, former Tripolitans who are settled on moshavim, but such mobility had taken place in Libya as well.

Available demographic data do not include community of origin, so that knowledge concerning other groups is only impressionistic. In a brief survey of moshavim performed five years ago, in which I attempted to locate former residents of Tunisian towns, I was struck by the number of times that I was told that, in a given moshav, people from the city of Tunis used to live there, but had moved to Ramle, or some other city, leaving the moshav more homogeneous in terms of people from "small town" origins. It seemed as if people who originally had moved "from town to village," i.e., from the city of Tunis to a moshav, were more likely to move again to a city after becoming economically established in Israel, while the former small-town dwellers were more likely to continue to reside in moshavim.

It is likely that the same holds true for other ethnic groups (including Europeans). Very few Baghdadis are found in the moshavim categorized as Iraqi, and many Moroccan moshavim are inhabited by former residents of villages and small towns. If this is true, then there is a significant factor of self-selection based on expectations and values carried and reactivated from the past that has yet to be described. It may also mean that the concentration of ethnic groups in different development towns, analyzed by Spillerman and Habib (1976) not only reflects the lack of choice of the immigrants and the short-sighted absorption of policies of the bureaucracy, but may stem from a certain degree of self-imposed homogeneity on the part of the newcomers themselves.

Social Relations

In the realm of social organization we have several well documented studies showing the influences of history, which at the same time take full account of the present vortex of social forces. Shokeid (1972) and Goldberg (1972) have each provided studies of rural North African communities that were resettled in moshavim. In both instances, patterns from and references to the past had to be taken into account in understanding the contemporary situation. Shokeid explicitly makes theoretical allowance for what he calls "the reference situation." Despite the uniformity of the moshav framework into which both these communities were absorbed, the difference in social structure that emerged in each should alert us to the importance of history. Deshen's work in Ayara (1970), a town more complex than the moshavim cited above, has also attempted to relate meaningfully to the past. Several of Deshen's analyses stress the point that the past may make itself felt in a negative fashion, and not just as a straightforward replication of earlier patterns (Deshen and Shokeid, 1974). Deshen has shown how Tunisian immigrants evaluate their religious behavior with reference to past standards and, finding themselves wanting, have either relinquished patterns of behavior that they found themselves unable to maintain or have tried to recoup their sense of religious merit by adhering to modified forms easier to maintain in the Israeli setting. In either instance, the continuation of patterns from the past in the minds of individuals, reinterpreted as those patterns might be, is an essential ingredient in shaping the unfolding situation.

As stated earlier, the situation in development towns is more complex than that in moshavim, from an ethnic or stratification viewpoint, and one cannot expect to usefully view any single town as an example of a transplanted community. Nevertheless, there are a number of different towns in which a high percentage of the residents originate from Morocco and in which Moroccans have become prominent in running municipal affairs. One wonders what sort of description would emerge upon looking at these towns in terms of patron-client relations characteristic of Morocco's cities, as analyzed, for example, by Kenneth Brown (1977). More precisely, perhaps, it would be interesting to study the process of reinterpretation, whereby the Israeli system of patronage, rooted in party organization, was assimilated to a rather different model of dependency/manipulation relationships. In addition, it would be fruitful, perhaps, to look for threads of historical continuity in organizational forms other than those based on locality. Examples that come to mind are certain occupations (perhaps varying by city) or the many ethnic organizations that now exist, whether their purpose be economic, political or cultural (or, what is more likely, a combination of these). Focusing on these organizational forms in specific settings, and tracing networks of relationships backwards in time, as well as synchronically outward, are likely to reveal ties to the past, both at the sociological level and in the realm of the conceptualization of social relationships.

Cultural Continuity and Non-Jewish Communities Abroad

It has been suggested that certain aspects of ethnic phenomena may be understandable in terms of patterns characterizing the general, non-Jewish society abroad. Here, if anywhere, a more up-to-date view of cultural transmission and transformation is required. Of course, there are some simple examples of individual culture traits relating to food, dress and speech forms that were common to a society as a whole, and have been perpetuated to a greater or lesser (usually lesser) degree in Israel. It is suggested, however, that certain features of the non-Jewish environment may have become prominent in Israel, even though they were not common to Jews in their original setting. Palgi (1975) has analyzed how the smoking of hashish, virtually absent among Jews in Morocco, became accepted in certain circumstances among Moroccan Jews in Israel. Kimur (1980) has shown how some Persian Jews began to organize and participate in a ceremony associated with the discipline of a Moslem religious order in Iran, after these Jews had been settled in Israel. It is possible that examples of this cultural transposition may be found in the realm of social relations as well.

We recall once more the thorny issue of the *hamulot* (Middle Eastern patrilineages) discussed by sociologists and anthropologists with reference to immigrant moshavim in the 1950s and 1960s, and the question of whether these forms of social organization were to be understood as the continuation of patterns from the past, or as a species of factionalism induced by the pressures of social change in a new situation (see Shokeid, 1968). While it now appears that there is probably no single answer to this question, Moroccan "hamulot" may not be the same as Kurdish "hamulot," and so forth, it probably is the case that nowhere in recent times were Jewish communities organized along the model of classic lineages familiar to anthropologists. In particular, as landowning on the part of Jews in the rual Middle East was limited or nonexistent, the organization for access to, and defense and regular transmission of land, is not likely to have been prominent. Upon arrival on a moshav, however, these Jews were instantly placed in a situation somewhat similar to that of their non-Jewish neighbors abroad (or at least perceived by them as such), whereby land and water became crucial and, perhaps, open for competition. The possibility of forming coalitions with others, in order to maximize one's own interests or prevent encroachment by others, became available. In such a situation it is possible that people were first guided by models of organization employed by their non-Jewish neighbors abroad, even though these forms had not been common within the Jewish community itself. Hence, the appearance of "hamulot."

At present this line of analysis is offered only as a suggestion. I should note, however, that this interpretation is similar to the often cited notion that Israel political organization is (was) reminiscent of politics in Eastern

Europe, despite the limited direct experience of Jewish immigrants to Palestine with these political forms. In any event, the claim that the continuity of historical influence is often more complex than that of the inertia of a set of traits within a specific social group is further underlined.

The importance of this question is highlighted by Geertz's recent remarks (Geertz *et al.* 1979:164) concerning communal organization in Sefrou: "The Jews were at once Sefrouis like any others and resoundingly themselves. . . . Many of their institutions were direct counterparts to Muslim ones. . . . But the way those institutions were put together was in such sharp contrast to the Muslim way as to be almost an answer to it." Such a formulation certainly raises important issues about the interpretation of forms of "Jewish" behavior in the immigrant situation, to say nothing of the understanding of Jewish life in North Africa itself.

Ethnic Boundaries

The previous discussion of how "non-Jewish" traits abroad became the markers of Jewish ethnic groups within Israel brings us to one of the most complex questions concerning ethnicity in modern society, that dealing with group boundaries. The term "ethnic," divorced from the semi-racial connotation that once characterized it, has had at least two main associations in modern social science. One is the concern with ethnic groups in modern societies—the case of the U.S. and its many immigrant populations being one of the best studied instances. The other meaning is closely linked to the anthropological term "culture," in the combined sense that "culture" was often used in American anthropology as both a group of people and a characteristic set of lifeways.

In recent work, these two perspectives have become analytically sorted out, following, in large part, Barth's seminal essay on the importance of ethnic boundaries (1969). The focus on ethnic boundaries shows how cultural traits may persist, even in reshaped form, not so much because of intrinsic value assigned their content, but because they mark and help perpetuate boundaries between social groups, which are useful for these groups to maintain for economic, political or other reasons. This is an example of cultural transformation *par excellence* which, in addition, has the capability of hiding the social factors that give it its potency. A culture trait (food, celebration, holiday and so forth) that may have simply been part of a non-ethnicized inventory of traits turns into a symbol of

belongingness and rootedness in the past. In doing so, it creates an illusion
of distinctiveness, while at the same time disguising the fact that in modern industrial social settings ethnic groups frequently have entered into the
same arena of competition for culturally-defined valued resources, so that
what they have in common (but care not to admit) is the presupposition
of the newly developed emblems of their particularity.

This analysis would seem to argue against the importance of culture
in understanding modern ethnic phenomena, but such a conclusion is
hasty for several reasons: First, even granting that the definition of ethnic
boundaries and the highlighting of culture traits that mark these boundaries is a process that is manipulated in the striving for economic gain and
political advantage, it does not appear that there is an unlimited ability to
create or dissolve categories at will. Manipulation normally takes place
within the limits of cultural definitions considered acceptable, plausible,
or real by the actors in question. This point will be exemplified shortly.

Secondly, even if it is true that many ethnic groups have become similar
to one another in their basic definition of valued societal goals, it cannot
be overlooked that these goals are no less cultural for being widespread
or even universal. Thus, we should not forget Weber's lesson that the
modern Western configuration of cultural symbols that motivate economic
behavior arose in specific historical conditions, and therefore must be
recognized as a particular complex of meaning (no matter how it has
spread), which does not characterize all societies at all times. The fact that
universality does not equal non-cultural should be recognized in the case
of Israeli society as well. The question of how similar ethnic groups have
grown to one another in terms of their basic values, definitions of reality
and so forth, can only be assessed with the aid of adequately documented
studies of how different they were to begin with. It is my feeling that, if
such studies were possible to carry out, we would find many commonal-
ities at the deepest levels of culture among the Jews of Europe, North
Africa and the Middle East, despite the obvious superficial differences
distinguishing them. If so, the formation of a common core of meanings
in the new society and State of Israel must be understood at a more basic
level than the evaluation of the effectiveness of one or another policy or
institutional framework in bringing about "absorption." This, too, as we
have said, is a task still to be done.

Thirdly, the flexibility and manipulability of culture does not necessarily call for its demotion in importance. On the contrary, that cultural
forms can be added to, subtracted from, turned on their heads, and

invested with new meanings, perhaps points to culture as the most significant mechanism of all in understanding how people adapt to new settings. Is it not this plasticity of human behavior, made possible by the lack of genetic fixity upon which culture flourishes, that anthropologists celebrate as the hallmark of our humanity, and the special quality of our behavior in comparison to other social animals? To ignore this special feature of culture, just because it is so "slippery" and difficult to demonstrate by the methods borrowed from experimental sciences, is to take for granted precisely those features of culture that are in the greatest need of explanation.

Ethnic Definitions: Inside, Outside and Structural Views

I have discussed some of the theoretical implications of the manipulability of the symbols of ethnic boundaries. It was argued that even though the symbols are plastic, their plasticity is not infinite. This is true if for no other reason than that very often the manipulators of ethnic symbols who are pushing in one direction are opposed by other manipulators who have different, or even opposite purposes. The collection of studies of Arabs and Berbers, edited by Gellner and Micaud (1972) shows, on the one hand, how the French had an interest in hardening these ethnic categories in a way that did not accord with traditional usage and, on the other hand, how they were unsuccessful in this redefinition, despite their political domination of Moroccan society during the colonial period. We thus see that the generalization that "a group of people discriminated against because of their origin will eventually identify themselves as an ethnic group" (Peres, 1976:43) requires much further specification in terms of the given historical circumstances.

In the case of Israeli society, too, we have found that a new social situation has resulted in new attempts to define ethnic boundaries, but that the outcome of these attempts are not necessarily in accord with the intentions of the manipulators. A case in point is the category of *edot hamizrah* ("Eastern communities" or "ethnic groups"). It has been argued vigorously that this term has little meaning as a legitmate historical classification (Ben-Sasson, 1979). Even those who find it a useful notion to bring together research efforts in directions that hitherto have been neglected, do not deny the important differences in the historical contexts shaping (for example) the development of Jewish life in Morocco, Yemen and Iraq. The term *edot hamizrah* may best be seen, in its initial usage, as a way of labeling a bewildering medley of "others" who, in the space of a few years, had a massive impact on the previously ethnically homogeneous Jewish population (Willner, 1969). At this same period, there was a vague anxiety that all the Middle Eastern immigrants would organize and thereby dislodge the (old-timer) Europeans from their established political positions, or severely alter the existing balance of forces among the then extant parties. For this reason, there was an agreement among the old-timers to disperse the newcomers, insofar as was possible, within the existing party structure. This complex of events, in itself, raises the question of whether the creation of ethnic categories always serves the expressed purpose of the manipulators, for surely one way to set a group of people on the road to political self-consciousness is to put in practice a policy based on a designation that presumes their unity.

In terms of the actual developments within Israel society, I believe it is fair to say that the notion of Israeli society being divided into two broad segments has received general acceptance, among Middle Easterners as well as among Europeans, but not in any simple way. It is significant that it receives legitimate recognition in specific contexts, and that it appears in different linguistic and conceptual guises in the various contexts where it is acceptable. In this way the sense of a basic split running from one end to another of the social fabric is, so to speak, patched up.

For example, the Central Bureau of Statistics (and many other sociological studies) divides the immigrants into those who have come from Asia-Africa and those who have come from Europe-America, while the Ministry of Education recognizes the category of *te'unei tipuah* (those who require special care of "culturally deprived").

Another division of the same ministry has been set up to enrich the general curriculum with *moreshet yahadut hamizrah,* materials dealing with the tradition of the Jews of the East, where the absence of the term *edot* (ethnic communities) is conspicuous. Thus, the ambivalence inherent in the view that the society is divided into two halves, and that one half is preferable to the other, is situationally overcome by rephrasing the notion in terms appropriate to the issue in question. We also see how a sociological generalization (such as that concerning self-identification, above) must be refined in terms of the specific cultural and linguistic forms that constitute the social process in question.

The situations just discussed, in which the division of the society into two components, an Eastern and a Western, is institutionalized and thus, to a significant degree, acceptable, are all related to public policy and administration. It seems, however, that the closer one gets to Middle Eastern Jews' self-labeling, the more one finds that narrower categories such as Yemenite, Moroccan and Kurd are meaningful. One gets the impression that the notion of *edot hamizrah* is found as a form of self-definition among the young, and is associated with social protest as in the case of the Israeli Black Panthers (Mendes-Flohr, 1976), but that Middle Eastern individuals who are married and who have families are more likely to place themselves within the context of a specific ethnic group or see themselves as non-ethnic Israelis (Ben-Rafael, 1980). It is, of course, the case that these more specific categories also partially reflect the impact of European Israelis (Goldberg, 1977), but we argue that the legitimacy of these labels, too, is a function of their acceptability to the groups in question, and that this acceptability relates to the ease with which these categories can be seen as making sense given the meanings they carry with them from the past.

Ethnic Stereotypes

If we take a step back from the preceding analysis, we see that it is based on several methodological assumptions basic to modern cultural theory. Individual terms are placed in a field of meaning, and their interpretation depends on their relationship to other terms in the field. The fact that they come from separate institutional spheres (Moroccan from the sphere of ethnicity, *te'unei tipuach* from the sphere of education), does not preclude them from being analyzed as a part of the same semantic field at the cultural level. Finally, while each of these terms has its own history, a historical analysis is not incompatible with a synchronic analysis, which aims to find structural relations between the various cultural elements in a field of meaning. We believe that it is useful to maintain this perspective, not only with regard to standard ethnic labels, but also with regard to well known ethnic stereotypes in Israel society.

While from a demographic point of view Israeli society is made up of immigrants from scores of different countries, there are a few ethnic categories that are prominent in the public consciousness, and which carry strong value-laden associations, while other terms are relatively less salient. On an intuitive basis, it seems to me that among the three most prominent stereotyped categories of Middle Eastern Jews are Moroccans, Yemenites and Kurds. This is very clearly something that changes with time, as the notion of *Gruzini* gained attention only after the Georgian Jews began to leave the Soviet Union in large numbers, and one gets the impression that *Parsi* (Persian) is used with much greater frequency these days than in the past The discussion that follows assumes that at a given time period (1950s-1960s) the *Morokkai, Teimani* and *Kurdi* (Moroccan, Yemenite and Kurd), were simultaneously prominent, and that these stereotypes may be understood as a part of a field of meaning, and not as individual items whose approximation to correctness is open to assessment.

In an earlier paper (Goldberg, 1977), it was pointed out that in Israel the ethnicity of Jews, coming under the rubric of *edot,* and the ethnicity of Arabs, known as the question of *mi'utim* (minorities), were seen as two separate "topics," despite various *prima facie* reasons for treating them within the same terms of reference. To my knowledge, only Peres (1976) has sought to find meaningful links among these categories. His work focuses on the social-psychological level and shows a tendency of Middle Eastern Jews to reject the qualities that might identify them with Arabs. I believe this line of thought can be developed at the cultural level, placing the terms of ethnic stereotyping within a broad field of meaning relating to basic problems of Israeli society.

Today we are acutely aware of the basic question concerning the place of the Arab population within Israeli society. From an objective point of view, the question has always been present and basic, but at certain periods of time before 1967 it seems to have had the status of an after-thought in large segments of Israeli Jewry. If this "denial" reflects a kind of cultural defense mechanism, and not simply innocent neglect, then we would expect, following the Freudian analogy, an expression of the re-pressed cultural energy in another sphere. We suggest here, in a tentative way, that the heavy and problematic focus on the question of the ethnic-ity of Middle Eastern immigrants in the 1950s and 1960s, in part repre-sented a transformed concern, on the part of European Israelis, as to the "Jewishness" of the society, with the implicit assumption that the "oppo-site" of "Jewish" is "Arab." There were, of course, explicit statements of this concern, such as the problem of "Levantinization," which clearly has euphemistic functions, suggests, these issues could only be brought into the public sphere in a limited degree, with frequent shifts in terminol-ogy, providing a smokescreen for the abiding anxiety over the "Arabiza-tion" (a term that no one used) of the society on the part of the new im-migrants.

While the terms Arab and Jewish may often appear as paired opposites in Israeli contexts, the content of the relationship between the terms, from the Jewish point of view, is by no means simple. On the one hand, there is the element of aggression perceived by Jews as emanating from the other side, in spite of a lack of any evil intentions on the part of the Jewish settlers. The Jews, for their part, cannot understand why someone should resent them, when they are mostly interested in the development of the country, a notion that takes for granted Arab backwardness. The clinging on the part of Arab peasants to traditional ways, however, is not only negative in the eyes of Jewish Israelis, but symbolizes rootedness, which the Jewish newcomers (notably those of the first *Aliyah*), paradoxical as it may sound, strove to achieve. The opposition, then, of Arab versus Jews, whose meaning also changes over time, carries within it a complex of associations wrapped, as it were, into a single bundle. This bundle of meaning, we suggest, is also relevant to understanding the Jewish ethnic stereotypes, mentioned above.

Recalling the three *edot* mentioned earlier, we suggest that each of them corresponds to one of the main strands of the Jewish-Arab bundle. Thus, Moroccans were associated with aggression (*marokkai sakin,* Moroccans wield a knife), Kurds with simple backwardness ("Primitiviut" signalled by *ana kurdi*), and Yemenites with rootedness, a concept summed up in the recently fashionable notion of *giz'i* (somewhat parallel to the notion of "soul" in the United States, but used in different contexts). Thus, the same cathexes, to use an old Freudian/Parsonian term, directed at the Arabs by European Jews, were also directed at Middle Eastern Jews, but in a separate and individual manner. In this way, the similarity between the two sets of evaluations was hidden, and the official notion of Jews being different from Arabs left unchallenged. At the same time, the similarity was asserted at a non-conscious level so that the Middle Eastern Jews were not fully aware of the source of their victimization or, in the case of the Yemenites, of their favored status. The European Jews, for their part, were protected from the guilt of treating fellow Jews "as Arabs," and were allowed to believe that these stereotypes had a basis in objective characteristics of the different ethnic groups. This cultural mechanism also contributed to the separation of identities of Middle Eastern Jews and Arabs, a process that built upon the firmly established religious identities that had separated the two groups abroad. This line of interpretation, of course, should be tested with field data and/or with more structured types of investigation. The main claim is that contemporary cultural theory suggests that ethnic stereotyping is not only a pan-human sociological tendency, but takes on specific content in given cultural/historical conditions.

Religion

The topic of religion provides the last example of the importance of appreciating the cultural dimension of ethnic phenomena. The subject of religion in Israel has been discussed in relation to ethnicity from a number of different perspectives. Deshen has documented how religious parties manipulated traditional symbols in the effort to win and maintain the loyalties of North African immigrant groups (1970). Peres (1976) has noted that the religious split and the ethnic split in Israeli society cross-cut one another, thereby mitigating the conflict that might result were these divisions to correspond with one another. A number of authors have claimed that the religious split in Israel is the most basic one in the society's value system (Abramov, 1976; Leslie, 1971; Zucker, 1973) over-riding other issues such as "socialism" vs. "liberalism", or even the ethnic segmentation. It is useful, I maintain, to specifically identify the cultural aspect of these questions.

First, it should be noted that, while diverse religious, ethnic and political categories exist in many societies, the conceptualization of the interrelationship of these different domains of action is a cultural matter. The organization of religion into political frameworks, taken for granted by many Israelis, is strange, if not abrasive, to many immigrants from North America. It is not only a question of which cultural conceptions are linked together, however, but a matter of their hierarchical arrangement. In Dumont's terms (1970) one would want to know which of these culturally defined spheres of social action is encompassing and which is encompassed. From this perspective there is little question that the religious/political split is hierarchically prior to the ethnic split, so that the religious/political division shapes the conception of ethnicity more so than the other way around. An example of what is meant can be found in the realm of education.

There has been a recent awakening to the lack of attention paid to the history of Middle Eastern Jewry in the Israeli educational system, and everyone is agreed that this situation should be changed. The split between the state elementary schools, and the state religious elementary schools (Klineberger, 1969), an outgrowth of the basic cultural conceptions (themselves a historical product), just discussed, has a distinct effect on how the question of Middle Eastern Jewish culture is treated in the curriculum.

A school defined as religious would have little difficulty in incorporating into its curriculum topics such as learned rabbis, communal organization centering on the synagogue, kosher slaughtering, and charity linked to the Sabbath and holidays, institutions that were important in the organization of most of the traditional Middle Eastern communities. As these topics are familiar to their students and teachers, it is "natural" to discuss them in the context of Middle Eastern Jewish communities. A school defined as "non-religious" has a certain discomfort with these topics, and even though these subjects are a central part of understanding the social history of Middle Eastern Jewry, cannot easily present these topics within the existing curriculum. Instead, the development of a curriculum of programs to deal with Middle Eastern Jewish cultures in a secular school is likely to seize upon food, dance, dress and other "folklorist" items. The intellectual bankruptcy of such a forced division is apparent. Our main point, at the present, however, is to indicate how the religious split in the society, at the cultural level, is hierarchical in its relationship to the ethnic split (and not crosscutting in the sociological sense), in that it dominates the form that the latter takes.

It is the nature of central cultural conceptions that they are taken for granted and become common sense in the societies in which they are found. Even when explitictly pointed out, members of a society may not appreciate the peculiarity of their own conceptions. This is particularly the case when those who point to these special configurations are immigrants from a putatively "less educated" background. For example, it was often cited, in discussing the "naivete" of the Middle Eastern immigrants in the 1950s, that an individual asked the question of why he became less observant in Israel than he had been abroad would reply with the statement: "*Ani lo data; ani Mapai*" (I am not religious; I belong to the Mapai party). A European Israeli describing such an incident would paternalistically smile at the unfamiliarity with modern politics demonstrated by his newly arrived, but still "backward" fellow citizen. The argument can be made, however, that the perception of the Israeli scene reflected in this statement is veridical, that in Israel "religion" in many ways is politics, and that it is the smug European who was deceiving himself. Since that time, many Middle Easterners have been "coopted" into the system on the cultural level in the sense that they too view the concept *dati* (religious) as an undifferentiated religious/political bundle. This holds true for those who see themselves as "dati" as well as those who label themselves as non-religious, and who may find ethnic identification in activities like football (Deshen 1978). This cooptation reflects the hierarchical nature of the religious split vis-a-vis the ethnic. If the ethnic division were to encompass the religious segmentation (rather than the other way around), the nature of the social splits and alliances would be quite different from those at present (perhaps more akin to the Black-White situation in the United States). In any event, it is claimed that explicit attention to a cultural level of analysis is critical to the understanding of ethnic phenomena, not because it replaces interactional or statistical analysis, but because it illuminates the contexts in which the social action revealed by these other methods becomes meaningful.

Conclusion

We have discussed various aspects of ethnic phenomena in Israel from historical and cultural points of view. Our theoretical stance sees culture as a system of meanings, embodied in symbols, which are analytically separate from social structure, though they constantly interact with it. Schneider (1969) has stressed that patterns of meaning that are linked together (or separated) at the cultural level may not be isomorphic with the structure and interlocking of institutions at the social level. With regard to ethnicity, which, at the very least, is a mode of identifying sub-units within a larger collectivity, this has two interrelated implications. First, ethnicity, at the cultural level, in any given society, has to be seen in terms of the central values and dilemnas of that society. Secondly, the way that cultural conceptions of institutional spheres (politics, stratification, religion) are linked together in a given society is a historical and, hence, variable matter, so that ethnicity, in any given instance, must be viewed in the context of these broader configurations, and cannot be fully understood in isolation. This has been stressed in our last two examples, suggesting links between ethnicity and religion in Israel and between "Jewish ethnicity" and the Jewish-Arab cleavage in Israeli society. This is not to say that ethnicity can be understood only as a particular phenomenon in each society, with no contribution from cross-cultural comparisons. What it does claim is that such comparisons which ignore the historical and cultural dimensions of these questions are likely to be superficial and misleading.

References

Abramov, A. Z. 1976. *Perpetual Dilemma: Jewish Religion in the Jewish State.*
Cranbury, N.J.: Associated University Presses.
Barth, F. 1969. "Introduction" to F. Barth (Ed.), *Ethnic Groups and Boundaries.*
Boston: Little, Brown, pp. 9-38.
Bar-Yosef, R. 1966. "Social Absorption of Immigrants in Israel" in H. P. David (Ed.),
Migration, Mental Health and Community Services. Geneva: American Joint Distribution Committee, pp. 55-70.
———. 1968. "Desocialization and resocialization." *International Migration Review.*
2:27-43.
Ben-David, J. 1953. "Ethnic differences or social change?" in C. Frankenstein (ed.),
Between Past and Future. Jerusalem: Szold Institute. Reprinted in S. Eisenstadt
et al. (Eds.), *Integration and Development in Israel.* New York: Praeger, pp. 368-385, 1970.
Ben-Rafael, E. 1980. *Beyond the Melting of Edot: Ethnic Conflict and Social Reality
in Israel.* Mimeograph. Department of Sociology and Social Anthropology, Hebrew University of Jerusalem.
Ben-Sasson, H. 1979. "The Oriental Jewish Heritage: Problems and Possibilities,"
Pe'amin, I:85-97. (In Hebrew).
Brown, K. "Changing Forms of Patronage in a Moroccan City" in E. Gellner and J.
Waterbury (Eds.), *Patrons and Clients in Mediterranean Societies.* London: Duckworth, pp. 304-328.
Deshen, S. 1970. *Immigrant Voters in Israel: Parties and Congregations in a Local
Election.* Manchester: Manchester University Press.
———. 1974. "Political and Cultural Ethnicity in Israel During the 1960s" in A. Cohen
(Ed.), *Urban Ethnicity.* London: Tavistock, pp. 281-309.
———. 1978. "Israel Judaism: Introduction to the Major Patterns," *International Journal of Middle East Studies* 9:141-169.
——— and Shokeid, M. 1974. *The Predicament of Homecoming: Cultural and Social
Life of North African Immigrants in Israel.* Ithaca: Cornell University Press.
Dumont, L. 1970. *Homo Hierarchicus.* Chicago: Chicago University Press.
Eisenstadt, S. N. 1953. *The Absorption of Immigrants.* London: Routledge and Kegan
Paul.
Geertz, C., Geertz, H., and Rosen, L. 1979. *Meaning and Order in Moroccan Society:
Three Essays in Cultural Analysis.* Cambridge: Cambridge University Press.
Gellner, E., and Micaud. C. (Eds.). 1972. *Arabs and Berbers.* Boston: Heath.
Goldberg, H. 1972. *Cave Dwellers and Citrus-Growers: A Jewish Community in
Libya and Israel.* Cambridge: Cambridge University Press.
———. 1977. "Introduction: Culture and Ethnicity in the Study of Israeli Society" in
H. Goldberg (Ed.), *Ethnic Groups,* pp. 163-186.
Kimur, R. 1980. "The Meaning of the Zurhaneh Ritual Among Iranian Jews in
Israel." Paper delivered at the Annual Meeting of the Israel Anthropological Association, Jerusalem, March.
Klineberger, A. 1969. *Society, Schools and Progress in Israel.* Oxford: Pergamon
Press.

Leslie, S. C. 1971. *The Rift in Israel: Religious Authority and Secular Democracy.* London: Routledge and Kegan Paul.

Mendes-Flohr, R. 1976. "The Courtyard Youth. A Study of Adoptive Strategies in a Market Environment." Unpublished M.A. Thesis. Dept. of Sociology and Social Anthropology, The Hebrew University of Jerusalem.

Palgi, P. 1975. In V. Rubin (Ed.), *Cannabis and Culture.* The Hague: Mouton.

Peres, Y. 1976. *Ethnic Relations in Israel.* Tel Aviv: Sifriat Poalim. (In Hebrew.)

Schneider, D. 1969. "Kinship, Nationality and Religion in American Culture: Towards a Definition of Kinship," in V. Turner (Ed.), *Forms of Symbolic Action.* Proceedings of the Annual Spring Meeting of the American Ethnological Society. Seattle: University of Washington Press, pp. 116-125.

Shokeid, M. 1968. "Immigration and Factionalism: An Analysis of Factors in Rural Israeli Communities of Immigrants," *Brit. Journal of Sociology* 19:385-406.

——. 1972. *The Dual Heritage.* Manchester: Manchester University Press.

Spillerman, S., and Habib, J. 1976. "Development Towns in Israel: The Role of Community in Creating Ethnic Disparities in Labor Force Characteristics," *American Journal of Sociology,* Vol. 81, No. 4, pp. 781-812.

Turner, V. 1969. *The Ritual Process: Structure and Anti-Structure.* Chicago: Aldine.

Willner, D. 1969. *Nationbuilding and Community in Israel.* Princeton: Princeton University Press.

Zucker, N. L. 1973. *The Coming Crisis in Israel: Private Faith and Public Policy.* Cambridge, Mass.: The M.I.T. Press.

10

Folk Models of Habbani Ethnic Identity[1]

Laurence D. Loeb

Over the past century, Jews have migrated to Israel from all over the world. The ingathering of the exiles has brought succeeding waves of immigrants who have been stereotyped and have accepted stereotypes of themselves and others. One popular classificatory mechanism in the Israeli model has been "country of origin." The Polish, Russian, German, American, South African, French, Moroccan, Iranian, Kurdish, Cochini, Bene Israel, Georgian, Syrian, Turkish, Iraqi and Yemenite Jews among others have been singled out from the conceptual community of Jews, *Klal Yisrael,* and marked with distinguishing labels and assumed customs and behavioral patterns attributed to those of the category. It is not the purpose of this paper to defend or attack the existence or accuracy of these folk models. They exist because in a society people need to pigeonhold and categorize individuals different from themselves. That complex society operates to a large extent on these stereotypic models is unquestionable, though their importance may vary with demographic and other considerations.

Within the Israeli popular ethnic model each designated group carries its own model of "reality," further distinguishing many ethnic subsets of the categories designated by society at large. Yemenites, for example, carry folk models that distinguish among San'anis, Haidanis, Sharabis, Dhamaris, Ibbis, Giblis, Adanis, and Bedhanis.[2] These models carry perceptions of "other," but concomitantly evoke culturally shared images of self. These shared images comprise what is generally referred to as "ethnic identity." "Cultural self-image" is used to describe an individual's application of ethnic identity in reference to self.

Evidence will be presented in this chapter demonstrating that the Habbani in Yemen evolved a strong positive self-image, which, with some modification, was accepted and reinforced by coreligionists elsewhere. The Muslim population likewise respected and confirmed the Habbani Jewish self-perception. However, that which was adaptive in a social milieu where social segregation was the norm, became a source of contention in Israel where integration is the goal. Strong motivation to pursue cultural persistence, a need to cultivate greater *Temani* identity and resistance to secularism complicated by an active proselytizing program by HaBaD has evoked an intensive struggle to reformulate a Habbani model of ethnic identity more responsive to the contemporary Israeli situation. This presentation purports to explore the contrasting sociocultural milieus of Yemen and Israel and the kinds of change Habbani ethnic identity is undergoing.

Contrasted with North Yemen's almost continuously woven carpet of hundreds of Jewish communities, South Yemen (the Aden Protectorate) was rather sparsely populated by Jews. Except for Aden proper[3] and the nearby town of Lahj, Jews were to be found only in the villages and towns near Dhala and Bedha (on the southeastern Yemen border), Abiyan, in a few villages of Dathina, and in Habban and nearby villages, probably less than 7,000 Jews altogether. Almost all other sites were temporary quarters (sometimes so inhabited for years) of itinerants, the most wideranging of whom were the Habbani.

Habban,[4] probably first settled by Jews in pre-Islamic times, was an isolated community, located more than 100 kilometers to the east of its nearest Jewish neighbor and some 340 kilometers east of Aden. Habbani Jews were consciously different from their coreligionists in the nearest settlements in the areas of Behan, Bedha and Dathin and claim to have "colonized" these and other communities of South Yemen (Cf. Yavnielie, 1963:223-224). The indigenous Jew of these sites often support this contention, testifying to frequent Habbani visits, reputed family ties, etc. Visitations from non-Habbanis to Habban, on the other hand, were rare; those who came were by and large Bedhani, though a San'ani teacher reputedly spend an extended time in Habban in the late 19th century. Habbani patronymic groups claim origin in Dhofar, Gahalan, Aden and Assala, but Habbanis feel closest to their "colonies" and peculiarly to the Haidanis, at the far end of North Yemen.[5]

Having spoken with San'anis, Adanis Bedhanis and Behanis about how they perceived Habbanis before coming to Israel (for San'anis it was hear-say only), the following stereotype emerges: strangeness (e.g., clothing, lack of head covering, long hair covering *pe'ot* (side locks), dialect), cour-age, tenacity, piety, inflexibility, naivete, lack of extensive scholarship—but a good grasp of limited areas of study and inept Tora reading. Physi-cally they were perceived as tall and gaunt, of proud bearing, etc. Their silversmithing was considered crude. In sum, they were viewed as approxi-mating the stereotypic "country bumpkin" or "hick".

In fact, from the Yemenite Jewish perspective, the Habbani were "strange". The Habbani man dressed distinctively in a kilt, an open turban of indigo, walked barefooted or with special sandals, wore unique jewelry, was barechested with a *tallit* (prayer shawl) thrown over a shoulder and sported long unkempt hair. The women's costume was likewise unusual, but similar in many respects to indigenous Muslim women's dress and orn-ament. Habbanis readily admit to having been naive and markedly differ-ent from Jews elsewhere, yet their self-esteem was considerable. They viewed themselves as tough, pious, more meticulous in observance than others, independent and self-reliant. They attest to their need for oc-casional outside rabbinical opinion, but only when their own scholars were partisan to the issue. Thus, in the early 1900's, when the two lead-ing patronymic groups contested the validity of using municipal cistern water in the *miqveh* (ritual bath), rather than private cistern water, and the manner of moving the water to the bath proper, they eventually elected to send a delegation to San'a for a decision. They got only as far as Bedha, received a written opinion, which was lost or stolen by the losing faction en route home and were thus eventually forced to arrive at their own solu-tion; they built a second *miqveh*. On the other hand, at Hashid refugee camp near Aden in 1950, the Habbani were so appalled at the ritual slaughter and inspection of other Yemenite *shohtim* (slaughterers), they forcibly evicted them, and resorted to their own slaughter.

Habbanis explain, with considerable pride, that more than forty percent of the adult males in each generation were ordained *shohtim* and nearly that many were competent *mohalim* (circumcisors). They created marve-lous religious poetry; their poet laureate and sage, Mussa ben (Rom) Shamakh, a contemporary of and correspondent with Shalom Shabbazi, is said to have actually been the author of some of the songs entered into the latter's *Diwan*.

The Habbani mode of subsistence was unique; every adult male was an itinerant silversmith, plying his craft from Aden to the edges of Wadi

Hadramaut. It was unusual except for the periods of Pesah and Tishre for more than two or three adult males to actually reside in Habban. Neither the wandering men nor their unchaperoned women were molested. They formed strong alliances with local royalty and the powerful tribal confederacies.

The arrival in Palestine in 1945 of Yihye ben Awad al-Adani, the first Habbani, created something of a sensation. Other "Habbani," residing for generations in Bedha, Behan and Dathina, who had maintained their original identities, began arriving in the 1920s (some may have come to Palestine from Habban in the 17 or 18th Century), but they were relatively acculturated to their local norms. Yihye, now known as Zkharya Habbani (see Ashkenazi, 1947) told the Yishuv of this unique outpost of Judaism, hundreds of kilometers to the east of Yemen, subsisting in a desert town, all but cut off from the outside world. Zkharya was instrumental in arranging the complicated two-pronged rescue operation, which eventually brought them out in the summer of 1950.

Dominant Factors in the Traditional Habbani Self-Image

After more than five years of research with the Habbani, I find myself convinced that the place itself, the town of Habban, is a central focus of their identity. The older generation of Habbani live an almost dual existence; one "real" and tangible but meaningless—in the present; the second, "ideal" and intangible, but meaningful—in mentally reconstructed Habban. In actuality, through reliving experiences shared there rather than continuing by developing new experiences, Habban serves as the religious experience par excellence, conforming closely to Geertz's definition of religion: "A religion is: a system of symbols which acts to establish powerful, pervasive and long-lasting moods and motivations in men by formulating conceptions of a general order of existence and clothing these conceptions with such an aura of factuality that the moods and motivations seen uniquely realistic" (1966).

Despite this strong attachment to Habban, the town seems unremarkable in a physical sense. Informants' descriptions supported by photographs depict a barren desert landscape; a town of less than 4,000 (probably less than 2,500) located on the heights overlooking Wadi Habban, having no permanent water resources and wholly dependent on sporadic precipitation to fill the municipal cistern. The Jewish quarter was located on the highest and best ground, between the cisterns and the Sultan's palace. Food resources were limited in kind, quality and quantity; drought and starvation were frequent visitors. Habban's sole historic claim to fame was its position astride a Khimyarite trade town and informants report many ruins in the nearby mountains of Khimyar. Informants likewise report ancient Jewish sites near Habban and large Ashuri-script carvings in the cliff face, announcing to one and all: *thum Shabbat,* "the Sabbath boundary" (Cf. Miles and Munzinger, 1971:222). Those Habbani men who traveled west to Dathina, with its springs and vegetation, and the towns of Behan and Bedha, found a populace receptive to the itinerant Habbani who eventually settled those areas 200 and more years ago. Yet despite the extreme hardship of subsistence in Habban, nobody desired to leave. Even after news trickled back to Habban of the massive aliya from all over Yemen, no one expressed real desire to depart. By 1949, no more than ten to fifteen percent of the Habbani had drifted down to Aden and from there to Israel. When the elders discussed the merits of leaving Habban in early 1950, the convincing arguments were not those of religious or political Zionism, but the fear of real isolation; that they would remain the last Jews on the Arabian peninsula. That fear was the major factor which overcame numerous overtures and outright bribery by neighbors, royalty and the tribes to remain.

In common with many other immigrants, nostalgia for place of origin sometimes masks the discomforts once faced by the Habbani Jews. Habban, the place in reality, tended to be hot and dry, frequently infested with mosquitos, famine prone, disease-inflicted with smallpox, guinea worm, influenza and pneumonia, where two of three live births failed to achieve maturity, resulting in a true survival of the fittest; and, while open murder of Jews was strictly prohibited, clandestine testing of poison on unsuspecting Jewish victims was not unheard of and pressure to convert to Islam waxed mightily in periods of famine and stress. All of these and many other problems are acknowledged readily by informants, and yet the Habbani sincerely believe that they gave up too much in coming to Israel. They view the harsh reality of Habbani life as the trial that forged "communitas" (Turner, 1973), that tested the physical and spiritual endurance of the individual. Habban was a place of piety and innocence, where, despite all hardships, pristine Judaism flourished, where men and women trusted each other completely with absolute faith in the morality and behavior of fellow Habbani Jews in the most tempting of sexual circumstances. Habban was also a time: when men studied while they worked and at every moment of leisure, and where women evolved elaborate structures of dance, song, poetry and narrative embodying law and lore to while away the weeks and months of male physical and/or emotional absence. Habban thus was the space/time coordinate of simple piety—an attitude of achievement not obtained (perhaps not attainable) elsewhere.

Habbanis nostalgically remember their Muslim neighbors. Here, too, we are not faced with a typical immigrant nostalgia syndrome, but rather a contention well borne out by a vast body of materials. The relationship was not and is not viewed as idyllic. Problems occurred and Jews were sometimes victimized. But, for the most part, Habbani Jews were respected and treated well. They were granted freedom of movement throughout the Western Aden Protectorate and through part of the East as well. Unlike other Jews, they were allowed (though few ever did) to wear the *gambiya* (dagger), a symbol of independence and self reliance. In the South Yemen caste system, they ranked rather high, below royalty, Sa'ids and Mashaykh—but at the same level as the Gaba'il, the Bedouin tribesman, the majority populace. They ranked higher than many townsmen and agriculturalists. They were well protected under Dhimmi status, and their total annual *gizye* (poll tax) for the entire town totaled 16 rials, a pittance (one smith could earn that much in a normal month). The folklore is replete with tales of the serious protection offered by royalty and pastoralists. Most non-Jews were prepared to accommodate them in their travels and invite them to their celebrations, providing special utensils and food for Jewish guests. Habbani Jews were never humbled by Muslims and were sometimes protected by them even in face of their own laws, e.g., in cases of conversion where children of the convert should also be compelled to convert to Islam, tribesmen and others extended hospitality and protection to refugees from forcible conversion. Elders of the community, 30 years after emigration, wonder what has become of their friends and neighbors and wish them only well.

In Habbani culture, sharing and communication of the "real" is "a metaphor for the true—and not identical with it" (Crapanzano, 1981:130). This served them well during the first generation in Israel, much as it sustained them in their diaspora. In present day Israel, the Habbani elders cling to their ideal of rugged piety but, as we shall see, its application has undergone modification and reevaluation.

Modifying Habbani Perceptions of Ethnic Identity in Israel

Upon coming to Israel, the Habbani were viewed by other Jews as exotic and even somewhat eccentric. Early newspaper reports (Jerusalem Post 7/30, 8/27, 9/25, 1950), pictures and films marvel at a group of primitives from the remote wilderness of Hadramaut. They are presented as tall, proud, happy, peculiarly dressed and rather primitive in their technology. Allegedly, they were the mythical Bene Dan desert tribe. Their initial adjustment in Israel was difficulty; they did not like Ein Shemer and were then moved as a group to Zarnuqa, outside of Rehovot. After a year or so, they found themselves involved in physical confrontations with other groups over religious and other problems and demanded their own settlement. They finally selected Baraqet, sited on the abandoned Arab village of Tira, 2.5 kilometers east of Ben Gurion Airport. A minority settled in Salameh, a suburb of Tel Aviv.

The early years in Baraqet were trying ones. The younger generation of mature adults seized the political initiative from the elders who appear to have agreed to this change because the experience in Israel was beyond their ability to cope. Health conditions were poor, communications rotten, security along the nearby border was spotty, and subsistence inadequate. The first Arab terrorist raid in 1952 was the last; they were frightened off by the intense resistance of this strange group. Baraqet was originally set up as an agricultural moshav, but it quickly became clear that, given the available technology and land, agriculture was doomed to failure. Labor for males had to be found in nearby villages and on reclamation projects. As communications improved, men sought work in nearby industry and women, rarely engaged in income-producing labor in Habban, found employment as part-time housemaids in nearby Tel Aviv suburbs. In Baraqet, traditional dress was gradually abandoned by men, though women merely adopted it stylistically to Israeli modes.

Most Habbani continued to marry endogamously and live in patrilocal extended families. Gradually they have extended their social network to the surrounding. villages, to employers and coworkers, and to school and military acquaintances. The smaller Habbani group in Salameh proceeded to acculturate much more quickly, while maintaining close ties with their kinsmen in Bareqet. Habbani renewed their relations with long lost kinsmen from Bedha, Behan, Abiyan, Aden and Dathina as well, who proudly reaffirmed their Habbani roots.[6]

Israelis evolved a new stereotype of the Habbani. On neighboring settlements they were referred to as "wild Indians." Their naivete was proverbial, their "primitiveness" in custom and sanitation and their fidelity
to tradition were considered remarkable. In short, their behavior was
viewed by neighboring settlements, Oriental and Ashkenazi, as "stone
age Judaism," if the use of hyperbole is not out of place. To some extent,
this view has been communicated to Israeli born Habbani, who both
resent and are embarrassed by it.

No discussion of Habbani ethnic identity in Israel would be meaningful without reference to HaBaD. Elsewhere (Loeb, 1978) I described the
impact of Lubavitch (HaBaD) Hasidism on the Habbani community. Within a few months after arriving in Israel in 1950, HaBaD began proselytizing among the Habbani successfully convincing a number of parents to
send their adolescent sons to HaBaD ritual schools. HaBaD emphasis on
Klal Yisrael, piety and ritual observance and a simple, though rather
mystical acceptance of the divine inspiration of the Rebbe, has been
perceived by many Habbani as a kindred, spiritual experience possessing
a force and commitment rivaling the traditional Habbani one. While
HaBaD motivations may initially have been largely altruistic, intending
to defend the Habbani and other Oriental communities from the encroachment of Israeli secularism, they ultimately resulted in cultural
self-aggrandizement and consequent denial of the validity of indigenous
Habbani values and norms. With perhaps fifty percent of Habbani affiliated in some way with HaBaD on a regular basis, Hasidism has reached
deeply into community life and has impacted Habbani self-evaluation
in every situation.

The following cultural self-images of present day Habbani are derived by means of extensive interviews, but have not yet been tested by
survey/questionnaire. There is, nevertheless, considerable confidence in
the material presented. The emerging picture applies primarily to Habbani
living in Bareqet and not necessarily to those Habbani who have left Bareqet with the intention of assimilating to another cultural milieu, nor to the
community living in Salameh, where, for the most part, only the aged effect strong ties and commitments to Habbani lifeways and values.

Habbani ethnic identity can be measured in a number of ways, but
two readily available parameters include informants' verbalization and
actual behavior. Furthermore, it is clear that the Habbani are by no
means presenting a monolithic position on any point. Factors such as age,
sex, and social experience seem significant in differentiating self-image. A
matrix could thus be constructed with the elements shown in Figure 1.

		Male		Female	
		HaBaD	non-HaBaD	HaBaD	non-HaBaD
Born:	(A) before 1935				
	(B) between 1935-1949				
	(C) after 1950				

Figure 1. Self-image Matrix.

The two really significant variables in present-day self image are age and HaBaD affiliation. The age categories consist of: (A) those born before 1935 and raised and married in Habban shortly after arrival in Israel; (B) those born in Habban (between 1935-1949), but who spent a significant part of their childhood or at least adolescence in Israel; and (C) those born in Israel after 1950.

Each category of persons in the matrix might be expected to possess differing self-perceptions. For those in category (A), now in their late forties or above, whether HaBaDnik or not and without obvious gender differentiation, Habbani pride and chauvinism is boundless. Most express some sense of guilt that their piety, scholarship, creativity and strength are not as great as their forebears'. They further admit that they are not in Israel what they were in Habban in terms of religious piety. Israel is viewed as a mixed blessing at best. They appreciate the relative luxury they enjoy, low mortality, bountiful subsistence, and the presence of myriads of other Jews, but Israel has in many cases "corrupted" their children through secularism and materialism and even corrupted the generation raised and matured in Habban. The pious and meticulous observance of commandments, the *mitzvot,* has diminished as reflected, for example, in reduced attendance at daily worship, even during the penitential period (this, despite the probability that Bareqet is the most observant and caring Oriental community in contemporary Israel). Habban is viewed by the mature and elders as a spiritual paradise of perfect adherence to the simple pursuit of *mitzvot* (the commandments). "Habbani" conveys to this group a proud image of adherence to the law in the face of vicissitudes, of scholarship and poetic creativity, of spiritual glory in the face of economic deprivation. Habbani see themselves as a family (eighty-eight percent of the marriages have been with fellow Habbanis) with attendant veneration and shared love. In searching for the secret of Habbani cultural perseverance in Israel, the most important clue has been the dominance of these concepts among the elders.

Something slightly different begins to emerge in the young adult group (B), born in Habban but matured in Israel. This group includes a number who reached their teen years in Habban. Most attended school in Israel and some completed Yeshivot. Among this group are the young leadership of the community, including the central committee chairman and some of the membership. Most have strong sentimental ties to their childhood in Habban, but their memories are often fuzzy. Some who have become HaBaDniks have evolved an ambivalent attitude about "Habbaniness." The Rebbe and Hasidism take priority. Habbani ways, when in conflict, are often seen as deficient. Some will not eat food at their parents' table, although, after considerable observation, I, for one, doubt whether HaBaD slaughtering is any way more meticulous than Habbani practice. Some have affected HaBaD dress and have moved out to HaBaD communities. Still, the young pietist HaBaD attitude merely echoes traditional Habbani piety, so that to some extent the two buttress each other. In this group, the HaBaDniks express some pride in the accomplishments of their forebears and express the sentiment that HaBaD is the new way to maintain religious intensity in the Israeli environment. On the other hand, the majority in this group, still living in Bareqet, reject the cultural imperialism of HaBaD and seek to intensify their identity with "Habbaniness." They seek to do this through iconoclasm in ritual, demanding that authentic Habbani practices be restored where replaced. They seek to create a Habbani cultural center. Some are even beginning to study their own cultural/historical traditions. It is in this age category that the Habban vs. HaBaD controversy is strong.

The pro-Habban group is itself somewhat religious, hoping to break down the last vestiges of patronymic controversy. Many have adopted new Israeli family names. This category includes young pietists and some less observant but strongly committed "cultural" Habbanis. Some have consciously chosen not to pray in their lineage synagogue. Yet, they do recognize the unique nature of their tradition and its importance in maintaining a perceived religious and social superiority as contrasted with neighboring populations. They actively and often successfully seek material wealth and there is some doubt expressed by elders as to the moral quality of this group. For the most part, the positive Habbani self-image remains intact, and eighty percent are married endogamously. One contingent has recently established a new West Bank settlement, but it remains to be seen how important homogeneity will be there.

Category (C) was born and raised entirely in Israel. For them, Habban is little more than the tales told them by their elders. Despite a conscious degree of isolation in Bareqet, this generation has been totally exposed for their entire lives to Israeli education, technology, media and social relations. There is still a surprisingly high degree of endogamy in the group,[7] reflecting strongly the positive self-image. Those who wish to marry out have no great difficulty doing so, but an overwhelming preference for endogamous mating reinforces "Habbaniness."

The biggest problem faced by the generation born in Israel is the remoteness of the Habban experience. Living in a homogeneous community, they are brought up with the same shared experience and traditions, but the intensity of involvement with the tales and values so important to previous generations is diminished by being second and third hand. Self-consciousness and severe embarrassment sometimes set in as young, modern, sometimes even chic Habbani attempt to bridge the gap between the Ashkenazi-culturally-dominated Israeli world with the traditional, and only gradually evolving, Bareqet environment. Some Habbani brides no longer want to be decorated with henna since this calls attention to their "primitive" origins when they return to work. Others rebel against unstated but very apparent dress codes. A few reject restrictions on heterosexual contact. In fact, much of the discontent is found among females whose role orientation has gradually shifted from wholly domestic to a productive-domestic mix. Their mothers strongly resent the Ashkenazi *geveret* for whom they clean house; they disparage their ignorance of ritual and impiety, thereby reinforcing their own ethnic pride. Their daughters, however, have been socialized through school and the media to respect and admire the possessions and values of the Ashkenazi world, which somewhat weakens that pride.[8] Young men have sought to rebel through a rejection of ritual observance and religious values. While the number of rebels is small, they are quite vocal. The older Habbani have been unable to develop a procedure to deal with this problem. This small group tends to have a strongly negative Habbani self-image.

In the final analysis, a trend toward weakening ethnic pride and negative self-image is growing in the Habbani young generation. Even so, the extent and kind of rejection of Habbaniness is relatively small as contrasted with the pace of acculturation among other immigrant groups in

Israel. Furthermore, the Habbani population, which has more than tripled to nearly 1,600 people in 30 years, is committed to the contemporary revival of Yemenite culture in Israel, marked by the establishment of ethnic *yeshivot*, publishing of religious and secular works by Yemenites and about Yemen, increasing distribution of tapes and records of Yemenite music, and the holding of Yemenite cultural events around the country. It is not inconceivable that concerned Habbanis might further impede the acculturative dimension of Israeli life and spur some sort of nativistic revitalization. Already, annual Habbani pageants and displays grace the Bareqet scene. Plans for a small museum and archive are being considered. Two Habbani are attempting to construct a history of the community from oral sources.

In Yemen, the folk model of Habbani ethnic identity was strongly positive; Habbani pride reflected not only self-esteem, but complimentary perceptions by Muslim neighbors and coreligionists elsewhere. This kind of chauvinism undeniably reinforced the determination to survive and persist in isolation from other Jews and under hazardous subsistence conditions. In Yemen, where social segregation was the norm, such an Habbani world view may be evaluated as adaptive. In Israel, where social integration is a national goal and cultural pluralism is, at best, tolerated as transitionary in its pursuit, Habbani ethnicity and pervasive, vigorous indigenous folk models of ethnic identity become a source of contention.

What is most unusual about the Habbani in the Israeli setting is that they resisted integration from the outset, unlike most immigrant groups who accepted it for a generation and, only then, having experienced the loss entailed by surrender of identity, began to espouse the cause of cultural pluralism. The Habbani feel good being together, even when problems ensue from the contact. They view themselves as an extended family and proffer similar sentiments to the groups with whom pervasive ties exist: the Bedhanis, Behanis, Adenis and Dathinans. The only wider circle of identity they actually cultivate is that of *Temani* (Yemenite). The only acceptable, strongly organized force for integration is HaBaD, and its ideology is clearly on the periphery of mainstream Israeli life. Whether Habbani ethnic identity now rooted in the past can evolve into a strongly positive one imbued with contemporary pride may prove the critical ideological component of continued Habbani existence.

Implications for Futher Research

Sammy Smooha (1978) suggests that Israel is a country strained by ethnic tension. He visualizes a simmering conflict between large blocs of once disparate but now coalescing ethnic entities, e.g., Ashkenazim of European/Western Hemisphere extraction and Orientals of Afro-Asian extraction. The research discussed in this article brings into question the underlying assumptions and validity of these categorizations.

While the Habbani are certainly unique in some respects, the processes of folk modeling and reinforcing of ethnic identity are replicated widely throughout Israel. The Habbani are *Temani*, yet they are not totally comfortable with that identification. Efforts to enlist support for *Temani* political candidates and for a *Temani* party have met with only minimal enthusiasm. Habbani are torn by desire to support the party of their Moshav Movement (NRP), Gush Emunim, strong defense (Likud) and social benefits (Ma'arakh). But even *Temanim* with weaker commitment to regional or village identity and strong cultural self-image rarely identify with the aspirations of Moroccans, Tunisians, Iranians, Syrians, Turks, etc. Each of these ethnic groups has internal loyalties, and in most contexts they see little that unites them with other ethnicities. I have never met an informant who would characterize himself as "Oriental."

Although there are many subcategories of Ashkenazim, e.g., Yekke, Polish, Rumanian, Russian, Anglo-Saxon, etc., they seem to possess a greater consciousness of kind, and awareness and recognition of themselves as an in-group sharing a nexus of common interests than do the "Orientals." Ashkenazi" as a folk taxonomic category is far better defined and understood than "Oriental." It is really the major ethnic reference category.

Many of the attempts to assign a label with implications of commonality and social cohesiveness to non-Ashkenazim are clumsy and contrived.[9] The convenience of such an identification is overbalanced by the evidence suggesting that it is wholly artificial and must, therefore, be utilized with caution. A valid formulation of ethnicity and the nature of interethnic relations in Israel must carefully assess the important role played by folk models in structuring cultural identity and in shaping social relations.

Notes

[1] Research carried out in Israel in 1974, 1975, 1976, 1977-78 and 1980 was supported by the Memorial Foundation for Jewish Culture, a Fulbright Faculty Research Grant, the Social Science Research Council, the University of Utah Research Committee, and other funding from the University of Utah.

[2] In fact, one of the unfortunate concomitants of the extensive research on processes of sociocultural change initiated in Israel during the 1950s and early 1960s was

the ignoring of basic research (for the most part) regarding traditional culture. Social scientists must share the blame for presenting Yemenite culture in monolithic
terms—even papering over social and historical differences long ago alluded to in
the travels and studies of Tabib (1973), Yavnielie (1963) and others.

[3] Aden's Jewish population was approximately ten percent of the urban total, e.g.,
2,000 in 1871 (Von Maltzan, 1873:176); 4,120 in 1933 (Phipson, 1934:72).

[4] Habban refers not only to the town itself, but the occasionally inhabited nearby
villages of Lih'yeh, BaSafa, Hauta, Rauda, Yashbum and, more especially, al-Gabiya
in Hadhina where one sublineage was permanently settled for some four generations.

[5] Haidan lies at the northern terminus of the old "incense route" connecting Belhaf
(Cana) with Najran, by way of Habban. It might be speculated that at some time
these communities may have been in contact or perhaps even settled by the same
group.

[6] Among the Habbani men who settled in Bedha, Behan, Aden, Abiyan and Dathina
in the 19th century, more than twenty-five percent selected mates from among
fellow Habbani emigrants, despite the obviously limited selection of potential mates
in this pool. Many of these Habbani expatriates dropped their patronyms and
adopted the surname "Habbani."

[7] Nearly sixty percent have chosen mates from within the wider Habbani community.
Those living off Bareqet for whom I have less complete data have managed only
forty-five percent and this figure is probably inflated. For Israel, this, nevertheless,
remains a rather high rate of endogamy for second generation immigrants.

[8] An attitudinal survey of a sample of young women from Bareqet was administered by Cathy Clark of the University of Utah during the summer of 1980. Many
young women with high school education expressed iittle desire to remain within
the confines of Bareqet or the restriction of Habbani life. They expressed some
pride in their tradition and the strength of kinship ties, but wanted to be integrated with their potential spouses and children into the greater Yemenite community and Israel as a whole. Whether they will act on these sentiments to an appreciable degree remains to be seen. A number of young married women who had
expressed comparable sentiments to us several years ago nevertheless married close
kinsmen and remained on the moshav. It is unclear in any case how representative
the sample is for unmarried females generally, since those who chose not to respond
might represent, in part, those who do not seek to integrate, i.e., the Habbani
chauvinists who consider even Ms. Clark's form of inquiry "too modern."

[9] It may, of course, be politically expedient and socially valuable, but that requires
a different order of evaluation.

References

Ashkenazi, T. 1947. "The Jews of Hadramaut," *Edoth* 2:58-71.
Cale, Ruth. 1950a. " 'Habanim' Coming from Aden," *Jerusalem Post,* July 30.
———. 1950b. "Plane Load of Immigrants from Hadramaut Arrives," *Jerusalem Post,*
     August 27.

Crapanzano, Vincent. 1981. *Tuhami: Portrait of a Moroccan.* Chicago: University of Chicago Press.

Geertz, Clifford. 1966. "Religion as a Cultural System," Michael Banton (Ed.), *Anthropological Approaches to the Study of Religion.* London: Tavistock.

Loeb, Laurence D. 1978. "Habban and Habad: The Influence of the Lubavitcher Hasidim on a Yemenite Moshav." Paper delivered to the Israel Anthropological Society.

Miles, S. B., and Munzinger, Werner. 1971. "Account of an Excursion into the Interior of Southern Arabia." *JRGS,* pp. 210-243.

Orgel, Hugh. 1950. "Last Flight of Magic Carpet," *Jerusalem Post,* September 25.

Phipson, E. Selby. 1934. *A Medical Survey of Aden.* Aden: Cowasjee Dinshaw and Bros. Press.

Smooha, Sammy. 1978. *Israel: Pluralism and Conflict.* London: Routledge and Kegan Paul.

Tabib, Victor. 1973. *Galut Teman.* Tel Aviv: Emanut.

Turner, Victor. 1973. "The Center Out There," *History of Religions* 12:191-230.

Von Maltzan, Heinrich. 1873. *Reise nach Suedarabien.* Braunschweig: Friederich Biewig.

Yavnielie, Shmuel. 1963. *Masa' Lteman.* Tel Aviv: Am Oved.

11

Ethnicity, Culture, and Adaptation among Yemenites in a Heterogeneous Community[1]

Herbert S. Lewis

Introduction

Numerous attempts have been made to restrict the scope of the concept of ethnicity and to limit particular aspects of it. There are those who see ethnicity primarily as an interest group phenomenon, of economic or political origin and significance, and deny its having any basis in sentiment, affect or "primordiality" (v. Glazer and Moynihan, 1975:19-20; Yancey *et al.*, 1976; Patterson, 1975). Others have seized upon Barth's distinction between ethnic boundaries and cultural content in order to remove any consideration of "culture" from the study of ethnicity (Bennett, 1975:8-10). Still others argue that modern ethnicity is no more than a symbolic residue lacking deeper substance (e.g., Patterson, 1979; Gans, 1979). While these tendencies are typical of the literature on ethnicity generally, there are similar attitudes to be found in the literature on ethnicity in Israel as well (e.g., *Sverski*, n.d.; Smooha, 1978).

Attempts to limit the meaning or scope of ethnicity are self-defeating. They represent rearguard actions, as scholars of various schools have been taken unawares and confounded by the now obvious (though previously unexpected) significance and persistence of the phenomena we call "ethnicity." Neither the "liberal expectancy" nor the "radical expectancy" of the end of ethnicity have proven to be correct (Glazer and Moynihan, 1975).

What is ethnicity? Is it political or "primordial"; basic and cultural or "merely" symbolic? Simply, ethnicity is not either this or that, but is the full range of relations, feelings, boundaries, behaviors, movements, identities and customs that grow from the presence of populations of differing origins and identities within single sociopolitical systems. This is not to say that each case presents us with a full range of cultural, social, political and behavioral phenomena. Rather, we contend that once there is more than one ethnic group or category within a system named by themselves and others, there is then the possibility that various other elements may be present and play roles in behavior (cf. Epstein, 1978:111-112; Greeley, n.d.; 1972).

These elements include:

1. Identification. The basis of ethnicity is the recognition that there are categories of people of different origin, of separate common backgrounds. These are named categories, and for ethnicity to work there must be recognition by many that "they are the X," and "we are the Y," or "I am a Y; he is an X." Without such mutual awareness there would be no ethnicity.

2. Social relations. In any situation we may ask the question: To what extent does the fact of common ethnic origin guide or effect social relations? Is there greater than chance possibility that members of the same ethnic group will join together for various activities and in social relationships, whether they do this consciously or not? This may vary from almost exclusive involvement within a group to very little. It remains, however, a significant researchable problem, and one that is all too often ignored.

3. Conscious concern with the traditions and heritage of an ethnic group. In this case, too, there may be no particular interest, or involvement may be natural and constant. Members of an ethnic category may feel that there is nothing of value worth preserving or even, at times, may actively deny and flee their ethnic heritage. Others, or the same people at other times, may become very involved with their histories, traditions and symbols.

4. Politicization. An ethnic group may not serve, in any dubious way,

as a political or economic resource at a given time, but the mere existence of ethnically identified individuals and groups means that the potential exists for the politicization of ethnicity.

5. Culture and ethnicity. Here we have in mind, not primarily heritage or customs and costumes, but those codes, plans and rules that many anthropologists consider the guides to behavior and basis for perceiving, predicting, judging and acting (Goodenough, 1966:259). There may not be much in the way of custom and culture that distinguishes one group from another at the obvious, surface level, as Barth has noted (1969:14), but there may be different codes or behaviors, at least partly based on ethnically derived cultural differences. These may not be evident to the casual observer, but may be significant in choices made by members of a society.

If students of ethnicity find it easy to accept political ethnicity, perhaps the aspect of ethnicity they find most difficult is that of culture. The idea that members of the same society may differ in patterned ways with respect to their values, attitudes, ideas and behavior is resisted alike by Marxians, social anthropologists interested in symbolism, those impressed by Barth's separation of ethnic boundaries and content, and social scientists afraid that to speak of cultural differences is to "blame the victim" (v. William Ryan, 1971).[2]

Yet, culture remains a key anthropological concept. We teach our students that the transmissions of culture, the inculcation in children of specific codes of behavior is a *sine qua non* of human existence. We read about how the Javanese become Javanese, how the Subanun learn to quench their thirst, and of the imponderabilia of native life in the Trobriands. We accept that the codes and bases for perceiving, judging and acting must be shared and transmitted by parents, siblings, kinfolk, peers and others in an individual's environment. Nevertheless, we encounter uneasiness, if not outright resistance, when it is suggested that, in a complex, multi-ethnic nation-state, parents, kin, peers and neighbors may be transmitting attitudes, values and behaviors that are, in part, at least, ethnically based, and that may vary from one subgroup within the population to another (cf. Greeley, 1972:7-8). Those who transmit these ethnically derived tendencies may not be aware that they are doing so. Indeed, if they live in an ethnically homogeneous enclave they may not even be aware that their behavior or values are different from others in the wider population.[3] Furthermore, these may not be at all obvious to the outsider. That doesn't mean, however, that they are not of considerable potential interest for social science. To assume, *a priori,* that they cannot exist is to unnecessarily limit our understanding and our ability to predict.[4]

This chapter deals with a case in which all the aspects of ethnicity enumerated above are present—with the possible partial exception of politicization. It is the contention of this paper that the Yemenite Jews of a small city in Israel, called here Kiryat Eliahu, have chosen to live much of their lives in the company of their co-ethnics and that these social relations form a powerful reinforcemnt to the maintenance of Yemenite identity. This Yemenite reference group has a strong sense of values and attitudes (culture), which guide the actions and choices of many members of the group. It is also argued that this situation is neither transitional, nor purely a reaction to their economic or structural position in Israeli society. Finally, although the patterns outlined below are not typical of other Israeli Jewish immigrant communities, these groups may, at some time in the future, come closer to the Yemenite pattern than is now the case.

In this chapter, I will discuss some elements of a code shared, in varying degrees, by people of Yemenite origin in a small city, and suggest some of the implications for behavior of this code.[5] I am not suggesting that there is a simple set of rules by which all Yemenites live, or that social life and behavior merely represent the performance by individuals of the rules of their culture (cf. Turner, 1974:13). I envision a far more flexible, open-ended and variable situation in which individuals choose behavior as they perceive their situations, in the light of circumstances and in the light of culture and sentiment. Decisions are made in relation to the ideas, principles and values that were taught and in terms of the perceptions of how others will view those choices. In the complex pluralistic multi-ethnic world of the Yemenite of Kiryat Eliahu, the paradigms come from many sources. Their values and their significant others are not merely Yemenite and not merely Israelis. In the case under consideration, however, I shall be stressing those elements and expectations derived from Israeli-Yemeni culture and, more specifically, its Kiryat Eliahu variety.

Background

Kiryat Eliahu was founded after the establishment of the State of Israel as a place of settlement for new immigrants. Located near a major industrial zone, not far from a major city, a variety of work is available, and the city has grown to municipality status, with a population of over 25,000, as it continues to absorb immigrants from every part of the world. Indeed, the population of Kiryat Eliahu is virtually a sample of that of the whole country, with substantial numbers of residents from Morocco, Romania, Poland, the USSR, and smaller groups from Yemen, Egypt, Turkey, Tunisia, Germany and elsewhere. The 1300 or so Yemenites comprise 5% of the population of Kiryat Eliahu, about the same as their proportion in the nation.

The institutional and physical arrangements of the city are such that there is considerable residential and social integration. People of all backgrounds are constantly thrown together in public places and institutions; the schools are generally ethnically integrated (though relatively few Ashkenazi children are found in the religious schools), and the political institutions (the municipal council and government) mirror the ethnic composition of the city to a considerable extent.

In this heterogeneous city the Yemenites are among the veterans (*vatikim*). Although some of them moved to Kiryat Eliahu from other areas after the first decade of the town' existence, most of the Yemenites arrived during the first five years, and thus shared the hardships and the camaraderie of the difficult early years. This period seems to be remembered fondly by the old settlers, of whatever origin. The pioneering experience, therefore, is not remembered as particularly traumatic by the Yemenites of Kiryat Eliahu; on the contrary, it enhances their self-esteem.

In Kiryat Eliahu everyone has potential access to the institutions and opportunities of the city and the nation: these include residential areas, work, schools, the army, political activity and facilities for religious, entertainment and "cultural" activities. The population is not isolated in a remote development town, nor are they isolated through ethnic homogeneity. In practice, however, the choices the Yemenites make guide them in certain specific directions.

The Yemenite Community

Although the Yemenites of Kiryat Eliahu represent only 5% of the population and some adults spend their workdays outside of the city in settings in which they are even less well represented, many individuals live in intense contact with fellow Yemenites. More than 90% of the Yemenites of Kiryat Eliahu live in one section of the town—the one in which they originally settled. Although they share that section with many others (they constitute about 30% of the population there), Yemenites have continued to be loyal to the district and live there even though most can afford to move to other parts of the city. It is not a fashionable part of town, children of other *vatikim* tend to leave, but it contains the six Yemenite synagogues, kin and community.[6]

The Yemenites of Kiryat Eliahu thus live amidst fellow ethnics. Although they are a small minority in the town as a whole, in their neighborhood they form a substantial bloc, as they are the largest single ethnic group, and they have easy access to each other. Their neighborly relations are primarily with people of the same background.[7]

Religion plays an important role in guiding the social interactions of the Yemenite population. Most Yemenites send their children to only one of the two religious primary schools, and to the religious secondary school. In these settings they may comprise as much as 10-15% of a given class. While they are not isolated from children of other backgrounds in school, they have the opportunity to interact with age-mates of their own ethnic background.

The synagogues are ethnically homogeneous and since virtually every male below the age of 14 and above the age of 25 goes to synagogue every Sabbath (and on every major festival) Yemenites spend at least every Sabbath morning together. Furthermore, since most Yemenites of Kiryat Eliahu do not travel on the Sabbath, they spend the day visiting within their community and elsewhere in town. Even those who live outside the neighborhood are likely to come back to visit their parents and friends on the Sabbath.

There are other occasions, however, when the local Yemenites get together. Family occasions such as the celebration of births, ritual circumcision (*brit mila*), weddings, as well as funerals, bring people together in groups that are invariably almost ethnically homogeneous. In recent years there has been a growth in the importance of the *h'inna,* a party given a week or so before a wedding. Basically an occasion for women to sing, dance and celebrate, these affairs draw increasingly large crowds of males and young people. Whereas the weddings, held in halls, may include coworkers and friends from the army and school who are not Yemenite, the *h'inna* tend to be ethnically homogeneous.

Another institution, called *ja'ale*, involves men more than women, and may occur on any Sabbath or be associated with any other celebration. For *ja'ale,* men gather in someone's house, snack on a variety of foods, drink and sing traditional songs from the Yemenite songbook, the *diwan.* The work contains the works of Yemenite poet-composers, especially Shalom Shabazzi. While this a preferred activity of older men, some younger men also participate. *Ja'ale* has its ritual and its etiquette, and a Yemenite from Kiryat Eliahu can find the same activity anywhere in the country where other Yemenites are found.

The patterns of social interaction in the neighborhood, in the schools on the Sabbath and during the distinctive ceremonial and recreational activities of these people form the basis for a pattern of intra-ethnic interaction. In addition, casual observation leads to the conclusion that children's play groups within the community, and the majority of friendships, tend to be ethnically homogeneous. When people leave town for a weekend or a vacation it is often to visit kinsmen living in other communities or, perhaps, to attend *h'inna* and weddings. Thus, the Yemenites maintain networks of kinsmen and *Landsmann* all over the country.[8]

It is important to emphasize that this style of life has been chosen by the Yemenites themselves, and not forced upon them by outsiders. Most outsiders are quite unaware of the life style of their Yemenite neighbors. There are Yemenites, young and old, who claim that they would like to get away from all this Yemenite togetherness, and some do, but the pressures to be involved are from friends, kin and community, not from outsiders. Israeli society at large provides the possibility for escape for those who want it. It is generally not the lack of resources or alternative that keeps people within the community.

The Yemenite Code of Kiryat Eliahu

The Yemenites of Kiryat Eliahu are quite conscious of and articulate about their values and culture. They frequently speak of *arachim* (values) and of their belief that they developed *arachim* in Yemen that are important and should not be lost in Israel. They are aware of their traditions and heritage of the accomplishments of members of their *edah* (ethnic group) in Israel, and of the manner in which others (especially Ashkenazim) view them. Their images of themselves are not unmixed with criticism (e.g., "we are primitive," "we are too simple and let others take advantage of us," "we are too envious of each other," etc.), but on the whole, the estimation is a positive one. Perhaps not surprisingly it comes close to the stereotypes that other Israelis commonly hold about Yemenites: "This image sees the Yemenite as hard-working, self-respecting . . . well educated in Jewish faith and practice, traditional in his behavior, and strongly identified with family, ethnic group and the Jewish people."[9]

To this description Yemenites and others might add: cheerful, content with their lot and modest in dress and comportment.[10]

In the following pages I will concentrate on a discussion of several Yemenite values. These include: the attitude toward work, contentment with little, education and loyalty to Judaism and to the Yemenite community and its traditions.

In describing these attitudes and values, I am not claiming that there are not some people who turn their backs on these values, or that the expression of these in practice works out the same for everyone. I am suggesting that these are widely shared sentiments and ideas, that one can see them in operation in many contexts, and that the members of the community tend to judge themselves and others by these standards.

The Yemenite Work Ethic

Yemenites in Kiryat Eliahu express a belief in the value of working well, hard, responsibly and without complaint. Work itself is not glorified, nor are long hours prescribed for their own sake, but, rather, work is accepted as a vital part of life. It is felt that those who work hard and well will be appreciated, perhaps recognized and advanced to more responsible positions. Those who cannot work or the few who will not work are pitied. Welfare is not seen as a respectable alternative.

Yemenites do not feel that it is demeaning to engage in work that others regard as humble. Traditionally a man was not measured by the status of his job as much as he was by how he raised his sons, supported his family, and by his religious piety and knowledge (Caspi, n.d.; Katz and Zloczower, 1961:306). This traditional attitude may be changing to some extent as Israeli standards of occupational prestige make inroads, but it has certainly played a role during the first three decades in Israel. For example, when the Yemenites arrived in Israel, some men took menial jobs in sanitation and some women became domestics, but their children don't look down on them for this. Even today, young women may work as domestics while continuing in school, and middle aged couples sometimes "moonlight" at janitorial jobs in order to earn extra money. The general attitude seems to be that, menial or not, it is a job, it pays, and one should get it done quietly and efficiently.

Menial jobs do not involve honor and shame. I do not recall any comments indicating shame at having to work in garbage collection, street cleaning, or in the back-breaking labor of afforestation and road building, which many older men did when they first came to the country. One is more likely to hear of pride in their pioneering role.

Yemenites of Kiryat Eliahu know that part of the stereotype others have of them is that they are hard-working, and they are generally proud of it. It is true that there are some, more cynical than others, who say, "Sure, they like us for this. We are suckers, *frayerim,* working hard and not complaining." But even they see this as a distinctive trait.[11]

Today younger Yemenite men are not usually employed at unskilled labor. Indeed, while some of the older men (in their 60s and older) still work in sanitation, most men in their 50s have trades. They are electricians, tile setters, carpenters, painters and sometimes factory workers. Those still younger are skilled craftsmen (electricians, welders, crane operators, etc.), teachers, clerks and officers in the military (noncommissioned and commissioned). Some are factory workers with developed skills. There are more university graduates and students among them, and some have become technicians, engineers and architects, though these are, as yet, a small minority.[12]

"Histapkut b'mu'at"—Contentment with little

This phrase comes readily to the lips of those Yemenites who list their *edah's* outstanding traits. One evening, before an audience of several thousand Yemenites, Yisrael Yeshayahu (a Yemenite of national prominence, then speaker of the Knesset) explained the situation as follows: "It is not that Yemenites are so simple that they don't want the same things that other people want. But they know how to do without, if need be, and not blame others for their troubles, but work to improve their situation." There are, however, further implications of this.

The Yemenites of Kiryat Eliahu are not avid consumers. This is especially evident from the interiors of their homes. A Yemenite home is almost instantly recognizable by the lack of wallpaper (*tapetim*), the bareness of the floors, the sparseness of the furnishings and lack of knicknacks. Apparently, in Yemen household rooms were largely bare, and this almost seems the case now. The drapes, rugs, *tapetim,* heavy upholstered sofas and chairs, the buffet, the dining room set and the fancy coffee table—

the full Israeli dining/living room complex–is rarely encountered. Not only are the furnishings sparse, they are often shamelessly old and worn, even in the homes of young people with education and position. That this is not the product of poverty can be demonstrated by a house to house survey in Kiryat Eliahu. The homes of Moroccan Jews, for example, are typified by dense, rich, colorful furnishings, which fill their rooms with color and things. This is generally true for poor families on welfare as well as for those who are better off.

To Yemenites of Kiryat Eliahu, "tapetim" is often considered to stand for "frivolous expense" and "chasing mindlessly after the appearance of 'modernity'." Not only does the Yemenites' esthetic sense control the furnishing of their homes, but they may also express disapproval of those who chase after these "externals." The willingness to do without, to put off buying, is indicative of the thrift that others remark in them. Indeed, other peoples are often wont to call the Yementies *kamtsanim,* stingy folks.

If Yemenite contentment with less makes those who are better off feel less guilty, there is also some evidence that the attitude of thrift encourages saving, and has resulted in considerable relative wealth for those who practice it. In a city where much of the housing is owned by the Ministry of Housing and rented by the government rental agency, almost every Yemenite family owns its own home. In addition, quite a few own more than one apartment, and it is common for parents to present their newly married children with modest apartments of their own.

An investigation into poverty status in Israel, based on 1963 data, indicated the following striking result: If poverty were measured in terms of income, the Yemenites showed the highest rate of poverty of any ethnic group on the list. When measures of wealth were introduced their rate was much lower; indeed, they came close to those from the Balkans, and to Europeans, while those from Iran/Iraq and Morocco appeared far poorer (Habib *et al.,* 1977:26).[13] Wealth was measured by savings, stocks, imputed value of owner-occupied dwellings, and durable goods. This study suggests that the tendency of Yemenites to control their consumption of goods and save had the result of increasing their actual wealth. While I have no comparable material for Kiryat Eliahu, my observations on housing, building (it is typical for members of the community to expand their apartments by adding more rooms), and with the claims of both Yemenite and other informants, are consistent with these findings.

Identification with Judaism, the Yemenite edah and the family

It is difficult to separate elements here, as it is clear that they are, to some extent, mutually reinforcing. For example, parents are honored because it is a tenet of Judaism, but Judaism continues to be respected and practiced in part because of respect and concern for parents. It is clear that the Jewish religion and its ethics play a major role in certain aspects of Yemenite life.

As a people, the Yemenites are among the most observant ethnic group in Israel today. In Kiryat Eliahu, at any rate, the observance of the Sabbath through synagogue attendance and maintenance of the prohibitions is virtually universal in the Yemenite community, except, perhaps, for those young men who are going through a rebellious period before settling down to family life. The skullcap is worn in public by almost all males, including most of the young men, at least when they are in town. This degree of observance contrasts sharply with the general trend among other residents of Kiryat Eliahu.

The maintenance of the Sabbath and *kashrut* (dietary laws) demands a certain kind of order and discipline. It involves self-control, cleanliness, respect and obedience. Whether all do it in an ungrudging manner or whether they believe in it or merely do it for the sake of their parents, they follow these traditions. People will articulate the values involved and why it is important there be a Sabbath family gathering at home, and so on.

Most striking is the continuation of the tradition that a father is responsible for teaching his son(s) synagogue ways, prayers and, above all, preparation for each week's Torah portion (Gotein, 1953:118). Here the mutual obligation and the mutual discipline is manifested most strongly. During the week the father should drill the child and explain the Torah portion (*parsha*). During the service the son sits across from his father, as the father calls his attention to the passage and tries to keep his son's mind on it. From about the age of seven, boys are expected to be able to read from the Torah publicly. In fact, a boy is also expected to read aloud the Onkelos Aramaic translation, on a line by line basis, as adult readers read the Hebrew.[14] It is no exaggeration to say that the Yemenite men who have paid attention and done what is expected of them are virtuosi of the synagogue. They know the services by heart, are able to read the Torah in Hebrew and Aramaic, have Yemenite cantorial skills, and perhaps can pray and sing in other ethnic traditions (*nusachim*) as well, having learned them in school and the army. Since they do not depend upon rabbis to lead the service, but take turns leading prayers (and competing and bidding for the honor of doing so) any man of substance who wishes to maintain his prestige must be able to lead services, as well as to read from the Torah.

Education

Through Judaism and through their concern with Torah, the Yemenites had respect for learning, and literacy in Hebrew was said to be virtually universal among men in Yemen. This learning was tied to Judaism, however, and was not secular, or learning for its own sake.[15] Women were not formally educated in Yemen. It seems, therefore, that attitudes about education have not been simply transferred unmodified to Israel, but in Kiryat Eliahu there is a clear connection between the Yemenite community and education. More specifically, since the Yemenites are so involved and well educated in Judaism, the religious education system offers an occupational niche for many.

There is virtually a whole generation of Yemenite teachers and nursery school teachers in Kiryat Eliahu. Young women who are today in their mid-thirties and early forties, perhaps born in Yemen but educated in Israel, went to teachers' colleges, often after days of work, and became teachers. There are at least 45 such women teaching in schools and nursery schools. Today younger women are still going to teachers' colleges, but a growing number are continuing for full university degrees. A number of less well educated women work as aides to nursery school teachers.

While more women than men have gone into teaching, there are at least 15 male teachers in the town. It is harder to count the men because more of them have left Kiryat Eliahu for other parts of the country, but Yemenites from Kiryat Eliahu are working today as principals, regional nursery school supervisors and teachers in seminaries. Of 55 couples in one sample born between 1930 and 1944, 12 have one or both spouses in education. (Up to 1939, 7 out of 38; after 1940, 5 out of 17. The percentage of teachers among those born since 1945 is higher still.)

It is worth speculating on the effect that a generation of nursery school teachers will have on their own children and those of their siblings. At a time when Israeli educators are organizing programs to teach parents to play with and talk to their children, these women are specialists, very much aware of the social and intellectual needs of young children and concerned about their own children's development.

Although I have not seen data on the actual school achievement of Yemenite students as compared with others, discussions with teachers, advisers, school social workers and the truant officer have indicated that Yemenite children are generally good students and do not present behavioral problems. They are underrepresented in the case loads of the social workers and hardly to be found in the special classes for problem students. If Yemenite children have problems with mathematics and English (which both the students and the teachers seem to believe to be the case) they are considered superior students in Hebrew and subjects related to history and Torah.

So concerned are Yemenite parents about the education of their children that an increasing number are sending their sons to boarding schools or better religious schools in nearby communities. Most do this with their own savings, but some have begun to request scholarship aid from the State. Parents are more likely to keep their daughters at home to attend schools in town.

Loyalty to the ethnic group

The Yemenites of Kiryat Eliahu are not only loyal to their families and local community, they are proud of and involved with the Yemenite tradition as well. They are proud of having lived in a sea of non-Jews (*gabayil*) for over 2,000 years, while retaining their identity and Judaism. They are proud of their spoken Hebrew, with its distinctive pronunciation, and of their prayer traditions, their foods, music and poetry. Throughout the country, dance groups are flourishing, composers are writing music on Yemenite themes, and Yemenite boys and girls are trying to emulate popular Yemenite performers, Boaz Sharabi, Tsadok Tsubeyri, Yitshar Cohen, Uri Shevach and Ofira Gluska. This is not merely a fossilized continuation but a burst of creative musical activity. Organizations for the advancement of Yemenite culture in Israel are increasing their activities and membership, and attracting educated young couples. The Yemenites of Kiryat Eliahu complain that they are not organized and therefore lag behind other Yemenite communities, but they are interested and anxious to participate, and aware of what is being done elsewhere.

The adaptive value of Yemenite traditions

The adaptive implications of the Yemenite code, even where not explicitly alluded to earlier, are generally obvious. The willingness to work hard, responsibly and cheerfully makes Yemenites valued employees.

(Some complain that the *Shiknozim*—Ashkenazim—see them fit only to be low level workers, but, if so, it is unlikely to remain the case.) The willingness and ability to manage on little and, above all, to save, means that they are frequently able to invest in apartments and other property and to save for the education of their children. A generation that includes so many teachers from such humble beginnings is likely to expect higher levels of achievement in their children and be able to give more tactical guidance than their parents gave them.

The element of ethnic pride may be rather less obvious in its importance, but this pride is conducive to self-confidence. As Katz and Zloczower wrote, "Evaluating themselves in these terms—particularly with respect to familial, religious and national loyalties—the Yemenites do not pereceive themselves wanting, and this self-respect (though it is not unmixed with feelings of inferiority) contributes substantially to the picture presented here" (1961:306), (i.e., a picture rather similar to the one portrayed here). To people who look upon them as simple and miserly, Yemenites respond "We may be (have been) simple, but we are (were) good. We know about values, about education, about correct conduct (*derech eretz*) and Torah, and about hard work. We know about the interior values involved in modernization, not just the externals, the *tapetim* and the cosmetics." They contrast what they see as the coldness of the Ashkenazai population with their own warmth and concern for family.

It may be argued that these attitudes are, in fact, a product of the Yemenite experience in Israel; a response to life in a class stratified society, which the Yemenites entered at the bottom as unskilled and menial workers (and agriculturists, in some areas) (cf. Yancey *et al.,* 1976). Under such circumstances it would be advantageous to appear to work hard and to suffer cheerfully. But if this behavior was reinforced, or selected for, in the Israeli context, it is most unlikely that it was created *de novo* after immigration. Not only are these attitudes consistent with what we know of Yemenite Jewish attitudes previously (v. Goitein, 1953, 1955; Caspi, n.d.), but similar employment and economic conditions have not necessarily produced the same constellation of attitudes among other ethnic groups who entered the country and the work force at the same time and at the same level. This complex of attitudes and social and cultural traits seems unique to the Yemenite population. It is not characteristic, for example, of the other immigrant groups from Asia or Africa such as those from Morocco, Egypt, Turkey and Iraq.

Comments and Conclusions

The preceding pages contain a generalized description of various aspects of the life of Yemenites living in Kiryat Eliahu. This description is an abstraction from observed reality and it should be clear that the elements of the Yemenite code do not lead to simple, automatic or universal performances by all individuals. Although not everyone works hard, saves, studies well or becomes a teacher, many do, or they judge themselves and others in these terms. Furthermore, performance according to elements of the code may lead to measurable results. One example is the study cited regarding Yemenite savings and wealth. Discussions with workers in welfare, education and public health and a study of the relevant records, reveal that Yemenites are hardly represented on the welfare rolls, that their children are rarely problems for the truant officer, the school social workers or teachers. In an area of relatively high delinquency, there are very few Yemenite problem children out of a population of 1300. All this contrasts strongly with the Israeli stereotype of "Oriental Jews" as people sunk in poverty, disorganizationa and in need of special nurturing.

To some extent the description given here can probably be duplicated in many Yemenite communities around the country. There are, of course, sources of variation, such as: the degree of isolation or homogeneity of a community; its economic and educational standard; whether it is a moshav, a small town, or part of Tel Aviv or Jerusalem; the history of a community and the time of arrival of its members; and the place of origin in Yemen.

Some Yemenite communities seem worse off economically, socially or in terms of their morale, although few studies are available to document this. Others appear better off than Kiryat Eliahu in terms of occupational status, education, and organization.

As the case of Kiryat Eliahu demonstrates, Yemenite ethnicity is not being maintained through spatial or social isolation. Whereas such isolation may be seen in the case of Rosh Ha'Ayin or in many moshavim, this is clearly not the case in Kiryat Eliahu. The Yemenites of Kiryat Eliahu are involved almost daily with Israelis from other backgrounds, on the job, in school, when shopping, and through the mass media, but despite this they maintain their own networks, groups and activity systems.

The Yemenite social and cultural patterns described here are neither

"Oriental," "traditional," "working class," nor a "culture of poverty." These patterns represent a distinctive complex, shared among people of common origin, who participate in all of the institutions of the State of Israel (economic, educational, military, political) but whose "intimate culture" and private social relations are still lived within their own distinctive sphere.

This is certainly not a simple carryover from life in Yemen. The lives and conditions of Israeli Yemenites are completely different from what they were in Yemen, and while many institutions are directly traceable to Yemen, they are certainly much modified in form and meaning today. Many patterns are new, creative responses to new conditions in the new land. They are, however, unique to this group, developed among them, from a baseline of practice, values, attitudes and social relations derived originally from Yemen.

Any attempt to attribute this distinctive cultural/social complex to particular structural or economic conditions of the Yemenites in Kiryat Eliahu is not likely to succeed. It was reasonable for Katz and Zloczower to suggest that the conditions of isolation and educational and occupational inequality in Sha'arayim permitted ethnic continuity of the sort they described (1961:306), but this is not the case in Kiryat Eliahu, where no special treatment or educational, residential, occupational conditions distinguished the Yemenite settlers from those coming from Turkey, Egypt, Morocco, Romania, Poland or elsewhere.

Moreover, Yemenite ethnicity shows no sign of progressive weakening and in certain aspects is becoming intensified. Although some members of the first generation to grow up in Israel went through a traumatic period and turned their backs on their parents' culture, trying to become "modern" and "Israeli," this period has passed and many of these same people have come to have a more positive appreciation of their *edah* or ethnic group. To some extent Marcus Hansen's "principle of third generation" has taken place within the life cycle of the first generation (1952). Practices and traditions that had become unpopular with the young have come back into fashion. (*H'inna* and Yemenite music and dance are two such examples.) Whereas the parents of Yemenite children 25 years ago seemed to their children unworldly, unknowledgeable, *primitivi*, today's Yemenite parents are school teachers, clerks, skilled workmen, technicians, reserve soldiers, who passed through the difficult adjustment period and have returned or maintained their Yemenite-ness. I predict further intensification of identification and involvement with Yemenite culture in the immediate future, even though the rates of intermarriage are likely to rise (as will occupational and educational status), and although some individuals will leave the Yemenite community altogether.

Finally, on a more general level, certain elements of the code presented here have adaptive value and could be considered strategies or coping mechanisms, pursued whether consciously or unconsciously for the positive results they bring through education, savings and a good reputation. But necessity is not necessarily the parent of invention, and not every immigrant group operates in the same way, with the same values, making the same educational and occupational choices, no matter how useful they may be. Not every group has great pride in their traditions and communicates them to their children the way the Yemenites do.

This ethnically based cultural complex is more than just a set of strategies, or a reflex of economic and political conditions [as, for example, Williams claims is true of the return to Welshness in the Chubut Valley of Argentina (1978)]. For the person brought up in the community it comprises a part of a way of life, with a myriad of associations, emotions, expectations and understandings. It is through this distinctive Israeli-Yemenite cultural code that members of the community judge themselves and others, and it is in terms of it that they make choices and guide their actions.

Notes

[1] This paper is based on field research conducted in Israel in 1975-77 and funded by the National Science Foundation. Thanks are due to that institution, as well as to Arnold Strickon and Sidney Greenfield, who read drafts of this paper. I regret that I was not able to incorporate more of their suggestions. Above all I am indebted to Eli Malkhi for aid and advice.

[2] Barth correctly notes (1969:11) that ethnic boundaries may exist even in the absence of apparent cultural differences. It does not follow, however, that cultural differences do not exist, although a number of writers seems to have made that assumption.

[3] Such differences may be manifest, above all, in what Epstein (1978:112) calls "intimate culture" rather than "public culture." Much of it is seen "backstage," at home, or in ethnically specific places of worship. Thus, those who encounter others only in public places (work, school, market) may not be aware of how they differ from each other (cf. Izraeli 1979).

[4] Examples of studies in the United States, which point to significant cultural differences, include: Greeley (1972), Kobrin and Goldscheider (1978), Laumann (1973), Gambino (1975), Mindel and Havenstein (1976).

[5] I hope that this discussion will, in a small way, respond to Alex Weingrod's call for "the specification of ways in which ethnicity orients behavior in the broad range of everyday social situations (Weingrod, 1979:64).

[6] Berdichevsky (1977) and Katz and Zloczower (1961) report similar loyalty from the Yemenite community of Sha'arayim.

[7] During the past few years a number of better educated young couples have moved from the old neighborhood and now live near each other in another part of town. This may result in the development of a new Yemenite section, one marked by higher socioeconomic status.

[8] More than 75% of marriages are ethnically homogeneous. Sometimes intermarried couples stay in the neighborhood and participate with the community, especially if the husband is Yemenite and can be involved in the synagogue, raising his son to know the Yemenite ways.

[9] This was written by Katz and Zloczower twenty years ago (1961:294).

[10] These characteristics are commonly attributed to Yemenites both by themselves and by other Israelis. They are encountered in the press and in casual conversation. The same attributes were listed by Kiryat Eliahu high school students of mixed ethnic background when asked to typify various Jewish groups.

[11] In his paper on the work ethic among British Jews, Kosmin cites the Talmud: "Great is work for it honors the workman" and the Rabbinic dictum "Love Work" (Aboth, 1.10). He sees this as an early form of Protestant ethic, attaching merit to the work and the reward. This could well be the same source for the Yemenites (Kosman, 1979:39).

[12] Very few Yemenites have shops and none are engaged in selling outside their own shops. Selling is not regarded as a way to make a living.

[13] Habib and his associates had to use data from 1963, when most Yemenites had been in the country only 15 years. It would be interesting to see the results of such a study today, 30 years after their arrival in Israel.

[14] In other Jewish communities a boy is not called up to read from the Torah until he is *bar mitzvah* at the age of 13. It is also common in other communities for a special cantor to do the actual reading while the person honored by being called up merely says the blessings before and after the actual Torah reading. It is usual, however, for each Yemenite man to chant directly from the Torah himself. As the reading must be perfect both in pronunciation and melody, it takes considerable preparation. The reading of the Onkelos translation, which has been dropped by other communities, involves a different melody and style from that of the Hebrew Torah reading.

[15] Knowledge was gained through long hours of learning from special teachers (*mori*) who taught reading, but not necessarily understanding of the texts), and from fathers. For an extensive discussion of Jewish learning in Yemen see Goitein (1953).

References

Barth, Fredrik, 1967. "On the Study of Social Change." *American Anthropologist,* 69:661-669.

——. (Ed.). 1969. *Ethnic Groups and Boundaries.* Boston: Little, Brown.

Bennett, John W. (Ed.). 1975. *The New Ethnicity: Perspectives from Ethnology.* 1973 Proceedings of the American Ethnological Society. St Paul: West Publishing Co.

Berdichevsky, Norman. 1977. "The Persistence of the Yemeni Quarter in an Israeli Town," *Ethnicity* 4:287-309.

Caspi, Michael. n.d. "Growing up in Traditional Jewish Yemenite Society?" Manuscript dedicated to Professor Joseph Silverman.

Cohen, Percy. 1962. "Alignments and Allegiances in the Community of Sha'arayim in Israel," *Jewish Journal of Sociology*, 4:14-38.

Epstein, A. L. 1978. *Ethos and Identity: Three Studies in Ethnicity.* London: Tavistock.

Gambino, Richard. 1975. *Blood of My Blood: The Dilemma of the Italian-Americans,* Garden City: Doubleday.

Gans, Herbert J. 1979. "Symbolic Ethnicity: The Future of Ethnic Groups and Cultures in America," *Ethnic and Racial Studies* 2:1-20.

Glazer, Nathan, and Moynihan, Daniel P. 1975. *Ethnicity: Theory and Experience.* Cambridge: Harvard University Press.

Goitein, Shlomo D. 1953. "Jewish Education in Yemen as an Archetype of Traditional Jewish Education," in C. Frankenstein (Ed.), *Between Past and Future.* Jerusalem: Henrietta Szold Foundation.

———. 1955. "Portrait of a Yemenite Weavers' Village," *Jewish Social Studies* 17: 3-26.

Goodenough, Ward H. 1966. *Cooperation in Change.* New York: John Wiley and Sons.

Greeley, Andrew H. 1972. *That Most Distressful Nation.* Chicago: Quadrangle.

———. n.d. "An Alternative Perspective for Studying American Ethnicity." Unpublished manuscript.

Habib, Jack, Kohn, M., and Lerman, Robert. 1977. "The Effect of Poverty Status in Israel Considering Wealth and Variability of Income," *Review of Income and Wealth,* Ser. 23, No. 1, March 17-38.

Hansen, Marcus L. 1952. "The Third Generation in America," *Commentary,* XIV: 492-500.

Izraeli, Dafna N. 1979. "Ethnicity and Industrial Relations: an Israeli Factory Case Study," *Ethnic and Racial Studies* Vol. 2. 80-89.

Katz, Elihu, and Zloczower, Avraham. 1961. "Ethnic Continuity in an Israeli Town," *Human Relations* 14:293-308.

Katzir, Yael. 1976. *The Effects of Resettlement on the Status and Role of Yemeni Jewish Women: The Case of Ramat Oranim, Israel.* Unpublished Ph.D. Dissertation, University of California, Berkeley.

Kobrin, Frances E., and Goldscheider, Calvin. 1978. *The Ethnic Factor in Family Structure and Mobility.* Cambridge: Ballinger.

Kosmin, Barry. 1979. "Exclusion and Opportunity: Traditions of Work Amongst British Jews," in Sandra Wallman (Ed.), *Ethnicity at Work.* London: Macmillan.

Laumann, E. O. 1973. *Bonds of Pluralism.* New York: John Wiley.

Light, Ivan H. 1972. *Ethnic Enterprise in America.* Berkeley and Los Angeles: University of California Press.

Mindel, Charles H., and Havenstein, Robert W. 1976. *Ethnic Families in America: Patterns and Variations.* New York: Elsevier.

Olneck, Michael R. and Lazerson, Marvin. 1974. "The School Achievement of Immigrant Children: 1900-1930," *History of Education Quarterly,* 14:453-482.

Patterson, G. James. 1979. "A Critique of 'The New Ethnicity'," *American Anthropologist* 81:103-105.

Patterson, Orlando. 1975. "Context and Choice in Ethnic Allegiance: A Theoretical Framework and Caribbean Case Study," in Nathan Glazer and Daniel P. Moynihan (Eds.), *Ethnicity*. Cambridge: Harvard University.

———. 1977. *Ethnic Chauvinism: The Reactionary Impulse*. New York: Stein and Day.

Ryan, William. 1971. *Blaming the Victim*. New York: Vintage Books.

Sverski, Shlomo. n.d. "Orientals and Ashkenazim in Israel: An Emerging Dependency Relationship." Haifa University.

Smooha, Sammy. 1978. *Israel: Pluralism and Conflict*. Berkeley and Los Angeles: University of California Press.

Strickon, Arnold, and Ibarra, Robert A. 1980. "Norwegians and Tobacco in Wisconsin: The Changing Dynamics of Ethnicity." Manuscript.

Turner, Victor W. 1974. *Dramas, Fields and Metaphors*. Ithaca, N.Y.: Cornell University Press.

Weingrod, Alex. 1979. "Recent Trends in Israeli Ethnicity," *Ethnic and Racial Studies* 2:55-65.

Williams, Glyn. 1978. "Industrialization and Ethnic Change in the Lower Chubut Valley, Argentina," *American Ethnologist* 5:618-630.

Yancey, William L., Ericksen, E. P., and Juliani, R. N. 1976. "Emergent Ethnicity: A Review and Reformulation," *American Sociological Review* 41:391-403.

12

Iranian Ethnicity in Israel: The Performance of Identity

Judith L. Goldstein

A scheme of our experience is a meaning-context which is a configuration of our past experiences embracing conceptually the experiental objects to be found in the latter but not the process by which they were constituted. The constituting process itself is entirely ignored, while the objectivity constituted by it is taken for granted. (Alfred Schutz, 1967:82).

In 1975 I passed through Israel on my way back to the United States from Iran to look up the relatives of Iranians with whom I had become acquainted.[1] Whereas older Iranians in Israel were eager to hear news I might have and had very specific questions about people, places and social conditions, younger people disavowed any interest in Iran and in the Jewish past there on the explicit grounds that it did not concern them. They told me their Persian language ability was poor and left the room when I showed pictures of the town of Yazd where I had done my fieldwork. Five years later, many of these same young people were among the enthusiastic audiences that went to see a Persian language theater troupe play in Jerusalem, Tel Aviv and smaller towns throughout Israel. When I showed my slides in a development town with a substantial Iranian population, more than 300 people, mostly young, turned out to see them; a far cry from the extended family of twenty I had been told to expect.

237

These young people illustrate the recent emergence of ethnic group consciousness among Iranians in Israel. They are joined by an increasing number of middle class[2] Iranians who participate in activities organized by the Iranian community, which are themselves becoming more frequent. In this paper I will describe how Iranians are consolidating their identity through "definitional ceremonies"[3] in which they present themselves to themselves in a variety of cultural performances.

The Iranian community in Israel, since the 1978 revolution, is composed of old immigrants, the bulk of whom came during 1950-1951; young adults who were born in Iran or Israel, but were raised in Israel; and new immigrants who have come within the last three years.[4]

I speak of an "emergence" of ethnic group consciousness because Iranians are an example of an Israeli group that has maintained a low ethnic profile. Analysts of Israel ethnicity have noticed the growing bifurcation between Ashkenazim and Sephardim, and the greater differentiation according to country of origin among Middle Eastern as opposed to Ashkenazi Jews, but they have not remarked that Jews from certain Middle Eastern countries have very low saliency as an ethnic category.

Iranian Jews have not been subsumed in the Oriental Jewish stereotype (itself stereotyped). Oriental negative characteristics catalogued by Patai, for example, include "instability, emotionalism, impulsiveness, unreliability, incompetence, habitual lying, cheating, laziness, boastfulness, inclination to violence, uncontrolled temper, superstitiousness, childishness and lack of cleanliness" (quoted in Lewis, 1980:16). These terms are not used for Iranian Jews who, if anything, bear the stamp of the calculating capitalist, which does not imply lack of control at all. Traits associated with Iranians are stingingess and deceit. What these traits imply is that the Iranians march to a different drummer—for some they exhibit the lack of open hospitality which makes for camaraderie; for others, lack of commitment to a collective socialist ideal; for yet others, their ability (and this is positive) to provide apartments for all their children, and so on. Iranians do not see themselves in the Oriental stereotype. In fact, they attribute their lack of success in obtaining benefits from the Israeli bureaucracy to their inability to be like the Moroccans who, they say, shout and push over chairs, rather than being polite like Iranians, and get what they want. The ability of the Iranians to maintain a low ethnic profile was made easier because they were classed neither with the Ashkenazim nor, in any consistent way, with the Sephardim.

In abandoning their low profile, Iranians have been influenced by Israeli forms of being ethnic, particularly by ethnic festivals and the revival of cultural forms within a national framework.

The Iranian identity being forged in cultural performance links Jewish history in Iran with contemporary Iranian life in Israel. An ethnic group, according to a much cited definition, is:

> a collectivity within a larger society, having a real or putative common ancestry, memories of a shared historical past, and a cultural focus on one or more symbolic elements defined as the epitome of their peoplehood. (Shermerhorn, quoted in Aronson, 1977, and Cohen, 1978)

Though a concept of a "shared historical past" appears to be a central constituent of ethnic identity (at least to people within an ethnic group, if not to scholars who prefer a more political definition), I would deny that this must be based on "memories of a shared historical past." Rather, it seems as if a shared historical past can be created in the process of ethnic incorporation. I would argue that Jews of Iranian origin are doing this through the medium of definitional ceremonies, which try to unite Iranians with varying definitions of self, different pasts, and different interests in the present.

Thus, my concern is the definition of ethnic identity from the natives' point of view. To study this I focus on two hitherto underanalyzed aspects of ethnicity: the process of self-ascription of ethnic categories and the effect of the increasing emphasis on ethnic identity for a group that is internally differentiated.

Cultural Models: Ashkenazi, Moroccan and Israeli Ethnic

Some observers claim that the general dominance of the Ashkenazim in Israel have left the Sephardim without fitting models for themselves. Toledano referred to the "present Ashkenization of the Sephardim" and called for programs, especially in the schools, which would "help restore the cultural balance in Israel" (1973:346). Smooha also argued that Ashkenazi "middle class life style is the dominant model in Israeli society today. . . . The prevailing social ideals are completely Ashkenazi—a small middle-class urban family, a kibbutz member, the sabra, the socialist society. The Oriental Jew cannot recognize himself in such images of Israel" (1972:32,

35). The model was Ashkenazi, these authors claim, and what was "left over" was ethnic. Thus, Kol Israel would present a reading of the Megillat Esther in the Ashkenazi style, then announce "And now we will chant chapters according to melodies of the ethnic groups" (Toledano, 1973: 342).

However, recent developments, including the Black Panthers in the political sphere, and ethnic revivals in the religious/cultural spheres, make this one-model view questionable. These developments make increasingly difficult to maintain that the "Oriental Jew cannot recognize himself" in the other available images. The Black Panthers have been described by Smooha as providing a countermodel for Middle Eastern Jews in the political arena. Others have pointed to what they call an ethnic "revival" and Weingrod (1979:61) observed that ethnic festivals seemed to arise in the mid-60s when cultural pluralism was no longer considered "dangerous."

These ethnic festivals—the Moroccan *Mimouna* and Kurdish *Seranna*—have political and cultural functions. They provide occasions for ethnic politicians to publicize themselves and renew contact with national leaders who attend while also demonstrating the electoral power of the group (Weingrod, 1979:61). *The Jerusalem Post* of April 20, 1979 (Yudelman, 1979) ran its articles on the Moroccan *Mimouna* and Iranian *Ruz-e bagh* (like the *Mimouna,* an outdoor festival following Passover) celebrations back to back, emphasized the number of people who attended each event, and provided pictures, not of the thousands of picnickers, but of the politicians. The Moroccan, Kurdish and Iranian festivals are similar in form. They are celebrated in the spring with picnicking, singing, dancing and political speechmaking. They are public and take place in the open air in contrast with the more private ceremonies in ethnic synagogues, but nonetheless "can also be viewed as spiritual occasions where cultural symbols become elaborated" (Weingrod, 1979: 61). They are confused with each other by observers; a number of Israelis reported to me that the Iranian festival which was held in Tel Aviv was a Moroccan *mimouna*. When told the festival was Iranian, they responded, "Oh, it's their *mimouna*!"

And so, in a way it is. After all, the Moroccan *Mimouna* had appeared before the others in Israel, and along with the example of Moroccan political organization, inspired other "ethnic" groups. There was, in this sense, a Moroccan model of considerable importance that could be considered along with the Ashkenazi model to which Smooha and others refer.

The model they present for the Iranians is one of the achievement of visibility. The Moroccans can be said to have turned negative visibility into a more positive one by re-presenting themselves to the Israeli public. They re-presented themselves in that they presented themselves a second time, and in that they have offered another image of themselves for both popular and internal consumption. The Moroccan example influenced the Iranians who had maintained a low profile.

The ethnic revival of the 1960s can be seen as having a general Israeli form that encapsulated the particular content of each ethnic group. This revival was expressed "in such activities as the publication by different immigrants associations of matters related to their particular religio-cultural heritage, and in the increasing popularity of particular traditional festivities of various immigrant groups" (Deshen:284). The different ethnic groups expressed their particularism in these shared forms. Thus, one can point to an Israeli form of manifesting ethnicity, a form that covers the range of ethnic activities from mundane association meetings to colorful ethnic festivals. The Israeli form of the events, and the Israeli motivation for the events (the reason for having the festivals in Morocco and Iran are different from those in Israel) make it possible to apply to Israel ethnic groups what was said about American ethnic groups: "The so-called 'foreign heritage' of ethnic groups is taking place in this country" (Yancey et al., 1976:400).

Two arguments merge here. One argument assumes the relationship of the festivals in the country of origin and Israel is similar enough to be described as a "revival." The other questions the "authenticity" of these festivals in their Israeli versions (Goell, 1981). The term "revival" distorts the living nature of these festivals—they should not be compared with their former versions by means of a point-by-point checklist alone, but should be placed in their former and current historical and social contexts. When this kind of comparison is made the issue of authenticity is transformed. The festivals are not and cannot be exactly what they were in the old country, but are "authentic" creations in the new country. For example, the public Iranian festival observed is a blend of what were two festivals in Iran. In Israel, the celebration is referred to interchangeably as *Ruz-e bagh,* a Jewish day in the garden following Pesach, and as *Nowruz,* the celebration of the traditional Iranian New Year. The confusion in terminology allows the two traditions, one Jewish and one

Iranian, to merge. In Israel *Ruz-e bagh* "competes" with the Moroccan *Mimouna,* while *Nowruz* connects Israelis of Iranian origin to a-other "great tradition."

In creating a group identity for themselves, Iranians are influenced by Ashkenazi and Moroccan models, and act within Israeli modes of being ethnic. According to Sartre,

> The constitution of an elite group (on the basis, of course, of real, material conditions) as an ensemble of solidarities has the dialectical consequence of making it the negation of the rest of the social field and, as a result, of occasioning in this field so far as it is defined as *non-grouped,* the conditions for an antagonistic grouping ... Everything becomes clear if we situate the non-grouped who discover themselves to be a collective through their impotence in relation to the group which they reveal. (1976:346-347)

Both the Ashkenazim and the Moroccans were potent (to keep within Sartre's terminology) cultural models for the Iranians. The Ashkenazim may have formed a ruling elite (Weingrod and Gurevitch, 1977) with an enviable life-style (Smooha, 1972; Toledano, 1973), but the Moroccans helped show the Iranians what to do about it. The non-grouped embarked upon the process of becoming grouped. Young people may say that they are discriminated against because they are Oriental Jews and within certain contexts the Iranians form a bloc with Oriental Jews, but as a whole they are more interested and feel they have more to gain in grouping as an Iranian ethnic group—the *eda ha Iranit.*

Definitional Ceremonies: The Intersection of Ethnicity and Culture

However Israeli the form of ethnic activity may be, the content is ethnic. The Iranians are becoming visible to themselves through "definitional ceremonies," which are performed interpretations of themselves. Through these performances the Iranians involved are presenting themselves as an *eda,* or ethnic group, and not as a collection of people who have, somehow, an Iranian background in common.

It may help to state this somewhat differently. It is my contention that Iranians in Israel are making the effort to move from what Alfred Schutz called "contemporaries" to what he called "consociates." Consociates are "the other selves of the world of directly experienced reality," but, although contemporaries have ideas about each other, they do not meet since they share a community of space, not of time. The crucial difference for the argument at hand is that "actions between contemporaries are only mutually interrelated, whereas actions between consociates are mutually interlocked" (Schutz, 1967:180).[5] The attempt to form an *eda* is equivalent to the attempt made to interlock Iranians in Israel.

Schutz said that contemporaries are related by the assumption of a "shared interpretive scheme." I am claiming here that it is the creation of a shared interpretive scheme that provides a means by which contemporaries can be transformed to consociates. One of the functions of the Iranian cultural performances, which I will describe, is precisely to construct a shared schema of experience.

Before I discuss the definitional ceremonies that are acting to interlock individuals of Iranian origin, I must turn briefly to the ways in which Iranians can be said to have been interrelated. The category "Iranian" refers to an individual's country of origin (or if second generation in Israel, the origin of his/her parents), personal life, religious life and family life. The category "Iranian" is itself specific to Israel and not to Iran as Iranians follow the pattern of "In Iran I was Jewish; in Israel I'm Iranian." Among themselves they continue to refer to themselves by city of origin. To an extent this illustrates the general proposition that "members tend to know more their own and adjacent categories, and less about those more socially distant" (Handelman, 1977:191), but it also reflects the Jewish past in Iran.

The Jews of the Iranian cities were relatively isolated before the changes that occurred within the past generation brought them together in Teheran and Israel. The customs, dialect and Persian accents of the Jews of the cities of Iran were marked, identifiable and, therefore, of course, different. Even in spoken Hebrew, Jews of Iranian origin preserve the habit of identifying themselves by city of origin (in my experience more than Israelis of other countries) and refer to themselves "incorrectly" as the *eda ha yazdit,* the *eda ha isfhanit,* and so on. "*Eda*" to them glosses cultural distinctions and covers differences that are "within the eda" to non-Iranians.

The possibility for creating a salient *eda* was based on the attributes of Iranianness, and although an image of the past for the present is being created, it is founded on some formally articulated shared understanding of what an Iranian is and does. Thus, the definition of ethnicity as both subjective and objective is pertinent here. Defining oneself as Iranian is a subjective, relational choice based on what is taken by the actor as objective characteristics. Although the relevant objective characteristics change according to situation, the varying definitions of self are seen as being, in each case, objective and present. Thus, in relation to Moroccans, Iranians ,might see themselves as hardworking and thrifty; in relation to Ashkenazim, as having a strong family life and high morals among unmarried girls; in relation to secular, as religious, and so forth. But this kind of identification is not enough to form an *eda* in the way we have been considering the term as a consciously formed gorup with some sort of collective objectives in mind. This Iranianness is, if anything, weakening in the face of adaptation to Israel.

The interpretive schema is the creation of a mutually agreed upon and a mutually shared common past. This past, related to equally mutually agreed-upon customs, forms the "heritage" (*moreshet*), a core symbol of the Iranian Jews in Israel. These new schemes of experience are created in Iranian activities—in weekends, seminars, evening entertainments—which themselves become the truly experienced past that interlocks the participants. The sharing of these activities reinforces the reality of the created past, which then becomes the "objective" base for Iranianness, and is "naturally" called "Iranian ethnicity."

The Ceremonies

The ethnic activities, which are reframed here as definitional ceremonies for the Iranians are:

1. The first conference on Iranian Jews, which took place at the Van Leer Institute in Jerusalem, fall 1978. (The second conference took place during summer 1980, although in the interim similar conferences took place elsewhere.)
2. The first "weekend" retreat for Iranians, which took place in spring 1979.
3. Iranian cultural performances, which feature comedies in Persian, and Iranian music and dance.

Only this third category is organized by Iranian Jews without intervening outside organizations.

The Conference

The Van Leer "Conference on the Jews of Iran" was sponsored by the Committee on Sephardic and Oriental Jews. The format was a series of academic lectures by professors who teach in the university system and by professional organization men. The Oriental Jews and the Iranians are a relatively new addition to the sponsoring committee, which used to concern itself with Sephardic Jews more rigorously and traditionally defined. There were lectures on the subject of Judeo-Persian literature, on the relation between the form of Muslim and Jewish poetry in Iran, on Jewish folklore, on Jewish history in Iran and on traditional and modern Jewish education. The day concluded with a discussion of the current revolutionary situation in Iran (1978). The Iranian Knesset member who had been asked to speak was unable to attend, as he was in Iran at the time. The audience participated actively, sometimes heatedly.

In the audience were university students who were members of Iranian Student Associations, merchants who were members of the Committee on Sephardic and Oriental Jews, relatives of the speakers, and a handful of non-Iranians who had a professional interest in the proceedings. A number of young people who were "just interested" had taken the day off from work to attend. Three of them told me their interest was recent. A couple of years ago they were "ashamed" to say they were Persian, but now they were "interested" in learning more about their heritage.

Two issues encouraged debate among the members of the audience: the relations between Oriental and Ashkenazi Jews and the plight of the Jews in Iran. Ultimately these issues overlapped as the Ashkenazim were blamed for ignoring Jewish education in Iran and this provided an explanation for the fact that fewer Iranian Jews than might have been expected (or hoped) had come to Israel after the Revolution. The groundwork for Zionist ideology, it was claimed, was not laid by the members of Jewish organizations sent to Iran. These Jewish organizations had not been sufficiently concerned with the condition of Persian Jews and had not sent representatives of sufficiently high quality to Iran. The poor state of Jewish education in Iran was not placed in the context of recent Iranian history, but at the feet of foreign (Ashkenazi) Jews.

At issue in this debate, I believe, was a public definition of self within the Zionist framework of Israel. Iranians who held positions within state organizations had tended to express the point of view that Iranian Jews would realize that they should come to Israel and, as Zionists, they felt gratified that the State of Israel could perform this rescue function for Iranian Jews. The danger faced by the Jews of Iran focused positive public attention on the Jews of Iranian origin in Israel. It became increasingly obvious, however, that while many Iranian Jews would come to Israel, the entire community was not coming and many who did come were waiting to see what the future would bring, rather than immediately adopting the status of new immigrants. Concerned with the image of Iranian Jews in Israel and genuinely anxious about their future in Iran, many Iranian Jewish leaders sought to explain why the Iranians were not arriving en masse. One reason given was the neglect on the part of Zionists and foreign Jewish institutions of Iranian Jews. Later in the year (as we shall see in the discussion of the "weekend"), the debate took a different turn.

The Weekend

The "Weekend" was sponsored by the Histadrut, and was one of a series of weekends dedicated to particular ethnic groups. It took place in a vacation spot in the north during a shabbat. The Iranian weekend was like others of its kind—a cross between a children's summer camp and an adult package tour with some educational lectures thrown in. It was advertised in the Iranian community before the event, but chiefly spread by word of mouth. Chartered buses brought Iranians from the major cities and converged on the retreat late Friday afternoon. The weekend provided a mix of sacred and secular activities—speeches on Iranian culture and history, Shabbat events, singing and dancing. The weekend was distinguished from others by the mix of people who attended; both young and old *vatikim* and new immigrants showed up and the event was plagued by language problems. Half the speeches were given in Hebrew and half in Farsi, which left out half the poeple at any given time, as most of the young Israelis were not fluent in Farsi (they might understand their grandparents, but not the more formal speeches) and the new immigrants did not understand Hebrew. However, the Shabbat services were well attended by both young and old and most of the younger Israelis knew the songs and dances, which were mostly from the secular Iranian tradition shared with Muslims.

The Iranian weekend I attended in the spring of 1979 was the first of its kind for the Iranian community. Said the lead speaker: "This is the first time we are having a meeting with people from all over the country—the *eda Iranit*." This appelation—the *eda ha Iranit*—can be

understood as an "authoring" of the group, in this case, from the top
down. The term *eda Iranit* unites the Iranians, while at the same time it
separates them from the *edot ha mizrach*. I say this naming of the group
is "from the top down" because the lead speaker is also the head of an
Iranian organization and is the spokesman for Iranians on other occasions.
That his concern for establishing an Iranian "eda" within the larger body
politic is not limited to the weekend is shown by a remark he made to
the press during the Iranian celebration held after Pesach (*Ruz-e bagh,
Nowruz*). He told *The Jerusalem Post* that the 20,000 Iranian participants in the festivities "represented the 150,000 Israelis of Iranian origin" (Yudelman).

The concept that any Iranian can in this sense stand for another is a
relatively new one. The Iranians have not formed long-lasting association
in comparison with other groups.[6] Said a Persian leader:

It may be surprising but the Persians have no organized national
framework such as the Yemenites or Western Europeans, nor does
this derive from self-deprecation, but rather from the subtle feeling of need to rely upon the hidden capacities of the nation as a
whole, and not upon the capabilities of one unit. The Jews of Persia (for example) adopted the mode of prayer common in Palestine, and did not preserve the Persian order of the prayers or the
melody of the Psalms. (Halper, 19   :11-12)

The weekend attempted to reverse the facts of this observation by
organizing a national framework and reviving Iranian cultural forms.

The most explicit meaning of the weekend was that is was Iranian,
and this was understood to be important both politically and culturally. Said the lead speaker: "This Shabbat we'll have poetry, *minhagim*
and *masoret* of the ancient Jews, perhaps the oldest Jews." He hoped
that more meetings of this kind would follow and described previous
attempts at discussing Iranian culture as "academic" while this weekend was "practical." At the same time he said that the weekend was
sponsored by the Histadrut and "It's part of a common endeavor. Jews
from North Africa and Yemen have had their weekends and this is our
Shabbat. I have no doubt that more meetings will follow from this Shabbat." According to the welcoming speech given by the Histadrut representative (the one non-Iranian with the exception of the anthropologist
and her husband) they were in fact the seventh group to come because
he congratulated them on getting the lucky number of the seventh Sabbat.

The choices evolving from the discussions at the weekend were not
those that have been discussed elsewhere as typifying the dilemma of
ethnic identity: how and when are we Israeli, Iranian, Oriental. What was
at issue was a version of history, and that history was seen as affecting the
decision about identity in the present. Two main paradigms emerged from
the lectures. The first one combined a negative view of the way Muslims
treated the Jews with a positive, even sentimental, view of Jewish life in
Iran. The second presented a positive view of an Iranian culture in which
the Jews participated and which they shared.

The first paradigm was expressed in one of the speeches in the following way:

> There were three sides to the everyday life of the Jews in Iran. . .
> One was the synagogue, the second was the home, and the third
> was the bazaar. Two sides were full of strength and one side—the
> basaar and *xiaban* (street)—caused damage to the other two. Two
> built and one destroyed. The synagogue was the center of Jewish
> culture, the center of Jewish feeling. The house had internal rich-
> ness. But in the street and bazaar a Jew walked in a world that was
> against him.

The speaker representing the contrasting point of view first quoted Persian poetry, and then reminded the audience:

> We have no right to forget the ethics (in this poetry). We lived in
> Iran for 2500 years and we should not diminish it. It is not right
> to do that to the country which raised us. It is a mistake from the
> point of view of morality, a mistake from the point of view of so-
> ciety, and a mistake, today, from the political point of view.

The negative view of the Jewish experience among small town Muslims
and the warm picture of Jewish life in Iran appealed to the old immigrants
who remember the environment of Teheran or who left their home towns
to attend university while they were in Iran. The speaker who presented
the second view had attended university in Israel and had spent much of
his life outside of his native provincial town with its circumscribed Jewish
community life.

Both views merge, however, because their goal is integration within the
larger Israeli community. Neither approach asks that Iranian culture be
forsaken—the *misug ha galuyot* at which they aim is of a different sort.

The first perspective places itself within a Zionist framework which sees the Jews as unsafe anywhere but in Israel. The disintegration of Jewish life in Iran is similar to its disintegration everywhere and the danger the Jews face in Iran is similar to the insecurity found anywhere outside of Israel. The second paradigm locates similarities among Jews very differently. It sees Jewish emigration to Israel as voluntary, and not forced upon most Jews, although it states that Jews can be "pushed or pulled" to Israel. It finds unity among Israeli Jews insofar as they freely chose to make Israel their home. They are united by the moral and historical correctness of their decision, not by their adverse situation.

The first paradigm wants to preserve Iranian culture because it accepts a pluralistic definition of Israel—Israel is made up of diverse communities. The second wants to preserve Iranian identity because it sees a rejection of self in a rejection of Iranian culture, and it fears that a rejection of self will lead to a rejection by others.

The cultural performances

The evening entertainments, featuring plays in the Persian language and Persian singers oriented completely toward the Iranian community, are not sponsored by any outside organizations. These activities are only meant for Iranians. They strongly parallel the ethnic synagogues and ethnic religious forms, which are kept alive by members of the group itself. If a range of relevant ethnic activities is posted, the evening entertainments and ethnic synagogues can be seen as the secular and sacred embodiments of the most unmediated forms of Iranian ethnic identity. The secular entertainments are not only secular as opposed to sacred, but they draw upon the general Iranian culture; they have among their sources non-Jewish Iranian culture.

The songs are mostly classic and modern popular music of a type that could be heard on Iranian radio in the early 1970s. In addition, visiting singers, sometimes Muslims, who pass through Israel, are invited to sing, and bring with them new songs, some of which have political significance. The words of these songs are very important and require more than an appreciation of the music alone.

I first attended these plays in 1978. The plays I have seen and the scripts of those I have read but not seen come in two forms. Some of the plays have Jewish content while others resemble standard Iranian farces and could have been performed without change in Iran. Others are classic farces with stock figures of fun, and indeed some of the plays were written by Muslims. In one of these plays, for example, the tyrannical father forbids his daughter to marry anyone but a deaf man because he himself is deaf. In another a stingy "hajji" is torn between his two wives, the newest of whom he is trying to conceal from his first wife. These plays take place in "Iran"–the figures wear Iranian dress and Iranian "types."

The other form of the play takes place in Israel, and they generally embroil the main character in the Israeli bureaucracy. The standard figures are still there, but now they are Jewish. The antagonistic element is the Israeli bureaucracy. The downfall of the central character is not only just punishment for his antisocial ways–paternal tyranny, greed, etc.– but also demonstrates his inability to adjust his tactics to the new environment. In one such play an Iranian merchant and fortune teller is arrested by the police for swindling and is hauled in by the tax collectors for tax evasion. In his ignorance of his new culture he does not realize that the woman who comes to him to have her fortune told is an unlikely type to come for such aid and is, in fact, a police officer in disguise. He confuses the tax collector with an intermediary in matchmaking and exaggerates his assets to impress his potential bride's family. He is embroiled more deeply in all his troubles by the Iranian "*vatik*" (old immigrant) who translates for him and, for all his airs of expertise, does not, when the crunch comes, understand that much more than the new immigrant.

The plays present a negative stereotype of certain presumably Iranian character types to an audience that is composed only of Iranians. These stereotypes are not simply reflections of a stereotype circulated in the general Israeli culture. The Iranians are not necessarily included in the stereotype of Oriental Jews, nor do they have an elaborated category of their own in non-Iranian eyes. One reason the plays are so appreciated by the audiences is that they are truly "in-group"–no one else can understand the language and even young people raised in Israel cannot fully appreciate the types dressed in Iranian costumes. Part of the humor comes from seeing these Iranian figures so out of place in the Israeli context. These plays present the family "secrets" to a preselected audience and demand a knowledge of the past from the audience.

One of the "secrets" seems to be that the character traits are indeed Iranian or, at least, that persons with these traits can dominate the lives of other Iranians even though they are in a minority. The greedy patriarch is a dominant figure: he does not win within his household, to be sure, and the tricker is tricked, but the actions of others are nonetheless oriented around him and most of their energies are devoted to acquiring money or favorable decisions from him.

The fact that the "bad" character loses is a common motif and much of the comedy derives from his downfall. When the traditional characters find themselves in Israel their downfall seems to acquire a new meaning. The characteristics of greed, concern for self to the detriment of others, and lying to avoid or get out of scrapes are shown to be non-adaptive. In the four plays that take place in Israel, the central "Iranian" figures lose to official representatives of various kinds—bureaucrats, housing officials, customs inspectors, doctors in hospitals. The theme is not how the sly and clever fellow wins, but how he thinks he is winning when he is not.

The audience can identify with how the central character becomes tangled up in red tape and misunderstanding, both linguistic and cultural. But it is with the central person's situation, and not with his character, that they identify. The "bad" Iranian character loses, and the "bad" character is not them—he is someone at whom they can laugh. Thus, they at once accept and reject the stereotype of the calculating Iranian, a stereotype which is, to a certain extent, shared with non-Iranian Israelis as well.

The Definitional Ceremonies and Issues of Identity

The definitional ceremonies accomplish three things. They answer a need for older Iranian immigrants who want to feel a connection to a remembered past, they place young Israelis in an ethnic context that is valued in the contemporary Israeli framework, and they provide a bridge for new immigrants who would feel lost without this contact.

In all three of these definitional ceremonies the past was presented to the participants in a way that is relevant to the construction of an Iranian identity. The past may be idealized or criticized, but it is seen as central to any evaluation of the position of Iranian Jews in a Zionist framework in modern Israel. What differs among the three activities is style and form.

The conference style was informational; lecturers presented their views of Iranian history as the products of objective research. The form of the conference was "Israeli", or rather unmarked as "ethnic," although the sponsors (the Committee on Sephardic and Oriental Jews) clearly accepted a division of the population into Ashkenazi and Sephardi (Oriental). The event was secular.

The weekend was a combination of many things. Although the format of the lectures resembled the Conference—speakers in front of microphones facing a large audience—the tone was partisan. The lecturers did not all agree with each other and members of the audience took sides. The

master of ceremonies had said the occasion was "practical," unlike the
Conference, which was "academic," and the audience pushed him and the
speakers further in this direction than they wanted to go by demanding
immediate action. Young teachers, for example, wanted the weekend to
provide curricular materials for the teaching of the Iranian heritage. Although the content of the event was Iranian, its form was not. The Iranians were, as has been pointed out, the seventh in a series of similar weekends. These weekends are marked as "ethnic." The weekend audience
was more exclusively "ethnic" than was the audience at the Conference
and was expected to understand both Hebrew and Persian. Because it took
place over Shabbat, it was not a purely secular event. The Shabbat rules
were obeyed, Shabbat prayers were said over candles and synagogue services were held in Persian style. Family groups came and the atmosphere
was festive.

The entertainments were not informational in the direct sense that the
Conference and the weekend were. The participants were more exclusively
Iranian. Whereas half the proceedings of the weekend took place in Hebrew, the plays are performed in Persian and use a little Hebrew only if
they take place in Israel. The music is Iranian. Attending the plays satis-
fies more of an emotional and less of an intellectual need. University students and teachers participated animatedly in the discussions following the
lectures, but it was high school students who joined their parents at the
entertainments because they were hooked by the music. Adolescents
sometimes claim that what interests them most about being Iranian is the
music.

"The Constituting Process": Interrelating
and Interlocking

The very process of meeting in a group makes the ethnic message, which is
a collective one, seem to be "real." As Moore and Myerhoff (1977) wrote
about secular ritual, the "formal properties mimic the message." The problem of uniting very different people under one heading has already been
discussed.   The forms that definitional ceremonies take address yet
another fact of modern Iranian Jewish life. A strong strain of individualism
has challenged the traditional focus on the community itself as the center
of Jewish life. This trend toward individualism has affected traditional
Iranian Jewish life in Iran because it was predominantly as individuals (or,

if not, as family partnerships) that Jews (and Muslims) achieved wealth in the past generation in Iran and Teheran. Social mobility among Oriental Jews in Israel has also taken place at the level of the individual, not the group. "The way *misug galuyot* is applied in Israel (is) as individual assimilation, the absorption into the prevailing social and cultural structure of certain qualified members of the out-groups individually, one by one" (Toledano, 1973:237).

Thus, the emphasis on a collective identity comes after the recent stress in Iran and Israel on individually achieved success and is, like the move from a low to a high profile "Iranianness," something new. The collective dimension being created is neither the collective dimension of the traditional Iranian Jewish community, nor the collective dimension of all Jews inherent in Zionist ideas. It reflects instead the use of *eda* to mean "ethnic group," rather than "local community." Therefore, it can be said about the definitional ceremonies and Iranian meetings, which take place within a national framework, that their "very occurrence contains a social message" (Moore and Myerhoff, 1977:8).

This collective "social message" also speaks to young adults. They have, more than either of the other two groups, grown up in an environment in which ethnic and group action has been linked to demand for rights and power. What Ronald Cohen says about the effect of ethnic politics on democratic political theory is relevant here:

> Democratic theory and ideology has shifted to include both individual and group rights. In this sense, ethnicity has been legitimized in political theory making it a means not only of anti-alienative, diffuse identity but also a means of asserting one's rights in a political community in which ethnicity is a recognized element. (Cohen, 1978:402)

Young Iranians often remark upon the tension they feel between their traditional parents and the goals of the rest of Israeli society. One educated young woman who is a teacher said to me: "I'm between two worlds, and it gets worse, not better. I've disappointed my family by not marrying and continuing my education. They liked me better ten years ago. On the other hand, I like a household in which the father is 'king' and there is respect for the parents. And outside I'm affected by discrimination and by the negative traits associated with Persians. I don't want to marry a Persian and I don't want to marry an Ashkenazi." This woman is one of the group of university students who frequently attend Iranian activities. For her, these activities can be said to provide an "anti-alternative, diffuse, identity" as well as a "means of asserting (her) rights in a political community."

It is the experience of attending these meetings, as much as the cognitive framework they produce as secular rituals, which make this possible. For young adults, an Iranian *eda* exists, insofar as it does, because they meet united by these concerns of identity and political effectiveness. They share these concerns and not a bundle of culture traits. It is attending these Iranian functions that produces a "shared schema based on an experienced past," for these young adults and for old and new immigrants.

Conclusions

Certain aspects of the way Iranian ethnicity had developed are peculiar to the Iranian situation. The Iranian community has always included Iranians of different classes who have come at different times, unlike the mass exodus "at one time" which some other Jewish communities in Islamic lands experienced. However, the Iranian revolution caused a sudden influx of immigrants who might otherwise not have come to Israel. One of the reasons Iranian organizations have had to help in the absorption process is that hard-working, long-suffering Israeli relatives do not always welcome their (formerly) wealthier relatives who, as the usual oral history puts it, "didn't throw their relatives in Israel even a small part of the millions they made".

What does this study of Iranian ethnicity tell us about Israeli ethnicity? Even more broadly, what does it tell about Israel?

First, becoming an *eda* is not just doing what comes naturally. The statement that, "In Iran I was a Jew, in Israel I'm an Iranian" may be about identity or prejudice, but it does not make anyone a member of an ethnic group—and does not make an ethnic group even if enough people say it. It is worth asking more generally who needs to be ethnic to be Israeli, or who needs to take the ethnic route in order to feel assimilated in the Israeli context.

Second, there are many ways to be ethnic. Iranians seem to have chosen to hold in-group Persian language entertainments and not to folkdance in public festivals. These qualitative distinctions need to be analyzed.

Third, in this chapter I have noted Ashkenazi, Moroccan and Israeli ethnic models. Ashkenazim are by no means the only source of emulation;

"becoming Israeli" is not the only cultural fate which Oriental Jews have in store for them. Moroccans have served as a model not just for the achievements of visibility, but (in conjunction with former Iranian relig-ious customs) in the religious sphere as well by suggesting the legitimacy of synogogue ritual as a source of identity and local-level community organi-zation.

I have argued that the crucial issue in the construction of Iranian eth-nicity is group agreement about identity in the past ("what was our posi-tion in Iran?") and in the present ("where do we fit in the range of con-temporary ideas about Zionism?") Analysts of Israeli ethnicity have been looking for continuity in the wrong places: continuity is not located in particular customs which are "revived", but in the search for what it means to be a Jew in the Diaspora and an Israeli in Israel. In this sense, non-ethnics too are involved in the basic business of ethnicity.

Notes

[1] Fieldwork was done with Iranians in Israel in spring of 1975, from June 1978 to August 1979, and June to August 1980. The summer 1980 research was funded by a Mellon Grant from Vassar College. Many of my informants in Israel were original-ly from Yazd, Iran. I had become acquainted with them or with their families dur-ing my fieldwork in that city from 1973 to 1975, funded by the Fulbright Com-mittee and the National Institute of Mental Health. I would like to thank Yitzhak Cohen, Motti Golan, Moshe Katsav, Batya Khalili, Suleiman Mottahedeh and Moshe Omivdar for their help with my work in Israel.

[2] The common assumption that the people involved in ethnic activity in Israel are lower class is incorrect for the Iranians. The assumption is, in my opinion, arrived at incorrectly in that it is based on the public visibility of mass outdoor ethnic festi-vals and the idea that these activities compensates for low status in other areas of social life. It ignores the prevalence of other activities such as the ones described in this paper.

[3] This term was used by Barbara Myerhoff in a paper presented at the 1980 American Anthropological Association Meetings. According to its precis, the paper examined "the ways in which people define themselves in public, ceremonial terms, drawing from historical, chaotic and accidental events a web of meaning which eventually become the reality they claim to be." I take the term from her although I do not use it in exactly the same way she does.

[4] The Iranians are an instructive example for the study of Israeli ethnicity. Previous work has distinguished between immigrants who migrated at one time as a com-munity with its leadership intact from those who came without leaders. The Yemen-ites and Iraqis are presented as an example of the first type of immigration, the Mor-occans as the second. The Iranian aliyot do not fit into either category. Unlike the Moroccans, a cross section of the Iranian community migrated in each of its succes-

sive migrations before 1948, after the declaration of the State of Israel, 1967, 1973, and 1977 and after. As the list of dates shows, the Iranians did not come all at once as did the Yemenites and Iraqis. Although the poor outnumbered the middle class and the rich in the mass immigration after 1948, there were community leaders in all the migrations, starting from the earliest ones described in Raphael Hacohen's *Evenim be Homa* in which local religious figures led groups from their cities in Iran to Israel.

[5] Schutz's terms have been applied to social life in Bali by Geertz who described the "anonymization of persons," the treatment of consociates as if they were more distant contemporaries. In contrast, Rosen found that Moroccans tend to see contemporaries as potential consociates and seek to personalize passing interactions. In this chapter, I follow their use of Schutz's categories, but, instead of directing my attention to an ongoing pattern of relationships, I try to catch the "constituting process" at work and point to a change in Iranian perceptions of the people in their social world.

[6] For a history of Iranian community organization in Jerusalem, see Hacohen's *Evenim be Homa* (1970).

References

Aronson, Dan. 1977. "Ethnicity as a Cultural System: An Introductory Essay", in Frances Henry (Ed.), *Ethnicity in the Americas*. The Hague: Mouton.

Avineri, Shlomo. 1973. "Israel: Two Nations?" in Curtis and Chertoff (Eds.), *Israel: Social Structure and Change*. New Brunswick: Transaction Books.

Bloch, Maurice. "The Past and the Present in the Present," *Man* (N.S.) 12, 278-292.

Cohen, Ronald. 1978. "Ethnicity: Problem and Focus in Anthropology," *Annual Review of Anthropology*, 7:379-402.

Deshen, Schlomo. 1976. "Ethnic Boundaries and Cultural Paradigms: The Case of Southern Tunisian Immigrants in Israel," *Ethos* 4:271-294.

———. 1974. "Political Ethnicity and Cultural Ethnicity in Israel during the 1960s," in Abner Cohen (Ed.), *Urban Ethnicity*. London: Tavistock.

Geertz, Clifford. 1973. *The Interpretation of Cultures*. New York: Basic Books.

Goell, Yosef. 1981. "Passing of the 'ethnic ear'." *Jerusalem Post International Edition*, May 3-9, p. 15.

Hacohen, Raphael Hiam. 1970. *Evenim be homa*. Published by author, Jerusalem.

Halper, Jeff. "The Role of the Neighborhood in the Process of Ethnic Adaptation: The Persian and Kurdish Jews of Zichronot." Unpublished paper.

Handelman, Don. 1977. "The Organization of Ethnicity," *Ethnic Groups*, Vol. 1, pp. 187-200.

Heller, Celia. 1973. "The Emerging Consciousness of the Ethnic Problem Among the Jews of Israel," in Curtis and Chertoff (Eds.), *Israel: Social Structure and Change*. New Brunswick: Transaction Books

Lewis, Arnold. 1980. "Phantom Ethnicity: 'Oriental Jews' In Israeli Society." Paper presented at the Conference on Ethnicity in Israel, Ben Gurion University of the Negeve, Beersheva, Israel.

Moore, S. F., and Myerhoff, B. (Eds.). 1977. *Secular Ritual.* Amsterdam: Van Gorcum, Assen.

Myerhoff, Barbara. 1980. "Definitional Ceremonies: Life not Death in Venice." Paper presented at AAA meetings, December.

Poll, S., and Krausz, E. (Eds.). 1975. *On Ethnic and Religious Diversity in Israel.* Ramat Gan, Israel: Bar Ilan University.

Rejwan, Nissim. 1964. "Israel's Communal Controversy: An Oriental's Appraisal," *Midstream,* June.

Rosen, Lawrence. 1972. "Muslim-Jewish Relations in a Moroccan City," *International Journal of Middle Eastern Studies,* 3:435-449.

——. 1973. "The Social and Conceptual Framework of Arab-Berber Relations in Central Morocco," in Gellner and Micaud (Eds.), *Arabs and Berbers.* London: Duckworth.

Sartre, Jean-Paul. 1976. *Critique of Dialectical Reason.* London: NLB.

Schutz, Alfred. 1967. *The Phenomenology of the Social World.* Evanston, Ill.: Northwestern University Press.

Smooha, Sammy. 1972. "Black Panthers: The Ethnic Dilemma," *Society,* Vol. 9: 121-134.

Toledano, Henry. 1973. "Time to Stir the Melting Pot," in Curtis and Chertoff (Eds.), *Israel: Structure and Change.* New Brunswick: Transaction Books.

Weingrod, Alex. 1979. "Recent Trends in Israeli Ethnicity," *Ethnic and Racial Studies,* 2:55-65.

——, and Gurevitch, Michael. 1977. "Who are the Israeli Elites?" *Jewish Journal of Socioloty,* Vol. xix:31-40.

Weller, Leonard. 1974. *Sociology in Israel.* Westport, Conn.: Greenwood Press.

Yancey, W. L., Ericksen, E. P., and Juliani, R. N. N. 1976. "Emergent Ethnicity: A Review and Reformulation." *American Sociological Reviews,* Vol. 41.

Yudelman, Michal. 1979. "20,000 Gather for Iranian New Year," *The Jerusalem Post,* April 20.

13

The Druze in Israel as Arabs and Non-Arabs: Manipulation of Categories of Identity in a Non-Civil State[1]

Jonathan Oppenheimer

Ethnicity, variously defined and often ill-defined, underlies a significant quantity of published material in anthropology and sociology. Much of this literature stresses the political interests of members of ethnic categories which lead them to adopt strategies of ethnic organisation in order to achieve political, economic or social goals (e.g. Barth, 1969; Cohen, 1969, 1974; Glazer and Moynihan, 1975). There are also those who stress the significance of modernisation, bureaucracy and the rationalisation of political processes as factors tending to reduce the relevance of cultural difference, and hence of ethnicity itself. These include both Marxist analysts, who see ethnicity as a form of false consciousness and predict its disappearance in the context of class struggle, and liberal scholars, who predict the reduction of ethnic tension through such aspects of modernisation as education and the dissemination of a universalistic ethnic. The persistence of ethnicity as an organising dimension in many societies seems to belie such predictions, but most of the literature on this topic has not addressed itself to the question of why, often in the face of apparent socio-economic facts, such a 'cultural' phenomenon may retard or distort participants' perceptions of class interests and conflicts.

In this paper I examine some contradictions in the status of the Druze in Israeli society, in which they appear in some contexts as part of the Arab minority and in others to be differentiated from it. I hope to show the importance of analysing the kind of state in which the particular confrontation of ethnic identities occurs, as well as the relevance of focussing on the negotiations between state administrations and ethnic leaderships. In the present case, that leadership had a prior existence as a loose collection of local notables, but in the course of negotiations with the State administration it was to some extent transformed into an institutionalised community leadership. It is important to note the character of these negotiations. The administration deals with certain parties who claim to represent the membership of the ethnic category as a whole, but in reality may only represent relatively small interest-groups within it. It is therefore inadequate to analyse ethnic groups as if they are undifferentiated in this respect. One must take care, in examining the emergence and development of political processes predicted on ethnicity, to identify the interests at work as precisely as possible. Otherwise the use of a concept like ethnicity may simply obscure underlying political and economic contradictions.

The Druze in Israel, who number some 50,000 persons, are members of a religiously-defined community with co-religionists in Syria and Lebanon. Their religion is secret, with no provision for conversion. Linguistically, culturally and historically they are part of the Arab population and of the Israeli State itself. Most Druze live in seventeen villages in the North of the country, nine of which are truly Druze villages, since Druze comprise 90% or more of their populations. In these villages the remainder of the population is composed mainly of Muslim refugees from villages destroyed during and immediately after the war of 1948. In another five villages, the Druze are the majority. In the villages where they are the minority, the largest other element in the population is Christian; in this area, on the margin of Druze settlement, Druze traditionally preferred to live among members of another religious minority, rather than among the politically dominant Sunni Muslims. It must also be remembered that until 1957 when Israel recognised the Druze as an autonomous religious community, they had the legal status of Muslims; thus, in these mixed villages, they *were* jural representatives of dominant Islam. Recent events in Lebanon have shown that whatever the real causes and deeper nature of the conflict may be, at the level of perception of ethnic/religious categories, the Druze have easily been re-included (both by themselves and other participants and by outside observers and commentators) within the Muslim fold. In Israel itself the situation changed after 1948 in that the displaced "internal refugees" became economically and politically the weakest element in the generally weakened Arab population, and whether they were Sunni Muslims or not, they presented no threat to the Druze villages in which some of them sought sanctuary. On the contrary, in the early years of Israeli Statehood, the Druze, whose leader had previously negotiated the survival of their own villages with the new Jewish authorities, enjoyed a stability and security unknown to the rest of the Arab population, and were able to act as patrons and protectors for the fragmented refugee groups which clustered around them.

Sociological and anthropological analyses of Israeli society by Israeli scholars have included several approaches to ethnic phenomena. First, Arabs in Israel have often been treated as marginal to the analysis of Israeli society (e.g. Eisenstadt, 1967). Such analyses have concentrated on the building of Jewish society in Israel, the establishment of the State and the formation of its institutions, the development of collective and communal settlements, and, in particular, the absorption of immigrants. In respect to the latter, the work of Israeli sociologists has often stressed the importance of modernising and integrating features, such as the army, collective agriculture and parliamentary democracy, in creating a melting-pot (Eisenstadt, 1954; Eisenstadt, Bar-Yosef, and Adler, 1970). It was expected that cultural and ideological differences would soon be overshadowed by the development of common institutions and a common commitment to the new emerging national society. Such predictions have not been born out, but some Israeli scholars have continued to claim that cultural differentiation is of little political significance compared with unifying forces, particularly when induced by crises and wars (e.g. Deshen, 1974). This represents only a modification of the earlier view, since it is maintained that the emerging society can withstand and even encourage the preservation of diverse cultural traditions, at least within limited contexts such as religious ritual.

Two trends in those studies which relate directly to the Arab population are particularly striking (Nakhleh, 1976). The first stresses elements of modernisation in Arab society in Israel, which are explained as resulting chiefly from contact with Jewish Israeli society, and from the policies and actions of the Israeli administration (e.g. Standel, 1972; Peres, 1970; Israel Government, 1968). In this view, lack of integration of the Arab population into Israeli society is a result of the continued hostility towards Israel of the surrounding Arab states, which creates problems of divided loyalty for the Arabs and a problem of security for the administration.

Two flaws in this view must be noted. First, it is not true in any simple sense that the Arabs are not "integrated" into Israeli society. In reality, they are integrated, mostly at the lowest socio-economic level, as a significant section of the Israeli proletariat, and the process of this integration has, to a great extent, been the other side of the coin of these processes which main-stream Israeli sociologists have regarded as central to Israeli society. It is not really surprising that the literature on nation-building, on the development of collective and communal settlements, and on the building of development towns, makes little mention of the massive disruption in traditional Arab society brought about by these processes. These have included the wholesale disappearance of entire villages and the expropriation of the agricultural land of many more, the marginalisation of Arab agriculture and the emasculation of Arab political and economic institutions. Those same processes which have been wrought upon the Arabs in Israel have also played an integral role in the shaping of Israeli society. It is the concentration of Arabs in agricultural labour on Jewish farms, in the building trade and in services such as garages that has made it possible for some of them to become self-employed artisans or small contractors (Rosenfeld, 1978). At the same time the common fate of Arabs in Israel has retarded class differentiation among them, and the upwardly mobile Arab artisans and contractors do not share the status of the Jewish petty bourgoisie. It is quite impossible to understand the dynamics of Israeli society *without* taking account of this integration of the Arabs, although this involves a view of that society which is ideologically unacceptable to many Israeli scholars. Moreover, the loyalties of many Israeli Arabs are by no means divided—a growing number are openly committed to Palestinian liberation. The possibility of maintaining a dual loyalty—"proud Arabs and loyal Israelis"—(Zu'bi, 1964; Bastuni, 1964), has always been an explicit tenet of Zionist political orthodoxy and of Government-sponsored Arab "leaders". However, this possibility has never had much substance for most Israeli Arabs and even as political fiction it is more than ever undermined by Israel's massive military operations against Palestinians in Lebanon and its repressive expansionism at the expense of the Palestinian population on the West Bank.

A second approach among some Israeli scholars also identifies a continued lack of integration among the Arabs, but explains it in terms of deep-seated differences of culture, including language and social institutions. This view is reflected in the work of Smooha and Hofman (1976), and it involves a premise of basic conflict emerging from these cultural differences rather than from a power-struggle for territory, rights and autonomy. Smooha also claims that stratification in the emerging society necessarily follows lines of ethnic cleavage, as one or another of the culturally defined groups achieves political dominance. The struggle is seen as cultural rather than as a matter of political economy. A combination of the two approaches is found in Abner Cohen's book *Arab Border Villages in Israel* (1965), but here a causal relationship is posited between the hostility of the Arab states to Israel, and the continued structural and cultural differentiation between Arabs and Jews within Israel. The former is characterised by Cohen as the 'border situation'. With regard to the latter, he maintains that the Arabs are led by political insecurity and by their increased incorporation in the State's economy to revive old and previously weakened structural forms, which have meanings in terms of their own traditional culture. In reality, cultural distinctions and social separation are maintained and reinforced by the State through mechanisms such as separate education (with Arab education having inferior resources), separate communal religious courts with jurisdiction over matters of personal status, and the absence of alternative, secular and universally available institutions in areas like marriage, divorce and inheritance.

Within the Jewish population, cultural differences are not seen as determinants of the eventual form of the society—their divisive force can and should be overcome by modernisation. In explaining the relations between Jews and Arabs, however, such differences are seen as paramount (and it is traditional Arab culture which is seen as the barrier), together with the hostility towards Israel among the surrounding Arab states. Thus, selective recourse to theories of ethnicity brings sociological analysis into line with the political ideology of the State. The nature of that State itself is scarcely considered. Its relations with its own Arab population and with Palestinians outside its borders, or in territory which it has occupied, are not treated as determining factors. This bias is well-exemplified in the work of the Israeli political scientist, Jacob Landau, who, in his book, *The Arabs in Israel,* almost always refers to Arab nationalism as 'extremist', while Jewish nationalism is never thus qualified (Landau, 1969—see in particular his discussion of the suppression of the *al-Ard* (The Land) Movement, pp. 92-106).

The Druze in Israel are treated by the Israeli administration and by local scholars as a special category, distinct from both the Arab and the Jewish sectors of the population. Here also, the distinction is posited on cultural and historical grounds. Druze ethnicity tends to be explained as a spontaneous development from a long tradition of separatism and communal solidarity (e.g. Ben Dor, 1973, 1976; Blanc, 1952, 1958). In accordance with this view, Israeli policy towards the Druze is seen as legitimate insofar as it respects Druze aspirations for a formally institutionalised separate status and permits their realisation—policy is seen, in other words, as a *response* to Druze demands, rather than a determinant of Druze destiny (cf. Israel Knesset, 1975; Falah, 1967).

It would be both simplistic and in error to say that such aspirations do not exist among Israeli Druze. They do, but they are ambiguous. In part, both the aspirations themselves and the view of Druze history on which they rest result from the situation in which Druze in Israel find themselves. Both the scholarly analysis and the official view are products of an ideologically distorted understanding of Druze history, by which it is transformed into a charter for the administrative and political separation of the Druze from the rest of the Arab population. Against this, I hope to show that the Druze share most aspects of their political and economic situation with the rest of the Arab population of Israel, and that such problems as can be regarded as exclusively Druze stem largely from the very administrative separation which is supposed to solve them and to realise Druze aspirations.

Israeli administrators have selected and emphasised certain elements of Druze culture and history as a basis for the development of a 'special relationship' between the Druze and the Jewish State. In pursuing this course, they have found partners with whom to negotiate alliances among traditional Druze notables, and more recently among some elements of the emerging younger intelligentsia. In pre-Israeli Palestine the Druze were one of several religiously-defined categories which made up the heterogeneous village and urban populations. None of these categories was organised as a political community although all developed and maintained intra-category networks of relations based on agnatic and affinal kinship, personal friendship and trade, expressed and maintained through mutual visiting and assistance. Only the relations based on kinship were normatively confined to members of the same religious category, because of the general preference for religious endogamy. For the rest, these networks tended to merge into one or another of the broad but unstable polyethnic alliances so typical of the region. In such a situation, the question of whether Druze were or were not Arabs would have been meaningless, and politically relevant distinctions were those between rival polyethnic factions (the clients and followers of competing landowners) or between local persons and the agents of successive alien administrations. It is clear that in the context of the emergence of mutually hostile nationalist movements, and their development into equally hostile nation-states, the political significance of the labels 'Arab' and 'Jew', and in their wake, that of Druze identity, has been transformed.

Christian and Muslim religious identities have not been politicised in Israel in the same way, or to the same extent, as has the Druze identity. That this is so in spite of events in neighbouring Lebanon is another indication of the power of Palestinian nationalism to transcend religious divisions. Politically, the separateness of Muslims and Christians has tended to become submerged in their common Palestinian–Arab experience, and in their common aspirations for nationhood. In the case of the Muslims this is not surprising, since Islam is also the religion of the vast majority of Arabs outside Israel. Christians, however, form minorities in all Arab states in which they are found, and sectarian differences abound within these minorities. However, as the Nazareth municipal election of 1975 showed, even the civil war in nearby Lebanon did not foment politically separatist organisation among Christian Arabs in Israel.

In this election, the non-sectarian alliance of the Communist Party (RAQAH) and members of the local professional intelligensia was successful in a town with a mixed Christian and Muslim population. This happened in spite of attempts by Government representatives to exploit the tragic events in Lebanon in order to persuade the electorate that the real issue in Nazareth was the religious division, in the hope of thereby splitting support for the radical list and attracting Christian votes for Labour-sponsored candidates.

In what can be thought of as their secular culture the Druze share most traits with their neighbours: all speak Arabic, build their houses and farm their land in much the same way, and in food and dress are distinguished from each other only by certain differentiating prohibitions and dialectical features. These differences would be meaningless in isolation, but derive their meaning from the shared system of ideas of which the differentiation itself is an integral part. This is also true of the stereotyped jokes which members of the different categories make about each other–they belong to a common cultural repertoire, and their humour relates to the fact of close continuous contact between the different groups (cf. Zenner, 1972). Similarly, the different social categories have the same type of kinship structure, with the same terminology, generating kin-groups of similar kind and order. Thus they are part of one society, interacting across religious boundaries and interlocking within the composition of many villages. The growing importance of the concept of Palestinian identity is also crucial here, since it is explicitly said (by those who claim it) to override sectarian or ethnic distinctions. It is tempting to compare this, by analogy, to Jewish ethnic groups, yet there is a profound difference: Jewish groups are united by a common religious tradition but divided by different histories and different secular cultures, whereas Palestinian subgroups are divided by religion but united by common historical experience and centuries of proximity.

Since the Druze and "the Arabs" share broad features of one common culture, it is not surprising that some Druze, both in 1948 and today, have included themselves in the latter category in its clash with Zionism. However, even before the establishment of the State of Israel, other Druze had been establishing friendly relations with Jewish leaders (in particular, commanders of the Haganah, the military underground of the Jewish Labour Movement) and negotiating informal terms on which they would support the Zionists. Some of these leaders or their sons took an active part in the fighting of 1948-49 on the Jewish side. Unlike the Palestinian nationalists. Zionism claimed to combine an essentially religious heritage and nationhood in one identity, which was, moreover, exclusive and generally ascribed by birth. In this respect the Druze religion and Judaism have something in common, at least in regard to their boundary definitions. Once Zionism had made religion, endogamy and ethnic continuity the basis for political organisation and for the achievement of almost Messianic goals, some Druze, although their own goals were more limited, may have adopted the model of ethnic political organisation as a conscious response. In any case, it was Zionism which gave these criteria a new political significance.

Most Druze shared an interest in maintaining the strength of their exclusive boundaries whether or not they approved of the increased politicisation of their identity. In this respect, Druze identity harmonised better with Jewish than with Arab nationalism, and this harmony became a cornerstone in the manipulation of Druze identity by the Israeli administration. Thus, the deterioration of relations between Druze and other Arabs in some villages during the Mandate period can itself be regarded as an expression of the growing awareness of the potential political significance of ethnic/religious distinctions, in which some Druze saw themselves in a less problematic relation to Jews than to other Arab categories. The political manipulations of ethnic distinctions by the French mandatory power in Syria (Longrigg, 1958; Tibari, 1969) and by the British in Palestine, also contributed to this growing awareness. By the end of the fighting in 1949, some of the Druze from outside Palestine who had entered with the Arab forces from Syria, had withdrawn, while others had gone over to the Israeli side, joining those Palestinian Druze who had been directly involved in the fighting. Even those Druze villagers who had not sided actively with the Israelis, offered no resistance to Israeli occupation of their villages, and according to Druze and Christian eyewitness they received better treatment from the occupying troops than did other Arab villagers. Practically no Druze left the country as refugees, and thus they were the only Palestinian community to remain intact after the 1948 war. Since then the relationship between Druze and the rest of the Arab national minority in Israel has acquired a new ambivalence.

Cultural and Institutional Expressions of Druze Status in Israel

The establishment of a special official status for the Druze in Israel, specifically as non-Arab non-Jews, has been achieved and expressed through the manipulation of categories of identity and attributes of culture. In particular a local Druze religious hierarchy has been created from among the notables who engaged in the initial process of negotiating Druze status with the Israeli administration.

A brief historical review is needed in order to understand the importance of religious autonomy in Israel. In seeking recognition, first from the British authorities during the Mandate and later from the Israeli Government, traditional Druze leaders were trying to achieve for their community a status similar to that held by Muslims, Christians and Jews under the Ottoman administration; that is, the status of a *millet,* a religiously defined community with its own courts and jurisdiction, particularly in matters of personal status. In the past, the absence of such courts, and the fact that officially they had been regarded as part of the Muslim community, bound by Sharia law in these matters, had probably not been much felt by Druze villagers. At the local level, problems of personal status, and indeed all matters of customary law, were generally dealt with informally through mediation and arbitration by local religious sheikhs and secular leaders. Among these were individuals whose personal prestige, acquired through their wise resolution of disputes, was such that their services as mediators were sought by individuals outside their own local and religious communities.

In the Israeli context, Zionist concerns with religious/national exclusiveness, as well as the vested interests of the religious establishments of the recognised *millets,* gave this system continued currency. The basis for the separation of the Druze from the rest of the Palestinian Arab national minority, and their integration into Israel as a separate community, was expressed in religious terms both by Israeli officials and by Druze themselves. Thus, formalisation of Druze religious status provided an institutional expression for the separation of the Druze from the other autonomous religious categories. At the same time, it provided a framework of offices and influence for the traditional notables within the wider structure of the state, and thus became a basis for their claims to community leadership. In 1957, official recognition of Druze religious autonomy was granted, and this was followed by the establishment of a Druze Religious Council and religious courts under the supervision of a special department within the Israeli Ministry of Religions.

State recognition of Druze religious autonomy also facilitated the political separation of the Druze from the rest of the Arab minority in "national' terms. In the registration of individuals, and hence in the classification of the Israeli population, two criteria are used: religion (*dat*) and nationality (*le'om*). Both appear on birth certificates and the latter is used on the identity card which every resident in obliged by law to carry. Druze religion had now been added to the list which already included Muslims, Christians, Jews and several other small groups. Until the early 1960's the principal officially-recognised *national* distinction was between Jews and Arabs—there being no universal category of Israeli nationality. There is also another criteria of identity, which is used in Israeli sociological writing and in the classification of some official information about the population, but which has no legal force. This is '*eda*': an ethnic group or community. Thus, the Jewish population is sometimes classified by '*eda*', broadly into Sephardim and Ashkenazim, or more narrowly, by country of origin. The term *eda* is also used to refer to the various Christian sects, the Muslims and the Druze. However, given that the goal of negotiations between Druze leaders and the administration was the establishment of a special status for the Druze in Israel, the question of Druze nationality was a problem. If they were merely a religious *eda,* since they were not in national terms Jews, they must be Arabs, and they were indeed registered as such until the early 1960's. Beginning at about that time their apparent harmony with the model of the Jewish category, in which religion and nationhood were seen to coincide was given official recognition, and therefore from about 1962 "Druze" began to replace "Arab" as their national label on identity cards and birth certificates.

The single most powerful symbol of the separation of the Druze from the rest of the Arab national minority has been the service of Druze in the Israeli army. This practice became compulsory for Druze males in 1956. According to official claims this followed the request of the Druze themselves. It is clear, however, that the community has never been united on this question, and those who made the demand (if demand it was) were the same traditional leaders who had previously become clients of the Israeli administration and, in particular, of the then dominant Labour Party, MAPAI. A popular account of this development among Druze who oppose the officially recognised leadership suggests that traditional leaders were pressed into making the request in exchange for specific favours, and in particular, the granting of religious autonomy which was finalised the following year.

The developing status of Israeli Druze must therefore be seen as the outcome of negotiations between two parties with some complementary interests, but with totally different resources of power. The Israeli administration was interested in the subdivision of the minority population, the establishment of lines of patronage and control within the different divided sections, and the cooperation of more marginal sections such as Bedouins, Circassians and especially the more numerous Druze. This latter interest was no doubt partly for cosmetic reasons–it "looked good", especially abroad, to demonstrate that the possibility existed of cooperation between the Jewish State and at least some of its non-Jewish citizens. However, there were also more practical considerations–not least the significant military contribution that these cooperative sections of the non-Jewish population could and did make. On their part, traditional Druze notables, such as village leaders, petty landowners and religious sheikhs, were interested in winning the security and stability for themselves and their people that had been denied to so much of the Palestinian Arab population. They were also interested in the establishment of an institutional framework which would provide them with offices and hence resources for the broadening and legitimation of their leadership and influence, and for channeling favours to themselves and their supporters.

Nonethless, official Israeli policies towards the Druze were ambivalent and even inconsistent from the outset. Although the latter were encouraged or even compelled to distinguish themselves from other Arabs in a number of ways, in other respects they continued to be treated as an undifferentiated part of the Arab minority. Until 1972, the Druze, like other non-Jews, were excluded from full membership within the Labour Party, and their parliamentary candidates were placed on 'minorities' lists, sponsored, selected and effectively controlled by the Labour Party organisation. Moreover, like other Arabs, in some villages Druze have suffered major losses of land through government expropriation (for example, as a result of implementing the policy of "Judaisation of the Galilee", Yehud ha Galil). The Druze village in which I worked lost about two-fifths of its arable land after 1948, and this area included almost all of the village's cereal land).

Official ambivalence is also expressed in the brief history of the administrative status of the Druze in Israel. Until 1966, all but two Druze villages came within the control of the military government that was established in 1948 to administer "border areas", but which in practice controlled most of the Arab population. Gradually the affairs of the Druze and other Arabs were transferred to civil administration in the form of "Minorities' Departments" established in the various ministries, under the overall supervision of the Prime Minister's Advisor for Arab Affairs. The official justification for the existence of these departments has been that the Arab population has special problems which are best dealt with by a specialist staff. However, Arabs have repeatedly objected to the existence of a separate administrative framework, charging that it is really a mechanism for discrimination, particularly in budgetary allocations. They argue that such administrative separation makes it easier to use funds originating in foreign aid and donations from Jews outside Israel exclusively for development within the Jewish sector. Druze have been particularly hostile to the Minorities' Departments, and the removal of Druze affairs from their control has been the principal aim of more than one Druze ethnic association. The Druze argue that they fulfill the obligations of citizenship, including military service, and hence should be entitled to all the rights and privileges enjoyed by Jewish citizens. Apart from a minority which has supported RAQAH, the predominantly Arab Communist Party, and more recently, those who have supported the Druze Initiative Council—a radical group which will be discussed later—the Druze have not actively opposed the existence of Minorities' Departments or even of discrimination as such. In 1970 their affairs were removed from the control of the Minorities' Departments following a promise originally made by the then Prime Minister, Levi Eshkol, to leaders of the community after the 1967 war (Landau, 1969). However, this move did not resolve the problems of the community, and in fact created new ones. Druze ex-servicemen who had previously competed for employment with Arabs in the Minorities' Labour-Exchanges, and who had been able to use their veteran status to advantage, now found themselves in competition with Jews who also were mostly ex-servicemen. After a year, this change was reversed. More recently, following the recommendations of a Knesset (Parliamentary) Committee of "experts", Druze affairs were once more removed from the Minorities' administration. A temporary coordinating body for the Druze was established as a prelude to their administrative integration with the Jewish population—and total administrative separation from the rest of the Arab minority.

Apart from the formal, institutional framework, the special position of the Druze in Israel has been given emphasis in terms of those cultural attributes which are said to distinguish them from other Arab categories. These traits include markers which are more or less absolutely distinctive, most of which are selected from the traditional cultural repertoire, although some are new symbols. These symbols include, for example, indicators of identification such as minor distinctions of dress, or dialectical features of language. Others are expressed in boundary-defining features of religious organisation, and their rules of ascription. The central position of religious legitimisation, which previously was discussed in connection with the granting of relgous autonomy, is further demonstrated by the fact that more religious and secular Druze office-holders have been or become members of the category of religious initiates (*'uqqal*), "those who are admitted to the secrets of esoteric religious knowledge". This is remarkable because it contrasts with the traditional separation between religious and secular authority which appears to have characterised Druze ideology in the past and is still often referred to by Druze today. This separation may also be related to the contradictory interpretations of religious ideology that have recently emerged. Religious precepts have been used to legitimate two quite different responses to the Israeli state. On the one hand, some Druze, including the officially-recognised leadership, claim that loyalty to the constituted authority of the State is a principle of their (secret) religion. On the other hand, those Druze who oppose what they regard as excessive cooperation with an alien administration refer to a conflicting principle according to which the Druze religion is committed to social justice, and a religious man should hence accept nothing from secular rulers whose power is inevitably tainted by exploitation.

During recent years there appears to have been a marked increase in the number of young men undergoing religious initiation, adopting religious dress and taking an active role in the congregation, all of which were traditionally regarded as actions more appropriate to older men. Some of these younger men have begun to develop their own cohesion in opposing the support given to the Israeli administration by the 'official' spiritual leaders. Religious piety among the Druze demands the abrogation of violence and, like rabbinical study among Jews, can be used in Israel as grounds for exemption from military service. It seems clear that some undergo initiation for this reason alone. However, the young religious radicals have joined with many secular Druze in opposing conscription for the Druze altogether. In this regard they allied themselves with the Communist Party (RAQAH), and one result was the establishment in 1972 of the Druze Initiative Committee, whose leaders included a religious sheikh and veteran communists. The Committee's main aims have been the abolition of the religious life of the community, and the fostering of cooperation between Druze and the rest of the Arab population in order to resist Government measures such as the expropriation of land.

Other symbols of Druze identity used to represent their relationship to the Israeli State include the Druze flag, the emblem of the Minorities' Brigade in the Israel army and the annual pilgrimmage to the tomb of Nabi Shu'eyb. The flag consists of five horizontal stripes of different colours, which are said the represent the hierarchy of five supreme cosmic principles in the Druze religion. This flag plays little part in everyday life but features prominently in the celebrations of the annual pilgrimage. The latter was formally a religous gathering of initiated Druze from all over the area, accompanied by a meeting of uninitiated Druze (Oliphant, 1887). As such, it was an example of a cultural element shared with Muslims, Christians and Jews; all made pilgrimages to the tombs of saints, holy men and religious prophets, and many of these shrines were venerated by members of all three religions. Nabi Shu'eyb himself is traditionally identified with Jethro, the father-in-law of Moses, and this identification has served as yet another element in the representation of the relationship between Druze and Jews as "special". The Druze believe that prior to the full revelation of the true religion in the 11th century, there had been a series of "true prophets" whose identity was masked behind that of the "revealed prophet", and through whom they imparted a partial revelation. In accordance with this belief, they claim that Jethro/Shin'eyb was the "true" concealed prophet behind the secondary, revealed prophet, Moses.

After the establishment of the State of Israel, the annual pilgrimage acquired a new and different character. It became a regular and institutionalised representation of the 'official' view of the relationship between the Druze and the State. In addition to the traditional gathering of religious leaders, the following day was marked by visits to the tomb by Israeli officials and public figures such as the Prime Minister and Minister of Religions. These distinguished visitors and their Druze 'hosts' (the official religious leadership and Druze members of the Knesset), made speeches extolling the brotherhood between Druze and Jews and the part played by Druze youngsters in the defence of the State. An honour guard of Druze soldiers stood at attention, and the flags of Israel and of the Druze themselves, flags of equal size, were draped side by side over the walls of the shrine. The significance of this 'performance' was also recognised by those opposed to closer cooperation between the Druze and the State. In 1975, these celebrations were interrupted by a noisy demonstration of young Druze againse compulsory conscription and the use of the pilgrimage as a platform for the government and for the Druze establishment which it sponsored. Conscription of Druze men has continued, but as far as the pilgrimage is concerned the demonstrators achieved their aim: in 1976 and 1977 it resumed much of its traditional character, and there were neither government representatives in attendance, nor speeches, parades and flags.

The emblem of the Israel Army Minorities' Brigade—a pair of crossed scimitars—is displayed on the uniforms of Druze soldiers who form the bulk of its members. It also takes the form of a mounted ornament in many homes (along with portraits of Israeli statesmen and generals) or as a sign on the rear window of cars and taxis belonging to Druze who wish to stress their loyalty to the State. This emblem has, however, become a controversial and perhaps outdated symbol, since many young Druze soldiers protest that the Minorities' Unit symbolises segregation and limits the scope of their military careers. Indeed, these Druze demand that they be freely absorbed within other units throughout the Israeli armed forces. On the other hand, Druze who oppose conscription relate that for them the crossed swords had an ironic significance, symbolising a kind of mercenary status (in Hebrew, mercenaries are *skhirei herev*, literally, "hirelings of the sword").

Thus far I have discussed cultural elements held in common by Druze and other Arabs, and cultural expressions of the special relationship which is claimed, both by the Israeli administration and the Druze leaders aligned with it, to exist between the community and the State. I have also shown some of the administrative processes whereby this relationship has been institutionalised. Other features of this kind, such as efforts to construct a special educational programme aimed at raising the consciousness of separate identity among Druze children, could also be mentioned. In order to complete my analysis I turn briefly to consider features of the economic situation that characterizes the Druze.

Druze villages in Israel have undergone processes of change similar to those experienced by other Arab villagers. The main features of this change include the shift from subsistence village agriculture to involvement in the Israeli national economy, including wage labour outside the village, some sale of agricultural produce on the Israeli market, and the purchase of most commodities on the same market. In agriculture, the Druze face the same problems as other Arabs in competing with the heavily capitalised and technologically sophisticated farming of the Jewish sector. In both the agricultural sphere and in the labour market, they share with other Arabs many disadvantages, compared with Jewish workers and farmers. They also suffer the general subordination of their political and economic interests to those of the Jewish population. This subordination is expressed in land expropriation, budgetary discrimination, and restrictions on political expression. Druze, like other Arabs, fit Rosenfeld's description of a rurally-resident proletariat dependent largely on skilled and semi-skilled non-permanent wage labour, coexisting with a residual peasantry as well as with a small but growing group of independent artisans and small contractors who organise the labour of their kinsmen and neighbours, plus government employees who often fill roles of political middlemen (Rosenfeld, 1964, 1978; cf. Zureik, 1976).

As early as in 1961, 53% of employed Druze, in comparison with 54% of Muslims and 40% of Christians, worked outside their settlements of residence. In the village in which I did most of my fieldwork, in 1970,

64% of employed villagers worked outside the village; moreover among the 24% who continued to regard farming as their principal occupation, most also took seasonal or casual outside employment. Within the national labour force Druze, like other rural Arabs, are prominent as agricultural and building labourers, dockers and to a lesser degree, factory workers. The only prominent occupational difference between Druze and other Arabs stems from Druze conscription. A few follow a military career, particularly among those who achieve officer rank during their period of compulsory military service. Others join the border police and many of these drift between the border force which offers occupational security and regular pay but hard conditions, harsh disciplines, physical danger and prolonged absence from home, and wage labour, which is insecure but offers greater individual freedom. In the village in which I worked, 22% of the employed population were in the armed forces and the police and prison services, *excluding* national servicemen. This is a far higher proportion than in the Jewish population, and the political importance of this difference from other Arabs has already been noted. Its economic significance lies in the fact that it has provided the Druze with an alternative to civilian wage labour which is not open to other Arabs. The working histories of Druze men often show this: in years of recession, such as 1966-67, instead of returning to their small village plots many unemployed Druze entered or re-entered the ranks of the border police.

Thus, in terms of secular culture and class position, the Druze are a part of the largely proletariat and rural Palestinian Arab minority. It only remains to examine the political behaviour of Druze themselves in voting and their relationship to the Israeli political parties and in the formation of goal-oriented ethnic associations.

The Druze have formed three different kinds of relationships with Israeli political parties. First, the Labour Party has repeatedly placed Druze on at least one of its sponsored lists of Arab parliamentary candidates. The most prominent of these Labour-sponsored representatives belonged to the traditional leadership of village notables. This leadership was based mainly upon support drawn from the leaders' home villages and surrounding settlements. In the first few Knesset elections, a major proportion of Druze votes went to lists on which these men were placed. Voting was often divided within villages between the lists of rival leaders, each receiving support from one or other of the local-level factions which are such a prominent feature of this part of the Middle East. Support for these lists was, in part, a pragmatic effort by individuals and groups to establish good relations with the then-dominant Labour Party. However, it was also an act within the network of patronage through which such relations were to be implemented, and through which, it was hoped, the rewards for political loyalty would flow.

In later elections, there has been increasing support for other parties, and in particular for the National Religious Party (NRP) and, in some villages, for the right-wing GAHAL bloc (later the Likud, a broader alliance of right-wing and right-centrist groups which now dominates the Israeli Government). This support, and especially that for the NRP, is largely an expression of mutually opportunistic material relations, devoid of ideological content. The NRP, which has dominated the Ministry of the Interior and the Ministry of Religions throughout successive administrations, has had control of funds for village councils and other developments, and has also offered favours and material benefits to village leaders in return for the votes of their supporters. Thus a paradoxical situation arose in which a religious Jewish Zionist party with the least commitment to the interests of Israeli Arabs received, in 1969 and 1973, nearly has high a proportion of votes in the smaller Arab villages as it did in the country as a whole. In many Druze villages the NRP received two, three and even four times its national percentage of the vote.

A third political party which attracts Druze and wider Arab support is RAQAH, the New Communist List. As in the Arab electorate as a whole, not all those who vote for RAQAH are committed Communists. However, this party provides practically the only organised and legal alternative to Zionist parties, and thus comes closest, in spite of its internationalist ideology, to being a party of the Arab national minority in Israel. It is also the only party to make a serious and constant attempt to give young Arabs a political education, and some of the results of this, in terms of discipline and the control of chauvinist or vengeful impulses, are truly impressive. Support for RAQAH has remained much lower among the Druze than in the Arab population as a whole. Nonetheless, in Beit Jann and Yirka, for example, each with populations which are over 90% Druze, support for RAQAH has, in some elections, exceeded the percentage for Arab villages of comparable size, while in Li-Bqe'a with a population which is over 60% Druze, it has well exceeded the percentage among Arabs as a whole.

Beginning with the 1950's a number of Druze associations also emerged. The relatively recent Druze Initiative Committee, with its anti-conscription and pro-Palestinian stand, has already been mentioned. The earlier movements, which were mostly founded by young Druze ex-servicemen and professionals, had different goals. These associations provided younger Druze, who were excluded from the government-sponsored traditional leadership or from prominent positions on lists of parliamentary candidates, with an organisational framework for conducting their own negotiations with the administration. Their aim was to obtain certain privileges —in particular, resources such as government positions and economic aid for their members in fields such as housing. Some younger Druze, and especially members of the intelligentsia, also sought to maintain a special relationship with the state, and some individuals have obtained prominent positions (a Druze became the President's Advisor on Minority Affairs, for example). Recently, a small group of Druze from the two villages on Mount Carmel formed an association called "The Druze Zionists". This group declared itself in favor of total integration of the Druze into the Israeli State and "ultra-loyal" support for the government. In return for this support they demanded land for the establishment of a cooperative agricultural village, modelled on the Jewish *moshav*.

The varied relationships with political parties and the proliferation of ethnic associations are eloquent expressions of the political ambivalence of Druze in Israel. A false political consciousness has been generated among many Druze. They enter into opportunistic alliances for limited and particularistic ends, while avoiding criticism of the fundamental nature of the Israeli State and their position within it—a position from which arise the basic problems of social, economic and political discrimination which they share with the rest of the Arab minority in Israel.

Conclusions

In this chapter I have tried to show that in terms of their secular culture and socio-economic status, the Druze form part of the Arab national minority in Israel. On the other hand, their political and jural status, and the framework in which they are administered, has remained ambivalent. A similar ambivalence is found in Druze self-identity as expressed in voting behaviour and in ethnic organisations. This ambivalence results from an increased stress on the political significance of Druze ethnicity, an emphasis produced by the administrative actions of successive Israeli governments. The State has created and maintained a religious-communal hierarchy and facilitated ongoing negotiations with particular interest groups within the minority populations. The effectiveness of this emphasis on a separate Druze political identity is reflected in the fact that political groups such as the Palestinian- or the Communist-oriented opposition within the community has to organise itself in explicitly ethnic terms (the Druze Initiative Committee, for example). The irony of this situation is not lost on the Committee's members. This subdivision of the Arab population enables the administration to relate to the non-Jewish minority in Israel as if it lacks any overall Arab identity, and specifically to the Druze as if they are at once Arabs and non-Arabs. An analysis of this situation which sees Druze ethnicity simply as an internally generated product of Druze history and culture, or as a product of some independent Druze strategy, and which ignores the nature of the Israeli State, is bound to obscure the latter's manipulative role in the generation of political consciousness.

Notes

[1] This paper originally appeared in English in Cambridge Anthropology Vol. 4, No. 2, in May 1978, and later in Hebrew in *Machbarot le-mehkar ve-b-bikoret* No. 3 in December 1979. Much has happened to the Druze both in Israel and elsewhere—especially in Lebanon—since then. I have made some minor changes and additions to this paper for its reappearance in the present volume.

References

Barth, F. 1969. *Ethnic Groups and Boundaries: The Social Organization of Culture Differences.* Boston: Little, Brown.
Bastuni, R. 1964. "Integrating Israel's Arabs," *Jerusalem Post,* 25 Sept. 1964.
Ben Dor, G. n.d. *The Druzes in Israel.* Mimeographed: University of Haifa.
——. 1973. "The Military in the Politics of Integration and Innovation: the Case of the Druze Minority in Israel," *Asian and African Studies* Vol. 9, No. 3.
Blanc, H. 1952. "Druze Particularism: Modern Asepcts of an Old Problem," *Middle Eastern Affairs,* pp. 315-321.
——. 1958. *Ha-druzim* (The Druze). Jerusalem: Office of the Prime Minister's Advisor for Arab Affairs.
Cohen, A. 1965. *Arab Border Villages in Israel.* Manchester, Manchester University Press.
——. 1969. *Custom and Politics in Urban Africa.* London: Routledge and Kegan Paul.
——. (Ed.). 1974. *Urban Ethnicity* (A.S.A. Monograph No. 12). London: Tavistock.
Deshen, S. 1974. "Political Ethnicity and Cultural Ethnicity in Israel" in A. Cohen (Ed.). *Urban Ethnicity.* London: Tavistock.
Eisenstadt, S. 1954. *The Absorption of Immigrants.* London: International Library of Sociology and Social Reconstruction.

THE DRUZE AS ARABS AND NON-ARABS 279

——. 1967. *Israeli Society.* London: Weidenfeld & Nicholson.
——, Bar-Yosef, R., and Adler, C. (Eds.). 1970. *Integration and Development in Israel.* New York: Praeger.
Falah, S. 1967. "Druze Communal Organization in Israel" *New Outlook,* Vol. X: 40-45.
Glazer, N., and Moynihan, D. P. (Eds.). 1975. *Ethnicity: Theory and Experience.* Cambridge, Mass: Harvard University Press.
Israel Government. 1968. *Ha-Hevra ha-'arvit be-yisrael tmurot u-mgamot* (Arab Society in Israel: Changes and Trends). Jerusalem: Office of the Prime Minister's Advisor on Arab Affairs.
Israel Government Yearbook, 1968.
Israel, Knesset. 1975. Report of a Parliamentary Committee on the situation of the Druze. (In Hebrew.)
Landau, A. 1961. "Ha-shiput ha-'adati shel ha-druzim be-yisrael" (Communal Jurisdiction of the Druze in Israel) *Ha-mizrah he-hadash,* Vol. XI.
Landau, J. 1969. *The Arabs in Israel* London: Oxford University Press.
Longrigg, S. H. 1958. *Syria and Lebanon under the French Mandate.* London: Oxford University Press.
Nakhleh, K. 1976. "Anthropological and Sociological Studies on the Arabs in Israel: A Critique," *Journal of Palestine Studies,* Vol. VI, No. 4.
Oliphant, L. 1887. *Haifa, or Life in Modern Palestine.* New York: Harper.
Peres, Y. 1970. "Modernisation and Nationalism in the Identity of the Israeli Arab," *Middle East Journal,* Vol. 24, No. 4.
Rosenfeld, H. 1964. "From Peasantry to Wage Labour and Residual Peasantry: The Transformation of an Arab Village" in Robert A. Manners (Ed.), *Process and Pattern in Culture: Essays in Honor of Julian Steward.* Chicago: Aldine.
——. 1978. "The Class Situation of the Arab Minority in Israel," *Comparative Studies in Society and History,* Vol. 20. pp. 374-407.
Smooha, S., and Hofman, J. 1976. "Some Problems of Arab-Jewish Co-existence in Israel," *Middle East Review,* Vol. 9, No. 2.
Standel, O. 1972. *The Minorities in Israel* (Hebrew) Jerusalem: The Government Information Office.
Tibawi, A. L. 1969. *A Modern History of Syria, including Lebanon and Palestine.* London: Macmillan.
Weingrod, A. 1965. *Israel, Group Relations in a New Society.* London: Institute of Race Relations.
Zenner, W. P. 1972. "Some Aspects of Ethnic Stereotype Content in the Galilee: A Trial Formulation," *Middle East Studies,* Vol. 8, No. 3.
Zureik, E. 1976. "Transformation of Class Structure among Arabs in Israel: From Peasantry to Proletariat," *Journal of Palestine Studies,* Vol. VI No. 1.
Zu'bi, A. A. 1964. "Talking Frankly and Facing Facts" *New Outlook.* Vol. VII:32-34.

14

Aggression and Social Relationships among Moroccan Immigrants[1]

Moshe Shokeid

Moroccan Jews, the largest group of immigrants to have arrived in Israel since the establishment of the State in 1948, have long been stereotyped as a hot-tempered and uncontrollable people. During the 1950s and early 1960s, this was symbolically represented by the appelation *morocco sakin*, literally "Morocco knife."

Their violence was interpreted as a sign of the breakdown of family and communal ties, the continuation of a process of disintegration which had started in Morocco with the migration from rural areas to the coastal cities (Bar-Yosef, 1959; Weingrod, 1960; Palgi, 1966; Elam, 1978). Bar-Yosef (1959), commenting on an outburst of riots and violence by Moroccan immigrants in an urban slum, noted that the migration to cities had led to the breakdown of the traditional Jewish economy in Morocco, a growing identification with unattainable middle class ideals and standard of living, and a desire to achieve political equality. Those who came to Israel transferred these aspirations to their new society, but their hopes to quick improvements in economic, social and political status were soon shattered. Moreover, the notion of relative deprivation grew immensely with the change of reference group. Marx (1976), who studied Moroccan immigrants housed in a new town with limited employment opportunities, interpreted minor personal violence as a strategy employed by the individual for extracting material benefits from bureaucrats responsible for the allocation of various resources; or as a way of attracting the attention of other members of the family and community to his predicament and his inability to provide for his family. Existing studies, which are based on a vaguely defined hypothesis of social disintegration and aggression, have thus mainly emphsized the situational aspect of Moroccan violence.

Another common view has considered Moroccan violence to be a product of the conditions of personal danger that for many generations typified great parts of Morocco, due to the weakness of the central government (see, for example, Marx, 1976:33). However, studies carried out in Morocco (Rosen, 1972; Geertz, 1973:3-32), as well as my own data (Shokeid, 1980a), substantiate a common anthropoligical observation: the weakness of central governments does not necessarily imply chaos and lawlessness in the lower levels of social organization, and particularly in the life of local communities. Studies on the relationships between Jews, Berbers and Arabs in Morocco demonstrate that, except during particular instances of political turmoil, violence was carefully checked at the local level, even in the most remote tribal areas. Moreover, in this social environment there were no "strangers," in the sense that travelers were easily identified as members of certain social units (Jewish or Muslim), whose relatives and patrons would demand revenge or compensation for any damage or injury.

Instead of employing the usual procedure, which is to consider the particular types of violence reported among Moroccan immigrants (such as aggression employed against bureaucrats, or aggression in terms of social protest), I intend to tackle the issue of "Moroccan violence" through the examination of the totality of aggressive acts as they were observed in the routine of daily life in two Moroccan communities. I believe that this approach provides a better understanding of the features and norms of aggressive behavior in various ethnic groups.[2]

This objective is further facilitated by the composition of the study population, as it comprises two separate rural communities, both of which were less subject to acute processes of social disintegration and economic deprivation than were the Moroccan groups analyzed in other studies. These communities were partially transplanted from Southern Morocco. The immigrants were not subject to the process of urbanization in Morocco, nor were they totally dispersed in Israel. Moreover, their economic situation was better than that of the immigrants settled in towns. The

the settlers, protesting this action, gave the rabbi a light shove—again, causing offense rather than injury.

These incidents illustrate that, while the Moroccans studied might physically assault close kin, they generally refrained from assaulting members of their own community with whom they had no family ties. However, there were some incidents of violence involving outsiders. It seems that outsiders, perceiving their Moroccan protagonists' deafening screeches and bodily expressions as signs of imminent violence, responded with a defensive stance that actually exacerbated the dispute, and triggered off a counterreaction of aggression, which might otherwise not have taken place. This stance differentiates the inexperienced and disoriented outsiders from unrelated Moroccans; we assume that in the absence of such a response, the outsiders would also have been spared physical assault. Nevertheless, the outcome of these confrontations was generally offense rather than physical injury. This observation is supported by Marx's (1976) findings with regard to Moroccan immigrants' action towards officials: aggression toward them was minor and often only demonstrative (such as brandishing a chair with the apparent intention of hitting an official).

On the whole, the outburst of physical aggression was usually unexpected and was much regretted by all those involved. The attacker, his relatives and others were generally upset with a turn of events that ended in unrestrained violence.

Verbal aggression

While physical assault was never considered excusable, and was an embarrassment to all concerned, verbal aggrewsion was unanimously considered natural, a sign of purity of motives and sentiments. This attitude was expressed in statements such as: "Dirty mouth—clean heart"; "he who has evil in his mouth does not have evil in his heart"; "I scream but I don't keep a grudge"; "our people don't know how to talk, they don't conceal their thoughts." Other common sayings stressed the connection between verbal aggression and reconciliation: "If we scream at each other we can later meet and talk again, that's how we are"; "as much as we Moroccans quarrel, when we eventually meet at a celebration we eat together and make up." This was given impressive expression in the frequent parties in Romema, many of which were arranged by those involved in disputes as a gesture of conciliation for their uncontrolled mouths (Shokeid, 1976).

This mode of behavior was clearly demonstrated by a wealthy farmer in his late forties, a shrewd politician who was frequently carried away by violent outbursts of anger and was involved in more disputes than anyone else. He was, however, a generous party giver; after a quarrel with the rabbi he insisted on holding the annual party of the Zohar (text of Jewish gnosticism) Study Circle in their house and at his expense, even though he rarely attended their meetings. In contrast, the very few settlers who refused to reconcile with their disputants were condemned and regarded with suspicion by the rest of the community.

Frequently, verbal aggression appeared to express a fleeting emotion, and its impact was no less fleeting. Having screamed out their protest, settlers would frequently calm down and head for home, or engage, often good-humoredly, in discussion on another issue.

The Amranites were inclined to interpret more permanent disaffection in terms of a wider political confrontation rather than personal enmity. Thus, Daniel Sebag, experiencing Levy Biton's persistent opposition to him taking office in the moshav organization (opposition that had severe personal consequences for Daniel Sebag as it meant the loss of badly needed money as well as prestige), interpreted it not as personal animosity, but rather as part of the Biton's resentment of the Sebag family's aspirations for leadership. In arguments with Biton, Sebag was very careful to suppress the release of the frustration and anger apparent in his facial and bodily expressions. Sometimes, at the peak of a heated argument in the village meetings, he would leave abruptly so as to avoid the escalation of a personal dispute. Later, he would rejoin the meeting and resume discussions with the participants, Biton included. Sebag's great control in encounters with Levy Biton and other members of the Biton family was in sharp contrast to his lack of restraint in arguments with his own relatives. Thus, at a public discussion of a decision made by the village committee, he rudely attacked his elder first cousin and brother-in-law, Shlomo, as stupid and incompetent; but within a few weeks the two were reconciled at a family celebration. By that time, Daniel had told his close associates that his attack on Shlomo was, in fact, a strategy he employed in order to gain Levy Biton's support in another matter, beneficial to the Sebags, which he would have otherwise opposed. Shlomo seemed inclined to accept this face-saving interpretation. Had Daniel expressed his anger with Levy Biton in the same uncontrolled fashion, reconciliation would have been much more difficult.

This restraint in verbal disputes with unrelated individuals despite

longstanding rivalry contrasts keenly with the uncontrolled aggression
with close relatives. As such, it is akin to the pattern observed in physical
aggression.

Aggressive neighbors—forgiving relatives

Eight aggressive encounters (18 percent) between members of nuclear
families, in-laws, and other relatives followed disputes over the neglect of
family responsibilities and family commitments. Thus, for example, Levy
Biton beat his wife and threw her out of the house for nagging him to
switch off the radio as an act of respect to her father who had been taken
to the hospital. The furious woman and her children found shelter at an
uncle's house. Despite talk of calling the police, the wife was back home
within a few hours of the incident. Someone suggested that her husband
must have been drunk. This was an unlikely explanation, since he rarely
drank, but it was a welcome face-saver for all concerned.

Reuben Mahluf carried on a bitter quarrel with his relative and neighbor, Yehuda Mahluf, because the latter offered to supply water to a Sebag
to farm land ceded to him by Reuben as the result of a village decision.
Reuben claimed emphatically that Yehuda, as a kinsman, should not have
helped the Sebag who had taken his land.

While the Amranites preferred close relatives as neighbors (see map in
Shokeid, 1971:65), residential proximity between kin was a constant
cause for dispute. Disputes between neighbors from different families were
frequently far milder than those between neighbors from the same family
group. Thus, Daniel Sebag had two Mahluf families (Yehuda and Itzhak)
as next door neighbors, while his first cousin Nahum Sebag lived opposite.
Daniel's contacts with his Mahluf neighbors were usually cordial, but his
relationship with his cousin gradually deteriorated, largely because of
Nahum's habit of borrowing farm tools without asking permission. When
Itzhak Mahluf died, a young, still unmarried first cousin of Daniel Sebag
moved into the house. To Daniel's astonishment, the newcomer soon
claimed that Daniel's hothouse (built a few years earlier) encroached on
his land. Unable to resolve the dispute, which escalated under its own
momentum, the two finally sought legal advice. Daniel's bitterness was exacerbated by the fact that his cousin only received the house because he,
Daniel, and his brother had persuaded the other members of the village
committee to make an exception and allocate a house and farm land to
an unmarried candidate.

Family disputes were not limited to the Sebags. While Yehuda Mahluf

got along well with his Sebag neighbor, Daniel, he was continuously involved in disputes with his neighbor and relative, Reuben Mahluf. Yehuda
complained, for example, that Reuben's poultry battery was too close to
his courtyard, and the refuse too close to his windows. Thus, while Daniel
Sebag and his Mahluf neighbors seemed to avoid aggressive encounters,
both were engaged in disputes with neighbors from their own family
group. But, as a teenaged Sebag commented, "Sebags do quarrel, but within a fortnight it is all forgotten," or as Aziz Sebag commented disparingly,
"the Mahlufs conceal their envy and contempt for each other, unlike the
Sebags whose mouth is a true agent of their heart." Thus Aziz tried to
justify his own frequent involvement in disputes as an expression of affective relations with his kin.

As much as the Amranites were quick to support their relatives when
in dispute or competition with strangers, they sometimes competed with
their own kin. For example, a young Amranite in Yashuv was concluding
negotiations for the acquisition of a farm from a retiring European settler.
To his dismay, he discovered that his older cousin had tried to interfere
with the deal in order to get the farm for his unmarried son. Nevertheless,
he did not consider severing his relationship with his relatives. This incident was one of several between them, of which the most serious had
occurred about a year earlier when the same cousin had beaten the informant's sister and mother. The aggressor's 10 year old son had called the
other's 16 years old sister a whore. She had lashed out and spanked him,
and the child ran home to his father; the father ran straight to the girl's
home and hit both her and her mother (his aunt). However, in spite of
the injury and abuse, the aunt finally decided to drop the case.

It is interesting to note another ethnographic source that supports our
data: the analysis of the description of family relationships in the folktales
of the different ethnic groups in Israel. The proportion of tales whose
theme indicates intrafamily confrontations (mainly between husband and
wife, parents and children, siblings and in-laws) is significantly higher
among North African and Middle Eastern Jews than among European
Jews.[7] According to Shenhar (1972:406), this is due to the prevalence of
the extended family in North African and Middle Eastern society, a situation prone to dispute because of the conflict that stems from the contradiction between individual goals and the structure of social and economic
cooperation. The results obtained from the analysis of Moroccan folktales
seem compatible with the observed high frequency of conflict and disputes

among relatives who, in their new environment, seem to continue practices associated with the traditional extended family.[8]

In the search for an explanation of the observed frequency and intensity of aggressive acts as related to the social distance between the protagonists, we should consider two major variables: structural expectations
and bystanders' reactions. Thus, opposition, lack of support, or inconsider-
ate behavior from close relatives shattered patterns of social relationships
and norms of role expectations. The perception of breakdown in the social
and moral order intensified the reaction of the individual who felt himself
wronged, and affected his control of aggressive expressions.[9] Second, the
role of bystanders: in cases that involved members of different family
groups or strangers, any relatives who happened to be present acted almost automatically to restrain the escalation of conflict and the release
of aggression. But in those disputes in which the protagonists shared a
common and closely-knit social network, confused loyalties on the part
of bystanding relatives and an unwillingness to get involved on the part of
outsiders delayed the restraining mechanism. However, in disputes involving strangers, even if the bystanders were members of the community not
closely related to the local protagonists, they would sometimes intervene
to restrain him, thus assuming the shared status of Moroccan community
members.

Conclusions

The Moroccan Jews studied here did not undergo the acute process of family and community distintegration characteristic of a large segment of
Moroccan Jewry, nor were their experiences in Israel as traumatic as those
described in most other reports. Their family and communal bonds were
not drastically disrupted; nor did they endure economic deprivation and
severe decline of personal social status. The absence of these situational
factors in this study may therefore permit better insight into the "culture"
of aggressive behavior among Moroccan Jews.

The data reveal two main related observations. First, in spite of a cultural code that apparently allows for and professes the free release of
verbal aggression, in practice the release or restraint of either verbal or
physical aggression seems to be conditioned not so much by the extent
and type of provocation, but rather by the social relationships connecting
the protagonists. Second, as with the cases of more severe violence, homi-

cide in particular, reported for example by Bohannan (1968:28) and Wolfgang and Farracuti (1967), the outburst of uncontrolled verbal aggression
and minor violence has an intragroup direction. The individual encounters
numerous aggressive stimulations in the cycle of daily life involving close
or distant relatives, covillagers from the same or different ethnic groups,
or outsiders who render him various services. Although these encounters
may be considered equally frustrating, he nevertheless tends to select as
targets for the release of aggression those with whom he is integrated in a
web of social relationships.[10] While the Amranites were easily triggered
toward aggressive responses, their control in the selection of target and
the extent of the aggression released is indicative of great restraint in
that sphere of expressive behavior.[11]

   In his study of aggression among Moroccans in an immigrant town,
Marx considered aggression mainly in terms of a strategy instrumental
in obtaining material and social support. Debating some leading psychological theories, and particularly the frustration-aggression hypothesis,
he searched for the social context of aggression and came to emphasize
the goal-directedness and rationality of aggressive behavior. Thus he
states: "Most of the aggression I studied served a more or less clearly
defined purpose ... the aggressors sought to produce some effect on
their social environment" (Marx, 1976:109).

   No doubt, some forms of aggression, like other affective mechanisms,
may be instrumental in reorganizing the social and emotional order. Moreover, the circumstances in the town Marx studied may have left the immigrants with few alternative effective personal resources. However, it is
likely that under the relative prosperity of the moshav, most outbursts
of aggression could not be interpreted in terms of rationality and instrumental goal-directedness; rather, it was the control and inhibition of aggression that carried an element of rationality.[12]

   Elam (1978), in comparing the patterns of violence among Georgian
Jews with the cases of the violence in the town described by Marx (1976),
argued that the Moroccan aggressors, in using force, were actually trying
to establish a particular social relationship with the universalistically
oriented bureaucrats. This seems consistent with our discussion. While research among Moroccans settled in villages (Weingrod, 1966; Shokeid,
1971) demonstrates that family ties provide the individual settler with a
powerful asset (as much or even more than in Morocco), it appears that
in towns, family ties lost much effect and came to be replaced by growing
dependence on the services and support provided by government and

municipal officials. A clear indication of this is found in Cooper's (1978) study of Moroccans in a development town. He states that "kin roles are sometimes projected beyond the range of real kin and applied as formulas for generating behavior" (p. 156). He brings up the case of a desperate man, married to a blind woman and father of eight children, who jumped on a table and shouted at the town council chairman, "Micha, you are my father, you must find me a job" (p. 47).

During the period with which I had contact with the villages presented here there were no attacks on bureaucrats representing outside agencies such as the Ministry of Agriculture, the Jewish Agency Land Settlement Department, the regional municipal and economic organizations, etc. This is in stark contrast to the frequency of aggression directed against relatives, even though they were also major sources of support to the individual settler in his claims on outside agencies and in his struggle for economic and political resources in the moshav organization. In contrast with the relatively advantageous economic and organizational conditions of the moshav, the bureaucrats in Israel's new and often depressed towns have assumed the roles of benevolent yet often incomprehensible sponsors responsible for the individual allocation of most material resources (such as employment, housing and welfare). Considering the evidence available from other studies of Moroccan Jews it appears that when aggression is employed by Moroccan immigrants, it may well imply the cognitive confusion of social categories. In that liminal state of social passage in the life of Moroccan immigrants who have been abruptly cut off from their old communal and occupational life, when the instrumental and affective perception of the role of relatives is considerably reduced, clients grant bureaucrats an affective property which often forces them to react also in terms of personal relationships.

Thus, while current interpretations of aggressive actions among Moroccan immigrants have considered these a mode of reaction produced from the frustration of social and political expectations, as a rational strategy for obtaining material and social support, or as a traditional response of self-defense, I have emphasized the affective dimension of Moroccan aggression. While the regulation and the modes of these expressions of affective behavior may be altered by drastic changes in economic and social circumstances, they nevertheless reveal a completely different phenomenon from that presented in earlier interpretations of Moroccan aggression. As much as aggressive behavior may sometimes serve to gain material and social benefits and possibly to respond to frustrations which follow the breakdown of various social, economic and political expectations, it is a dramatic expression of the deep changes which affect the individual's modes of interaction and commitment with those who impinge upon his world.

The interpretation of Moroccan aggression in terms of a mode of affective behavior which regulates the individual's social relationships with kin and strangers leads to a general theoretical discussion of the sources and meaning of aggression in society. While that discourse is beyond the scope of this chapter, it demonstrates the relevance and the possible contribution of the study of apparently specific ethnic phenomena to wider sociological issues.

Notes

[1] This ongoing research was facilitated by a Ford Foundation grant received through the Israel Foundation Trustees, a grant from the Pinhas Sapir Center for Development, and by a fellowship at Manchester University, financed by the Bernstein Israeli Research Trust. I am grateful to Shlomo Deshen, Samuel Cooper and Alex Weingrod for their comments and to Connie Wilsack for help with the editing.

[2] For a similar approach, see Levy (1973).

[3] Participant observation extended over 21 months (October 1965 to March 1976, June 1976 to September 1976) in Romema. Fieldwork in Yashuv was conducted during sporadic visits over one year (1979).

[4] For more details about the moshav pattern of settlement and about the adjustment of Middle Eastern and North African immigrants to that model of organization, see for example, Weingrod (1966); Willner (1969), Shokeid (1971,1980b).

[5] For more details about these events, see Shokeid (1971:41,43; 1976:210-235).

[6] See Romanucci-Ross (1973:28-29) who differentiated between "bound conflict" when the individuals act as members of a larger unit and "unbound individual conflict" when the individuals act on their own behalf.

[7] According to Shenhar (1972), of the 455 folktales recorded among Moroccan immigrants, 24 percent (108) deal with intrafamily confrontation, as compared with 27 percent among the folktales of Tunisian immigrants, 45 percent among those of Iraqi immigrants, and 25 percent among those of Yemenite immigrants. Among European Jews, the proportion is much lower: for example, 11 percent among Rumanian Jews, 10 percent among Russian Jews and 8 percent among Jews from Poland.

[8] In fact, aggression and violence involving strangers and outsiders are rather rare in the general corpus of Moroccan folktales. Thus, there is a story of an Arab strongman who wanted to confront a Jew from Marrakesh who was reputed for his physical endowments (Noy, 1964:43); he chose to avoid that confrontation in a jocular way, and the two ended up close friends.

[9] A relevant observation has been made by Bilu (1979) in his study of demonic ex-

planations of disease among Moroccans in Israeli villages. His observations revealed that fights and quarrels constituted a frequent context for the emergence of demonic disease. But most interesting, the impact of these discords and their development into a demonic disease have been influenced by the fact that they have "usually evolved within the patient's inner social circle and rapidly escalated to physical violence" (p. 369).

[10] This mode of the selection of targets for the release of aggression is reminiscent of witchcraft accusations, which also tend to involve people who are closely related and often by consanguineous, affinal or territorial ties. See, for example, Gluckman (1963:81-109).

[11] I do not discuss here the role played by women in aggressive encounters. While the men refrained from the escalation of dispute with unrelated disputants, women were much less inhibited by social distance. Moreover, women sometimes intervened aggressively in disputes involving their menfolk where the men themselves had refrained from the release of aggression. Their low status in the community may explain the widespread toleration of such spontaneous outbursts. See my discussion on the position of Amran women in Morocco and in Israel (Shokeid, 1971:165-215; Deshen and Shokeid, 1974:122-150).

[12] Cooper (1978), observing Moroccan immigrants in a development town, makes brief reference to outbursts of violence. He also suggests that the expression of violence is patterned in such a way that control is guaranteed (p. 154).

References

Bar-Yosef, R. 1959. "The Moroccans: The Background of a Problem," *Molad* 17: 247-251 (in Hebrew). (Revised English version, 1979, in S. N. Eisenstadt, *et al.,* (Eds.), *Integration and Development In Israel.* Jerusalem: Israeli Universities Press, pp. 419-428.

Bilu, Y. 1979. "Demonic Explanations of Disease among Moroccan Jews in Israel," *Culture, Medicine and Psychiatry* 3:363-380.

Bohannan, P. 1969. *African Homicide and Suicide.* Princeton: Princeton University Press.

Cooper, S. 1978. *Newgate: An Old-New Town in the Negev.* Ph.D. Dissertation, the Catholic University of America.

Deshen, S., and Shokeid, M. 1974. *The Predicament of Homecoming: Cultural and Social Life of North African Immigrants in Israel.* Ithaca, N.Y.: Cornell University Press.

Elam, Y. 1978. "Use of Force among Moroccan and Georgian Immigrants," *Megamot* 24:169-185 (in Hebrew).

Geertz, C. 1973. *The Interpretation of Culture.* New York: Basic Books.

Gluckman, M. 1963. *Custom and Conflict in Africa.* Oxford: Basil Blackwell.

Levy, R. I. 1973. *Thaitians: Mind and Experience in the Islands.* Chicago: University of Chicago Press.

Marx, E. 1976. *The Social Context of Violent Behavior: A Social Anthropological Study in an Israeli Immigrant Town.* London: Routledge and Kegan Paul.

Noy, D. 1964. *Jewish Folktales from Morocco*. Jerusalem: Bitfuzot Hagolah.

Palgi, P. 1966. "Cultural Components of Immigrants' Adjustment" in H. P. David (Ed.), *Migration, Mental Health and Community Services*. Washington: International Research Institute, pp. 71-82.

Romanucci-Ross, L. 1973. *Conflict, Violence and Morality in a Mexican Village*. Palo Alto: National Press Books.

Rosen, L. 1972. "Muslim-Jewish Relations in a Moroccan City," *International Journal of Middle Eastern Studies* 3:435-449.

Shenhar, A. 1972. *Family Confrontation and Conflict in Jewish Folktales*. Ph.D. Thesis, The Hebrew University.

Shokeid, M. 1971. *The Dual Heritage: Immigrants from the Atlas Mountains in an Israeli Village*. Manchester: Manchester University Press.

——. 1976. "Conviviality versus Strife: Peacemaking at Parties among Atlas Mountains Immigrants in Israel," *Political Anthropology* 1:101-121.

——. 1980a. "Jewish Existence in a Berber Environment" in *Les Relations entre Juifs et Musulmans en Afrique du Nord*. Paris: Editions Du Centre National De La Recherche Scientifique, pp. 62-71.

——. 1980b. "Reconciling with Bureaucracy: Middle Eastern Immigrant Moshav in Transition," *Economic Development and Cultural Change* 29:187-205.

Weingrod, A. 1960. "Moroccan Jewry in Transition," *Megamot* 10:193-208 (in Hebrew).

——. 1966. *Reluctant Pioneers: Village Development in Israel*. Ithaca: Cornell University Press.

Willner, D. 1969. *Nation-building and community in Israel*. Princeton, N.J.: Princeton University Press.

Wolfgang, M. E., and Ferracuti, F. 1967. *The Subculture of Violence: Towards an Integrated Theory in Criminology*. London: Tavistock.

15

The Benefits of Attenuation: Continuity and Change in Jewish Moroccan Ethnopsychiatry in Israel

Yoram Bilu

The traditional heritage carried by Jewish immigrants from Morocco to Israel includes beliefs, practices and social roles that a "modern" observer might consider to be interrelated elements in a system of folk psychiatry. My concern here is with the vicissitudes undergone by this system in Israel since the first waves of immigration from Morocco in the early 1950's. The analysis that follows is based on field work conducted in two settings during the years 1974 to 1977 (Bilu, 1977, 1978). In the first setting, ninety inhabitants of two *moshavim* (small holders' cooperative villages) founded by Jews from southern Morocco, who employed the services of traditional healers in Israel, were interviewed about their problems, the assumed etiologies of the problems and modes of treatment. From these interviews, information concerning thirty-eight healers, most of whom were Moroccan-born rabbis living outside the *moshavim*, were derived. The work patterns of eight of the healers were also carefully examined. Thus, an attempt was made to describe and analyze the traditional system of folk medicine from both the patients' and the healers' points of view.

In order to continue in a modern context, any system of folk medicine must undergo significant change. The mainstream ideology, which is reluctant to accept the cultural premises of folk medicine, and the existence of a modern medical system, impose crucial challenges on the traditional system. As powerful as this challenge is, however, various forms of folk medicine may be flexible enough to surmount it. Irving Press, who studied urban *curanderos* in Bogota, has contended that, unlike the relative isolation of modern medicine from its socio-cultural milieu, close contact exists between systems of folk medicine and other institutionalized sectors in the society. "As open systems, folk medical systems should thus be especially capable of adapting to novel environments or threats and of affording continuity of old functions while offering new ones to meet the needs of populations experiencing new pressures and opportunities" (Bilu, 1978:72). Indeed, the literature in medical anthropology abounds with successful cases of persistent folkways despite the pressures of modernization.

Landy (1974), who reviewed this literature, has suggested three general adaptation patterns typical of traditional healers under the impact of Western medicine. 1) The adaptive curing role characterizes those traditional healers who have managed to find some *modus vivendi* with modern agencies. 2) The emergent curing role refers to healers who could even add novel functions to this role as a result of pressures and frustrations in rapidly changing settings. 3) The attenuated curing role designates those situations in which healers must forego some significant aspects of their role in order to survive. Although all three patterns can be identified in our small sample of healers (see below), attenuation appears to be the most potent factor in the current Israeli situation. This does not mean, however, that the traditional system inescapably moves toward its vanishing point. Rather, I shall try to show that a recurring pattern is operative, according to which the very process of attenuation leads to better prospects of preservation for the remaining parts of the system.

The General Background of Attenuation in the Traditional Healing System

In Israel, high status and prestige are given to medical practitioners by all the population, including traditional segments. (Shokeid, 1971;125; Shuval, 1970). It is no wonder therefore that major areas of affliction, mainly somatic in nature, once considered pertinent to the rabbi-healer, have been taken away from him in the new country. Yielding to the constraints imposed by the new medical reality, patients and healers alike adopted the idea that the two systems are more complementary than exclusive. Although many of them refer to "physician's illnesses" and "rabbi's illnesses", it became evident that, in practice, the borderline between them is empirically, not conceptually, delineated. In more than eighty percent of the problems eventually treated by a folk healer, the priority in referral was given to the modern agent.

According to Romanucci-Schwartz (1969) this pattern, from the modern practitioner to the traditional one, designates an "acculturative sequence" in which the degree of acceptance of modern medical practices by traditional segments is indicated. While this sequence attests to the dominance accorded to medical resources, it also points to the actual failures of modern medicine and psychiatry, which contribute to the maintenance of the traditional alternative. Interestingly enough, in Israel, the fact that a modern practitioner cannot deal successfully with a given problem has become the central criterion for defining it as demonically caused. The healers typically accept and even encourage the priority accorded to their modern colleagues-rivals. Only after a standard examination of the scope and results of the physicians' prior involvement with the case, does the healer decide whether he will intervene or not. All this undoubtedly reflects an attenuated curing role, but, at the same time, this attenuation renders the traditional role more secure—the probability of directly competing with the modern practitioner is thus reduced—and also more positively valued. In addition to the instrumental aspect of increasing the salience of a therapeutic alternative after other pathways have been exhausted, the medical failure authorizes the healer as the appropriate agent, since it constitutes a diagnostic sign that the problem pertains to him.

It should be emphasized that the majority of these cases have a psychological component. In many cases this component has simply been left unnoticed by the physician because of the conspicuous somatic manifestations of the ailment (as with some psychophysiological and conversive problems). Even when the psychiatric nature of the problem has been acknowledged and some sort of psychotherapy administered, the success rate has been quite low. While biochemical medical therapy may work cross-culturally, psychotherapy rarely does. As a result, the contemporary version of the once all-embracing curing role does become similar to that of a modern psychotherapist.

With this background in mind, I turn to examining particular elements of Jewish-Moroccan ethnopsychiatry and their changes in the Israeli setting. First, the position of two major etiological agents of disease in Morocco, demons and witchcraft (see Westermarck, 1926), will be discussed. Second, an attempt will be made to account for the differential adaptability and success of folk healers in the new country.

Changes in the Position of Traditional Agents of Affliction

In Morocco, demons (*Jnun*) had been considered responsible for a wide spectrum of ailments, most of which were psychiatric in nature. *Jnun*-produced diseases were divided into *tsira* (demonic strike) and *aslai* (possession) according to the offending agent's mode of attack, the focus of which was either external (injuring the victim from the outside) or internal (entering his body and taking control of him). The typical symptoms of *tsira* were anxiety reactions as well as somatic complaints, centering around various organic dysfunctions and pains. The classical form of *aslai,* called "evil spirit disease" by our interviewees, involved a short but intense phase of altered consciousness. During this dissociative episode, the possessive demon manifested its presence through relatively complicated trance-like behaviors.

Focusing on the prevalence of these diseases in our sample, a clear-cut trend became evident: whereas the incidence of (*tsira*) strike diseases has not significantly decreased, "evil spirit diseases" have almost totally vanished from the Israeli scene. In accounting for this differential incidence, the following generalization is suggested: Given the pressures of mainstream Israeli society, demonic phenomena in which *Jnun* are "visible" or strongly felt, and which represent a "participational mode of responsibility" (Crapanzano, 1973:151), are liable to disappear, while the covert aspects of the demonic traditions, those that reflect an "explicative mode of responsibility" (*Jnun* as a logical construct) are preserved. Indeed, the explicative mode applies to most of the persistent strike diseases, where the role of the demon must be inferred from indirect signs, such as the abrupt onset of symptoms and ineffectiveness of medical treatment. In possession, the role of the *Jnun* is central as it is visibly and dramatically participating in symptom formation. The decline of the "participational demon" is lucidly seen in many other phenomena beyond the context of disease. Thus, diagnostic methods based on the summoning of the demons by the healer or spontaneous face-to-face encounters with *Jnun,* which were quite common both in Morocco and Israel during the first post-immigration years, have also rapidly diminished (Bilu, 1980:31 32).

As with the other modes of attenuation discussed above, it might be argued that these changes may warrant the more tenacious preservation of the *Jnun* in Israel. On the one hand, demons are no longer accorded a central role in constructing daily events of reality; their "existential facets" have been corroded and blurred. Only a small segment of the older population in the *moshavim* is aware of the once continuously pronounced presence of the *Jnun* and care to maintain the behavioral norms regulating the relations between humans and demons. The weakening of the *Jnun* in Israel have been alluded to by many traditional patients in our sample. "There are not as many demons in Israel as in Morocco", and "Only Moroccan Jews are haunted by demons here", were typical responses. One credulous interviewee gloomily depicted the current situation as he sees it: "Today's demons are terrified of men, not vice versa! In Morocco, people were afraid to leave their homes after sunset. Here they do not hesitate to go outside, even to burgle and steal under the cover of night. Why do the *Jnun* refrain from injuring these people?!" (In this statement, the role of demonic beliefs in encouraging obedience to social norms is clearly revealed). Yet on the other hand, in crisis situations, when facing problems in living otherwise inexplicable, many people in the *moshavim* (including youngsters) would return to the *Jnun* and use it as explanatory construct. As I have shown elsewhere (Bilu, 1979) demonic explanations of disease offer a theory of causation that is comprehensive, logical and internally consistent. It is not too bold a prediction to assume, therefore, that in certain areas of human misery, long life is believed to be determined by the demons in their attenuated explicative role.

The course that beliefs in witchcraft (*Skhur* in Moroccan Arabic) have taken in Israel follows the same rule of attenuation. Traditionally, this type of explanation was mainly employed in two spheres of human grievance, one of which concerns romantic, marital and sexual problems, and the other centering around material losses of various kinds. Here too the decline has been selective and has to do with the "visible front" of the phenomena. Two antagonistic factors participate in molding the patterns that *skhur* formulations taken in the *moshavim.* On the one hand, witchcraft is conceived as sheer superstition by the Israeli mainstream (this is what pupils are taught in the *moshav* school). On the other hand, socio-

L

psychological factors favoring a climate of witchcraft have a fertile ground in the *moshavim*. Following Evans-Pritchard (1937) and Mary Douglas (1970), in the *moshavim* one finds relatively intense social relations, marked by competition and sharpened by a dense concentration of people who were formerly more sparsely distributed. (In Morocco, the contemporary inhabitants of the *moshavim* had lived in very small communities scattered over the entire western High Atlas.) In addition, the breakdown of traditional stratification (Shokeid, 1971) and the emergence of egalitarian norms (Goldberg, 1972) result in a marked ambiguity in social-role definition. Finally, the socio-economic organization of the *moshav,* dictated by the ideology of government settlement agencies, is conducive to adopting a "notion of limited good" (Foster, 1972), out of which a witchcraft-fostering atmosphere may easily emerge.

The net result of this equivocal situation, where the contemporary socio-psychological determinants of a strongly disabled traditional belief are still very potent, seems to be a situation in which *skhur* suspicions are being continuously generated but not easily transformed into explicit accusations. In this respect, witchcraft has attenuated into a private affair, since people who are more open to (and more aware of) the disapproving and even derisive responses of others who identify with the mainstream ideology, are more reluctant to openly and explicitly specify their accusations. It should be emphasized that this suppressive tendency also played a role in circumscribing social responses to witchcraft in Morocco. But it is my impression that this has grown considerably in the post-immigration era. Today, open, unrestrained *skhur* accusations are critically evaluated in the *moshavim,* and they are often considered the product of a sick mind. Detrimental to social relations as *skhur* suspicions are, normatively they remain an unpronounced secret.

Success and Failure in Maintaining the Traditional Curing Role in Israel

Shifting our focus to the rabbi-healers, it might be conjectured that one aspect of their successful adaptation is reflected in the restrained and limited use of *Jnun* and *skhur* etiologies (compatible with the hitherto described changes). This is only partially true, since differential success in maintaining the curing role is influenced by other variables as well. One critical variable is the healer's place of residence. In the *moshavim*, we can witness the gradual extinction of the traditional curing profession since local healers face enormous difficulties in preserving their role. Although readily available, their potential clientele usually prefers to turn to healers living in nearby urban areas. This phenomenon, also documented in other parts of the world (see, for example, Spiro, 1967:207-8; Press, 1971), may be partially explained by the fact that therapeutic effectiveness and, consequently, healers' prestige are heightened by the process of going out to a remote agent. As Frank (1961) has noted, positive expectations, conducive to therapeutic success, are enhanced by the routine-breaking decision to go to a distant healer and the efforts invested in making the trip. This psychological mechanism does not seem to operate when the local healer is called. Also, local healers are deeply and inextricably involved in the intricate web of social relations in the *moshavim*. These settlements are typically plagued by bitter chronic struggles over political and socio-economic control. Local healers, like other *moshav* members, identify with one of the warring parties, which are organized along lines of kinship and former (Moroccan) neighborhood relations. This fact alone might take away potential clients belonging to rival groups. On the *moshavim,* healers are subject to the close scrutiny of neighbors and therefore must maintain high moral standards. This situation complicates their role in that any infraction will compromise their respectability and trustworthiness. Rabbi-healers, claiming their curing ability to be related to close contacts with the sacred (see below), must be pious and pure. It is much easier to maintain these attributes when patient-healer relations are limited to one or few therapeutic sessions rather than extended to all spheres of daily activities. Familiarity breeds contempt. (It might be argued that the strict isolation of therapeutic sessions from daily activities so feverently adhered to by many modern psychotherapists seems to serve the function of avoiding this contempt-provoking familiarity.)

Urban healers, therefore, are better equipped "ecologically" to keep their practice alive than their village counterparts. Yet their success in doing so is far from guaranteed. Let me briefly sketch three profiles of urban rabbi-healers in order to further illuminate determinants of differential success in preserving their role. The three all live in the same Israeli development town.

Rabbi David Amzaleg

Rabbi David is an old man, almost 80 years old at the time of this study, who came to Israel from a rural area in the western Atlas, not far from the town of Dimnat. His family geneology is resplendent with rabbis and sages, venerated by the local Jewish community for their erudition, piety and charismatic attributes. Several of his elders were elevated to the level of saint because of their miraculous deeds. Thus, Rabbi David's familial background has endowed them with a large quantity of *zekhut avot* (literally, "virtues of the ancestors"). This term designates a potentiality of Divine Grace, the manifestations of which are not unlike those of the Moroccan-Muslim *baraka*. (See Westermarck, 1926:1:35-262; Rabinow, 1975:17-30). Making the study of the Torah his sole concern, he has been proven worthy of his *zekhut* and is considered a religious authority, even though he has never been part of the rabbinical establishment. Rabbi David is also a renowed student of *Kabbala* (Jewish mysticism), the main source of Sacred Names and esoteric combination, the written manipulations of which constitute the basis of traditional healing in Judaism. In Morocco, he was sporadically engaged in "writing" (*ketiva*) cures. The "professionalization" of his healing activities in Israel was forced upon him since he could no longer rely on the financial support of his followers who were spread all over the country (nevertheless, many still pay him visits and present gifts on special occasions).

Rabbi David has made only minor concessions to the Israeli reality. Living in a tiny apartment in a working class neighborhood, he still wears a traditional black *jellaba* (gown) with a brown hood wrapped around his head. These garments, in addition to his long white beard, give him an impressive appearance. Rabbi David's life style is marked by spirituality: in addition to "writing", his entire day is devoted to prayers and religious study. Ailing patients, mostly Moroccan-born, come to him mainly from his town and neighboring areas, although others travel considerable distances to see him. His modest apartment is well adapted to take them in. While waiting in the guest-room, his patients are first served with food and tea from the ever-busy kitchen kept by the Rabbi's wife and daughters. Rabbi David receives the clients in his small room, seated on a bed. The respect and admiration he enjoys are clearly manifested in the conversation that ensues, which is short, parsimonious and problem-oriented. Having learned about the patient's ailment, he uncovers its underlying etiology by using his favorite diagnostic tool, a fairly standard, handwritten, Jewish traditional lot-book. Rabbi David's etiological explanations are particularly biased in the demonic direction, although an attempt is often made to incorporate them within a broader religious framework.

Thus, the ailment-provoking demonic attack may be presented by him as God-initiated punishment for a religious transgression.

After authoritatively stating his diagnostic conclusions and explaining them in detail to the patient, he turns to prepare the therapeutic intervention. In a solemn, almost ceremonial silence, he carefully writes two types of charms, based on Jewish-kabbalistic sacred formulae. One is for cure and should be burned or erased in water with certain demon-repellent incenses so that the patient can inhale the smoke, drink the water or smear it on his body at certain times. The other written piece is an amulet designed to immunize the patient against further attacks. This two-fold curing measure is the standard paradigm in Jewish folk-therapy, but Rabbi David applys it more rigorously and meticulously than all the healers I have studied. He is also more inflexible concerning the payment he charges which, although fairly decent, is fixed and non-negotiable. Because "writing" is his sole regular source of income, it seems that he cannot obey the prevalent norm of letting the patient determine the cost of the therapy. It is also possible that his high prestige and spiritual status enable him to be unyielding and demanding in this respect.

Indeed, the image of piety and holiness with which Rabbi David is accorded is unparalleled in the contemporary Israeli scene. Stories of his charismatic, miraculous acts feed and reinforce this image and draw to him a constant flow of clients.

Rabbi Yosef Amzaleg

Rabbi Yosef is Rabbi David's 67-year-old cousin. The fact that they were close neighbors in Morocco as well as in Israel, and that their curing role has emerged from the same cultural matrix, makes the comparison of their careers in the new country particularly interesting. More explicitly than his elder kin, Rabbi Yosef emphasizes his intimate relations with his holy ancestors, who recurrently appear in his dreams and guide him in his personal life and therapeutic work. He claims to be the true inheritor of their spiritual power, a claim that cannot be overstated since his cousin and close neighbor is Rabbi David, a most respected descendent of the Amzaleg family. Indeed, even though Rabbi Yosef's *zekhut avot* is amply acknowledged by his community, he cannot compete with the charisma of Rabbi David. Unlike his older cousin, whose entire life has been devoted to the worship of the Lord, Rabbi Yosef has pursued the more ordinary although highly respected career of a religious functionary. In Morocco, he was part of the local rabbinical establishment, serving intermittently as a ritual slaughterer, *mohel* (one who performs the act of circumcision), teacher of the Torah, performer of prayer rituals in the synagogue and executant of marriage ceremonies. Healing based on religious erudition constituted a natural part of this generalized role, which, indeed, had been assumed by most of the Moroccan-born healers in our sample. In Israel, Rabbi Yosef had been employed as a ritual slaughterer in the local municipality until his recent retirement at the age of 65. Now, he considers himself a "full-time" healer and actively seeks to enlarge his clientele.

Rabbi Yosef is a small, lean man, always dressed in the black costume and hat typical of religious public servants in Israel. The curative devices he employs, although based on the same tradition as that underlying Rabbi David's practices, are not identical with them, and reflect his distinctive personal style and preferences. Being methodical, pragmatic and cautious, he conceives of his job as an empirically-based endeavor in which therapeutic interventions must be carefully applied and continuously reassessed for their effectiveness. In the diagnostic phase, his caution is expressed in a determined refusal to use traditional tools, which purportedly disclose the origins of the patient's problems. Instead, he prefers a prognostic lot which, on the one hand, gives practical valuable information concerning curing prospects, but, on the other hand, bears conclusions that are irrefutable at the moment (unlike the former, past-oriented lots).[1]

Rabbi Yosef's empirical approach is manifested through his selection of therapeutic devices. As he himself admits, his arsenal is composed of limited and apparently simple versions of *ketiva,* but each of these items has been carefully examined by him and proven effective. Moreover, he deviates from the one-trial therapy design, typical of traditional treatment, as he conceives of healing as a sequence of consecutive interventions, each of which should be constructed according to the consequences of the preceding one. The therapeutic contact is thus extended over several sessions.

Rabbi Yosef's work style is more organized and systematic than that of any other healer I have met. All the *ketiva* versions he employs are alphabetically ordered in one booklet, which is kept, together with his other therapeutic tools, in a small suitcase. Whenever he goes out of town, be it for a family or social affair, he takes the suitcase with him, hoping to make use of its contents. In this way, he succeeds from time to time in arranging for clientele in other places.

On the whole, Rabbi Yosef is a conservative healer, proud of his therapeutic skills and family heritage. He radiates authority and self-assurance with his patients, although this is somewhat moderated by his cautious, quasi-experimental approach. Warmth and empathy are not his strong points, and a certain distance is always maintained between him and his patients. These personality attributes and work patterns are related to his current status as a folk healer.

Rabbi Chaim Elmaliach

Although a remote kin of the Amzaleg's and a native of an adjacent region in Morocco, Rabbi Chaim represents a different life-style and a different healing tradition. Forty-eight years old, beardless and always dressed in ordinary informal fashion, nothing in his appearance would hint that he had also functioned as a 'rabbi' before immigration, serving as a ritual slaughterer and teacher of the Torah in the town of Beni-M'Lal. His career as a healer, based on a solid family tradition, had been precipitated by a dream message from a venerated saint, Rabbi David u-Moshe, delivered to young Chaim's sick mother. In her dream, the saint inserted a pen into her son's mouth, thus indicating his destiny as a "writer" for cure. Since then Rabbi Chaim has been a devout disciple of this saint. He claims that the contributions he reluctantly receives from grateful patients are primarily dedicated to organizing Rabbi David u-Moshe's *Hillulah* (the annual celebration in memorial of the saint).

Unlike the Amzalegs, who strongly emphasized the Jewish character of their healing traditions, Rabbi Chaim was not deterred from studying under famous Muslim scribes and he willingly adopted many of their methods. Along with other rabbi healers, he considers Muslim practices superior to the Jewish counterparts in certain, non-disease areas of affliction (for example, romantic and marital problems). He also rejects the ascribed inherited aspect implicit in the idea of *zekhut avot,* emphasizing instead professional skills acquired through learning. In this respect, his approach is unique among his colleagues, who, while not underestimating the importance of acquired skill, perceive the *zekhut* as a prerequisite for its achievement. Rabbi Chaim's current occupational status adds to his peculiar profile: he is the only rabbi-healer in my sample who voluntarily shifted to a non-religious job in Israel. He is employed as a technician in a public construction company. Therefore, he receives patients only in the late afternoon and in the evening.

Rabbi Chaim belongs to the small sub-group of healers who prefer to divide the therapeutic encounter into two sessions. In the first, the patient delivers some identifying details (such as his name and his mother's name) on the basis of which fairly detailed diagnostic information is generated. This information is delivered to the patient in the second meeting, a few days later, together with therapeutic materials. For diagnosis, Rabbi Chaim mainly employs a Muslim lot called *Zenati,* which he has translated into Hebrew, together with a Jewish version of palm reading. Both tools convey information that is fairly "culture free". This accords with Rabbi Chaim's inclination to avoid traditional explanations of demons and sorcery. Because his therapeutic arsenal is based on both Jewish and Muslim sources, and as a result of his extensive use of the latter, Jewish sacred names and formulae play a relatively minor role in his interventions. It should be noted that the kernel of the therapeutic encounter in the cases of the Amzalegs, i.e. arriving at etiological and prognostic conclusions and preparing the curing materials, is transferred in this case to the interval between sessions and accomplished without the patient's presence. As a result, the formal, highly structured sequence of events in the traditional therapeutic setting (entailed from the fixed order in which the healer initiates his interventions during the session) is changed for a more flexible discourse, based on lengthy verbal interactions between the participants. In a prolix manner, Rabbi Chaim discusses his diagnostic conclusions and consequential modes of healing with the patient. He controls the conversation, but definitely urges the patient to comment and elaborate on the information presented.

The general atmosphere in the house is informal, warm and friendly. In the waiting room, Rabbi Chaim's wife chats freely with the patients about routine events. Extrovert, humorous and empathic, she offers the clients food and drink as well as a sympathetic ear for their troubles and complaints. The noise in the apartment is overwhelming, particularly because Rabbi Chaim's children are playing, doing their homework, watching TV and chasing each other in front of the waiting patients. None of the latter, however, seems deeply concerned by these "distractive stimuli". Rabbi Chaim's approach to the patients neatly fits (and, of course, contributes to) this atmosphere. He is an expert in establishing smooth and cordial interpersonal relationships, and his therapeutic style is based on persuasion and espousing broad, direct suggestions.

The three profiles depicted here represent the wide heterogeneity of healing styles in urban settings (Press, 1971). Our concerns, however, are variations in preserving traditional practices. To what extent do the rabbi healers succeed in maintaining their curing role in Israel?

Rabbi David and Rabbi Chaim might be considered successful healers, as they both enjoy a constant flow of patients who fill their waiting rooms. Rabbi Chaim, in particular, is an impressive case of the "emergent curing role". He proudly claims that his clientele has grown considerably in Israel. Rabbi Yosef, on the other hand, suffers a gradual diminution in his role, in spite of his respectable attempts to actively draw patients to his therapy whenever possible. I suggest that, far beyond idiosyncratic accommodations, these three profiles represent life styles and occupational careers typical of many other traditional therapists. Therefore broader conclusions can be drawn from them concerning differential success in preserving the curing role in Israel.

On the basis of my observations, successful healers are grouped under two rubrics: "conservatives" and "innovators". A typical healer in the first group (represented by Rabbi David) fervently adheres to traditional practices and insistently relies on his glorious familial heritage, which gives him a high level of ascribed, unconditional status (*zekhut avot*). He works in purity and impresses his potential clientele with his appearance and life style. Any anachronistic and dissonant feature in methods employed by healers in this group (i.e. overemphasis on demons) is compensated for by their charismatic image and the degree of spiritual supremacy ascribed to them. In order to survive within the traditional conservative paradigm, a healer must have this radiant aura of moral ascendency and unimpaired virtue. Without a thread of holiness, he is doomed to fail. This is one of the reasons why traditional therapists like Rabbi Yosef do not attract a wide range of clientele. Respected for his genealogy and skill, he nevertheless does not live up to the high standards of which his cousin, Rabbi David, is a living model. Thus, he lacks this charismatic image, which would constitute a protective shield under rapidly changing circumstances; but, at the same time, he is extremely reluctant to accommodate himself to these circumstances, being rigid, meticulous and cautious in his work style, and proud of his heritage. As a result, Rabbi Yosef, like other conservative colleagues, is engulfed in a situation which inevitably leads to an attenuated curing role.

Innovative healers, most of whom lack a bountiful image of "holiness", succeed in preserving their curing role by making adaptive changes in the traditional practices they employ. Divergent in form as these changes have been, they all represent attempts at responding to the challenge imposed by the changing cultural circumstances in the new country. Since among the three profiles illustrated previously, Rabbi Chaim represents the successful innovators, the "deviant" features in his work style will be pointed out and assessed for their adaptive potential.

In many respects Rabbi Chaim seems to challenge the very sources from which the Jewish Moroccan curing system was traditionally nourished. He rejects the idea of ascribed-inherited *zekhut avot* as a prerequisite for the curing role, emphasizing instead skills acquired through learning and experience. Manipulations of mystically derived Jewish sacred words, the gist of the traditional modes of Jewish healing, are accorded only a marginal role. In addition, he employs traditional explanations of *Jnun* and *skhur* quite parsimonously and with unmistakable reluctance. In Morocco, these reservations concerning the source of legitimacy in curing (the *zekhut*), together with its main etiological rationale and therapeutic measure, would have probably been deemed iconoclastic and met with disapproval. In Israel, however, a large portion of the traditional population might accept them less critically as they reflect the ambivalence many have experienced toward their native heritage. For example, the status that Rabbi Chaim accords demons and sorcery in his practice neatly fits into the general decline of the participational aspects of these entities in Israel. Like many of the interviewees in the *moshavim* he does not deny their existence, but, like them, he considerably circumscribes their role in explaining human misery. (Rabbi Chaim considers impotence, a typical *skhur* problem, as either physically-based, or emotionally instigated; in certain anxiety saturated disturbances, he replaces the old *Jinn* with "fright" and "imagination", psychological variables, as etiological agents).

Other peculiar aspects of Rabbi Chaim's life-style and work contribute to and reinforce his postively innovative image: the successful shift he made to a non-religious vocational career in Israel indicates his initiative and flexibility in utilizing novel opportunities in the new country. His claim that many of his therapeutic tools have been obtained in recent years, after his immigration to Israel, demonstrates a role orientation that is not past-located. The diagnostic methods at his disposal are clearly less culturally dependent than the typical Jewish divinatory techniques, and thus conclusions based on them may be easily addressed to clients who are fairly removed from traditional explanations of affliction.

Rabbi Chaim's curing arsenal is based on varied, heterogeneous sources. It represents a wide spectrum of methods bipolarly distributed: for some physical, quasi-somatic symptoms, he uses natural remedies extracted from organic substances; for emotional and interpersonal (particularly romantic) problems, he prefers Muslim devices, based on magical manipulations of certain materials together with written charms composed of "profane names".[2] Whereas his natural remedies enrich his work with medical flavor congruent with his innovative image, his prevalent Muslim-Moroccan practices represent the conservative aspect of Rabbi Chaim's curing role. Deviant as the latter may appear to rabbi-healers like the Amzalegs, they are based on solid traditions of the past. Thus, for an outside observer, at least, an uneasy gap exists between Rabbi Chaim's reluctance to employ magico-traditional explanations, like *skhur*, and his bountiful use of therapeutic interventions based on the same magical rationale. In effect, however, the typical client is not exposed to this incompatibility, since the therapeutic materials are not prepared in front of him, given Rabbi Chaim's work pattern of a two-session encounter.

Whereas this twofold division alleviates the vulnerable situation where traditional methods are preserved without their rationale-providing background, it does create a new potential threat: the basic ingredients of the Jewish traditional diagnostics and curing are contrived here in the absence of the patient, therefore, their therapeutic effectiveness is partially lost. In responding to this threat, Rabbi Chaim and some of his innovative colleagues draw near a modern conception of psychotherapy, as the vacuum created by the two-session encounter is filled with "psychological ether". Liberated from the necessity to exhibit his expertness in diagnostic and therapeutic minutiae vis-a-vis his patient, Rabbi Chaim can utilize the two meetings to amply and flexibly talk with him about his problems in a manner unknown to the Amzalegs.

Together with other healers, working in a similar way, Rabbi Chaim appeared to be an expert in creating rapport and warm atmosphere. He is both sympathetic and emphatic, provides ample opportunity for catharsis and generally emits hope-giving suggestions. Unlike the conservative healers whose suggestions are always technique bound (e.g. "no cure equals my writing"), he gives advice and instructions that are fairly autonomous from the therapeutic materials. Thus, relationships and "psychological" manipulations are being emphasized at the expense of technique and formal manipulations. In Rabbi Chaim's own words: "Giving hope is more important than giving an amulet". This flexible attitude cannot be adopted by traditional healers like Rabbi Yosef in whom the absolute adherence to old-time practices is reinforced by a personality make-up which seems quite authoritarian, reserved, rigid and cautious. It appears quite "natural" for Rabbi Yosef, who does not shed much warmth and empathy, to emphasize his techniques and his *zekhut*.

It should be remembered, however, that this growing psychological orientation among some innovative healers is still far removed from modern psychotherapy. The lengthy verbal interactions only thinly disguise the magico-religious remedies, and the gradual relinquishing of traditional etiologies and therapeutic rationale only highlights and accentuates the "miraculous-like" attributes of the healer, who is, after all, the source of these remedies.

Summaries and Conclusions

Throughout this chapter I have tried to show that various aspects of Jewish-Moroccan ethnopsychiatry have undergone a process of attenuation under the influence of mainstream Israeli medicine. The end-product of the entire process, however, is not total decline, but rather selective preservation. A dialectic trend has been detected, according to which the fact of partial attenuation makes the less vulnerable parts of the traditional system endurable. This has been demonstrated, first, in regard to the role boundaries of traditional curing, which have been considerably narrowed in Israel by the "acculturative sequence" of giving priority in referral to modern practitioners. This pattern, accepted by traditional patients and healers alike, leaves the "failures of medicine" as potential clients; but, at the same time, it smoothly regulates a potentially problematic relationship between two competing resources of therapy and ultimately enables the rabbi healer to survive under unfavorable circumstances.

Second, changes in perceiving the causes of affliction have also been conceptualized according to the pattern of attenuated preservation. This holds particularly for *Jnun* (demons), whose position has been gradually devalued with the increasing absence of visible "participational" demonic phenomena. Witchcraft explanations of human grievance have undergone similar permutations. As I have tried to show, the socio-economic and ecological conditions in the Israeli *moshavim* are particularly conducive to witchcraft accounts. Indeed, people have not ceased to employ the traditional idiom of *shkur* (witchcraft) to account for their misery and affliction; some have been obsessively engaged with questions centering around the identity of persons in the vicinity responsible for their unexpected economic impoverishment, their daughter's ongoing spinsterhood, etc.

Having been rebuffed by disapproving and derisive responses to their accusations, however, for most persons witchcraft is preserved as a private affair. The idiom is used for articulating suspicions, but not for publicly uttering accusations.

On the background of these two general foci of selective attenuation —curing-role boundaries and etiological agents of affliction—the rabbi-healer's careers can be properly analysed. Rabbi David represents that small ground of orthodox healers who enjoy a reputation of piety and holiness so immense and unshakable that they are exempt from any need to adjust their practices to the changing reality of the new country. Rabbi Yosef, on the other hand, is a pathetic example of a skillful healer who, despite his expertness and experience, is trapped in the attenuation process. Healers like Rabbi Chaim, who are willing and able to make innovative adaptive changes in their practices, enhance their prospects of survival. The patterns of change manifested in the work style of the innovators are legion, but it seems that one general trend has to do with more explicit utilization of "psychological manipulations" during treatment (See Reynolds, 1976, for a similar process among Japanese Morita therapists). Of course, "psychological" aspects could be seen in the conservative healers' therapeutic encounter as well, but these were covert derivatives of the formal technical therapeutic manipulations. Among innovators one finds that curative means such as warm, catharsis enabling discussions and hope-giving suggestions are more bountifully and willfully applied in relative autonomy from the formal intervention (i.e. "ketica").

It should be emphasized that the two types of successful healers—the "pious" conservatives and the "innovators"—are addressing their therapy to slightly different, although overlapping groups. Moroccans who turn to traditional healers in Israel are not necessarily acculturated and modernized to the same extent. While older, religious and more traditional people are overrepresented in Rabbi David's waiting room, Rabbi Yosef attracts also members of the younger, more modern segments of the population. The differences between these groups should not be overstated, however, since many patients share a common view of the essential nature of the curing role. In times of personal crisis, this view is translated into the wish to be assisted by a dominant authority figure, omniscient and omnipotent, who exerts a short-term, miraclelike intervention. In this pattern, persons can be fairly passive, without investing too much of their time, money and energy and without being asked to undergo profound changes. On this general level, traditional healers can meet their patients' expectations better than their modern colleagues. Nevertheless, since major ingredients of Jewish Moroccan ethnopsychiatry have been attenuated, it seems that in the future folk-therapists will follow the lead of Rabbi Chaim and the innovators; the personal attributes of the healer will be overrated at the expense of ascribed status and formal skills. Since the former are considered a most important, universal curative factor (Goldstein, 1975) healers who possess these qualities will have better prospects of maintaining their role when the traditional (Moroccan) idioms for its articulation lose their power.

Notes

[1] This particular hand written lot-book, called "*goral urim vetumim*" (lot of the oracle) is composed of matrices containing aggregates of Hebrew letters, ostensibly in random order. Through certain numerical manipulations, a selection rule is arrived at, according to which fifteen letters are obtained from the matrices. Any configuration of letters, when properly retrieved, generates a short sentence bearing prognostically meaningful conclusions. "*Goral urim vetumim*" also exists in standard printed form.

[2] Specifically, "profane names" are opposed to "sacred names" and allude to the impure forces of demons and spirits. Many Jewish informants, however, used this term to designate any form of Muslim-based "writing". This ethnocentric interpretation has been quite prevalent despite the fact that Muslim-Moroccans, on their part, also dichotomize sacred and profane names (Westermarck, 1926 1:208).

References

Bilu, Y. 1977. "General Characteristics of Referrals to Traditional Healers in Israel", *The Israel Annals of Psychiatry* 15(5)245-252.
——. 1978. *Traditional Psychiatry in Israel.* Unpublished doctoral thesis. Jerusalem: The Hebrew University.
——. 1979. "Demonic Explanation of the Illness Among Moroccan Jews in Israel", *Culture, Medicine and Psychiatry* 3:363-380.
——. 1980. "The Moroccan Demon in Israel: The Case of 'Evil Spirit Disease' ". *Ethos* 8(1):24-39.
Crapanzano, V. 1973. *The Hamadsha: A Study in Moroccan Ethnopsychiatry.* Berkeley: University of California Press.
Douglas, M. (Ed.). 1970. *Witchcraft Confessions and Accusations.* London, A.S.A. Monograph 9.
Evans-Pritchard, E. E. 1937. *Witchcraft, Oracles and Magic Among the Azande.* London: Oxford University Press.
Foster, G. 1972. "The Anatomy of Envy: A Study in Symbolic Behavior", *Current Anthropology* 13(2):165-186.

Frank, J. 1961. *Persuasion and Healing.* Baltimore: The Johns Hopkins University Press.

Goldberg, H. 1972. *Cave Dwellers and Citrus Growers: A Jewish Community in Libya and Israel.* Cambridge: Cambridge University Press.

Goldstein, A. 1975. "Relationship-Enhancement Methods" in F. H. Kanfer and A. Goldstein (Eds.), *Helping People Change.* New York: Pergamon Press, Inc.

Landy, D. 1974. "Role Adaptation: Traditional Curers Under the Impact of Modern Medicine", *American Ethnologist* 1,1:103-127.

Press, I. 1971. "The Urban Curandero", *American Anthropology* 73:741-756.

Press, I. 1978. "Urban Folk Medicine: A Functional Overview", *American Anthropology* 80(1):71-84.

Rabinow, P. 1975. *Symbolic Dominion.* Chicago: University of Chicago Press.

Reynolds, D. K. 1976. *Morita Psychotherapy.* Berkeley: University of California Press.

Romanucci-Schwartz, L. 1969. "The Hierarchy of Resort in Curative Practices: The Admiralty Islands, Melanesia", *Journal of Health and Social-Behavior* 10:201-209.

Shokeid, M. 1971. *The Dual Heritage: Immigrants from the Atlas Mountains in an Israeli Village.* Manchester: Manchester University Press.

Shuval, J. 1970. *Social Functions of Medical Practice.* San Francisco: Josey Bass Publications.

Spiro, M. E. 1967. *Burmese Supernaturalism.* New Jersey: Prentice Hall, Inc.

Westermarck, E. 1926. *Ritual and Belief in Morocco.* London: MacMillan and Co.

16

The Dynamics of Change in Jewish Oriental Ethnic Music in Israel[1]

Amnon Shiloah and Erik Cohen

Change in "Fourth World" Arts as a Subject of Anthropological Inquiry

In this paper we will describe and illustrate the principal directions of change in the music of Oriental Jewish groups in Israel. It is the first systematic attempt to undertake this formidable task, and is therefore, of necessity, a preliminary one.

Anthropologists and ethnographers were, until very recently, almost exclusively interested in the "authentic" or "traditional" cultural products of the "Fourth World" people—the tribal and ethnic minorities of the newly emergent nations.[2] In their endeavor to discover, describe and preserve the culture of the pre-contact period or the period preceding modernization, they discarded recent creations as unwelcome disturbances and alterations of the "original" tradition. The false impression was often unwittingly created that this tradition existed, static and unchanging, until contact with the Western world and the onset of modernization began to destroy it.

A similar orientation characterized the approach of the art historian and the ethnomusicologist; for them, the valuable artistic productions were those preceding modern influences on ethnic art. They regarded recent artistic productions as mere degenerate reflections of past glory or as bastardized concoctions devoid of "authenticity." Recently, however, as detailed investigations into the process of social and cultural transformation of tribal and ethnic peoples multiplied, students of arts and crafts gradually realized that their earlier judgments were often based on prejudices and oversimplifications. It turned out that tribal and ethnic peoples reacted artistically in a wide variety of ways to their emergence into and confrontation with the modern world. Their art underwent manifold permutations, which confront the student with new problems of theory and research. While the term "arts of acculturation" (Graburn, 1969:457) has sometimes been applied to the newly emergent art forms, it does not do justice to the wide variety of stylistic and other changes emerging under the impact of new conditions. The richness of these new productions has been excellently illustrated in a volume on *Ethnic and Tourist Arts* (Graburn, 1976a). In the field of music, too, some important studies of musical change have recently appeared (Kartomi, 1981; Katz, 1968; Merriam, 1955; Nettl, 1978a; Nettl and Shiloah, 1978; Neuman, 1976; Lomax, 1968; Slobin, 1976).

This diversity of new forms gives rise to the important problem of the different directions or types of dynamics to change in the "arts of acculturation." The problem has been dealt with on a theoretical level by Graburn (1976b) for crafts and by Nettl (1978b) for music. Our approach takes off from these beginnings, but attempts to extend their conceptual frame of reference, in order to accommodate a wider scope of empirical variation.

Traditional art and, more particularly, music, reflect the life of a society and its culture. Therefore, creative arts should be explored not only for their own sake, but also for a better understanding of other aspects of culture. It is regrettable that Israeli anthropologists have, in studying the processes of change and integration of Jewish Oriental communities, neglected the role of the creative arts in their lives. One can find some specific, descriptive studies of these traditional arts, but none has attempted to challenge the general problem—the processes of change in the arts of Jewish Oriental communities, whether prior to their immigration to the State of Israel or subsequent to it.

We deal here only with music and not with the whole spectrum of ethnic art. By narrowing the scope of our study, a better incursion into the matter can be achieved than would be the case had we covered the whole range of ethnic arts. But beyond this, the dynamics of music are of interest in themselves. As Merriam (1964:296) has pointed out, music is a language of feeling deeply rooted in the subconscious of an individual steeped in a certain cultural tradition. Music not only accompanies and enhances major events in man's life, but also plays an important role in all social happenings. Being so tightly related to the different aspects of life, music becomes a vital and indispensable element of the culture as a whole. The sharing of similar experiences and satisfactions from the same tunes provides, as Lomax argued, a sense of security and identification with the group. This observation led him to conclude: "An art so deeply rooted in the security patterns of the community should not, in theory, be subject to rapid change and, in fact, this seems to be the case. Musical style appears to be one of the most conservative of culture traits" (Lomax, 1959:930). Merriam reached a similar conclusion: "Music structure is carried subliminally and, since it is not objectified in most individual cases, it is resistant to change" (Merriam, 1964:297).

These statements do not imply that music does not change at all, but rather that it possesses a high degree of stability, at least in some of its major manifestations. If so much is granted, we can assume that in the case of the Jewish Oriental communities in Israel, attachment to pre-immigration music will, on the whole, be stronger than attachment to other facets of culture, including other art forms. Music does change, however, though perhaps at a slower rate than do other aspects of culture. Moreover, the change, as we shall see, is not complete: it is continuity-in-change, and even a return to tradition, albeit in a novel context.

The degree of stability of music is closely related to its function. Less change can be expected in religious music than in social and recreational music: "religious music is so much a part of religious practice that it cannot be altered without altering other aspect of ritual, while recreational music fulfills other needs which are not rigidified" (Merriam, 1964:308). An examination of Near Eastern music in general, with which the Jewish Oriental traditions interacted in the past, reveals that change has mostly affected the category of recreational music. This has, on the whole, also been the case with Jewish Oriental music in Israel.

A Historical Review

Jewish Oriental music has historically been associated with the "great tradition"[3] of Middle Eastern music. This tradition was characterized by

several major traits, common to all national musics in the region:[4] the
vocal component predominated over the instrumental; the musician is
both a composer and a performer; there are no time limits and no fixed
program in the performance; rather the performance is a display of solo-
ist virtuosity and the performer is permitted, and indeed encouraged, to
improvise spontaneously; in this he is helped by the continuous interplay
between himself and a limited, often intimate audience, which confronts
him directly, without any formal barriers; the music is orally transmitted
and was generally banned, for religious reasons, from institutions of formal education.

Throughout its history, the "great tradition" has been in a state of permanent, albeit slow, flux. Under the impact of the West and its music of
modern times, the pace of change quickened, while the changes were
deeper and became more pervasive than they had been in the past. The
changes which also affected Jewish Middle Eastern music even prior to the
immigration of the Jews to Israel, can be briefly summarized as follows:
(1) intimacy; (2) the emergence of a barrier between the artists and the
listeners through the introduction of the stage; (3) the introduction of
newer instruments and new playing techniques, which led to alterations
in the original interaction between the singer and the traditional instruments, such as the 'ud (a short-necked lute) and eventually even to changes
in the structure or size of the instruments themselves; (4) the necessity of
playing together in large ensembles shifted the accent from the display of
individual virtuosity and personal creativity to collective discipline, and led
to a growing emphasis on rhythmic and metric pieces instead of impro-
visational and nonmetric ones; (5) the emergence of an independent instrumental music (6) recourse to electronic means of amplification, which led
to the appearance of a new type of singer who does not rely any more on
the volume of his voice and its multiple nuances; (7) the introduction of a
time limit on programs in concerts on radio and television and on records;
and (8) the emergence of educational institutions in which traditional
music is taught by Western methods; the studies are based on notated
music, that is, fixed models, and not on oral transmission based on a variety of personal models. This new type of education necessarily leads to
standardization.

As a consequence of these changes and of the impact of some additional factors, such as the growing attention paid by musicians to folk
music, the Middle Eastern "great tradition" evolved in modern times into
the currently dominant "mainstream" style. This style is a confluence of

divergent stylistic elements deriving from the inherited great tradition, the diverse little traditions of various regional, ethnic and linguistic Middle Eastern groups and light and classical Western music. Nettl (1978a:149, diagram), for example, represents what he calls the "mainstream-popular" style in the city of Teheran as the point of merger of various musical styles; Racy (1980:85), in a study of the musical life of Cairo, attributes the same role to what he terms the "mainstream, multicolor" style.

Although belonging to a minority group, Jewish musicians were active participants in the musical life of their countries of origin, were much sought after in the large Muslim urban centers, and have participated in the modernization of the tradition. Muslims of the ruling class used to have recourse to non-Muslim musicians (mainly instrumentalists) to overcome religious prohibitions of the practice of music. Being of low social status in the wider society, Jewish musicians were also deprecated in their own community; behind this attitude stood theological and puritan arguments similar to those in the Muslim community. Nevertheless, the musicians were not banished, and the communities employed them to enhance the rejoicing at festive occasions and even for the performance of rituals in the synagogue. It seems that both the musicians and the listeners were aware of the distinction between music performed for the internal Jewish public and music performed for the external non-Jewish public.

The musical style of the surrounding society influenced Jewish music. Borrowings, however, were not mechanically adopted, but reflected and adapted. This is even true of a genre which at first sight appears entirely assimilated to the secular Near Eastern great musical tradition—the singing of Hebrew hymns with or without instrumental accompaniment. A thorough examination of that music, however, reveals some distinguishing traits: even when the melodical elements are wholly borrowed, the use of the Hebrew language necessarily introduces a new relationship between text and melody through word intonation and accents. Moreover, the content of the text and the solemnity of the occasion bear directly on the quality of the performance, whose function is to express and elevate the spirit of the religious occasion. This is also true when hymns and songs are in one of the Jewish dialects, and not in the Hebrew language. In synagogal music, the borrowing of external elements was also selective. The Jewish repertory, like that of other marginal Near Eastern cultures, which had been influenced by the Near Eastern great tradition, has thus preserved some features of the older, indigenous style. In the important urban centers it became part of the great tradition, but preserved some distinguishing traits of the little tradition from which it originated. Urban Jewish musicians in Iraq, Iran, Bokhara and Morocco, active both in their own communities and in the wider society, had a good command of both styles, and participated in both traditions. Some even contributed to musical modernization and the emergence of the mainstream style.

The little traditions have been paramount in the small Jewish communities, where only traces of the influence of the great tradition can be felt. The musical styles of the Jews of Kurdistan, Southern Morocco and even the urban centers of Yemen are instances of different little traditions. The Yemenite Jews usually make a distinction between the urban *San'ani* style and all other Yemenite styles, considered to be rural, and thus implicitly simple and inferior. No doubt, the *San'ani* style distinguishes itself by some refinement, but it has never attained the degree of sophistication of the great tradition of Near Eastern music.

If we wish to examine the changes in the music of Jewish Oriental communities in Israel, we should note that there were major differences between them in the extent to which their music changed prior to immigration. The extent of change depended primarily upon the nature of the relationship between the Jewish musicians and the cultural life of the surrounding society which, in turn, influenced the degree to which Jewish music participated in the great tradition and the emergent "mainstream" style. While some Jewish communities, originating in remote rural areas, were upon their immigration to Israel distant from the trend to musical modernization, for other groups the encounter with modern Western culture in Israel was not new, as their members, especially the intelligentsia, has already been in contact with it prior to immigration. They brought to Israel the mainstream style, to the elaboration of which they had themselves contributed, and continued to evolve it, both with relation to current developments in their countries of origin, and to the Israeli culture. Therefore, when speaking of change in Iraqi Jewish music in Israel, for instance, we cannot put together the Kurdistani Jews, who essentially belonged to a folk-tribal culture, and the Baghdadi Jews who, since the second half of the last century, played a determinant role in the musical activity of their non-Jewish environment, and participated in the evolution of its mainstream style.

The immigration of the different communities to Israel often proceeded in waves. The early immigrants, who came before the Second World War, became the absorbers of the newcomers, after having been themselves subjected to a process of change. Thus, in some cases, the "newcomers" adapted rapidly to the style in vogue among their predecessors. The great tradition and the "mainstream" style may have come to influence the little tradition of remote Jewish communities, through this mingling of immigrants, even subsequent to their arrival in Israel.

Immigration to Israel exposed these people to a new and complex reality. They had been removed from their natural environments and found themselves in a new one where, in the realm of arts, Western concepts enjoyed exclusive sway. Moreover, as a result of the state of belligerence between Israel and its neighbors, they experienced an emotional conflict. They had to reconcile their national identification and their emotional attachments to the culture of those who now became their enemy. To complicate matters, in Israel they were asked to be "integrated" into an alien, Western culture and it was frequently denied that they even had a culture of their own. In their countries of origin they had the status of a minority community; but in the creative arts many individuals were integrated and, in some cases, dominant. In the new reality, their civil status changed, but they became a cultural minority, because their culture was not legitimized by the establishment. In this respect they differed from the ethnic groups of the Fourth World, which are allowed to preserve their cultural particularity and sometimes even encouraged to do so in order to attract tourism, though they were economically and politically incorporated.

During the Mandatory period and especially the early phase of statehood, the official attitude of the Zionist establishment toward ethnic cultural traditions advocated their disappearance in the "melting pot" of a general "Israeli society." Nevertheless, some musicologists and devotees of Western origin were anxious to safeguard and preserve these traditions before they disappeared. Composers and arrangers of Western origin attempted to introduce Oriental elements into the realm of Western art with the aim either to elevate the Oriental or to lend color to the Western. These concerns, however, were exceptional within a general attitude of disregard if not denigration.

Despite that attitude, ethnic music preserved an attenuated existence in the immigrant communities. Especially in the realm of religious practices, particular musical traditions have been most fully perpetuated. The readers of the Bible, the cantors and the singers of religious poems have kept close to those expressive musical patterns and intonations to which the worshippers had been accustomed and in which they felt at home. These are patterns "acquired in childhood," (*girsa de yankuta* in Aramaic) and as such

they deeply mark the individual's subsequent musical sensibility. Therefore, even todav, people living far away from their group or origin will do
their utmost to pray on festive occasions in a synagogue where they can
hear the sounds which symbolize their earliest childhood memories and
their first religious experience.

Even outside the liturgical and paraliturgical domains, traditional music
continued to be vital in family and community rejoicings, and to a certain
extent became a vehicle through which the traditional poet-singers expressed the experiences of their encounter with the new environment and
the emotional impact of the changes in their lives. However, during the
period dominated by the melting pot ideology of the Israeli establishment,
the status of the professional ethnic musicians (those who lived by means
of their art in the countries of origin) became seriously affected. The established society did not recognize or appreciate their talents and their
previous status. Their original audience was scattered to different localities and anyhow could not support them economically. Nevertheless,
their activity was not completely interrupted, but only impeded. Unfortunately, this has not been the case in most of the other folk arts of Oriental communities. As a result of the rapid process of modernization, the
demand for traditional goods decreased. Most of the Jewish traditional
artisans, who used to produce for the market in their countries of origin, were compelled to abandon their original occupations in Israel. Today one finds, for instance, only very few traditional Jewish silversmiths,
goldsmiths or coppersmiths. In contrast, it seems that the indispensabil-
ity of music on ritual occasions, and its relative independence from economic factors, has helped it to overcome the shock of the encounter with
the new cultural environment and to survive under the new conditions.

Though some of the traditional musical forms survived with little, if
any, alterations, there was considerable change in a variety of directions
in most forms of Oriental Jewish music under the impact of the new environment. The mutual encounter of the different Oriental traditions
resulted in some alterations in the original pre-immigration music of each
group. In localities of mixed ethnic populations, musicians and cantors
from one community participated in the festivities of the others. This
permanent exposure to other styles gradually led to mutual borrowing
and the adoption of various musical elements. One of the consequences
of this process, in the realm of synagogue music, is the emergence and
gradual dissemination of the so-called "Jerusalemite-Sephardi style"
(see below), popular particularly among the younger generation of Orien-

tal cantors. Another major direction of change has been the conscious modernization of ethnic musical styles (Nettl, 1978b:127), through the incorporation of Western elements into traditional Oriental tunes. While these types of change were often spontaneous and took place without outside encouragement and help, others occurred with the assistance and sometimes the sponsorship of outsiders (i.e., the transposition of Oriental musical styles into the realm of light music and, later on, the fine arts). The most recent developments of this kind are attempts by both ethnic musicians and outsiders to combine Oriental and Western elements in Israeli music in ways that reflect an ideology of cultural equality and pluralism. These take on a variety of forms to be discussed in our typology in the following section. Recently howerver, the opposite tendency to return to roots has also emerged. Some ethnic musicians endeavor to reconstitute particular traditional repertories, while ethnic ensembles strive to revive their old traditions, either on their own or with the support of national institutions. As a consequence of changed official attitudes, the frequency of ethnic musical performances on the stage, the radio and television has multipled. While most of these performances are destined for a general public, some are organized by scholars and folklorists, who strive to reconstitute for specialized professional audiences what they believe to be the authentic, pre-immigration versions.

The growing pressure for recognition of and wider exposure to the culture of the Oriental communities caused various new developments. On the one hand, it led to the official recognition of the need to preserve, cultivate and promote the cultural heritage of Oriental Jewry. This found institutional expression in the establishment of the "Center for the Integration of the Oriental Jewish Heritage in Culture and Education," which is located in the Ministry of Education and Culture. Its principal aim is to achieve full legitimation for this heritage on the part of the wider society. To that end the Center backs and promotes various cultural activities, whether initiated within the ethnic communities or sponsored from the outside. There, "serious" music is promoted. Concomitantly, however, the pressure for recognition, together with changing tastes among the younger generation, led to the emergence of a new, light commericalized musical style, expressed primarily in the form of "Oriental hits." The most important institutional framework for the performance of such works is the yearly "Festival of Songs in the Style of Oriental Communities." Since their style is widely popular and profitable, many non-Orientals have penetrated it. Even when the composers themselves are Orientals, the arrangers and orchestrators are usually of Western origin. The commercialized light Oriental style differs even less from other such music in Israel and sometimes completely loses its distinctiveness. The successful penetration of popular Oriental music into the national popular culture may thus eventually prove its undoing.

Directions of Change in Ethnic Music – A Typology of Stylistic Dynamics

Our preceding historical survey clearly indicates the intricacies involved in the problem of change of musical styles under the impact of various external forces. We shall now attempt to systematize this variety into a typology of stylistic dynamics.

The models for stylistic change in ethnic art and music current in the literature are based at least tacitly on the premise of unidirectinality, if not unilinearity of change. This is in principle true even of the most sophisticated approaches in the field. Thus, Graburn (1976) bases his typology on the concept of "acculturation," and despite his important distinction between arts produced for an internal and an external public, there is little doubt that his typology is unidirectional in conception. Nettl's (1978b:127) approach, couched in terms of "tradition," "modernization" and "westernization," seems to be based on a similar premise; interestingly, the very richness of concrete stylistic transformations that he lists raises questions as to the sufficiency of these three simple terms to account for the variety. Moreover, any assumption of unidirectionality or unilinearity suffers from a major theoretical drawback: it precludes the conceptualization of various types of stylistic dynamics emerging under different circumstances. Departing from the earlier work by Cohen (forthcoming) we base our typology of stylistic dynamics on four variables:

1) *Perpetuation vs. innovation* in musical production or performance. This variable relates to the extent to which musicians merely reproduce already existing stylistic elements or introduce novel ones.

2) *Orthogeneity vs. heterogeneity* of the process of musical change. This variable is adapted from the work of Redfield and Singer (1969 (1954)) and refers to the extent to which ethnic musical styles are replicated or further developed and elaborated under the new conditions (orthogeneity), or combined with extraneous elements to create new, original music styles (heterogeneity).

3) *Internal vs. external audience.* This variable, adopted from Graburn (1976), relates to the intended audience of the work: the internal audience is the audience of the musician's own ethnic group; while the external audience ranges from other Jewish Oriental groups to the general Israeli, Jewish or world public.

4) *Spontaneous vs. sponsored musical production.* This variable relates to the source of the initiative for new musical production, and is of much importance in Israel, where ethnic cultural events often do not occur wholly spontaneously, but are in various ways sponsored, as we have seen, by a variety of outsiders or public and national institutions.

A complete cross-classification of all these variables would be cumbersome and is in fact unnecessary. We have found that a ninefold classification, as presented in Table 1, does justice to most, or even all, of the important developments in ethnic music that came to our attention.

1) *Traditional.* Continuation of pre-immigration musical forms. This type includes the bulk of liturgical music, which is still regularly performed in ethnic synagogues and festivities, as well as some, albeit few, paraliturgical and secular musical pieces, such as functional songs and dances related to major family rituals: birth, circumcision, bar mitzvah, wedding ceremonies and death (dirges are still commonly used), songs related to the yearly festivals, like Purim and the Seder and the home hymns (*zemirot*), sung in Sabbatical repasts, cradle and epic songs, romances, pilgrimage songs, etc.

In the first period after immigration, under the impact, on the one hand, of the exhilaration of arrival to the Promised Land and, on the other, of the more prosaic hardships experienced there, some novel themes appeared in the secular music of the purely traditional type. A major example are the "Aliyah (Immigration) Songs," (Shiloah, 1970), which were created spontaneously and informally performed for an internal audience, particularly among Yemenite, Iraqi and Moroccan immigrants. The creation by gifted folk poet-singers of such "new" songs is characteristic of most musical cultures of the Near Eastern region. These poet-singers express the feelings and complaints of the community concerning current affairs by creating a new text that they associate with an old tune. Jewish poet-singers used to compose such songs in the Diaspora, and continued to do so upon immigration to Israel. Their works include diverse topics, sometimes expressing the enthusiasm of the immigrants and sometimes their protest, particularly against alleged discrimination and injustices perpetrated against them. Since no musical innovations are introduced in such

TABLE 1
A Typology of Stylistic Dynamics in Jewish Oriental Music in Israel

	Spontaneous-Internal Audience	Spontaneous-Sponsored External Audience	Sponsored External Audience
Perpetuation-Orthogenetic	(1) Traditional	(2) Conserved	(3) Museumized
Innovation-Ortho-Hetero-genetic	(4) Neo-Traditional	(5) Transitional	(6) Pseudo-ethnic
Innovation-Heterogenetic	(7) Popular	(8) Ethnic fine	(9) Fine

songs, we have classified them as "traditional"; moreover, even if new *literary* motifs are introduced, these too are expressed in stereotyped traditional forms. The scope of musical production in the purely traditional style diminished soon after immigration and various innovations appeared even in the spontaneous ethnic music.

2) *Conserved*. Deliberate preservation of traditional, pre-immigration musical styles, edited and adapted for a new, external audience. Though members of the ethnic group may be interested in the dissemination of their music, the editing and adaptation is usually done by outsiders, professional musicians with a Western musical education.

Major examples of such music are traditional tunes with certain characteristics removed or modified in order to facilitate their performance by outsiders, who are unable to perform them in their original form. The modifications range from simplification to stylization; microtonality, a large part of the ornamentation, rhythmic freedom and complexity, as well as inherited vocal intonations, nasal and guttural emissions and pronunciations are neglected. The long individual improvisations are shortened and heterophony in group singing is changed into monophony. This process starts by the intentional simplifications in transcriptions of traditional tunes into Western notation to make them accessible to outsiders (see, for example, Adaqi and Sharvit, 1981), and culminates in performances of these tunes from the simplified notation version. The "Center for the Integration of the Jewish Oriental Heritage" aims to propagate the musical heritage of the communities by helping to adapt it to a modern Western audience, while preserving its distinctiveness. In this sense the work of E. Avitzur, a modern composer sponsored by the Center, could be seen as performing a "conservational function." However, from another perspective, they are also original compositions, and will be discussed under the rubric of fine arts (Type 9).

Simplification and stylization along similar lines also characterize the staging of traditional dances. While in museumization (Type 3), the emphasis is on the strict preservation of the "authentic," conservation changes the original somewhat, as it strives to make it acceptable to a wider audience.

3) *Museumized*. Traditional, pre-emigration music, collected and preserved in its "authentic" form by ethnographically trained outsiders, in the interest of scientific and artistic documentation of ethnic arts and performed primarily for selected external audiences.

The movement to safeguard the authentic traditions before they disappear or change goes back to A. Z. Idelsohn, who came from Eastern Europe to Jerusalem in 1905. However, the movement received its major impetus in the wake of mass immigration after creation of the State of Israel. Traditional music and dances were collected, e.g., by Edith Gerson-Kiwi, Gurit Kadman and other ethnographers. Major collections were stored in several archives, including a national archive, affiliated with the National and University Library in Jerusalem. These thousands of documents now serve as material for research, musical education, and occasionally for the preparation of records edited by scholars. Composers use the archives in order to get acquainted with the disappearing "original" traditions, and sometimes use the melodies they like in their own compositions. Scholars like E. Gerson-Kiwi have also organized special concerts devoted to the performance of "authentic" music and dance in the framework, e.g., of international musicological congresses. Such performances took place at the East-West Encounter in Music (1963), the International Congress of Jewish Music (1978) and the International Days of Contemporary Music (1980). Gurit Kadman, who devoted herself to the collection of traditional dances, has, in the last ten years, initiated their revival in "authentic" forms performed by members of the various ethnic communities.

4) *Neo-traditional*. Innovative continuation of traditional musical styles, occurring spontaneously within the ethnic group, but absorbing

some outside influences; the synthesis is to a degree hetrogenetic. Thus, many immigrant groups, which prior to immigration had their own little musical traditions, adopted the so-called Jerusalemite-Sephardi style. This style has, in turn, developed at an earlier stage within the old established Sephardi community of Jerusalem and incorporated elements of the Middle-Eastern mainstream style with the Jewish Sephardi style, widespread throughout the Ottoman Empire. This style, enriched by additional Middle Eastern elements derived from the immigrants' traditions, now dominates the synagogal music of many Oriental communities, e.g., the Iranian, Bokharian, Moroccan, Yemenite, etc. It provides the basis for an emergent "pan-Sephardi" style in Israel, toward which most of the generation of Israeli-born Oriental cantors are included. A striking example is a young Yemenite who sings in perfect "pan-Sephardi" style.[5]

In addition to such homogenization, there is also a tendency towards various forms of syncretism in liturgical music, one of its most interesting forms being the penetration of elements of Ashkenazi *hazzanut*[6] into the synagogal music of some Oriental communities. A good example is a recorded collection of traditional Moroccan hymns sung by a famous Moroccan cantor, H. Luk. Here, the original style still predominates, but the cantor has purposely introduced Western instruments and stylistic elements borrowed from Near Eastern music and from Ashkenazi *hazzanut*. Thus, even in liturgical music, the one most resistant to change, some processes of heterogenization can be observed.

5) *Transitional.* This category, embracing the bulk of contemporary ethnic musical production, consists of music which, while still in many respects essentially orthogenetic, introduces so many extraneous elements that it becomes progressively heterogenetic. While directed primarily to an external, Oriental or general public, its production and performance is typically the result of a combination of spontaneous initiative within an ethnic group and sponsorship by institutions or individuals from the outside. Traditional tunes, melodic patterns, and ways of performance are fused into new popular songs, which are usually set to a Western accompaniment. Some top performers in this style, particularly singers such as Bracha Zephira (at an early stage of her career), Joe Ammar, and Yigal Ben-Haim, enjoy a wide popularity both within their group of origin and among the general public. Others, such as Soshana Dammari and Esther Gamlieli achieved an international reputation, and were among the principal popularizers of what is seen abroad as "typical" Israeli music.

The transitional style is widely disseminated through records and radio and television programs. Owing to the sponsorship of public and national institutions, special events for music in this style have been initiated. The principal one is the yearly "Festival of Songs in the Oriental Style." Due to borrowing and amalgamation of elements from various traditions, the differences between the "transitional" music of different ethnic groups tend to be gradually obliterated as a mainstream popular Oriental style emerges in Israel. Also, musicians from one ethnic community learned to perform the transitional music of the others and thus to diversify their programs. At the major ethnic festival of the Moroccan Mimuna (Ben Ami, 1976) a wide variety of transitional pieces are performed, in addition to some museumized ones, by musicians from various ethnic groups. A great deal of music in the transitional style is purely commercial, making money for producers and performers through popular concerts and the sale of records. Through the growing penetration of outsiders this style tends to be transformed into "pseudo-ethnic" music (Type 6).

6) *Pseudo-Ethnic.* The artistic transmutation of ethnic musical forms by producers and performers from outside the ethnic group for an external audience. While the works are presented as ethnic music, their form has undergone such far-reaching changes according to Western stylistic patterns that, properly speaking, they no longer belong to the realm of ethnic music. This is what happened to many of the songs, composed by Jews of Western origin or at least rearranged, harmonized and orchestrated by them at recent festivals of "Songs in the Oriental Style." This development was vehemently criticized by Ben-Moshe, who, in a review of the most recent Festival appearing in the "Ba'Ma'aracha" (the bulletin of the Sephardi and Oriental Jews), argued that "the 'style' of the festival had no connection whatever with the Oriental Jewry; even arrangers and performers were Western Jews (Ben Moshe, 1981:24). The "ethnic" label on music of this type refers, at most, to superficial imitations of traditional elements, incorporated in the new songs. The outsider composers, arrangers and performers are most anxious to meet the standards of the commercialized light music currently popular on the market, rather than render traditional ethnic musical patterns. Despite their similarities with other light music, such as the use of big orchestras, overwhelming sonorities, etc., pieces in the "pseudo-ethnic" style are fraught with stereotypic "Oriental" elements, such as Spanish rhythms and harmonies. Many so-called "Israeli" songs using adapted Oriental musical elements exemplify a version of the pseudo-ethnic style, still more remote from the original.

7) *Popular.* The spontaneous production or performance by members of one ethnic group, of music adopted from other musical traditions— Oriental, Mediterranean or even Western—for an internal ethnic audience. Contrary to all previous types, this music is alien in its origins to the traditions of the ethnic group and hence purely heterogenetic. A striking example is the wide adoption of modern popular Greek music by different Oriental Jewish communities. At big family rejoicings, Greek music performed by Jewish Oriental musicians is very popular. Indian popular music and Spanish flamenco also enjoy a wide popularity. Western pop music is popular among members of the younger generation of Orientals. Insofar as the musicians introduce no changes into such music, it is in fact perpetuative, rather than innovative, despite its heterogeneity.

8) *Ethnic fine.* This category includes the works of ethnic artists who, while making use of the musical heritage of their own group, fuse with elements taken from other, including Western, musical traditions, to produce works of an essentially innovative, heterogenetic character. While spontaneously initiated, the musical production of such artists is later frequently sponsored or helped by outsiders. A major characteristic of this type is the efforts of the ethnic musicians to "estheticize" folk music and elevate the traditional style to the rank of concert hall "fine art." These musicians, such as Bracha Zephira and Isaac Levy, who are animated by a desire to enhance the prestige of their own tradition, have frequently had recourse to outsiders—composers and performers—to transpose their work into new concert-hall forms. However, in the long run, some of the products of the products of this collaboration became more and more sophisticated and led finally to fine art compositions, with only some Oriental flavor left (Type 9).

A similar process occurred in Oriental folk-dancing; this is best exemplified by the "Inbal" dance company. Initiated by Sara Levi-Tanai and originally based on Yemenite folk-dances, the company soon employed choreographers of Western origin. Gradually it introduced musical elements from other Oriental traditions, and even some Ashkenazi ones. The sequences of the dances were presented in a "dramatic framework" (Manor, 1975). Inbal thus moved consistently away from folklore and into the realm of art. The recent appearance of the "Natural Selection" (*Breira Tivit*) ensemble, under the leadership of a Jew of Moroccan origin, Shlomo Bar, introduced another interesting variation to this type. The leader who serves as singer, drummer and flutist in the ensemble, joined with an American guitarist, an Indian Jewish violinist and an Israeli-born Jew of

Bocharian origin as contrabassist, to create an amalgamated, completely new style dominated by his powerful personality. The composer seeks to integrate widely different musical traditions, and yet endow his work with a pervasive "Oriental" spirit. It thus represents a balance of stylistic plurality and stylistic fusion.

9) *Fine*. This type includes modern Western music produced by composers of mostly Western origin who had formal musical training and who utilize ethnic thematic elements in their works.

In the 1930s and 1940s, as a result of their encounter with Oriental Jewish and other Near Eastern music, some of the composers who had immigrated to Palestine developed an ideology advocating the recourse to Oriental music as a way to form a new Eretz-Israeli style. At that early stage, the central figure through whom composers came into contact with Oriental musical traditions was Bracha Zephira. Born in Jerusalem to a Yemenite family, she had later studied music in Berlin where she met the composer and pianist Nahum Nardi with whom she made her first appearance on stage as singer of traditional tunes. She later cooperated with composers such as P. Ben-Haim, O. Partos and M. Lavry, and thus helped to introduce Oriental traditions into modern Western concert music. It should be stressed that the early encounter of the composers with Oriental traditions was not by direct exposure, but through a mediator who has already been "contaminated" by Western musical conceptions. Be that as it may, Bracha Zephira herself, a musician who originally strove to give an impetus to the fulfillment of the dream of cultural synthesis of Oriental and Western Jewish traditions, recently reached a skeptical conclusion concerning the success of her efforts. In an introduction to her collection of notated traditional songs she explicitly states: "In conclusion, despite our cooperation and contribution in the realm of art we did not succeed to create a true merger, neither cultural nor social" (Zephira, 1978:26).

In the last decade, new attempts to incorporate the Oriental tradition into Western music have been made by several composers, including H. Alexander, Y. Braun and E. Avitzur. Unlike the earlier generation of composers, these artists addressed themselves directly to the Oriental material without the help of a mediator. E. Avitzur has attempted a novel combination in which the traditional material is performed by the representatives of the ethnic communities, with an instrumental accompaniment written by himself and played by a small Western and Oriental ensemble. While in one sense serving the conservation of Oriental music, Avitzur works are also original artistic compositions, and he himself conceives of them as such.

M

Recently there have been some spontaneous attempts to raise ethnic music to a higher degree of sophistication through the introduction of Western elements. These were initiated primarily by representatives of the little musical traditions: Bracha Zephira, Itzhak Levi, Sara Levi-Tanai and others are all representatives of such traditions. It could well be the case that musicians representing the great Near Eastern musical tradition such as D. Buzaglo, E. Dardashti, and Z. Musa, did not deem it necessary to "raise" the level of their music, since it appeared to them as sophisticated as its Western counterpart. Indeed, as Seroussi (1981:65) found in his thesis on the *baqqashot* of Moroccan Jews, musicians of this tradition expressly claim that their music equals Western art music, arguing that "this is our concert music."

The sponsored introduction of Jewish Oriental musical elements into works by composers of Western origin underwent a more complicated process: the composers of popular Israeli folk songs borrowed exclusively from the little traditions. Composers of serious music initially also borrowed from the same source, but later turned increasingly to the great tradition. The latter is exemplified by attempts to introduce into art music the *maqam* and other basic patterns of the great Near Eastern tradition.

Discussion and Conclusions

Having outlined the major directions of change in the ethnic music of Oriental Jewish communities in Israel, we shall now consider a question of wider anthropological interest: what role do the emergent musical forms play in the formation of an encompassing national identity, on the one hand, and of particular ethnic identities, on the other?

We learn from the general literature that the fine arts of the people of the Fourth World are frequently utilized by their national institutions to help the formation of a distinct national identity. N. H. H. Graburn (in press) claims that Fourth World people, while failing to establish an autonomous national identity, "have become the 'totems' of the faceless modern nations which engulf them," helping the latter to achieve a distinguishing identity. By the same token the art of an ethnic group, as it comes to be oriented toward a new, external, national or international audience, creates an awareness of the group's existence in ever wider circles and helps to endow it with a new identity. This, in turn, may contribute to the transformation of its self-perception.

In Israel, however, some peculiar problems emerged with respect to Jewish ethnic groups. While the national institutions were keen on creating a distinct Israeli Jewish national identity, they were also, particularly in the early period of statehood, eager to "integrate" the various ethnic groups into one "nation". This created a dilemma with respect to ethnic cultures. While distinct ethnic cultural elements could be used, as they were elsewhere, to enrich the national identity by absorbing into "Israelness" certain types of dishes, designs, fashions or tunes derived from the culture of a specific Jewish ethnic group,[7] it was considered undesirable to perpetuate or emphasize the cultural distinctiveness of that very group. Such elements have often been unacknowledged. This was especially the case with pseudo-ethnic music (Type 6) and fine art music (Type 9), which were the most intensively sponsored during the Mandate and the early period of statehood. "Israeli" dance adopted elements of a variety of Jewish (for example, Yemenite) and even non-Jewish (Druse and Arab) ethnic traditions. Israeli folksong was frequently based on ethnic melodies to which new, Hebrew texts were adapted. In Hebrew song books the origin of the tune was frequently only vaguely mentioned as "traditional" or "Oriental" (for example, the song *Shir Noded,* based on the Bokharian song *Gudur Farona,* and the song *Bein Nehar Prath,* based on the Arab folk-tune *Aduq al Mayas*); in other cases, the specific ethnic group from which the song originated was pointed out (Sephardi, Yemenite or Persian), but the name of the original piece was generally omitted (for example, the song *Etz Harimon,* based on the Bokharian song *Shudam der Surtat Ushuq,* and the song *Yefeh Nof,* based on the Judeo-Spanish romance, *Tres Hermanicas Eran*). Traditional ethnic tunes were frequently appropriated by modern composers and published under their name; for example, the songs *Hitrag'ut* and *Sirati,* by the composer Nahum Nardi, are based respectively on the Judeo-Spanish romances *Mamma Yo Tengo Visto* and *Povereta Mucha Chica*; similarly, Isaac Levy's cycle of Hebrew songs, *Haktantana Hismiqa,* is based, as the arranger himself stated, on various Judeo-Spanish romances. In the field of fine arts, members of the so-called "Mediterranean School of Composition," which included such well-known names as P. Ben-Haim, M. Lavri, U. Boscowitz, M. Seter and O. Partos, frequently borrowed elements or whole tunes from specific ethnic groups, or from a variety of traditions, to endow their work with an "Oriental" flavor. Such borrowings, however, were highly selective, sporadic and tainted by a tendency to exoticism. They were not intended to bring the music of any particular group to the attention of the wider public. Indeed, the identity of the group from which the borrowings were made often remained obscure (except in cases where the composer merely arranged ethnic songs for concert performance). The borrowings had, therefore, little, if any, feedback effect upon the image of the group in the wider Jewish society.

The Yemenites are the only exception to this generalization. The Bezalel School of Arts and Crafts, dancing ensembles such as Inbal, and singers like S. Dammari and B. Zephira helped to propagate an image of the Yemenites as a versatile, artistically gifted people, whose tradition significantly enriched the emergent Israeli culture.[8] For many non-Oriental Jews the Yemenites came to symbolize Oriental Jewish culture in general. Indeed, it is quite possible that, in the popular mind, cultural traditions of other Oriental Jewish communities were mistakenly labeled "Yemenite."

The official attitude toward Oriental Jewish ethnic cultures, if not necessarily the attitude of the Western Educated public, began to change in the 1970s, largely under the impact of various forms of ethnic protest (Cohen, 1972; Smooha, 1978:208-216). As part of their demand for greater participation in the center of Israeli society, the Oriental ethnic groups demanded a wider recognition of their particular cultural heritages. Various ethnic institutes were founded for research and dissemination of the particular cultural heritages of various Oriental communities, such as the Iraqi, the Moroccan and the Yemenite. In response to the demand for greater recognition, several major cultural events were sponsored by various public and national institutions, such as the Moroccan Mimuna, a popular festival at which different ethnic groups make traditional appearances and, more recently, another traditional festival, the Kurdish Seherane. These events are attended by representatives of the State and the government, including the President and the Prime Minister. The Israel Museum staged major exhibitions of Moroccan and Bokharian Jewish culture and is now preparing one on the Kurdish Jews. In the field of music, there was a marked increase in the broadcasting of Oriental Jewish folklore on radio and television; while the "Center for Integration of Oriental Jewish Culture" sponsored performances and publication of records of ethnic music.

Oriental Jewish ethnic music and dance came to symbolize "Israeli" culture in festivals abroad. While preserving, to varying degrees, its particular ethnic identity, such music often undergoes considerable adaptation and change, which makes it more acceptable to a Western or Westernized audience. Rather than lead to a mere revival of tradition (Type 1 or 2), or pure museumization (Type 3), these efforts lead primarily to a proliferation of conserved (Type 2) and transitional music (Type 5). While these developments may contribute to a wider recognition of the various particular Oriental Jewish communities, their new "external" identities are to a degree slanted and differ significantly from the communities' traditional self-images; though it may be expected that, as in the case of some Fourth World groups who were given wide exposure, the former will eventually influence the latter—the self-image becoming gradually assimilated to the external identity. This might already have happened in the case of the most widely known Oriental Jewish community, the Yementies.

The latest development in the changing relationship between the general Israeli culture and ethnic culture in the field of music is the emergence of ethnic fine art (Type 8). While the composer's ethnic identity is clearly preserved and emphasized in its style of composition and performance, his claims are set higher than in the preceding cases. By weaving the ethnic element into essentially heterogenetic compositions, he claims recognition of his work as a stylistic variety of fine art music and thereby asks for legitimation of his own status as an "artist." If this is granted, Jewish Oriental ethnics will have penetrated the mainstream of Israeli music, not through acculturation to Western standards, but through the acceptance by the wider musical public of their composition as "art."

Our presentation indicates a trend away from the idea of mere amalgamation of different ethnic traditions into an overall "national musical style," and the gradual emergence of legitimate pluralism in music on the national level. This shows that the emergent Israeli cultural identity becomes less monolithic and more pluralistic than it has been conceived of in the past. The acceptance of diversity, however, is achieved at the expense of preservation of "authentic" traditional forms. Jewish Oriental ethnic music, like Fourth world arts, changes in response to altered conditions and audiences. Though his role may gradually achieve legitimation, the ethnic musician still faces the dilemma of making his world widely acceptable, without disturbing its distinct ethnic character out of recognition and thereby destroying his own particular ethnic identity.

Notes

[1] This chapter first appeared in *Ethnomusicology,* 27, No. 2 (1983), 227-52. Copyright © 1983 by the Society for Ethnomusicology, Inc. Reprinted by permission of the society.

[2] The concept of the Fourth World was first applied to the study of art by Graburn (1976a), who traces it back to Berreman (1972), Whitaker (1972) and Manuel and Poslums (1974). The concept has to be qualified when applied to the Jewish Oriental ethnic groups in Israel, since these are not full-fledged "minorities": though they possess distinct identities, they see themselves as belonging to an encompassing Jewish nation. In this respect they differ sharply from other minorities in Israel, such as the Arabs, Druse, Circassians, etc., or from minorities in Third World countries who are unrelated to the dominant national group.

[3] We borrow the term "great tradition" from the work of Redfield and Singer (1969-1954). In our context it designates the "high" and sophisticated musical art style elaborated in Near Eastern music after the advent of Islam and widely adopted by the cultures under Islamic influences, including the Jewish (see Shiloah, in press). The "great tradition" contrasts with the many specific "little traditions" of particular ethnic, linguistic, music." Both musical traditions are orally transmitted. In the past there was always some interaction between them.

[4] There exists a rich literature in Arabic on music, musicians and musical life; its beginnings go back to the ninth century. For further details, see Shiloah (1979).

[5] The boy is thirteen-year-old Yehiel Nahari, who sings *baqqashot* in the *maqamic* style, accompanied by an *'ud* and a *qanun*; his recordings appear on a commercial cassette, produced in New York.

[6] The term *Hazzanut* referred initially to the traditional form of liturgical chanting and later to professional cantoral singing.

[7] In a review of the contribution of Oriental Jewry to the "nascent Israeli culture," Smooha (1978:185), while arguing that this contribution is on the whole deficient, claims: "Only in the aesthetic field have Orientals had some minor influences, mainly in folk music and dance, arts and caraft. . . ."

[8] Thus Ben-Moshe (1981:24) points out that "The Yemenite song has long ago become the property of the nation as a whole." Smooha (1978:185) argues that the Oriental Jewish contribution to arts and crafts consisted "by and large in Yemenite embroidery and jewellry."

References

Adaqi, Y., and Sharvit, U. 1981. *A Treasury of Jewish Yemenite Chants.* Jerusalem: The Israeli Institute for Sacred Music.

Ben-Ami, I. 1976. "The Feast of the Mimuna of the Moroccan Jews," *Moroccan Jewry–Studies in Culture* (Jerusalem: Reuven Mass), pp. 139-52. (In Hebrew.)

Ben-Moshe, Sh. 1981. "Art and Theatre," *Ba'Ma'archa* 241:24 (in Hebrew).

Berreman, D. G. 1972. "Race, Caste and Other Invidious Distinctions in Stratification," *Race* 13:385-414.

Cohen, E. 1972. "The Black Panthers and Israeli Society," *Jewish Journal of Sociology* 14(1):93-109.

——. 1983. "The Dynamics of Commercialized Arts: The Meo and Yao of Northern Thailand," *Journal of the National Research Council of Thailand* 15(1), Part II: 1-34.

——. In press. forthcoming "The Dynamics of Commercialization of Folk Arts: The Hill Tribes of Northern Thailand" (provisional title).

Graburn, N. H. H. 1969. "Art and Acculturative Processes," *International Social Science Journal* 21:457-68.

——. 1976a. *Ethnic and Tourist Arts*. Berkeley: University of California Press.

——. 1976b. "Introduction, The Arts of the Fourth World," ibid.:1-32.

——. In press "Why Eskimos? Why Canada?" in M. E. Jackson (Ed.), *Graphic Arts of the Inuit*. Ann Arbor, Mich.: University of Michigan Press.

Kartomi, M. J. 1981. "The Processes and Results of Musical Cultural Contact: A Discussion of Terminology and Concepts," *Ethnomusicology* 25(2):227-49.

Katz, R. 1968. "The Singing of *Baqqashot,* by Aleppo Jews: A Study in Musical Acculturation," *Acta Musiologica* 40:65-85.

Lomax, A. 1959. "Folk Song Style," *American Anthropologist* 61:927-54.

——. 1968. *Folk Song Style and Culture*. Washington: American Association for the Advancement of Science.

Manuel, G., and Poslums, M. 1974. *The Fourth World: An Indian Reality*. New York: Free Press.

Manor, G. 1975. *Inbal: Quest for a Movement-Language*. Tel Aviv: Bank Leumi.

Merriam, A. 1955. "The Use of Music in the Study of a Problem of Acculturation," *American Anthropologist* 57:28-34.

——. 1964. *The Anthropology of Music*. Evanston: Northwestern University Press.

Nettl, B. (Ed.). 1978a. *Eight Urban Musical Cultures: Tradition and Change*. Urbana: University of Illinois Press.

——. 1978b. "Some Aspects of the History of World Music in the Twentieth Century: Questions, Problems and Concepts," *Ethnomusicology* 22(1):123-36.

Nettl, B., and Shiloah, A. 1978. "Persian Classical Music in Israel: A Preliminary Report," *Israel Studies in Musicology* 1:142-58.

Neuman, D. 1976. "Towards an Ethnomusicology of Culture Change in Asia," *Asian Music* 7(2):1-5.

Racy, J. 1980. "Contemporary Music of Cairo: The *Lawn* (color) Concept in a Patchwork Model," *Asian Music* 12(3):85 (diagram).

Redfield, R., and Singer, M. 1969. "The Cultural Role of Cities," in R. Sennett (Ed.), *Classical Essays in the Culture of Cities*. New York: Appleton-Century-Crofts, pp. 206-33.

Shiloah, A. 1970. "Aliya Songs in Folk Traditions in Israel," *Folklore Research Studies* 1:349-368 (in Hebrew).

——. 1979. *The Theory of Music in Arabic Writings,* RISM, Ser. B, Vol. X. München: Henle Verlag.

——. In press. "Transformation, changement et Phenomenes d'influence dans les musiques du Proche et Moyen Orient–hier et aujourdh'ui," *Intercultural Studies* (Paris CIPSM and UNESCO).

Seroussi, E. 1981. "Old and New in the Singing of the *baqqashot* Among the Moroccan Jews." M. A. Thesis, The Hebrew University of Jerusalem. (In Hebrew.)

Slobin, M. 1976. *Music in the Culture of Northern Afghanistan,* Tucson: University
of Arizona Press.

Smooha, S. 1978. *Israel: Pluralism and Conflict.* London: Routledge and Kegan Paul.

Whitaker, B. (Ed.). 1972. *The Fourth World.* London: Sedgewick and Johnson.

Sephira, B. 1978. *Many Voices.* Jerusalem: Massada. (In Hebrew.)

17

The Current State of Ethnicity: A Postscript[1]

Alex Weingrod

The conference on Israeli ethnicity that this book is based upon took place during the last week of June, 1980. One year later, almost to the day, on June 30, 1981, the elections to the Tenth Israeli Knesseth were held. Prior to the elections it was widely predicted that the major campaign topics would be internal matters like triple-digit inflation, or security problems such as the future of the West Bank. What Israelis usually think of as "ethnic problems"—issues such as the "social gap", or the disproportionately low rate of Easterners in high political and economic positions—did not then appear to be the major concerns around which the election campaign would revolve. To nearly everyone's surprise (including my own), however, ethnic group divisions and communal tensions rapidly became the central, almost dominant topics, in an increasingly volatile election campaign. Unexpectedly, perhaps, the divisions between the two major political parties followed along ethnic lines: the Labor Party received the bulk of its support from Ashkenazi voters, while the reigning Likud drew heavy support from the "*eidot mizrakh*", or voters from Eastern countries. In addition, although the high pitch of emotion was lowered following the election, a number of subsequent events signal the fact that the issues of ethnicity continue to be significant for many Israelis. Ethnicity, and the relationship between members of different ethnic groups, was once again thrust high on the national agenda.

341

   If the 1981 election was a watershed, then a series of factual and theoretical questions need to be asked. To begin with, what in fact happened
during the 1981 election and in the several years that have followed?
Second, why have ethnic-group tensions and a more outspoken "ethnic
consciousness" emerged sharply in the early 1980's? Finally, what is the
present-day range and meaning of ethnicity within Israeli society? These
are, to be sure, complex processual questions that are difficult to answer
since they are still being "played out" in daily events; to put it differently, any interpretation is at least partly speculative since novel and un-
anticipated trends are certain to develop.[2] Nonetheless, reflecting upon
these questions in this brief postscript brings many of the issues discussed
in this volume up to date.
   Let us begin with "the facts" themselves. What were the ethnic dimensions of the 1981 Knesseth elections?
   As other observers have also noted, a first sign of what was to come
took place during the *mimouna* celebrations in mid-April of 1981 (Arian,
1982). Although *mimouna* traditionally was a minor Jewish holiday in
North Africa, in Israel it has rapidly been transformed into a mainly
Moroccan ceremony of ethnic renewal; tens of thousands of Moroccan
Jews gather together to picnic and, at least implicitly, to demonstrate
their upward-moving social status and political power (Goldberg, 1978;
Weingrod, 1979). The main celebration is held yearly in Jerusalem's
Sachar Garden, near to the Knesseth, or Parliament, and over the years
Israel's national political leaders have come to address the crowds. Indeed, in recent years *mimouna* has been given an openly political slant,
and it was therefore not surprising that, in the spring of 1981, leaders of
both the government and the political opposition were invited to stroll
among the picnicking crowds and later address them from the central
stage. During this particular celebration, however, their speeches were received with divided emotion and anger: the leader of the opposition
Labor Party, Shimon Peres, was heckled and then showered with tomatoes
when he rose to speak, while the then Prime Minister, Menachem Begin,
was enthusiastically cheered by the crowd. It was an ugly moment—and,
in retrospect, it presaged the anger and ethnic division that grew during
the election campaign.
   As the political campaign moved into higher gear the "staging" took
a curious twist: instead of emphasizing the new electronic media of radio
and television, the main political protagonists chose the older style of
addressing crowds that assembled in public squares in the downtown sec-

tions of numerous Israeli cities and towns. Begin, a legendary orator who seemed to feast upon the crowd's cheers, was the first to "go out to the people", and Peres and his Labor Party colleagues soon followed. The response that each received was dramatically different: Begin filled the public squares with changing crowds, while Peres was frequently met with heckling, booing and what at times appeared to be deliberate attempts to break up Labor rallies. The television screens and newspapers were soon filled with angry, violent scenes—for example, the Labor Party spokesmen protested against those in the crowd who were making "obscene Oriental gestures" at their candidate. These disturbances, they implied, were incited by Likud riffraff—and, in fact, the Labor Party propaganda began emphasizing the spectre of violent *eidot mizrakh* who threatened the future of the "good Israel" (that is, Labor). The division gained momentum —Begin spoke to crowds of (apparently) Israelis of Eastern origin, while Peres and his colleagues were reaching those who were (apparently) Ashkenazi in background. The crowning moment came in the last days of the campaign when, in what may have been a fatal slip of the tongue, an entertainer addressing a Labor rally labelled the opposition with a demeaning ethnic slur ("chach-chachim"). The Likud quickly picked up the incident and used it to generate support among its own voters.

The results are, of course, well known: while the two major parties received an almost identical number of votes, the voting analysis shows that Ashkenazim mainly voted Labor, while Easterners tended to support the Likud (Arian, 1983). The political scientist Asher Arian, who has made a specialty of analyzing Israeli voting trends, puts it this way: "The 1981 elections witnessed an unprecedented crystallization of ethnic differences in Israeli politics", and again, "The 1981 elections witnessed the two major parties clearly identified with ethnic groups—the Alignment (Labor) with the Ashkenazi and the Likud with the Sephardi (1982:16,20). The voting was not entirely dichotomous—apparently about a third of each party's support came from the other ethnic category—but the "crystallization" was no less profound.

Israel is a nation traumatized by a seemingly endless stream of national crisis: whether mere paranoia or true danger, Israelis have grown accustomed to witnessing a parade of tumultuous, dramatic events. It is for this reason difficult to definitively select particular events for their special "ethnic meaning". Nonetheless, since the election two additional events stand out in this regard. Both of these were violent events, and to some extent they conform to the pattern that was indicated by the election.

The first of these incidents took place in the spring of 1982. The Tel Aviv Municipality sent a crew of workers to demolish an illegally-built home that had been put up in a low-income, ramshackle section of South Tel Aviv. (Tel Aviv is divided between its "North" which is high-income, primarily Ashkenazi and fashionable, and the "South" which is poor in income and city services, and mainly Eastern in origin). As the bulldozers approached to destroy the building some of the inhabitants began to wildly protest. A police officer who was at the scene feared that violence was about to break out; he pulled his gun and in the scuffle, a young member of the family whose home was being levelled was shot to death. This was a tragic, highly unusual conclusion—police normally do not use weapons in cases of this kind. The incident then took on distinct ethnic conflict dimensions: messages saying "Death to the Ashkenazim!", resplendent with swastikas, were scrawled on various public places throughout the country, and demonstrations held in the neighborhood also took on overtones of ethnic tension.

The second event is more difficult to interpret in strictly ethnic terms. In the turmoil that accompanied the publication of the Kahan Report pertaining to Israeli responsibility for the massacre of Palestinians in the Beiruth refugee camps, opponents of the war staged an evening protest march through downtown Jerusalem. It was a time of deeply divided opinions, and the marchers were almost immediately accosted by passers-by who cursed and threatened them. The marchers were accused of being traiters, fools, "Arab-lovers"—and not least of all, of being "Ashkenazim". It was another ugly scene, and it too ended in tragedy: a grenade was thrown into a crowd of demonstrators, and for the first time in several generations one Jew had killed another apparently for ideological political reasons.

If, as has been emphasized, the 1981 elections "reflect" (or "brought about": the meanings of these terms are quite different) an "ethnic polarization" in Israeli society, then these two additional events suggest that it may in fact be a serious social chasm. "Ashkenazi" and "Eastern" or "Sephardi" are associated in these incidents not only with different political parties, but also with different political outlooks and ideologies. In certain social circumstances or contexts ethnic group identity may intuitively be linked with a wide range of contrasting features. Writing recently in the *Jerusalem Quarterly,* Shoshana Avigal makes the point with depressing clarity:

> Between the two camps there exists now pure abysmal hatred. They
> could almost claim autonomy from each other, they were able to
> speak the same language. (1981:54)

The depths of the strain may be overstated by terms such as "two camps"
and "hatred", and yet many Israelis would recognize more than a glimmer
of truth in these remarks.[3]

Polarization between the two major political parties is only one of the
"ethnic dimensions" of the recent Knesseth elections. The other is the success of Tami, a new, almost exclusively North African political party, in
winning three "swing seats" in the Tenth Knesseth. In her analysis of
the historic development of "ethnic lists" in Iraeli politics (Chapter 8)
Hanna Herzog points out that since the elections to the Third Knesset in
1955 none of the ethnic parties have had any success—during most of its
history the Israeli electorate has voted against ethnic labels. It is therefore important to explain the reasons for Tami's election victory.

Tami differs from all of the previous Israeli ethnic parties in a number
of critical ways (Ben-Rafael 1982; Herzog 1983). First, the party was organized and headed by several prominent, highly successful political leaders; the leaders of the new party included previous Knesseth members and
government ministers as well as several mayors and others who were prominent in local politics. This elite group attracted their previous supporters,
and, in addition, were able to campaign as equals on the national level.
This stands in sharp contrast with the leadership of practically all of the
former ethnic parties; as Herzog and others have shown, they typically
were headed by aspiring politicians who were later co-opted by the major
political parties. Tami reversed this pattern by, in effect, drawing to it
persons who had already achieved prominence within established parties.
Second, although it entered late in the election campaign, Tami was well
financed and organized and consequently was soon able to function as a
national political party. Much of its financial support came from overseas
Sephardi donors who were deeply involved in the new party's organization. In this regard also, Tami differed from the previous ethnic lists which
were poorly financed and not effectively organized.

Equally important, the new party was successful since its appeal fell
upon many responsive ears. Tami's main leader, Aharon Abouhatzeira,
had previously waged a bitter struggle against opponents within the National Religious Party (NRP). Without presenting all of the details, Abou-

hatzeira, who had been Minister of Religions, was accused of having mis-used funds and was brought to trial. He, in turn, not only pleaded inno-cent (after the election a court found him guilty and sentenced him to a brief term in prison), but also accused his former NRP colleagues of failing to support him: in effect, Abouhatzeira accused the mainly Ashkenazi leaders of the NRP of being prejudiced against him and his North African followers. Many previous NRP supporters were convinced by his accusa-tions and therefore voted for him. Moreover, Abouhatzeira was a member of the most prominent Moroccan rabbinic family, and this too added to his appeal. Tami's election campaign stressed "ethnic pride" and religious traditionalism—for example, their television ads showed supporters praying at the grave site of a revered Moroccan saint. As the election results indi-cated, more than forty-five thousand voters found these appeals convinc-ing and voted for Tami.

This brief description indicates some of the major "ethnic events" that took place during and after the 1981 elections. The interesting question, of course, is why ethnicity and ethnic group tensions became accentuated during the early 1980's. What brought about the division into two "camps", and why did an outspokenly ethnic political party succeed while previous attempts had failed?

One explanation of the ethnic divisions that became apparent in the 1981 elections is that they do not signal a new development, but rather are the culmination of voting trends that had become apparent during the three previous national elections. Asher Arian develops this argument convincingly; his analysis shows that while Ashkenazim have persisted in supporting the Labor Party, the Likud began to attract Eastern-origin voters as early as the 1969 Knesseth elections (1982:20; 1983:97). What the 1981 elections really show, Arian concludes, is the ultimate power of demography: *eidot mizrakh* have now become the majority of the popula-tion, and since they continue to support the Likud the society has become polarized into two political camps.

What demography does not explain is *why* Easterners were attracted to the Likud, while the Ashkenazim continued to support Labor. One popu-lar theory has it that the Easterners—Jews from Yemen, Morocco, Iraq or Persia, for example—were kept outside of the reigning Israeli Establish-ment, and consequently they were drawn to the Likud which historically has been the party of the "under-dog". The proverbial "chemistry" be-tween the leader of the Likud, Menacham Begin, and the Middle Eastern voters, has also been explained in these terms: Jews from Persia or Morocco voted for Begin, the "Polish gentleman", since he symbolized the "out-sider" and consequently was closer to them. Among others, Daniel Elazar has argued this point forcefully:

> Sephardic Jews . . . see themselves as outsiders because that is how they have been labelled by the Labor-dominated Israeli Establish-ment. Hence their easy identification with Menachem Begin, the perennial outsider. (1981:1)

The Labor Party's "arrogance", Elazar concludes, produced the paradoxi-cal situation in which the party in power, the Likud, was perceived to represent the interests of the "outsiders", while the Labor opposition was seen as the repressive Establishment.

In addition to the demographic and "chemistry" theories one can also venture a more cynical explanation: ethnic polarization came to a head in the 1981 elections since the political parties discovered that "ethnic appeals" drew crowds and appeared to be "good politics". Begin's speeches drew tens of thousands of cheering supporters ("Begin, Begin") and the Labor Party's propaganda image of itself as the "good (Ashkenazi) Israel" also seemed to be having an effect. The politicians tactics, in other words, were to play upon ethnic feelings or emotions as a way of attracting vot-ers. The Likud and Labor practised the art subtly, while Tami "proudly" broadcast a more direct ethnic appeal. To return to terms that were used previously, the elections of 1981 did not "reflect" the existing polariza-tion but instead were an important factor in widening the ethnic rift (Arian, 1983:109).

Elections are "ripe events", overflowing with different shades and layers of meaning, and consequently they attract great interest.[4] The analysis that has thus far been developed pertains mainly to the "short run"–to an accounting of ethnicity as seen from the perspective of a na-tional election and several subsequent events. It is also important to assess the shape of ethnicity over the longer run. If the elections of 1981 were a watershed, then they may also have given impetus to new or different ethnic expressions. What do these events portend for the present and fu-ture of Israeli ethnicity? What wider trends may be associated with this unfolding series of happenings?

Several of the previous chapters develop evidence for a new and chang-ing Israeli ethnic sensibility. For example, in her analysis of Persian "week-end seminars" (Chapter 12) Judith Goldstein depicts some of the early steps in the process by which a new "Parsi" cultural identity is being fashioned. Similarly, in their analysis of the progression of "ethnic music" (Chapter 16) Amnon Shiloah and Erik Cohen trace a process through which new and different meanings are given to musical themes and performances. These are all part of the recent trend in which ethnic symbols are consciously designed and legitimately presented within the broader society. In one sense, this is a part of the process whereby Israeli society has become increasingly "pluralistic" during the period of the last decade or so (Lissak, 1973; Smooha, 1978). Beyond pluralism, however, the forces of ethnic difference appear to be carving a deeper impression upon the society as a whole. There are, indeed, signs of a "new ethnicity".

This term—"the new ethnicity"—was recently coined by Erik Cohen in a lengthy essay in which he marks some recent features of Israeli ethnic expressions (1983). His argument is worth citing in detail since it bears directly upon the topics being considered in this postscript. The problem that Cohen sets for himself is understanding why, for example, an unabashedly ethnic political party such as Tami could succeed in the 1980's while previous ethnic parties failed, or why ethnic celebrations such as religious *hiluloth* (festivities commemorating the memory of famous rabbis) have lately become widely accepted and proudly celebrated. During the lengthy period of the "old ethnicity" (presumably from the establishment of the state in 1948 until some time in the late 1960's) expressions such as these were blocked by the "symbolic domination" practised by the reigning Ashkenazi elites; ethnic group separatism and non-European traditions were negatively stigmatized as "divisive" and "primitive" while the Eastern immigrants were required to "adopt European culture" (Cohen, 1983:26). The "new ethnicity" developed as a progressively stronger reaction against the attempt to force Middle Easterners to reject their past. Indeed, according to Cohen,

> The principal objection of the new ethnicity against the old, Ashkenazi-dominated establishment is that the ideology of 'absorption of immigrants' deculturated (them). . . . The main effort of the new ethnic ideology is thus to establish Oriental Jewry as an equal but distinct partner with the Ashkenazim, (although) some of the more radical ethnics discard such pluralism as too moderate and advocate the formation of a new establishment, dominated by the Oriental Jews. (1983:30-31)

A successful North African political party such as Tami is symptomatic of this new ethnicity: Tami emphasizes the distinctive North African cultural past of its supporters, and its leaders appear on the national political stage with full assurance and legitimacy. It is therefore fair to suggest that a thoroughgoing ideological transformation has taken place: the "new ethnicity" is, in fact, only one feature of a deeper ideological change in which "particularistic, nationalist and orthodox religious values" are on the ascendancy (1982:32). Indeed, the "new Oriental ethnicity" has become "more legitimate and acceptable" since it conforms so well with the "shift to neo-traditional Jewish nationalism" (1983:33). Cohen views these developments darkly—they inevitably lead, he supposes, to "an Israel dominated by neo-traditional values" that will soon become just another "Middle Eastern country" (1983:34).

Whether one agrees with Cohen's long-range prognosis or not, his analysis points to potent forces that are at work within the society. It is pertinent to underscore the weight given to symbolic and cultural themes, on the one hand, as well as to politics and power on the other. These themes have often appeared in the analyses of Israeli ethnicity, just as they are prominent motifs in the study of ethnic social processes elsewhere in the world (Cohen, 1974). In an article published a decade ago Shlomo Deshen posited that, in Israel, a kind of "inverted correlation" existed between what he termed "cultural ethnicity" and "political ethnicity": from the vantage point of the early 1970's it appeared that "political ethnicity" had run its course whereas "cultural ethnicity" was on the rise (1974: 142). Now, a decade later, it would be difficult to sustain the argument that political ethnicity was "on the wane" in Israel. More to the point, it would appear that cultural and political features are equally a part of a single overall social process. The correlation between them is direct and potent—changes or developments in ethnic politics hinges upon changes in ethnic symbols and ceremonies, and vice versa. To be even more explicit, the swift rise to power of politicians such as David Levy or Aharon Abouhatzeira is connected closely with the prominence given to new cultural celebrations such as the *mimouna* or the resurgence of the tradition of *hilluloth* (Weingrod: N.D.).

What then is the current state of ethnicity within Israeli society? Ethnic sentiments and attachments continue to be strong forces. In the Israeli terms of discourse ethnicity increasingly means political power and political gain—when Israelis reflect upon or argue about "ethnic issues" they are in effect talking about power. To be sure, ethnicity "is not everything"— social class and ideology may be equally potent depending upon the actors and the context—but who would deny that, as Hanna Herzog puts it, there presently is a "tendency to construct social reality in Israel in ethnic terms" (1983:184).

Having become the population majority, new Eastern origin elites have entered the contest for political dominance and control. In a burst of cultural creativity, new ethnic symbols and performances have also been designed and launched. The Ashkenazi social and political hegemony has been challenged, and as a result group tensions and divisions are not far from the surface and sometimes emerge in conflict. The level of conflict should not be overestimated—and yet it is surely there, simmering. For better or for worse, the ethnicity genie is out of the bottle: it is by no means clear what new forms it will create or what tensions it may yet generate, but it does seem certain that in the future ethnicity will continue to be powerful and influential.

Notes

[1] At various stages in the preparation of this chapter Virginia Dominguez, Steven Sharot and Moshe Shokeid offered useful comments and suggestions. I wish to thank each of them for their help.

[2] New national elections are already in the offing. Elections to the Eleventh Knesseth are scheduled for July 23, 1984, and they will hence take place before this book is published. There are indications that "ethnicity" will again be a prominent feature of the campaigning; for example, there appears to be a trend to "Sephardize" the electoral competiton by including Eastern candidates in prominent places in all of the major political parties.

[3] The best source in this regard—what seems to be the most authentic "political ethnography"—is the novelist Amos Oz's reporting in his recent book *In the Land of Israel* (1983). See in particular Chapter 2, "The Insult and the Fury", where Oz records the comments of some residents of the town of Beth Shemesh.

[4] In their article on "The Ethnic Vote in Israel's 1981 Elections", Arian and Shamir list several other possible reasons for the split in voting. For example, they note that "Sephardim, who tend to be more traditional" responded to Menachem Begin's imagery of the "religion-sanctioned state" (1983:102). Taking a different direction, Amiram Gonen suggests that there has been a political-geographical slant to the election results; he points out that there have been geographical regularities in the Easterners swing to the Likud (1982).

One basic problem with all of these analyses is that the categories are much too broad; more specifically, "Easterner", "Sephardim" or "eidot mizrakh" is too inclusive and complex a category for proper understanding of group behavior. Indeed, lumping togehter different country of origin groups may mask significant differences between them. For example, it would be interesting to compare the voting behavior of persons who identify themselves as "Moroccans" with those who call themselves "Iraqis". These are two large-sized *edot,* and while they are both typically classed together as "Easterners" there is reason to hypothesize that their voting patterns (as well as other behavioral features) are distinctively different from one another.

References

Arian, A. 1982. "Elections 1981: Competitiveness and Polarization", *Jerusalem Quarterly,* No. 21, pp. 3-27.

——, and Shamir, Michael. 1983. "The Ethnic Vote in Israel's 1981 Elections" in A. Arian (Ed.), *The Elections in Israel 1981.* Tel Aviv: Ramot Publishing, pp. 91-112.

Avigal, S. 1981. "Moroccan 'Dybbuk' "? *Jerusalem Quarterly,* No. 21, pp. 48-55.

Ben Raphael, Eliezer. 1981. *"The Emergence of Ethnicity.* Westport, Conn.: Greenwood Press.

Cohen, A. 1974. *Urban Ethnicity.* London: Tavistock Publications.

Cohen, E. 1983. "Ethnicity and Legitimation in Contemporary Israel," *Jerusalem Quarterly,* No. 24, pp. 21-34.

Deshen, S. 1974. "Political Ethnicity and Cultural Ethnicity in Israel During the 1960's" in A. Cohen (Ed.), *Urban Ethnicity.* London: Tavistock Publications.

Elazar, Daniel J. 1981. "The 1981 Elections: Some Observations", *Jerusalem Letter: Viewpoints,* pp. 1-7.

Goldberg, H. 1978. "The Mimouna and the Minority Status of Moroccan Jews", *Ethnology,* Vol. 17, pp. 75-88.

Gonen, A. 1982. "The Geography of the Electoral Competition Between the Labour Alignment and the Likud in Jewish Cities of Israel, 1965-1981", *Medina, Mimshal V'Ihasim Benleumiyyim* 19-20, pp. 63-87 (in Hebrew).

Herzog, H. 1983. "The Ethnic Lists in Election 1981: An Ethnic Political Identity" in A. Arian (Ed.), *The Elections in Israel 1981.* Tel Aviv: Ramot Publishing, pp. 113-138.

Lissak, M. 1973. "Pluralism in Israeli Society" in M. Curtis and M. Chertoff (Eds.), *Israel: Social Structure and Change.* New Brunswick, N.J.: Transaction Books, pp. 363-378.

Oz, Amos. 1983. *In the Land of Israel.* New York: Harcourt Brace Jovanovich. California Press.

Weingrod, A. 1979. "Recent Trends in Israeli Ethnicity", *Ethnic and Racial Studies,* Vol. II, pp. 55-65.

——. N.D. *The Saint of Beersheba,* unpublished manuscript.

CONTRIBUTORS

Eliezer Ben Raphael teaches in the Department of Sociology and Social Anthropology, Tel Aviv University

Yoram Bilu has an appointment in both the Department of Psychology and the Department of Sociology and Social Anthropology, Hebrew University

Eric Cohen is a member of the Department of Sociology and Social Anthropology, Hebrew University

Harvey Goldberg teaches in the Department of Sociology and Social Anthropology, Hebrew University

Judith Goldstein is a member of the Department of Anthropology, Vassar College

Amiran Gonen is a member of the Department of Geography, Hebrew University

Majid al-Haj is in the Center for Middle Eastern Studies, Haifa University

Hanna Herzog is a member of the Department of Sociology and Social Anthropology, Tel Aviv University

Arnold Lewis taught in the Department of Sociology and Social Anthropology, Tel Aviv University. He now lives in the United States.

Herb Lewis is in the Department of Anthropology, University of Wisconsin

Laurence Loeb teaches in the Department of Anthropology, University of Utah

Judah Matras is at the Brookdale Institute for Gerontology and Human Development, Jerusalem, and the Department of Sociology and Anthropology, Carleton University

Jonathan Oppenheimer taught in the Department of Sociology and Anthropology, Haifa University. He now lives in England.

Yochanon Peres is a member of the Department of Sociology and Social Anthropology, Tel Aviv University

Amnon Shiloah is in the Department of Musicology, Hebrew University

Moshe Shokeid teaches in the Department of Sociology and Social Anthropology, Tel Aviv University

Shalva Weil is in the School of Education, Hebrew University

Alex Weingrod is a member of the Department of Behavioral Sciences, Ben Gurion University of the Negev

INDEX

360   INDEX

Persian Jew (see Iranian Jew)
Petah Tikva, 26, 29, 31, 33
"Pluralistic" society, 348
Pluralistic structure, 105
Poland, 53, 221, 232
Polish Jew, 201, 213
Political ethnicity, 70, 77, 78, 116,
        118, 119, 130, 131, 135-
        137, 159, 162, 165-171,
        173-175, 182, 187, 192,
        213, 218, 220-221, 341, 345
Popular Movement (political party),
        171
Prime Minister's Adviser for Arab
        Affairs, 124, 270
"Primitivity", 144, 147-150, 207,
        211, 223, 232, 348
Primordial identity, 57, 58, 62, 63,
        134-135, 149, 150, 217
Palestine, 111, 113, 120, 125, 126,
        130-131, 133, 138, 141-
        143, 160, 164, 166, 167,
        264, 267

Q

Q-Methodology, 81, 85-87, 89, 95, 98

R

R-Methodology, 85, 87
Ramat Gan, 86
Ramle, 186
Rehovot, 207
Rishon Letzion, 26, 29, 31
Rosh Ha'Ayin, 231
Roumanian Jew, 42, 213, 221, 232
Russian Jew, 43, 53, 142, 146, 194,
        201, 213, 221
Religious behavior, 22, 183, 187, 196,
        197, 198, 227

S

Saan'a, 163
Sa'ids, 206
Salameh, 207, 208
San'anis, 201-203
"Second Israel," 145

Sephardic Jews, 82, 165, 167-171,
        174, 238, 239, 245, 268,
        330, 335
Sephardic and Oriental Communities
        List (political party), 171
Sephardic Union, 171
Sephoris, 108
Sha'arayim, 232
Sharabis, 201
Sheli (political party), 168
Six Day War, 43
"Social gap", 133, 143
Social integration, 162, 163, 165, 171-
        173, 221
South Africa, 106
South African Jew, 201
Stigmatization, 169-173
Suburbs, 26, 32, 34, 36
Syria, 110, 121, 260, 267
Syrian Jew, 150, 201, 213
Stratification, 1, 2, 5-7, 16-20, 25-27,
        32, 34, 36, 39-41, 44-53,
        57-58, 73, 83, 86, 106, 107,
        114, 117, 125-131, 133,
        134, 136, 143, 145, 147-
        150, 164, 165, 171, 185,
        214, 226, 228, 230-232, 242
Stylistic dynamics, 320-337
Sua'ad tribe, 109, 110

T

Tami (political party), 345-349
Teheran, 243, 248, 253
Tel Aviv, 18, 27, 33, 86, 150, 165,
        207, 231, 237, 240, 344
Tel Aviv Municipality, 344
Tel Aviv-Jaffa, 26, 27
Te'unei t'puah, 192, 193
Torah, 203, 227-230
Tseirei Hamizrach, 162-163
Tripoli-Tripolitanian Jews:
        absorption process, 184-185
        images, 134, 137, 150
Tunisian Jews:
        aggressive behavior, 286
        cultural identity, 134, 137, 150,
        213
        demography, 186-187
        integration, 221
Turkaman, 109